Kant and the Foundations of Analytic Philosophy

ROBERT HANNA

CLARENDON PRESS · OXFORD
2001

OXFORD
UNIVERSITY PRESS

Great Clarendon Street, Oxford ox2 6DP

Oxford University Press is a department of the University of Oxford.
It furthers the University's objective of excellence in research, scholarship,
and education by publishing worldwide in

Oxford New York

Athens Auckland Bangkok Bogotá Buenos Aires Calcutta
Cape Town Chennai Dar es Salaam Delhi Florence Hong Kong Istanbul
Karachi Kuala Lumpur Madrid Melbourne Mexico City Mumbai
Nairobi Paris São Paulo Shanghai Singapore Taipei Tokyo Toronto Warsaw

with associated companies in Berlin Ibadan

Oxford is a registered trade mark of Oxford University Press
in the UK and in certain other countries

Published in the United States
by Oxford University Press Inc., New York

British Library Cataloguing in Publication Data

Data available

Library of Congress Cataloging-in-Publication Data
Hanna, Robert.
Kant and the foundations of analytic philosophy / Robert Hanna.
p. cm.
Includes bibliographical references (p.) and index.
1. Analysis (Philosophy). 2. Kant, Immanuel, 1724–1804. Kritik der reinen Vernunft.
3. Kant, Immanuel, 1724–1804—Influence. I. Title.
B808.5.H35 2001   142'.3—dc21   00–060632
ISBN 0–19–825072–X

1 3 5 7 9 10 8 6 4 2

Typeset in Minion
by Graphicraft Limited, Hong Kong
Printed by T.J. International Ltd
Padstow, Cornwall

T

1002825431

To MTH and ETH

The fundamental things apply,
as time goes by

PREFACE AND ACKNOWLEDGEMENTS

Since the late 1980s I have been deeply interested in the connections between Kant's *Critique of Pure Reason* and the historical foundations of analytic philosophy. What struck me like a slap in the face back then, just as now, is how the leading figures of the analytic tradition from the 1880s up through the 1950s and 1960s—Frege, Moore, Russell, and early Wittgenstein; Carnap and the Vienna Circle; later Wittgenstein and the ordinary-language philosophers; and Quine—quite self-consciously rejected the main doctrines of the first *Critique* and yet also quite unconsciously absorbed Kant's way of formulating the very distinctions and problems they were dealing with. Shining examples are the familiar and perhaps all-too-familiar dichotomies between analytic and synthetic, a priori and a posteriori, rationalism and empiricism, pure logic and empirical psychology, logicism and intuitionism, realism and idealism, and so on. Where would analytic philosophy be without these enabling contrasts and worries? In this sense, the analytic tradition is the reversed image of the first *Critique*.

In 1991 or thereabouts I read Alberto Coffa's important book, *The Semantic Tradition from Kant to Carnap*. Coffa's thesis is that the sort of philosophical semantics practised by Carnap and the other members of the Vienna Circle was the direct result of a long and subtle dialectical engagement with Kant's theory of the a priori. That, of course, was grist for my mill: it seemed to be only an instance of a more general fact. It also so happened that at the same time I was working my way through Stephen Schiffer's equally important book, *Remnants of Meaning*. Schiffer raises a very disturbing question—namely, what if the semantic project that lies at the heart of recent and contemporary analytic philosophy is in fact incoherent and impossible? As I read Coffa's book in parallel with Schiffer's, I gradually realized that our late-twentieth-century sense of the obvious wrongness of Kant's views on the crucial analytic/synthetic and a priori/a posteriori distinctions, and on all the others too, was based on a certain conventional understanding of the first principles of analytic philosophy. But if Schiffer is correct, then that conventional understanding is itself, at the very least, not *obviously* right. This in turn led me to the thought that, although Kant's doctrines had been officially trounced, they had not actually been refuted in any decisive way—not by a long shot. For these reasons, it seemed to me that a reconsideration of the connection between Kant's first *Critique* and the historical foundations of analytic philosophy from Frege to

Quine could usefully illuminate both Kant's theoretical philosophy and some topics of central contemporary concern. Hence, after a suitable period of time had elapsed, this book.

And while I am in the confessional mode, one other prefatory comment. Everyone has heard the equally wicked and witty remark, usually attributed to Quine, that there are two kinds of philosophers—those who are interested in the history of philosophy and those who are interested in philosophy. Part of my motivation for undertaking this project was to show how thoroughly that remark and the attitude it expresses misrepresent the real nature of our subject. For example: it is now clear that analytic philosophy as it was practised in 1950—the year of the first public presentation of 'Two Dogmas of Empiricism'—was in large part the result of working out to the bitter end a bold project initiated by Frege in the 1880s. But things might have gone very differently after 1950 if Frege's project had, in 1950, been placed in a broader historical perspective. I mean to say that we cannot do philosophy in the present without implicitly adopting an understanding of philosophy's past and also that we cannot *properly* do philosophy in the present without making this implicit historical understanding explicit—that is, without critically examining the intellectual origins and genesis we normally take for granted. So one might then say that there are two kinds of philosophers: those who are interested in the history of philosophy and those who *should* be.

Writing books is usually a solitary occupation, but philosophy is always a social activity; thus I have been helped by many people. I would particularly like to thank Paul Guyer, Christopher Shields, and Sir Peter F. Strawson for their comments on versions of Chapter 3; Mark Balaguer for his comments on a version of Chapter 4; and Alex Oliver for comments on a version of Chapter 5. Many thanks, too, are hereby directed to George Bealer, Jerrold Katz, Patricia Kitcher, Michael Potter, Peter Railton, and Christopher Shields for (for me anyhow) fog-lifting conversations about various aspects of the project. My editors at OUP, Peter Momtchiloff, Charlotte Jenkins, and Hilary Walford, have been unfailingly helpful, efficient, and pleasant throughout the several stages of the process of getting my manuscript into decent shape and then into print. Above all, however, I owe a personal debt of gratitude to Paul Guyer and Peter Strawson for their long-standing support of the very idea of this project.

Many undergraduate and graduate students participated in various versions of a repeating cycle of three seminars—on Kant's first *Critique*, on the semantics and epistemology of necessary truth, and on the historical foundations of analytic philosophy—that I ran at the University of Colorado at Boulder, at York University, and then back at Boulder again, from 1992 to 1999. Their intelligent comments and questions were a constant source of good ideas; and their appropriately directed expressions of bemusement and scepticism provided the perfect system of critical checks and balances. Thanks to you all. In a similar vein, I would like to thank audiences at the

University of Wyoming, University of British Columbia, York University, and Bowling Green State University, and also members of the Cambridge Moral Sciences Club, the Eastern Division of the American Philosophical Association, the North American Kant Society, and the UK Kant Society, for their comments on presentations of bits and pieces of this and closely related material.

I have also been aided by institutions. The Department of Philosophy at the University of Colorado at Boulder granted me release time from teaching during the Spring term of 1993, making it possible to compose the earliest drafts of Chapters 3–5. And both the University of Colorado and York University generously gave me travel money to test drive some of my ideas.

My indebtedness to my wife, Martha Hanna, and to our daughter, Beth, is of a different although ultimately more important nature. The quotation on the Dedication page is taken from the song 'As Time Goes By'. It was written by the little-known philosopher Herman Hupfeld, but—as everyone knows—memorably performed by Dooley Wilson in that most sentimental and wonderful of all old movies, *Casablanca*.

R. H.

1 January 2000
Boulder, Colorado

CONTENTS

A NOTE ON THE TEXT

For convenience I cite Kant's works infratextually in parentheses. These citations normally include both an abbreviation of the English title and also the corresponding volume and page numbers in the standard 'Akademie' (Ak.) edition of Kant's works. For references to the first *Critique*, however, I follow the common practice of giving page numbers from the A (1781) and B (1787) German editions only. And for references to Kant's *Reflexionen*—i.e. entries in one or another of the ten volumes of the (largely) untranslated *Kants handschriftlicher Nachlaß*—I give the entry number in addition to the Akademie volume and page numbers. For quotations from Kant's works I generally follow the standard English translation whenever one is available, but have also corrected or modified them slightly wherever it seemed appropriate. In the crucial case of the first *Critique*, however, I have sought both maximum translational accuracy and maximum philosophical flexibility by freely combining the two leading translations, Kemp Smith and Guyer-Wood, with my own terminological fine-tunings. Because the Akademie edition contains only the B version of the first *Critique*, I also consulted the following German composite edition: *Kritik der reinen Vernunft*, ed. W. Weischedel, Immanuel Kant Werkausgabe III (Frankfurt: Suhrkamp, 1968). The translations of the *Reflexionen* are my own.

ABBREVIATIONS

A   *Anthropology from a Pragmatic Point of View*, trans. M. Gregor (The Hague: Martinus Nijhoff, 1974)

Ak.   *Kants gesammelte Schriften*, 29 vols., ed. Royal Prussian (now German) Academy of Sciences (Berlin: G. Reimer (now de Gruyter), 1902–)

BL   'The Blomberg Logic', in *LL* 1–246

CJ   *Critique of Judgement*, trans. J. C. Meredith (Oxford: Oxford University Press, 1952)

CPR   *Critique of Pure Reason*, trans. N. Kemp Smith (New York: St Martin's, 1965)

        Critique of Pure Reason, trans. P. Guyer and A. Wood (Cambridge: Cambridge University Press, 1997)

CPrR   *Critique of Practical Reason*, trans. L. W. Beck (Indianapolis: Bobbs-Merrill, 1956)

DS   'Concerning the Ultimate Ground of the Differentiation of Directions in Space', in *TP* 361–72

DWL   'The Dohna–Wundlacken Logic', in *LL* 425–516

FS   'The False Subtlety of the Four Syllogistic Figures', in *TP* 85–105

GMM *Grounding for the Metaphysics of Morals*, trans. J. Ellington (Indianapolis: Hackett, 1981)

I.   'Inquiry Concerning the Distinctness of the Principles of Natural Theology and Morality', in *TP* 243–75; generally known as the 'Prize Essay'

ID   'On the Form and Principles of the Sensible and Intelligible World', in *TP* 373–416; generally known as the 'Inaugural Dissertation'

JL   'The Jäsche Logic', in *LL* 519–640

LL   *Immanuel Kant: Lectures on Logic*, trans. J. M. Young (Cambridge: Cambridge University Press, 1992)

MFNS *Metaphysical Foundations of Natural Science*, trans. J. Ellington (Indianapolis: Bobbs-Merrill, 1970)

NE   'A New Elucidation of the First Principles of Metaphysical Cognition', in *TP* 1–45

O.   'An Attempt at Some Reflections on Optimism', in *TP* 67–76

OD   'On a Discovery according to which any New Critique of Pure Reason has been made Superfluous by an Earlier One', in *The*

        Kant–Eberhard Controversy, trans. H. Allison (Baltimore: Johns Hopkins University Press, 1973), 107–60

OPA   'The Only Possible Argument in Support of a Demonstration of the Existence of God', in *TP* 107–201

OT   'What is Orientation in Thinking?', in *Kant: Political Writings*, ed. H. Reiss, trans. H. B. Nisbet (2nd edn. Cambridge: Cambridge University Press, 1991), 237–49

P.   *Prolegomena to Any Future Metaphysics*, trans. J. Ellington (Indianapolis: Hackett, 1977)

PC   *Immanuel Kant: Philosophical Correspondence, 1759–99*, trans. A. Zweig (Chicago: University of Chicago Press, 1967)

PM   'Physical Monadology', in *TP* 47–66

R.   *Reflexionen = Kants handschriftlicher Nachlaß*

RP   *What Real Progress has Metaphysics made in Germany since the Time of Leibniz and Wolff?*, trans. T. Humphrey (New York: Arabis, 1983)

TP   *Immanuel Kant: Theoretical Philosophy, 1755–1770*, trans. D. Walford and R. Meerbote (Cambridge: Cambridge University Press, 1992)

VL   'The Vienna Logic', in *LL* 249–377

Introduction

> Philosophy and the history of philosophy are one. You cannot do the first without also doing the second. Otherwise put, it is essential to an adequate understanding of certain problems, questions, issues, that one understand them genetically.
>
> *Charles Taylor*[1]

This book has two intimately intertwined topics. First, it is an interpretive study of Immanuel Kant's massive and seminal *Critique of Pure Reason*; but secondly and equally, it is a critical essay on the historical foundations of analytic philosophy from Gottlob Frege to W. V. O. Quine.

By Kant's own reckoning, the first *Critique* is an extended reflection on a single question: 'Now the real problem of pure reason is contained in the question: how are synthetic a priori judgements possible?' (*CPR* B19). Translated out of Kant's jargon, this question raises a deep and broadly applicable philosophical difficulty: how can the same judgement be at once necessarily true, referred to the real or natural world in a substantive way, yet cognizable by creatures minded like us apart from all sense experience? For easy reference, I will call this 'the Modal Problem'.

Kant's Modal Problem comprehends four important subthemes of the first *Critique*: (1) the nature of judgement—in all four senses of (i) a particular truth-evaluable 'judgement' (*Urteil*) or 'proposition' (*Satz*), (ii) an act of propositional affirmation or 'holding-for-true' (*Fürwahrhalten*), (iii) the mental state or process of 'judging' (*Beurteilen*), and (iv) the mental capacity for judging or the 'power to judge' (*Urteilskraft*); (2) the crucial distinction between 'concepts' (*Begriffe*) and 'intuitions' (*Anschauungen*); (3) the intimately related and equally crucial distinction between analytic and synthetic judgements; and, last but not least, (4) the protean distinction between a priori and a posteriori, which cuts right across the other three subthemes.

Ultimately, however, neither Kant's proposed solution to the Modal Problem, nor any of its implicated subthemes, fully makes sense except against the backdrop of Kant's doctrine of transcendental idealism. Hence a central feature of my account is a new interpretation of his special brand of idealism. The nub of that interpretation is that Kant's answer in the first *Critique*

---

[1] Taylor, 'Philosophy and its History', 17.

to his leading question about synthetic a priori judgements grows directly out of his long-standing engagement with an even more fundamental problem. In his pre-Critical work of 1763, 'The Only Possible Argument in Support of a Demonstration of the Existence of God', Kant speaks in passing of 'the deepest science of all, where the word "representation" is understood with sufficient precision and employed with confidence, even though its meaning can never be analysed by means of definition' (OPA Ak. ii. 70). A decade later, in a famous letter to his former student Marcus Herz, he returns to the same idea while describing the main topics of what eventually became the first *Critique*:

[I] was then making plans for a work that might perhaps have the the title, 'The Limits of Sense and Reason'. I planned to have it consist of two parts, a theoretical and a practical. The first part would have two sections, (1) general phenomenology[2] and (2) metaphysics, but only with regard to its nature and method.[3] . . . As I thought through the theoretical part, considering its whole scope and the reciprocal relations of its parts, I noticed that I still lacked something essential, something that in my long metaphysical studies I, as well as others, had failed to pay attention to and that, in fact, constitutes the key to the whole secret of hitherto still obscure metaphysics. *I asked myself: What is the ground of the reference of that in us which we call "representation" to the object?* (*PC* Ak. x. 129–30, emphasis added)

A representation is a *Vorstellung*—literally, a 'putting' (*stellung*) of something 'before' (*Vor*) a conscious mind. Later in the letter to Herz, Kant goes on to say that he is especially concerned with the question of how an a priori (that is, non-empirical or non-sensory) mental representation can correctly refer to real objects. He wants to know 'how my understanding may form for itself concepts of things completely a priori, with which concepts the things must necessarily agree' (*PC* Ak. x. 131). And the task of finding an answer to that question largely determines both the focus and the trajectory of Kant's intensive work in the so-called silent decade leading up to the publication of the *Critique of Pure Reason*. But the particular question about a priori necessary objective mental representations, crucial as it is, cannot be answered without first answering the question about objective mental representations in general; indeed, an answer to the latter question largely determines an answer to the former question. So the absolutely fundamental question of Kant's revolutionary new approach to philosophy as adumbrated in 1772—which 'constitutes the key to the whole secret of hitherto still obscure metaphysics'—is this: how are objective mental representations possible?

In the Critical period, Kant's technical term for any sort of objective mental representation is "cognition" (*Erkenntnis*): 'The genus is *representation* in general (*repraesentatio*). Subordinate to it stands representation with

---

[2] This corresponds to the Transcendental Aesthetic.
[3] This corresponds to the Transcendental Logic and the Transcendental Doctrine of Method.

consciousness (*perceptio*). . . . An objective perception is *cognition* (*cognitio*)' (*CPR* A320/B376–7).[4] If we abstract away for a moment from the purely mental or conscious component of a cognition—which Kant (slightly misleadingly[5]) calls its 'form'—then we are left with its 'content' or 'matter' (*Inhalt, Materie*). The representational content is the essential—or individuating—part of a cognition in the sense that it determines precisely which object the cognition refers to. That is, it determines the object directedness, aboutness, or *intentionality* of the cognition.[6] Put this way, and recalling that we have momentarily abstracted away from the purely mental or conscious aspects of a cognition, then we can clearly see that Kant's fundamental philosophical question is effectively equivalent to the question: how are *meanings* possible? In the philosopher's lexicon, 'meanings' are nothing other than object-directed representational contents, taken together with the formal or logical elements contained within such contents. This immediately implies that Kant's fundamental question belongs to the domain of *philosophical semantics*.[7] For this reason, I will dub the problem that Kant's transcendental idealism is ultimately designed to solve 'the Semantic Problem'. Now, as Kant makes quite clear in his letter to Herz, but also later in the first *Critique* itself (*CPR* Bxvi. B166–7), his underlying intention in the *Critique of Pure Reason* is that his solution to the Modal Problem will follow directly from his solution to the Semantic Problem. In this sense, Kant's transcendental idealism is at once a general *cognitive semantics* and a general *theory of necessary truth*.

Once we have isolated the Semantic Problem and the Modal Problem as the key difficulties that Kant is struggling with in the first *Critique*, then we are in a good position to see the segue between the twin topics of this book. If the *Critique of Pure Reason* is indeed at bottom a general cognitive semantics and a general theory of necessary truth, then it seems to me that we cannot properly understand the first *Critique* without undertaking at the same time a critical reassessment of the philosophical reception and fate of these doctrines in the tradition of analytic philosophy up to Quine.

---

[4] For more on the term "cognition", see Ch. 1 n. 13.   [5] See Ch. 1 n. 11.

[6] See Brentano, *Psychology from an Empirical Standpoint*, bk. two, Ch. I, esp. p. 88; Husserl, *Logical Investigations*, Investigation V; Aquila, *Intentionality: A Study of Mental Acts*; and Searle, *Intentionality*.

[7] For surveys, see Hacking, *Why Does Language Matter to Philosophy?*, and Kretzmann, 'Semantics, History of'. Kant's semantics falls into a mentalistic tradition that runs backwards through early modern philosophy (esp. Locke and Descartes) and the Scholastics (esp. Aquinas), to Aristotle; forwards in one track from Kant through von Humboldt to Chomsky, Fodor, and Jackendoff; and forwards in another track from Kant through Trendelenburg (Brentano's teacher) to Brentano, Husserl, Meinong, early Gilbert Ryle, Gareth Evans, Christopher Peacocke, and John Searle. For rejections of semantic mentalism, see Dummett, *Origins of Analytical Philosophy*; Dummett, 'What is a Theory of Meaning? (I–II)'; Quine, 'Mind and Verbal Dispositions'; and Quine, 'On Mental Entities'.

It is doubtless somewhat hazardous to attempt a comprehensive and uncontroversial formulation of the origins and nature of analytic philosophy, given both its complex historical development and the patent fact that one of the most vigorous and contentious debates in recent and contemporary analytic philosophy concerns precisely *what* the origins and nature of analytic philosophy really *are*.[8] But even granting that, at least two partial characterizations of it do seem to be unobjectionably correct. First, the analytic tradition is an Austro-German and Anglo-American philosophical movement that got underway in the late nineteenth and early twentieth centuries by promoting semantics and a theory of necessary truth based on mathematical logic together with a thoroughly conventionalistic construal of language to front-and-centre position in philosophy, thereby displacing to the periphery its traditional ontological, epistemological, and psychological concerns. Secondly, the leading figures in the analytic tradition are (1) Gottlob Frege in Germany in the 1880s and 1890s; (2) Bertrand Russell, G. E. Moore, and their Austrian-born student, colleague, and sometimes *bête noire* Ludwig Wittgenstein in England from the late 1890s into the early 1920s; (3) the 'logical positivists' or 'logical empiricists' (especially Rudolf Carnap) in Austria and Germany from the mid-1920s through the mid-1930s, and then later in the USA from the late 1930s until the late 1940s;[9] (4) Wittgenstein again and the Oxford-centred 'ordinary-language' movement (led by J. L. Austin, Gilbert Ryle, P. F. Strawson, and H. P. Grice) in the 1940s and 1950s;[10] and, finally, (5) W. V. O. Quine in the USA in the 1950s, 1960s, and beyond.

Where precisely do Kant and the *Critique of Pure Reason* come into this familiar picture of the analytic tradition and its Hall of Fame? One obvious

---

[8] See e.g. Bell and Cooper (eds.), *The Analytic Tradition*; Coffa, *The Semantic Tradition from Kant to Carnap*; Dummett, *Origins of Analytical Philosophy*; French *et al.* (eds.), *The Foundations of Analytic Philosophy*; Glock (ed.), *The Rise of Analytic Philosophy*; Hacker, *Wittgenstein's Place in Twentieth-Century Analytic Philosophy*; Pap, *Elements of Analytic Philosophy*; Rorty, *Philosophy and the Mirror of Nature*, esp. Chs. III–VI; and Tugendhat, *Traditional and Analytical Philosophy*, esp. pt. I. Dummett has argued in 'Can Analytical Philosophy be Systematic and Ought it to Be?', 441–2, and in *Origins of Analytical Philosophy* that analytic philosophy must be identified with linguistic philosophy. But this identification is almost certainly too narrow: see e.g. Hacker, 'The Rise of Twentieth Century Analytic Philosophy'; Monk, 'Was Russell an Analytical Philosopher?'; and Monk again, 'What is Analytical Philosophy?'

[9] Logical empiricism or positivism originated in the writings of members and associates of the Vienna Circle (*Wiener Kreis*), including A. J. Ayer, Gustav Bergmann, Carnap, Herbert Feigl, Kurt Gödel, Carl Hempel, Otto Neurath, W. V. O. Quine, Hans Reichenbach, Moritz Schlick, Alfred Tarski, and Friedrich Waismann. See Ayer (ed.), *Logical Positivism*; Coffa, *The Semantic Tradition from Kant to Carnap*, chs. 9–19; and Friedman, *Reconsidering Logical Positivism*.

[10] See Dummett, 'Oxford Philosophy'; Hacker, *Wittgenstein's Place in Twentieth Century Analytic Philosophy*, chs. 5–6; and Hanna, 'Conceptual Analysis'.

fact is that the rise of analytic philosophy decisively marked the end of the century-long dominance of Kant's philosophy in Europe.[11] But the deeper fact is that the analytic tradition *emerged* from Kant's philosophy in the sense that its members were able to define and legitimate their views only by means of an intensive, extended engagement with, and a partial or complete rejection of, the first *Critique*. So I think that the overall career of analysis up to Quine almost perfectly reflects Alberto Coffa's crisp dictum about the logical positivist or empiricist phase of the tradition—that it 'was born in the effort to avoid Kant's theory of the a priori'.[12] And essentially the same point is nicely encapsulated in a characteristically forthright self-observation made by Russell in *My Philosophical Development*: 'Ever since I abandoned the philosophy of Kant . . . I have sought solutions of philosophical problems by means of analysis; and I remain firmly persuaded . . . that only by analysing is progress possible.'[13]

Assuming that I am correct in closely connecting the rise and flourishing of analytic philosophy up to Quine with the extended and complex process of rejecting Kant's theoretical philosophy, this puts the contemporary student of Kant's *Critique of Pure Reason* in a philosophically rather odd but at the same time quite unprecedented and potentially exciting position. The Kant we study nowadays is manifestly a Kant who has been reworked and represented to us by those who participated directly in the analytic tradition's long and winding struggle with the first *Critique*. That is, by necessity we read Kant's theoretical philosophy from *within* the historical and conceptual framework of analytic philosophy. But two consequences seem to follow immediately from our becoming self-consciously aware of that fact, each of which partially determines the shape and subject matter of this book. First, those of us writing about Kant's first *Critique* at the beginning of the twenty-first century, and therefore 100 years after the beginning of the analytic tradition, cannot possibly ignore the dialectical interplay between Kant's views and those of his leading analytic critics without risking misunderstanding Kant's theories. Secondly, to re-examine several of Kant's key doctrines in the light of their critical reception and transmission by the leading figures of the analytic tradition is also critically to re-explore the foundations of analytic philosophy from a specifically Kantian point of view.

[11] I do not mean to underestimate the crucial importance of Hegel's philosophy during the early and mid-nineteenth century. Nevertheless, by the 1860s and 1870s—in Germany at least—Kant's ideas had made a decisive comeback, via neo-Kantianism. See Beck, 'Neo-Kantianism', and Köhnke, *The Rise of Neo-Kantianism*, chs. 3–7. The Hegelian influence survived somewhat longer in England than in Germany, but in the form of neo-Hegelianism—in which Kantian and Hegelian ideas cohabited very comfortably; see Passmore, *A Hundred Years of Philosophy*, chs. 3–4.

[12] Coffa, *The Semantic Tradition from Kant to Carnap*, 21.

[13] Russell, *My Philosophical Development*, 14–15. See also Hylton, 'Logic in Russell's Logicism'.

I have suggested that analytic philosophy up to Quine is to be partially identified with the thesis that semantics lies at or very near the centre of philosophy. So Ryle was not so very far from the truth when he wittily remarked that 'preoccupation with the theory of meaning could be described as the occupational disease of twentieth-century Anglo-Saxon and Austrian philosophy'.[14] I have also suggested that the other core element of analytic philosophy from Frege to Quine is a theory of necessary truth deriving from the fusion of mathematical logic and linguistic conventionalism. So in a Rylean tone of voice we might say that analytic philosophy is the joint product of two intimately connected occupational diseases: a preoccupation with the theory of meaning, and a preoccupation with the logico-linguistic theory of necessity. In order to be able to relate Kant's main doctrines in the first *Critique* to their later exciting adventures in the analytic tradition, we should have before us at least a schematic history of that two-headed obsession. Further fine points of detail, including chapter-and-verse references, and the inevitable qualifications needed for a richer and more fully adequate understanding of the analytic movement, can be added later as we go along.

As Coffa persuasively shows, the analytic tradition had its first stirrings in the early to mid-nineteenth century with Bernard Bolzano's criticisms of Kant's logic in his *Theory of Science* (1837),[15] and with Hermann von Helmholtz's criticisms of Kant's views on perception and geometry in the 1860s and 1870s.[16] Indeed, with the benefit of historical hindsight, we can see very clearly that Bolzano's focus on the philosophy of the formal sciences strongly anticipates the logicistic, rationalistic, and platonistic orientation of early analytic philosophy, and also that Helmholtz's focus on the epistemology of the natural sciences and non-Euclidean geometry just as strongly anticipates the empiricistic and exact-science-oriented slants of the middle and later phases of the analytic tradition.

If Bolzano and Helmholtz are the advance guard of analytic philosophy, then Frege is the first of its two Founding Fathers. Frege's claim to this status rests largely on three logical treatises in the foundations of mathematics—the *Begriffsschrift* (1879),[17] *Foundations of Arithmetic* (1884), and *Basic Laws of Arithmetic* (1893)—and his two essays, 'Function and Concept' (1891) and 'On Sense and Meaning' (1892). Of crucial importance in Frege's writings are his trenchant critique of 'logical psychologism' (i.e. the thesis that logic or

---

[14] Ryle, 'The Theory of Meaning', 350.

[15] See Coffa, *The Semantic Tradition from Kant to Carnap*, ch. 2.

[16] See ibid., ch. 3, and Hatfield, *The Natural and the Normative*, ch. 5. See also Sect. 5.5 below.

[17] "*Begriffsschrift*" means 'conceptual notation' or 'concept script'. The general idea is that mathematical logic must take the form of a universal ideographic symbolism—a *characteristica universalis*. See Boole, *The Laws of Thought*, and Frege, *Conceptual Notation and Related Articles*.

mathematics is fully explained by empirical psychology) as found, for example, in J. S. Mill's *System of Logic* (1843); his rejection of Kant's theory that truths of arithmetic are synthetic a priori; his theory of analytic truth as deductive derivability from logical definitions and universal logical laws; his logicism— that is, the project of theoretically reducing arithmetic to logic via his famous definition of number in terms of sets of one-to-one correlated sets; his ana- lytical strategy of contextual definition, obeying the dictum that a word or term has meaning only in the context of whole propositions; and last but not least his metaphysically realistic[18] theory of linguistic meaning—his theory of non- physical, mind-independent 'sense' (*Sinn*) or descriptive content, and mind- independent (although sometimes physical) 'Meaning' (*Bedeutung*) or reference.

Russell is the second Founding Father of the analytic tradition. His first philosophical book was a neo-Kantian study of the philosophy of space, *An Essay on the Foundations of Geometry* (1897). But he soon gave up what was left of his Kantianism under the powerful influence of Moore.[19] Moore was at this time a violent anti-idealist and a radical platonic realist.[20] According to him, concepts are literally the objective constituents of the world; proposi- tions in turn are essentially connections of concepts and thereby objectively exist in the world as well; and every object of sensation or perception is fully mind-independent. The writings of the Austrian philosopher Alexius Meinong[21] added fuel to the engine of Russell's platonic realism by convincing him that propositions are abstract or 'subsistent' ontic complexes containing both individual objects and concepts or universals; and also that most well-formed, meaningful mental presentations or verbal expressions stand for an object, whether that object actually occurs in space and time or not. And, perhaps most importantly of all, the works of the Italian logician and mathematician Giuseppe Peano[22] and Frege jointly convinced him that logicism was a fully viable philosophical programme. In the period 1900–14, Russell assimilated but also brilliantly synthesized these influences, particularly in *Principles of Mathematics* (1903), 'On Denoting' (1905), *Principia Mathematica* (1910–13),[23] *Problems of Philosophy* (1912), and *Our Knowledge of the External World* (1914). Russell's signal contributions to the foundations of the analytic tradition are his conception of philosophical analysis as the decomposition of logical,

---

[18] It is not quite accurate to call Frege's theory 'platonistic', although it certainly has some platonic features; see Ch. 4 n. 6.

[19] See esp. Moore's 'Critical Notice of B. A. W. Russell, *Essay on the Foundations of Geometry*' (1899), 'The Nature of Judgment' (1899), 'The Refutation of Idealism' (1903), and 'Kant's Idealism' (1904).   [20] See Baldwin, *G. E. Moore*, chs. I–II.

[21] See Meinong, *On Assumptions* (1st edn., 1902), and Russell, 'Meinong's Theory of Complexes and Assumptions' (1904).

[22] See Rossi-Landi, 'Peano, Giuseppe'; Russell, *The Principles of Mathematics*, 4, 10; and Monk, *Bertrand Russell: The Spirit of Solitude*, 129–31.

[23] Co-authored with A. N. Whitehead.

semantic, epistemological, psychological, or ontological complexes into simples or atoms; his sharp distinction between knowledge by description (conceptual or propositional cognition) and knowledge by acquaintance (intuitive or perceptual cognition); his denotational or (to use Ryle's phrase) ' "Fido"-Fido' semantics, according to which words have meaning solely by standing for objects; his theory of definite descriptions in 'On Denoting', which says that most or even all apparent singular terms can be theoretically eliminated by translating them into special contextually defined logically complex general terms; and finally his extension of logicism to geometry.

Then: enter Wittgenstein. From his arrival in Cambridge in 1911 through the publication of the *Tractatus Logico-Philosophicus* in 1921, Wittgenstein absorbed, refocused, and crucially transformed the Fregean–Russellian logic, metaphysics, and epistemology. Indeed, he turned analytic philosophy in a fundamentally new direction that initiated its second major phase. This Tractarian turn essentially contains four doctrines. They are a 'picture theory' of meaning for the denotational parts of language, according to which propositions are structurally isomorphic with what they are about;[24] a theory of logical constants as strictly non-denotational or functionally defined parts of language; two highly restrictive distinctions between logical sense and logical nonsense, on the one hand, and between 'saying' (= describing, stating) and 'showing' (= indicating, ostending) on the other; and lastly a closely related doctrine of logical truths as vacuous linguistic tautologies. The overall upshot, however, is a strong emphasis on the fundamental philosophical importance of language—especially 'ideal' logical languages or *Begriffsschriften*.

Wittgenstein's achievement significantly contributed to the creation of a new submovement within the overall analytic development—namely, logical empiricism or positivism.[25] This submovement began in the discussions and writings of the members of the Vienna Circle. In turn, the philosophical interests and outlook of the Circle had six main sources of inspiration and cognitive funding: Hume's epistemological empiricism, as updated by Ernst Mach; neo-Kantian philosophy;[26] the Helmholtzian conviction that philosophy should take its cue from the exact sciences and eschew speculative metaphysics; non-Euclidean geometry and Einstein's theory of relativity; Frege's and Russell's logicism; and, above all, Wittgenstein's *Tractatus*. Combining the intellectual

---

[24] Or at least that is the standard interpretation. See e.g. Hacker, *Insight and Illusion*, ch. III. But see also Diamond, *The Realistic Spirit*, Introduction II and ch. 6, for a revisionist reading of the *Tractatus* according to which everything propositional (including logic) is literally nonsense. If correct, this radically sharpens the contrast between what Frege, Moore, and Russell did and what Wittgenstein was actually up to.

[25] On the transition between the *Tractatus* and logical empiricism, see Coffa, *Semantic Tradition from Kant to Carnap*, chs. 8–12, and Friedman, *Reconsidering Logical Positivism*, ch. 8.   [26] See Richardson, *Carnap's Construction of the World*, chs. 4–6.

inputs from these sources with Wittgenstein's conversations with some members of the Vienna Circle in the late 1920s and early 1930s,[27] Carnap and the other empiricists then gradually developed three basic views. The first was the verificationist theory of meaning, according to which the meaning of a proposition is the method or rule by which it is empirically tested for truth; the second was the conventionalist, linguistic, or more accurately logico-linguistic theory of necessary truth, which holds that necessary truths are nothing but either truths of elementary logic or else theorems logically derivable from a set of arbitrarily chosen axioms or postulates for a given formal or natural language system; and the third was a blanket rejection of the very idea of the synthetic a priori[28] and of metaphysics more generally.

Wittgenstein returned to England in 1929, whereupon he promptly and rather perversely set about destroying his own earlier views.[29] The eventual positive result of this destruction was a strong emphasis on a painstaking, micrological description of the basic concepts implicit in 'ordinary' or natural languages and everyday speech practices, as opposed to the logical study of formalized languages.[30] But the negative result was a deep scepticism about the very possibility of systematic philosophy, including classical semantic and logical analysis in either its rationalist–platonist or empiricist–positivist versions.[31] Wittgenstein's new doctrines—or anti-doctrines—circulated in samizdat form and by word of mouth for many years, but were eventually published in the hugely influential *Philosophical Investigations* (1953).

The intellectually liberating ideas of the *Investigations* produced an odd interference pattern within the rolling wave that was the analytic tradition in the 1940s and 1950s, in the sense that they somewhat paradoxically at once gave it impetus and also tended subversively towards its dissolution. Still, even allowing for the important differences between Wittgenstein's early and later views, there remains an underlying thread linking both of them, and those of the intervening logical empiricists, together—namely, a primary focus on language, and on the thesis that all philosophical questions are ultimately— in some sense—questions of language. This crucially transforms Kant's famous Copernican Revolution in philosophy (*CPR* Bxvi), which says that all philosophical questions are ultimately questions about the origins, nature, scope, and limits of human cognition.[32] Hence it has been aptly called 'the linguistic

---

[27] See Waismann, *Wittgenstein and the Vienna Circle*.

[28] This is slightly overstated for expository convenience; for qualification, see Ch. 5 n. 10.

[29] This is not to deny the existence of many important continuities between earlier and later Wittgenstein: e.g. prop. 3.326 of the *Tractatus* (p. 57) strongly anticipates the intimate linkage of meaning and use in the *Philosophical Investigations*, etc.

[30] See e.g. Rorty (ed.), *The Linguistic Turn*, pt. III.

[31] If Diamond is correct, this deep scepticism about systematic philosophy infuses the *Tractatus* as well; see *The Realistic Spirit*, Introduction II.   [32] See Sects. 1.1 and 1.2.

turn'.[33] Viewed in this synoptic way, what otherwise appears to be a sharp or even unbridgeable dichotomy between the doctrines of the early and later Wittgenstein can be smoothly bridged by construing it as an essentially domestic difference between ideal language philosophy and ordinary language philosophy.

Influential as it was, the linguistic phase of analytic philosophy did not stay permanently in place. Just as Wittgenstein had transformed the logicist phase of analytic philosophy and initiated its linguistic turn, so Quine again transformed analytic philosophy and initiated its third phase. Quine's main intellectual influences were Frege's and Russell's logico-mathematical writings, on the one hand, and the writings of Carnap and the other members or affiliates of the Vienna Circle, on the other. But there were also lesser yet still significant elements of pragmatism, neo-Hegelian holism, and neo-Kantian verificationism in his work, perhaps more or less unconsciously inherited from Harvard's philosophical heavy-hitters of the previous two generations—William James, Josiah Royce, and C. I. Lewis.[34] In any case, particularly in 'Truth by Convention' (1935), 'Two Dogmas of Empiricism' (1951), *Word and Object* (1960), 'Carnap and Logical Truth' (1963), and 'Epistemology Naturalized' (1969), Quine thoroughly rejected the 'very ideas' of meanings or intensions, modality and modal logic, the analytic/synthetic distinction, atomistic verificationism, and the a priori/a posteriori distinction. Then on the ruins of logical empiricism he built a new form of empiricism—one that is thoroughly holistic, behaviouristic, and fallibilistic. Although Quine managed to retain an important element of linguistic philosophy in his great sensitivity to the 'use versus mention' distinction,[35] his version of analysis was above all guided by philosophical naturalism,[36] or the thesis that all serious metaphysical, epistemological, and methodological questions in philosophy can be answered only by direct appeal to the natural sciences. For this reason it seems highly appropriate to dub Quine's transformation of the analytic tradition the 'scientific turn'. Otherwise put, after Quine analytic philosophy is *scientific philosophy*.[37]

To summarize, we have three salient facts. First, there is the overarching explicit or implicit concern of all analytic philosophers from Frege to Quine with semantics and the logico-linguistic theory of necessity. Secondly, there is the overarching three-part symphonic structure[38] of the analytic tradition:

---

[33] The phrase is Gustav Bergmann's. See Rorty, 'Metaphilosophical Difficulties of Linguistic Philosophy'.   [34] See Kuklick, *The Rise of American Philosophy*.

[35] See Carnap on the material mode versus the formal mode of speech in *The Logical Syntax of Language*, sects. 64, 74–81; Tarski on object languages versus metalanguages in 'The Semantic Conception of Truth', 349–51; and Quine on semantic ascent in *Word and Object*, 270–6.

[36] See e.g. Kitcher, 'The Naturalists Return', and Papineau, *Philosophical Naturalism*.

[37] See Reichenbach, *The Rise of Scientific Philosophy*.

[38] i.e. the middle part of the analytic tradition up to Quine further divides into two subparts: ideal language philosophy and ordinary language philosophy.

(1) logicistic philosophy (led by Frege, early Moore, and early Russell); (2) linguistic philosophy (led in its first or ideal language phase by early Wittgenstein and Carnap, and then in its second or ordinary language phase by the later Wittgenstein); and (3) scientific philosophy (led by Quine). But, thirdly and perhaps most importantly, there is the underlying dialectical engine of philosophical analysis—namely, its ongoing critical struggles with the central doctrines of the first *Critique*. The first thing to go was Kant's philosophy of arithmetic, by Frege's means;[39] then Kant's idealism and theory of judgement, by Moore's means;[40] then Kant's philosophy of geometry, by Russell's means;[41] then Kant's doctrine of the meaningfulness of analytic or logical truths, by early Wittgenstein's means;[42] then Kant's doctrine of the synthetic a priori, by Carnap's means (although significantly prefigured by early Wittgenstein and Schlick);[43] and then finally Kant's seminal analytic/ synthetic and a priori/a posteriori distinctions, by Quine's means.[44] Seen in this light, it is scarcely an exaggeration to say that the inner drama of analytic philosophy from Frege to Quine and beyond[45] is its century-long love–hate relationship with Kant's theoretical philosophy.

I have one further point to make in this particular connection. It has been forcefully argued by several leading contemporary philosophers that analytic philosophy has now reached a stage of crisis[46] in its development. This crisis arises from the very unsettling fact that many and perhaps even most analytic philosophers now question the defensibility and ultimate intelligibility of the very idea of analysis. But how can there be analytic philosophy without a cogent and coherent conception of philosophical analysis? In this sense, the analytic consensus in contemporary philosophy—as intellectually vigorous, institution- ally secure, and one might even say bull-marketish, as it undoubtedly is— is speeding towards a crash. Michael Friedman has very plausibly traced the origins of this crisis back to analytic philosophy's rejection of Kant, via its intimate but stormy relationship with logical positivism.[47] Perhaps, then, our re-examination of the first *Critique* and the historical foundations of analytic philosophy up to Quine will also throw some light upon the underlying causes and possible remedies of this unwholesome situation.

---

[39] See Sect. 3.3.   [40] See Sects. 2.3 and 2.4.   [41] See Sect. 5.5.

[42] See Sects. 2.2 and 3.1.   [43] See Sects. 5.0 and 5.6.   [44] See Sect. 3.5.

[45] For the beyond, see Hanna, 'A Kantian Critique of Scientific Essentialism'. Scientific essentialists reject Kant's thesis of the strong equivalence between necessity and apriority (see Sect. 5.2).

[46] See e.g. McDowell, *Mind and World*; Norris, 'Doubting Castle or the Slough of Despond: Davidson and Schiffer on the Limits of Analysis'; and Putnam, *Words and Life*. Rorty's *Philosophy and the Mirror of Nature* and Schiffer's *Remnants of Meaning* laid the ground- work for this line of thinking.

[47] See Friedman, 'Kant and the 20th Century', 44–5, and Friedman, *Reconsidering Logical Positivism*, 1–14.

Before we get properly underway, however, I also have to lay down three caveats.

First, given its double-barrelled topic, my account does not follow in a perfectly strict way either the textual organization of the first *Critique* or the historical development of the analytic tradition. Instead its organization is thematic rather than textual-exegetical or conventionally historical.

Secondly, in order to avoid the ever-present danger of this book's becoming a loose, baggy monster, I have had to focus fairly selectively on certain key Kantian topics and also on certain corresponding key topics in the analytic tradition.

For these two reasons, however, a brief preliminary sketch of the contents of the chapters may help to orient the reader. In Chapter 1, I state and explicate my overarching interpretive proposal that Kant's positive theoretical philosophy as presented in the *Critique of Pure Reason* is at bottom a general theory of objective mental representation, or a general cognitive semantics; and then I begin the justification of that proposal by undertaking a preliminary discussion of Kant's theory of cognition, with a special emphasis on judgement. This is extended and widened in Chapter 2 with a discussion of the conditions under which cognitions are possible. This chapter unpacks in some detail my interpretation of Kant's transcendental idealism. Then I cover in sequence the natures of analytic (Chapter 3) and synthetic (Chapter 4) judgements. These two chapters also focus, respectively, on the cognitive semantics of concepts or descriptive terms, and the cognitive semantics of intuitions or directly referring terms. Chapter 5 deals with Kant's doctrine of necessary truth, and especially with his doctrine of synthetic a priori judgements. Here I argue on Kant's behalf for 'modal dualism'[48]—the thesis that there are two irreducibly different kinds of necessary truth. To confirm this thesis, I apply Kant's doctrine of the synthetic a priori to the highly controversial case of geometry and then look closely at the well-known objection(s) to Kant's doctrine from non-Euclidean geometry. Finally, in the Concluding Un-Quinean Postscript I offer a Kantian response to a radical worry—due of course to Quine—about the very idea of the a priori, and make a few tentative remarks about the broader implications of the first *Critique* for the future of analytic philosophy.

My third caveat is this. After much consideration, I have decided not to give a detailed or extended treatment of Kant's theory of the nature and justification of synthetic a priori truths of the transcendental metaphysics of nature—or, as he sometimes labels it, 'ontology' (*RP* Ak. xx. 260). Hence I present no detailed or extended interpretation of the Metaphysical Deduction, the Transcendental Deduction(s) of the pure concepts of the understanding, the Schematism of the pure concepts, the Analytic of Principles (Axioms of Intuition, Anticipations of Perception, Analogies of Experience, and Postulates

---

[48] This apt term was, I think, invented by David Chalmers.

of Empirical Thought), or the Refutation of Idealism. There are three reasons for this decision. First, the nature and justification of transcendental ontology is not a topic on which Kant has been directly engaged by Frege, Moore, Russell, Wittgenstein early or late, Carnap and the logical empiricists, or Quine. Instead, when dealing explicitly with Kant or with Kantian themes, they have focused almost exclusively on certain highly contested flashpoints: analytic versus synthetic; intuitions (or singular terms, directly referential terms) versus concepts (or general terms, descriptive terms); a posteriori versus a priori; the very idea of a synthetic a priori proposition; whether mathematics is grounded in pure intuition or in pure logic; the logical versus the psychological; realism versus idealism, and so on. Secondly, and somewhat more pragmatically, to work out Kant's theory of transcendental-ontological synthetic a priori propositions, with careful attention paid to all its aspects and implications, would take another book at least as long as the one I have already written. Thirdly, and perhaps most importantly, this is a topic already heavily and excellently covered by mainstream English-speaking Kant scholarship over the last 100 years.[49] It is not my task to tread this well-trodden ground again. Instead, I want to see what philosophical sense can be made of some key doctrines of Kant's *Critique of Pure Reason* in relation to the historical foundations of analytic philosophy from Frege to Quine. That is more than task enough.

[49] See esp. (in reverse temporal order) Guyer, *Kant and the Claims of Knowledge*; Allison, *Kant's Transcendental Idealism*; Strawson, *The Bounds of Sense*; Paton, *Kant's Metaphysic of Experience*; and Kemp Smith, *Commentary to Kant's 'Critique of Pure Reason'*.

1.

Kant and the Semantic Problem

If we discard [Kant's] antiquated terminology, and state his position in current terms, we find that it amounts to the assertion that *consciousness is in all cases awareness of meaning*.

Norman Kemp Smith[1]

1.0. Introduction

What is Kant's *Critique of Pure Reason* about? While the first *Critique* is notoriously long, dense, and difficult to grasp in its details, for contemporary readers there nevertheless seems to be an easy answer to this question. It is about the nature, scope, and limits of human knowledge—more precisely, about the problem of adequately justifying our scientific and more generally rational beliefs in the face of radical Humean or anti-metaphysical scepticism, on the one hand, and radical Cartesian scepticism about the external world, on the other. But as a matter of fact this pat answer is to a large extent predetermined by a certain long-standing and widely shared interpretive model of the first *Critique*. According to this canonical model, Kant is doing transcendental epistemology.[2] Bruce Kuklick plausibly speculates that in North America its proximal cause is C. I. Lewis:

After the [First World] war Hegel became, for Americans, a silly pompous, and *defeated* figure, unworthy of the great tradition. Indeed, the wonder is not that Hegel vanished, but that Kant remained. And in line with this development the Kant who remained was not the Kant pregnant with elements of transcendent metaphysics. It was the Kant

[1] Kemp Smith, *Commentary to Kant's 'Critique of Pure Reason'*, p. xli.

[2] See e.g. Allison, *Kant's Transcendental Idealism*; Beck, *Essays on Kant and Hume*; Beck, *Studies in the Philosophy of Kant*; Bennett, *Kant's Analytic*; Bird, *Kant's Theory of Knowledge*; Guyer, *Kant and the Claims of Knowledge*; Prichard, *Kant's Theory of Knowledge*; Strawson, *The Bounds of Sense*; and Van Cleve, *Problems from Kant*.

whom C. I. Lewis expounded, the austere transcendental epistemologist, not the transcendent metaphysician. To make the point in terms of the canon: the Kant of the canon synthesizes rationalism and empiricism; he is much less the father of Hegel.[3]

Kuklick's thumbnail gloss on Kant historiography also correctly indicates that there have traditionally been two distinct canonical ways of reading Kant: as a 'transcendent metaphysician'; and as an 'austere transcendental epistemologist'. According to the metaphysical reading, the *Critique of Pure Reason* is about the nature, scope, and limits of ontology—in particular, about answering the questions 'what basic sorts of beings are there?' and 'what is ultimately real?' This reading held sway in Germany from shortly after the publication of the first *Critique*,[4] through the Idealist period, until the emergence and flourishing of neo-Kantian philosophy in the mid- to late nineteenth century,[5] when it was gradually replaced by the epistemological reading. By contrast, in England and North America the metaphysical reading of Kant survived pretty much intact through the neo-Hegelian period until the early 1920s; but ever since then—Lewis's *Mind and the World Order* appeared in 1929—the epistemological reading has been the Anglo-American norm.

In my opinion, neither of these interpretive models of Kant's theoretical philosophy is wrong. Each, indeed, validly brings out an aspect of the first *Critique*. Nevertheless, each also presents a somewhat one-sided view—as it were, a flat or two-dimensional projection of a robustly three-dimensional object.

In addition to these two canonical readings of the first *Critique*, there is at least one other way of looking at Kant's theoretical philosophy—a way that is more fully explanatory and better rounded—that needs to be illuminated and explored. I make no special claims of originality for my third way; indeed, to a large extent it is merely the result of fusing two important pre-existing tendencies in recent Kant scholarship. First, it has been quite convincingly shown that Kant can be read as a *logico-semantic theorist*.[6] (For Kant, 'logic' includes not only the classical or Aristotelian/Scholastic theory of deductive entailment, sentential connectives, and monadic quantification, but also much of what we would now regard as semantics—the theory of concepts and their constituents,

---

[3] Kuklick, 'Seven Thinkers and How They Grew: Descartes, Spinoza, Leibniz; Locke, Berkeley, Hume; Kant', 133–4. The leading popularizer of Lewis's epistemic interpretation— even when he disagreed with Lewis—was L. W. Beck.

[4] See Beiser, *The Fate of Reason*.   [5] See Köhnke, *The Rise of Neo-Kantianism*.

[6] See e.g. Brandt, *The Table of Judgments: Critique of Pure Reason A67–76; B92–101*; Brittan, *Kant's Theory of Science*; Butts, 'Kant's Schemata as Semantical Rules'; Hintikka, *Logic, Language-Games, and Information: Kantian Themes in the Philosophy of Logic*; Longuenesse, *Kant and the Capacity to Judge*; McDowell, 'Having the World in View: Sellars, Kant, and Intentionality'; McDowell, *Mind and World*; Reich, *The Completeness of Kant's Table of Judgments*; Schwyzer, *The Unity of Understanding*; Sellars, *Science and Metaphysics: Variations on Kantian Themes*; and Sellars, 'Some Remarks on Kant's Theory of Experience'.

the theory of judgements or propositions, the theory of truth, and so on.) And, secondly, it has been equally convincingly shown that Kant can be read as a *philosophical psychologist.*[7]

Now Kemp Smith pointed out as early as 1923 that it is reasonable to regard the *Critique of Pure Reason* as a treatise about the conditions of the possibility of the human mind's conscious apprehension of meanings. What this strongly suggests to me is that, while the logico-semantic and psychological interpretations of Kant may seem on the surface disparate and incommensurable, they are really only two sides of the same coin. Kant's theoretical philosophy is at once thoroughly logico-semantic *and* thoroughly psychological in nature.[8] Or, as I put it in the Introduction, in my view the first *Critique* is a general theory of objective mental representation—a general cognitive semantics. In order to justify this interpretive thesis, in the rest of this chapter and in the next as well I will explicate the basic doctrines of the first *Critique* from an explicitly cognitive-semantic point of view.

1.1. Kant's Cognitive Semantics

The most obvious objection to my way of reading the first *Critique* is the charge of anachronism—that I am falsely imposing contemporary conceptions and distinctions on a quite foreign eighteenth-century outlook. So what we must see is how it is that Kant, from his earliest philosophical writings forward, is a cognitive semanticist.

As I mentioned in the Introduction, Kant's famous 1772 letter to Herz contains a working outline of the first *Critique*, and explicitly tells us that its 'key' lies in answering the question of how mental representations of objects are possible:

---

[7] See e.g. Ameriks, *Kant's Theory of Mind*; Aquila, *Matter in Mind*; Aquila, *Representational Mind*; Brook, *Kant and the Mind*; Falkenstein, *Kant's Intuitionism*; Gibbons, *Kant's Theory of Imagination*; Keller, *Kant and the Demands of Self-Consciousness*; Patricia Kitcher, *Kant's Transcendental Psychology*; Powell, *Kant's Theory of Self-Consciousness*; Waxman, *Kant's Model of the Mind*; and (leading the way in 1963) Wolff, *Kant's Theory of Mental Activity*. More generally, see Zoeller, 'Main Developments in Recent Scholarship on the *Critique of Pure Reason*', 457–66.

[8] See also Longuenesse, *Kant and the Capacity to Judge*, 6, 17–34, 398. Hence the first *Critique* shares much in common with recent works on the mentalistic side of the philosophy of language—see e.g. Evans, *The Varieties of Reference*; Fodor, *The Language of Thought*; Fodor, *Psychosemantics: The Problem of Meaning in the Philosophy of Mind*; Jackendoff, *Patterns in the Mind*; Jackendoff, *Semantics and Cognition*; Peacocke, *A Study of Concepts*; and Searle, *Intentionality*.

I noticed that I still lacked something essential, something that in my long metaphysical studies I, as well as others, had failed to pay attention to and that, in fact constitutes the key to the whole secret of hitherto still obscure metaphysics. I asked myself: What is the ground of the reference of that in us which we call "representation" to the object? (*PC* Ak. x. 129–30)

But what, more precisely, is Kant's conception of a representation? In one of his logic lectures in the 1770s, Kant remarks that 'what representation is cannot really be explained. It is one of the simple concepts that we necessarily have. Every human being knows immediately what representation is' (BL Ak. xxiv. 40). What cannot be explained in terms more basic, however, *can* be indicated and to some extent non-reductively analysed. So Kant continues:

Every representation is something in us, which . . . is referred to something else, which is the object. Certain things represent something, but we represent things. (BL Ak. xxiv. 40)

The object as we represent it is the *material*,[9] while the manner of the representation is the *formal*. If, e.g., I represent virtue to someone, then I can look in part to what I represent, in part to how I represent it; the latter is the *formal*, the former the *material* in the representation. . . . When we distinguish a representation and its object, with which it is concerned, from other representations, then we are conscious of the representation. *Consciousness* (*Bewußtsein*) accompanies each of our states; it is, as it were, the intuiting of ourselves. (BL Ak. xxiv. 40)

Four factors come forward here. The first and most obvious is that every *Vorstellung* is intrinsically referential or object directed; as he puts it later in the first *Critique*: 'all representations, as representations, have their object' (*CPR* A108). We can usefully think of this represented object as an intentional object, in the Brentanian or Husserlian sense that it is that to which the representation intrinsically refers, even if that object does not actually exist.[10] The second feature is that a representation is 'in us', in the sense that it is conscious or inherently mental in nature. Also in the first *Critique*, Kant characterizes representations as 'inner determinations of our mind in this or that temporal relation' (*CPR* A197/B242): they are what comes before the conscious mind as it lives through any temporal state or process of sensing, perceiving, imagining, remembering, thinking or understanding, judging, or reasoning. Thus every representation presents its object *to* some conscious subject—and this is the sense in which it *re*presents. Thirdly, the conscious subject always represents the object in some specific psychological mode or another. Kant calls this the 'formal' element of the representation (see also VL Ak. xxiv. 805 and

---

[9] Here I adopt Young's emendation: the text's "*das Objekt*" clearly should be read as "*das Materiale*".   [10] See Aquila, *Representational Mind*, chs. 1–2.

JL Ak. ix. 33).[11] But Locke's nice phrase 'postures of the mind' captures the same idea more accurately.[12] Locke's point, picked up by Kant, is that the mind has the capacity to adopt different subjective stances towards its own objective representations; and this psychological stance can vary while the represented object stays the same. For example, I can put forward the same judgement under the attitudes of mere entertainment, belief, or certainty (*CPR* A820–31/B848–59); or I can perceptually represent the very same object clearly or unclearly, distinctly or indistinctly (JL Ak. ix. 33–5). This brings us to the fourth, and most important, factor of every representation—its 'content'. The content of a representation is constituted by those elements within a representation that isolate and hold fixed the very object referred to—that yield a determinate package of information about the object and can retain it under various changes in psychological mode or posture. According to Kant's account in his Critical period, there are two distinct basic types of representational content: 'matter' (*Materie*) or sensory intuitional content (*CPR* A20/B34), and 'intension' (*Inhalt*) or conceptual content (*CPR* A63/B87, A77–8/B103; see also JL Ak. ix. 95).

As I also mentioned in the Introduction, in his Critical period Kant's technical term for any conscious object-directed representation (as opposed to the immediate inner consciousness of the subject's own mental state or condition) is "cognition" or "*Erkenntnis*" (*CPR* A320/B376–7).[13] Prime examples of cognitions are percepts, concepts, mental images, memories, thoughts, judgements, or propositions,[14] logical inferences or arguments, and theories. In every case, however, a cognition has the four-part structure sketched in the previous paragraph: a cognition is (1) a representation *of* an object, (2) *to* a conscious subject, who is thereby aware of that object, (3) *under* a certain psychological posture or stance, and (4) *through* an object-determining information content.

---

[11] The idea of 'form' is used in many different ways by Kant; see Pippin, *Kant's Theory of Form*. I focus primarily on the form of cognition, and in particular conceptual form, logical form, and intuitional form; see Chs. 2 and 3, and Sect. 4.3 below.

[12] See Locke, *Essay concerning Human Understanding*, bk. III, ch. vii, sect. 3–4, p. 472.

[13] Kant sometimes (esp. in the B edition) employs the notion of cognition more narrowly than he does at A320/B376–7, to mean specifically an *empirically meaningful* ('objectively valid') representation of an object (see e.g. *CPR* Bxxvii n., B146–8, B165). In this sense, the cognition of an object must involve our specifically human capacity for sensory intuition and sharply contrasts with the mere thought of an object and also with the intellectual intuition of an object. But it is useful to have a term for *any* mental representation of an object, whether that representation be objectively valid or not. For this reason I will very often use "cognition" in Kant's broader sense; but it should also be evident from the context when I am using it in the narrower sense.

[14] Occasionally, Kant distinguishes between judgements and propositions: judgements are said to be unasserted or 'problematic', while propositions are specifically 'assertoric' (VL Ak. xxiv. 934); or again judgements are merely 'senses', while propositions are 'posited' (*R.* 3100; Ak. xiv. 659–60). But since he usually ignores this distinction and treats all judgements as assertoric or propositional, I will too.

It should be clear by now that Kant's theory of objective mental representation is at once a theory of consciousness, a theory of intentionality, a theory of mental content, a theory of meaning, and a theory of cognition. Moreover, it includes within its scope our objective representational capacities for sense perception, memory, imagination, belief, judgement, knowledge (including a priori knowledge in natural science, mathematics, and pure logic), inference, theorizing, and even human language (*P.* Ak. iv. 322–3; see also *A.* Ak. vii. 192). This last point bears repeating: language is fully included within the explanatory scope of Kant's general theory of objective mental representation— but not all objective mental representation is linguistic. So Kant's cognitive semantics comprehends non-linguistic and linguistic meaning alike.

Now the letter to Herz also shows us clearly that, while the primary topic of Kant's first *Critique* is the theory of our mental capacities for representing objects, nevertheless he wants to focus especially on one particular aspect of it—how it is that a priori[15] concepts can correctly and necessarily represent their objects: 'As to how my understanding may form for itself concepts of things completely a priori, with which concepts the things must necessarily agree . . . this question of how the faculty of the understanding achieves this conformity with the things themselves, is still left in obscurity' (*PC* Ak. x. 131). If representations are caused by their objects, then it is at least on the face of it comprehensible how the former refers to the latter; but how can such a reference relation obtain when the representation is necessary and non-empirical? Or, as he puts it more bluntly in one of the *Reflexionen*: 'That a representation that is itself an effect of the object should correspond to it is comprehensible. But that something that is merely a birth of my brain refers as a representation to an object is not so clear.' (*R.* 4473; Ak. xvii. 564). In correspondence with Christian Garve in 1783 (two years after the appearance of the first edition of the first *Critique*), and with the benefit of hindsight, Kant reformulates this issue more narrowly as the question of how any *judgement* employing a priori representations of objects is possible:

It is not at all metaphysics that the *Critique* is doing but a whole new science, never before attempted, namely the critique of an a priori judging reason. . . . Absolutely no other science attempts this—that is, to develop out of the mere concept of a cognitive faculty (*Erkenntnisvermögens*) (when that concept is precisely defined) all the objects, [and] everything that can be scientifically known (*wissen*) of them. (*PC* Ak. x. 340)

Whether we formulate Kant's basic positive doctrine in the first *Critique* quite broadly as a general cognitive semantics, or more specifically as the critique of an a priori judging reason, that doctrine is captured by the conjunction of two basic theses. The first thesis is what I call 'representational

---

[15] Experience independence or apriority in Kant's sense is the strict underdetermination of representations by all sets or sorts of sense experience. See Sects. 1.3 and 5.2.

transcendentalism'. This is the claim that all representational contents, and thereby the contents of all cognitions, are strictly determined in their underlying structure by certain universal, innate,[16] a priori human mental capacities—in a word, transcendental capacities—that make experience itself possible:

I call all cognition *transcendental* that is occupied not so much with objects but rather with our mode of cognition of objects in so far as this [mode of cognition] is to be possible a priori.   (*CPR* A11/B25)

The word "transcendental" . . . does not signify something passing beyond all experience but something that indeed precedes it a priori, and that is intended simply to make cognition of experience possible.   (*P*. Ak. iv. 373 n.)

The second thesis I dub 'cognitive idealism' (or 'representational idealism'). This is the claim that all the proper objects of human cognition are nothing but objects of sensory experience (which Kant calls 'appearances' or 'phenomena'[17]). Appearances or phenomena in turn are numerically or literally identical with the intersubjectively communicable contents of sensory or experiential representations. Hence another way of expressing Kant's cognitive idealism is to say that *all the proper objects of human cognition are nothing but the intersubjectively shareable contents of sensory or experiential representations*:[18] 'You put the matter quite precisely when you say, "The content (*Innbegriff*) of a representation is itself the object; and the activity of the mind whereby the content of a representation is represented is what is meant by 'referring it to the object'"' (*PC* Ak. xi. 314).[19] This is the sense in which Kant's cognitive idealism is equally a *representational* idealism. The proper objects of cognition are nothing but what the total community of actual and possible human minds, construed at the appropriate level of idealization, could and would represent them to be. And in turn this implies immediately that these objects of cognition are specifically *not* beings that transcend the basic conditions and forms under which human sensory experience of apparent objects is possible, or that possess their natures entirely apart from any possible human or sensory cognizer. Kant calls such transcendent entities 'noumena' or 'things-in-themselves'.

The conjunction of representational transcendentalism and cognitive idealism is Kant's transcendental idealism—which he also sometimes calls

---

[16] Kant's conception of innateness is crucially different from that of the Rationalists, however; see Sect. 1.3.

[17] Kant employs a basic distinction between two types of appearances: (i) unconceptualized or 'undetermined' sensory objects (*CPR* A20/B34), and (ii) fully conceptualized or 'determined' empirical objects, the 'objects of experience' (*CPR* B161). See Sect. 1.4 below. Sometimes he also calls the fully conceptualized or determined empirical objects 'phenomena' (*CPR* A248–9).

[18] See also Longuenesse, *Kant and the Capacity to Judge*, 20.

[19] See Kant's letter to J. S. Beck, dated 20 Jan. 1792.

'critical' or 'formal' idealism in order to distinguish it sharply from Cartesian 'sceptical' idealism and Berkeleyan 'dogmatic' idealism alike (*P.* Ak. iv. 293–4, 375)—the nub of which is captured in this text:

By *transcendental idealism* I mean the doctrine that appearances are to be regarded as being, one and all, representations only, not things in themselves, and that time and space are therefore only sensible forms of our intuition, not determinations given as existing by themselves, nor conditions of objects viewed as things in themselves. (*CPR* A369)

Clearly, Kant believes that transcendental idealism follows directly from his fundamental thesis of the 'ideality' of space and time—the thesis that space and time are nothing but a priori subjective forms of sensibility (*CPR* A26/B42, A32–3/B49).[20] But what we need is a quite general characterization of transcendental idealism—that is, one that accounts for the fact that, for Kant, not only space and time, but also such fundamental ontological categories as 'substance' and 'cause', are transcendentally ideal in the sense that they are to be derived from our non-empirical cognitive capacities or faculties (*CPR* A76–83/B102–9). Therefore I shall say that Kant's transcendental idealism is the doctrine that the very forms or structures that are introduced into the contents of mental representations by the universal innate a priori cognitive capacities of the human mind are *also* introduced into the proper objects of our cognition. These proper objects of cognition are nothing but the intersubjectively communicable contents of sensory representations. Hence whatever supplies form or structure to the latter automatically supplies form or structure to the former. Otherwise put: Kant's transcendental idealism is the thesis that the proper objects of our cognition are *type-identical* with the human mind's universal innate a priori forms or structures, and *token-identical* with the particular intersubjectively communicable contents of the mind's sensory representations—the appearances or phenomena.

(As every student of Kant knows, transcendental idealism is by far and away the most controversial element of his theoretical philosophy. Consequently I will have to say a good deal more in explication and in defence of my interpretation—see Sections 2.3 and 2.4. For the time being, Dear Reader, please regard the above formulations as working assumptions.)

Transcendental idealism in turn yields a crucial consequence. Since the objects of our cognition are type-identical with the mind's universal a priori forms or structures, it follows immediately that any true judgements or propositions

---

[20] The ideality of space and time is derived by Kant from the notorious 'trilemma' proof (*CPR* A23/B58, A26/B42, A32–3/B49, A39–40/B55–7). In the Dialectic, by contrast, idealism is established by both (*a*) the proper critical diagnosis of the Antinomies, and (*b*) the positive solution to the Third Antinomy (*CPR* A490–7/B518–25). And in the *Prolegomena*, Kant says that idealism is entailed by his solution to the problem of synthetic a priori propositions (*P.* Ak. iv. 377).

that we can acquire about our mind's universal, innate, a priori forms or structures are automatically necessary a priori truths about the objects of our cognition. That is, since the mind's universal, innate, a priori forms or structures *are* introduced into the contents of mental representations, and since those contents just *are* numerically identical to the proper objects of our cognition (appearances or phenomena), it follows that truths about the mind's forms or structures are strictly guaranteed to be a priori necessary truths about the world of phenomena. This gives a clear interpretation of Kant's fundamental modal thesis that 'all necessity, without exception, is grounded in a transcendental condition' (*CPR* A106). And it in turn immediately implies that Kant's general cognitive semantics is really nothing other than his 'Copernican Revolution' in philosophy, as explicitly spelled out in the B edition Preface:

Hitherto it has been assumed that all our cognition must conform to objects. But all attempts to extend our cognition of objects by establishing something in regard to them a priori, by means of concepts, have, on this assumption, ended in failure. We must therefore make trial whether we may not have more success in the tasks of metaphysics, if we suppose that objects must conform to our cognition. This would agree better with what is desired—namely, that it should be possible to have cognition of objects a priori, determining something in regard to them prior to their being given. (*CPR* Bxvi)

Kant's Copernican Revolution of 1781–7 is in this way an all-things-considered answer to the fundamental semantic question he raised in 1772: how can mental representations—and more specifically necessary a priori mental representations—refer to their objects? And the answer is that mental representations refer to their objects because 'objects must conform to our cognition'; hence our true a priori judgements are necessarily true independently of all sense experience because they express just those cognitive forms or structures to which all the proper objects of human cognition automatically conform.

1.2. 'An Overview of the Whole'

In the A Preface, while explaining why the first *Critique* is long on dry scholastic argumentation yet short on 'examples and illustrations', Kant remarks that

the aids to clearness, though they may be of assistance in regard to details, often interfere with our grasp of the whole. The reader is not allowed to arrive sufficiently quickly at an overview of the whole (*Überschauung des Ganzen*); the bright colouring of the illustrative material intervenes to cover over and conceal the articulation and organization of the system, which, if we are to be able to judge of its unity and solidity, are what chiefly concern us.   (*CPR* Axix)

The purpose of this section is to give us an *Überschauung* of the whole of the *Critique of Pure Reason*. Like all bird's-eye views, it provides a schematic map that is slightly distorted, for it presents as clear and sharply differentiated much that in the muddy trenches of Kant scholarship is obscure and vague. But, although on the one hand this map neglects some fine-grained detail, on the other hand it offers a survey of 'the articulation and organization of the system, which, if we are to be able to judge of its unity and solidity, are what chiefly concern us'. Its sole purpose is to yield what Kant would call an 'orientation in thinking' (OT Ak. viii. 131–47).

One perfectly accurate feature of both the epistemological and the metaphysical interpretations of the first *Critique* is the idea that it contains Kant's attempt to work out, simultaneously, two fundamental and essentially interconnected philosophical projects: a negative one and a positive one. The negative one is a determination of the origins, scope, and limits of pure or a priori human representational reason, along with detailed diagnoses of the profound difficulties into which reason naturally falls if these constraints are not heeded. Let us call this 'the Critical Project'. Both the natural errors of pure reason and the nature of its self-criticism are vividly summarized by Kant as follows:

Human reason has this peculiar fate that in one species of its cognition it is burdened by questions that, as prescribed by the very nature of reason itself, it is not able to ignore, but that, as transcending all its powers, it is also not able to answer. (*CPR* Avii)

We can regard a science of the mere examination of pure reason, of its sources and its limits, as the *propaedeutic* to the system of pure reason. As such, it should be called a critique, not a doctrine of pure reason. Its utility in regard to speculation would really be only negative, serving not for the amplification but only for the purification (*zur Läuterung*) of our reason, and for keeping it free from errors—which is already a very great gain.   (*CPR* A11/B25)

Kant's idea is that human reason naturally yet tragically overreaches itself, by demanding or assuming a metaphysical knowledge of what utterly transcends the bounds of human sensibility, the noumenal; and, as a consequence, it falls into 'transcendental illusion' (*CPR* A293/B349) or even outright self-contradiction, 'the antinomy of pure reason' (*CPR* A406–60/B432–88). These errors can be prevented only by strictly limiting the application of theoretical or scientific reason to the phenomenal domain.

Retrospectively considered, this purgative and therapeutic conception of rational critique may strongly remind us of the later Wittgenstein's view that

the clarity that we are aiming at is indeed *complete* clarity. But this simply means that the philosophical problems should *completely* disappear.

The real discovery is the one that makes me capable of stopping doing philosophy when I want to.—The one that gives philosophy peace, so that it is not tormented by questions which bring *itself* into question.[21]

But the crucial difference between the later Wittgenstein and Kant is this: whereas Wittgenstein radically questions reason, and finally seeks to *cure* us of its tragic madness by going back to (what he takes to be) our essentially healthy everyday human practices,[22] Kant has the aim of clarifying, reforming, and ultimately *vindicating* human reason.[23] Indeed, for Kant our critically 'purified' theoretical reason even has a perfectly legitimate positive philosophical function.

What is that positive function? It consists in solving what Kant calls 'the real problem of pure reason':

Much is already gained if one can bring a multitude of investigations under the formula of a single problem. For one thereby not only lightens one's own task, by determining it precisely, but also the judgement of anyone else who wants to examine whether or not we have succeeded in our plan. Now the real problem (*eigentliche Aufgabe*) of pure reason is contained in the question: how are synthetic a priori judgements possible?   (*CPR* B19; see also *P*. Ak. iv. 276)

In other words, the basic positive aim of the first *Critique* is to offer us a transcendental explanation of a special class of objective mental representations, the synthetic a priori judgements. The general philosophical problem of how such propositions are possible is what in the Introduction I called the Modal Problem—the problem of accounting for necessary substantive (world-directed) non-empirical truths.

In turn, Kant's specific solution to this problem is what I will dub 'the Transcendental Project'. The Transcendental Project must not only produce a solution to the Modal Problem, but also contain the solution to the even more fundamental difficulty adumbrated in Kant's crucial 1772 letter to Herz. The Transcendental Project must solve the Modal Problem *by way of* solving the Semantic Problem. Therefore, if we can see the broad outlines of Kant's explanation of the synthetic a priori, then we will know in a synoptic way what his universal cognitive semantics is and how it constitutes the core of his transcendental philosophy.

In the letter to Herz Kant says that the working title of his treatise-in-progress is 'The Limits of Sense and Reason'. This title is in at least three ways more accurate than the published title of the first *Critique*. First, it indicates that his project has to do with two distinct sources of representations—sensibility *and* understanding or reason; secondly, it suggests that the two distinct

---

[21] Wittgenstein, *Philosophical Investigations*, sect. 133, p. 51.

[22] In this way Wittgenstein's later philosophy represents a direct recurrence to Hume; see e.g. *A Treatise of Human Nature*, bk. I, pt. IV, sect. vii, p. 269.

[23] See O'Neill, 'Vindicating Reason'.

sources of representations are inherently limited or constrained by one another; and, finally, it offers us the hint of a philosophical standpoint that is equally beyond the one-sided thesis that cognition is grounded solely on sensibility and also the corresponding one-sided thesis that cognition is grounded solely on understanding and reason.

It is a truism of the standard epistemological line of Kant interpretation— perhaps most clearly stated by Lewis White Beck[24]—that the basic strategy of Kant's theoretical philosophy involves both the culmination and the closure of the Cartesian tradition, in the sense that Kant attacks, reconciles, and then finally overcomes both classical Empiricism and classical Rationalism. This account, so far as it goes, is perfectly unobjectionable and easy to understand. What is more difficult, however, is to state quite precisely just *which* views Kant criticizes, just *why* he criticizes them, and just *how* he reconciles and overcomes them.

My proposal is that, in order to understand Kant's relationship to his predecessors properly, we must reconstruct their views from the standpoint of the seventeenth- and eighteenth-century history of cognitive semantics. Of course I am talking about the 'Way of Ideas'.[25] Again, it must be remembered that, for clarity's sake, I am stepping back from the nitty-gritty details and taking the bird's-eye view. But, when we do so, we can then see that seventeenth- and eighteenth-century Rationalists—especially Descartes and Leibniz[26]—held the following eight theses:

(R1) There exist two kinds of truths: necessary a priori 'truths of reason' (including all logical, mathematical, and metaphysical truths); and contingent a posteriori 'truths of fact' (truths about actual empirical states of affairs).

(R2) Truths of reason are of one kind only.

(R3) Truths of reason correctly describe the objectively real world; hence necessity objectively exists in the world.

(R4) Human cognitions always contain and are always mediated by 'ideas'—that is, mental representations.

(R5) Our veridical ideas—those that occur in our true judgements about reality—passively conform to the real objects.

(R6) Those veridical ideas are all *innate* ideas—ideas intrinsic to the mind. The contents of innate ideas describe purely intelligible, mind-independent objects: simple natures or essences. All intrinsic

[24] See Beck, 'Kant's Strategy'.

[25] See e.g. Cummins and Zoeller (eds.), *Minds, Ideas, and Objects: Essays on the Theory of Representation in Modern Philosophy*.

[26] See Descartes, 'Meditations on First Philosophy' and 'Principles of Philosophy'. See also Leibniz, 'Meditations on Truth, Knowledge, and Ideas', 'On Freedom'. 'The Principles of Philosophy, or, the Monadology', and 'The Source of Contingent Truths'.

connections between essences are objectively necessary, and all objective necessity in nature consists in intrinsic connections between essences. The innate ideas of essences are caused to exist in the human mind by God. Sensory representations of material objects are at best 'confused' or misleading images of essences and their intrinsic connections.

(R7) Our true judgements all have a single cognitive source.

(R8) That single cognitive source is pure or a priori reason, directed by means of innate ideas to essences and their intrinsic connections.

Correspondingly, we can also see that seventeenth- and eighteenth-century Empiricists—paradigmatically, Locke and Hume[27]—held these eight theses:

(E1) There exist two kinds of truths: necessary a priori truths of reason; and contingent a posteriori truths of fact.

(E2) Truths of reason are of one kind only.

(E3) Truths of reason are trivial and not reality describing, in that they involve semantic connections based entirely on stipulative or merely verbal definitions ('relations of ideas', 'trifling propositions').[28] Therefore there is no such thing as objective or real necessity. All truths about reality are contingent and a posteriori, because they describe empirical states of affairs.

(E4) Human cognitions always contain and always are mediated by 'ideas'—that is, mental representations.

(E5) Our veridical ideas—those that occur in our true judgements about reality—passively conform to the real objects.

(E6) All ideas begin in and are derived from sense experience, in the sense that they either refer directly to actual inner or outer sensory impressions, or else are built up by means of repeated mental operations upon ideas of sensory impressions.[29] Such impressions are, by means of an unknown process, distally caused by real material things. It follows immediately (*a*) that there are no innate ideas, (*b*) that the Rationalists' essences are at the very least uncognizable and quite

---

[27] See Locke, *Essay concerning Human Understanding*. See also Hume, *Enquiry concerning Human Understanding*, and *A Treatise of Human Nature*.

[28] According to Locke, a few necessary truths—including truths of geometry and such metaphysical truths as that God exists—are non-trivial; see the *Essay concerning Human Understanding*, bk. IV, ch. iii, sect. 8, p. 614, and ch. x, pp. 619–30. This brings Locke's position fairly close to Kant's, as Kant himself points out in the *Prolegomena* (*P.* Ak. iv. 270).

[29] Kant's major advance over Empiricism is that he is able to recover this notion of representation-building mental operations on sensory content ('synthesis') within a broadly rationalist perspective, by taking the rule-governed mental faculties for those operations to be innate. See Sect. 1.3 below.

possibly do not exist at all, and (*c*) that all propositions purporting to describe essences, or the necessary connections between them, are empirically meaningless or vacuous.[30]

(E7) Our true judgements all have a single cognitive source.

(E8) That single cognitive source is sensory or a posteriori experience.

It should be obvious enough from these lists of theses that Rationalists and Empiricists agree about some things, yet sharply disagree about others. They disagree about the possibility of substantive or reality-describing necessary a priori truths and the existence of objective necessity (R3 versus E3); about the type of ideas by means of which reality is represented (R6 versus E6); and about the internal cognitive source of our true judgements (R8 versus E8). But they also share five doctrines in common: (i) that there is a fundamental distinction between necessary a priori and contingent a posteriori truths (R1 and E1); (ii) that truths of reason are of one kind only (R2 and E2); (iii) that human cognition is idea based or representational (R4 and E4); (iv) that our veridical representations passively conform to real objects (R5 and E5); and (v) that our true judgements have a single cognitive source (R7 and E7). For convenience, let us call these points of agreement respectively (i) the Distinction Thesis, (ii) the Two-Pronged-Fork Thesis (aka 'Hume's Fork'[31]), (iii) the Representational Mind Thesis, (iv) the Mind-Conforms-to-Objects Thesis, and (v) the Single-Source Thesis.

Where precisely does Kant stand in relation to this debate? In agreement with Rationalists and Empiricists alike, he accepts the Distinction Thesis and the Representational Mind Thesis. Following the Rationalists, he also accepts R3—the thesis of substantive or essentially world-directed necessary truth and the existence of objective necessity—and correspondingly he rejects the Empiricists' thesis E3, the reduction of necessary truth to merely stipulative or verbal definitions. Nevertheless, he also takes on board the Empiricists' E6, the rejection of innate ideas and the uncognizability of essences, and thereby rejects the Rationalists' R6. But, although he fully accepts the Empiricist notion that all ideas begin in sensory experience of objects, he strongly rejects the Empiricist *reduction* of all the content of human cognition to sensory experiences or mere constructions upon them (E8), since it is inconsistent with recognizing substantive necessary truth and objective necessity. These various dialectical moves make Kant a *mitigated rationalist*. What this means is that Kant is (1) a defender of the claim that there are necessary truths, especially including substantive or world-directed necessary truths; (2) a defender of the

---

[30] There is a strong similarity between this Empiricist thesis and the later logical empiricist attack on the very idea of the synthetic a priori; see Sect. 5.0.

[31] i.e. Hume's doctrine of the exhaustive cognitive distinction between 'relations of ideas' and 'matters of fact'. See *Enquiry concerning Human Understanding*, 15–16.

possibility of human a priori knowledge of necessary truths; and (3) a recovered classical rationalist, whose own early tendencies towards epistemological and metaphysical excess regarding the origins, scope, and limits of human cognition—'my dogmatic slumber' (*P*. Ak. iv. 260)—have been trimmed back and tempered by an empiricistic theory of meaningfulness.

Beyond these modest or concessive moves, however, Kant also firmly rejects the Two-Pronged-Fork Thesis, the Single-Source Thesis, and the Mind-Conforms-to-Objects Thesis; he thereby undermines both unqualified Rationalism and unqualified Empiricism in one fell swoop. In their places he puts three successor theses. First (K1), there are two irreducibly different kinds of necessary a priori truth, in addition to empirical truths. This directly implies Kant's modal dualism; but, since it also includes a claim about empirical truths, I will call it the 'Three-Pronged-Fork Thesis'—or 'Kant's Pitchfork' for short. Secondly (K2), all true judgements have two irreducibly different cognitive sources—an intrinsically experience-independent or a priori source, and an intrinsically experience-dependent or a posteriori source—that are directly and respectively reflected in the 'form' and 'matter' of every representation. This is the 'Two-Source Thesis'. Thirdly (K3), all the proper objects of our cognition conform to our capacities for cognition. This I will call the 'Objects-Conform-to-Mind Thesis'. These three counter-theses contain the rudiments of his revolutionary theory of transcendental idealism.

This way of contextualizing Kant's Transcendental Project makes it easy to see what he wants to prove, and how he intends to prove it. His synthetic a priori propositions are substantive truths of reason. According to Kant's Pitchfork, this distinguishes them sharply from analytic a priori propositions, which he regards as indeed truths of reason but not as world-directed truths.[32] Since, according to the Two-Source Thesis, he accepts the Empiricist idea that all cognition begins in sensory experiences of objects, it follows that the sensible source operates as a supplier of primitive data and as a basic semantic constraint on any representational content whatsoever. Such representations are meaningful ('objectively valid' or 'objectively real'[33]) if and only if they apply to possible or actual objects of human sensory experience. Finally, since synthetic a priori propositions are world directed, and also necessarily constrained by the conditions of human sensibility, they are meaningful and true just in so far as they apply to all and only the objects of possible and actual human sense experience. And the strict guarantee of that application is yielded directly by the Objects-Conform-to-Mind Thesis.

To complete this overview, it remains only to map the main parts of the Transcendental Project onto the relevant parts of the *Critique of Pure Reason*, whose skeletal structure is as follows:

---

[32] See Sects. 3.1, 4.1, and 5.1.   [33] See Sect. 2.2.

Introduction

I. **Transcendental Doctrine of Elements**

The Introduction spells out the very idea of a synthetic a priori proposition, and carefully distinguishes such truths from analytic propositions, on the one hand, and from synthetic a posteriori propositions, on the other. The Transcendental Aesthetic performs four distinct but interconnected functions: (1) it sketches a theory of sensibility or intuition, in particular a theory of pure a priori forms of empirical intuition; (2) it develops the thesis that the pure a priori forms of empirical intuition are the representations of space and time; (3) it provides an argument for cognitive idealism by identifying space and time themselves with our a priori representations of space and time; and (4) it explains how synthetic a priori mathematical truths are possible by virtue of their cognitive-semantic dependency on one or another of the two pure subjective forms of intuition, space and time.

Transcendental Logic is the science of the necessary laws of reason and thought in so far as they apply a priori to objects. Transcendental Analytic, the first part of Transcendental Logic, adds the concept of truth to the doctrine of a priori thought. The first part of Transcendental Analytic, the Analytic of Concepts, begins by supplying a derivation of the pure concepts of the understanding (the categories) from 'pure general logic' or formal logic as Kant knew it—a derivation familiarly labelled 'the Metaphysical Deduction of the Categories'. The Metaphysical Deduction is incomplete, because, although it shows that the categories necessarily apply to any object whatsoever that is represented by means of a judgement or a concept, it does not adequately specify the type of judged or conceptualized object. The Transcendental Deduction of the Pure Concepts shows that the categories are necessarily applicable to all and only objects of experience, the fully determined sensory appearances. And the Schematism of the Pure Concepts of the Understanding supplies a further essential condition for the application of categories to appearances: partial interpretations, or partial models, of the several categories in terms of corresponding fundamental a priori imaginative schemata, which are in turn originally derived from the pure formal intuition of time. The second part of Transcendental Analytic, the Analytic of Principles, then explains how synthetic a priori truths in metaphysics and the natural sciences are possible by virtue of their cognitive-semantic dependency on the pure concepts of the understanding (together with their cognitive-semantic dependency on the pure forms of intuition, and on their transcendental schematization).

The Transcendental Dialectic completes the Transcendental Logic by carefully distinguishing between the legitimate synthetic a priori propositions explained by Kant's transcendental idealism, and the illegitimate ones that make up most of the content of traditional metaphysics. The latter are non-analytic propositions that could be meaningful, necessarily true, and a priori only if they applied to noumenal objects (for example, the immortal soul, spontaneous causality or freedom, and God). In turn, the representations of such objects are labelled 'ideas of pure reason'. Since noumenal objects are uncognizable by creatures with our specific cognitive constitution, and since the ideas of pure reason are objectively invalid or objectively unreal, hence empirically vacuous or 'empty', these propositions are all in fact empirically meaningless, and have no truth values. The assertion of them, or the use of them as premises in philosophical arguments, leads directly to fallacy and contradiction. The best that philosophy can do in this domain is to work out the etiology of empirical meaninglessness by unpacking the several different types of transcendental error.[34]

This completes the outline of Kant's cognitive-semantic explanation of synthetic a priori propositions; but what of the further question of the possibility of our *knowing them in the scientific sense (Wissen)*? In the Discipline of Pure Reason, the first chapter of the Transcendental Doctrine of Method, Kant argues (*a*) that scientific knowledge of synthetic a priori truths in mathematics is possible only by means of the activity or process of 'construction' (*Konstruktion*) and (*b*) that scientific knowledge of synthetic a priori truths in metaphysics is possible only by means of transcendental proofs or deductions. And in the second chapter of the Doctrine of Method, the Canon of Pure Reason, he describes the basic features of scientific knowing. *Wissen* is defined as an attitude of absolutely subjectively certain and a priori belief ('conviction' or *Überzeugung*) directed towards a necessarily true proposition; the addition of necessary truth to conviction equals objective certainty. But

---

[34] This is not to say that propositions containing noumenal concepts are *wholly* meaningless, however. See Sect. 2.2.

unfortunately this crucial account is sketched by Kant without regard to the different sorts of necessary truths, and without showing us precisely how conviction is possible. Nevertheless, he leaves us with two crucial epistemological hints to the effect that (i) all a priori scientific knowledge, whether of analytic or synthetic propositions, and including that by means of proof, is ultimately grounded on our cognitive capacity for 'insight' (*Einsicht*), and (ii) all a priori scientific knowledge via insight depends in one way or another on the activities of the imagination.[35] These two hints are contained in Kant's pregnant remark in the Preface to the B edition: 'reason has insight only into that which it produces according to a design of its own' (*CPR* Bxiii).

Let us now begin to recover some of these points in more fine-grained detail.

1.3. Kant's Epigenetic Model of the Mind

I have argued so far that the *Critique of Pure Reason* is most adequately interpreted as a treatise in general cognitive semantics—a general theory of objective mental representation—with a special focus on necessary a priori objective mental representations and in turn on synthetic a priori judgements. Essential to this theory is an explanation of how objective mental representations arise in the mind. Kant speaks of 'the act (*Actus*) itself, that is . . . the *generation*[36] (*Erzeugung*) of the representation' (*CPR* A103–4); and says that the representation in turn is the 'output' (*Wirkung*) of the generative act. In other words, for Kant the human mind is essentially active: it spontaneously generates its own representations, given sensory inputs. The act of representational generation, in turn, has a transcendental source. Kant's theory of the transcendental source of cognition starts with these fundamental claims:

Although all our cognition begins *in* experience it does not follow that it all arises *out* of experience. For it may well be that even our empirical cognition is made up of what we receive through impressions and of what our own faculty of cognition (sensible impressions serving merely as the occasion) supplies from itself.   (*CPR* B1)

That is, although necessarily every cognition is triggered or occasioned by sensory experiences, and although as meaningful every cognition must apply in some way or another to actual or possible objects of experience, nevertheless not every element in its representational content is determined by or derived

---

[35] For more details, see Hanna, 'How Do We Know Necessary Truths? Kant's Answer'.

[36] In this context, to say that a mental representation is 'generated' is to say that it is spontaneously yielded by the mind when triggered by sensory inputs, by following a set of determinate formal rules for operating on those inputs. Kant's notion of *Erzeugung*, or representational generativity, is later adopted in essentially this sense by Humboldt in the nineteenth century in his *On Language*, and then again by Chomsky in the twentieth century in his *Aspects of the Theory of Syntax*, 9.

from sensory experience. Rather, at least part of cognitive content—its underlying structure—is strictly underdetermined by experience because it is derived from a formal non-sensory source in the mind.

For Kant, the source of the underlying structure of cognitive content is a set of inherent capacities for synthesizing or processing sensory information— for organizing and transforming sensory data or inputs in accordance with certain dedicated,[37] or innate, protocols. These innate protocols fall into three basic types: (i) pure forms of intuition (the representations of space and time as structural wholes), (ii) pure concepts of the understanding (second-order concepts, or categories), and (iii) the transcendental schema of the imagination (the pure formal representation of time considered as a source of partial inter-pretations or partial models for the pure concepts of the understanding). The various distinct faculties, or distinct 'powers', within this dedicated information-processing capacity ultimately make up a well-ordered, well-coordinated cognitive unity or cognitive corporation, by virtue of an executive capacity for the unification of those elements of synthesis ingredient in the cognition of determinate objects—the 'original synthetic unity of apperception' (*CPR* B131–6). The basic function of the original synthetic unity of apperception is to be the a priori ground of self-consciousness, or the innate capacity for producing the representation 'I think . . .', which functions as an implicit prefix for every possible cognition.

It needs to be stressed how very different Kant's notion of a unified non-sensory source of cognition is from the classical rationalist conception of innate ideas—which, just to distinguish it terminologically from Kant's special brand of innatism, I will call 'INNATISM'. As early as his Inaugural Dissertation of 1770, 'On the Form and Principles of the Sensible and Intelligible World', Kant distinguishes sharply between two types of a priori mental inherence: (1) that according to which complete representations are originally inscribed in the mind at creation or birth, in order to be self-consciously grasped later under appropriate retrieval conditions; and (2) that according to which only a law or rule or procedure of mental processing is originally inherent in some capacity of the mind—a procedure whose application to raw content is trig-gered on the occasion of experience (ID Ak. ii. 395). In other words, the INNATIST theory of innateness is a doctrine of *content innateness*; by contrast, Kant's theory of innateness is a doctrine of *capacity innateness*, by which I mean that what is innate is not a mental representation but instead a mental faculty or power for generating representations according to rules (see also OD Ak. viii. 221–2). So, whereas the INNATIST view is based on a picture of the mind as a passive recipient or container of divinely caused ideas, Kant's innatist pic-ture is that the mind is essentially a set of active capacities or faculties, each

---

[37] See Patricia Kitcher, 'Kant's Dedicated Cognitivist System'. But for an alternative view, see Falkenstein, 'Was Kant a Nativist?'

of which contains some determinate formal procedures for the generation of representations.

In the Critical period, this contrast becomes the equally sharp distinction between what Kant calls the '*preformation system* of pure reason' (associated most closely with the metaphysical and epistemological doctrines of Descartes, Leibniz, Wolff, and Crusius), and his own 'system of the epigenesis of pure reason' (*CPR* B167). In the seminal 1772 letter to Herz, Kant observes that 'Crusius believed in . . . ready-made concepts that God implanted in the human soul just as they had to be in order to harmonize with things. . . . But the *deus ex machina* is the greatest absurdity one could hit upon in the determination of the origin and validity of our cognition' (*PC* Ak. x. 131). In other words, it is absurd to think that every cognition in our repertoire could be originally embedded in the human mind prior to sensory experience. Only an arbitrarily introduced transcendent Creator—that is, a Supreme Monad—could account for this cognitive plenitude. Not only is the preformation doctrine grounded on ad hoc metaphysical hypotheses, however. Such a view also requires a human cognitive storage capacity immeasurably larger than any empirical evidence indicates. And it further implies a highly implausible account of content acquisition whereby we cognitively anticipate all later experiences and then merely actualize those preformed representations under suitable empirical conditions. But 'on such a hypothesis we can set no limit to the assumption of predetermined dispositions to future judgements'; and each one of those dispositions would express at most a contingent subjective fact about us, not some necessary connection between us and what we cognize (*CPR* B167). Hence, paradoxically, a fully empiricist account of content acquisition would explain exactly as much as the INNATIST or preformation doctrine.[38]

By contrast, Kant's epigenetic model of the mind contains an explanation for cognitive content that appeals only to the idea of innate active capacities or faculties containing rules for synthesizing externally supplied sensory information. In its original biological context, epigenesis is the doctrine that living beings develop from simple seeds or embryos plus external influences or accretions. But what is essential to epigenesis is that each simple seed contains 'its own specific vital force', which guarantees that its development consists in a procedurally preprogrammed yet *materially and empirically interactive* process. As the historian of science Stephen F. Mason observes: 'the idea that an organism was ideally preformed by virtue of its own specific vital force implied that a real physical development, a material differentiation, should

---

[38] Despite the many parallels between Kant's and Chomsky's conceptions of the mind, Kant's critique of INNATISM also anticipates Putnam's critique of the Cartesian side of Chomsky's nativism. See Chomsky, *Cartesian Linguistics*; Putnam, 'The "Innateness Hypothesis" and Explanatory Models in Linguistics'; Block (ed.), *Readings in Philosophy of Psychology*, vol. 2, pt. 4; and Stich (ed.), *Innate Ideas*.

be observed empirically in the embryological growth of the organism.'[39] The theory of biological epigenesis is directly opposed to the biological preformationist theory—favoured by rationalistic and mechanistic philosophers—according to which living beings are genetically complete from the start and develop only by mechanically adding bulk. Transferred to a cognitive context, then, mental epigenesis is the doctrine that representations are the outputs of the active or vital operations of our innate capacities for implementing protocols of synthesis when triggered and fed by external inputs.

Abstracting away from its contrast with preformationism now, we can see that the core idea of Kant's epigenetic theory of the mind lies in his thesis that the sensory input to the mind *strictly underdetermines* the representational content of the manifest output of the mind. Hence the cognitive faculties must inherently contain a multiplicity of non-empirical or a priori formal rules sufficient for the generation of the manifest output.

The linguists Wilhelm von Humboldt in the nineteenth century and Noam Chomsky in the twentieth both make the extremely important point that sensory and behavioural inputs to our minds are far too limited and unstructured to explain our 'linguistic productivity' or 'creativity'—the surprising fact that all competent speakers and even very small children can generate an infinitely large number of novel grammatically correct sentences.[40] This point is sometimes called 'the poverty of the stimulus'. Given the poverty of the stimulus, according to Humboldt and Chomsky, any strictly empiricist explanation of our grammatical knowledge automatically fails.[41] The alternative explanation Humboldt and Chomksy offer is that our minds innately contain a finite set of grammatical rules that we repeatedly and recursively apply to inputs: an innate universal grammar. So from finite means we produce infinite outputs.

Kant's core idea is very similar to this, but even more radical. The sensory and more generally empirical inputs to our minds are utterly insufficient to explain how we are able to cognize a whole range of *categorial* features of our world, including the notions of unity, plurality, totality, reality, negation, limitation, substance, causality, strict reciprocity, possibility, existence, and (especially) necessity. And the same according to Kant is true of our ability to cognize *formal spatiotemporal* features of our world by means of pure sensible intuition. These representations radically exceed sensory or empirical inputs, particularly as regards their inherent strong modality or necessity. So those inputs alone obviously fail to explain the manifest facts of categorial productivity and pure intuitional productivity. Kant's system of the epigenesis of pure

[39] Mason, *A History of the Sciences*, 365. The theory of embryological epigenesis was first published in 1759 by Caspar Friedrich Wolff, a professor at the University of Halle.

[40] See n. 36. See also Chomsky, *Reflections on Language*.

[41] Chomsky repeatedly makes the point that when empiricists appeal to 'general learning mechanisms'—e.g. Hume's appeal to perception, memory, and imagination—to explain the acquisition of grammatical knowledge, they are *de facto* innatists. See Chomsky, 'Quine's Empirical Assumptions'.

reason is then offered as the all-around best explanation of these transcendental modes of productivity:

There are only two ways in which we can account for a *necessary* agreement of experience with the concepts of its objects: either experience makes these concepts possible or these concepts make experience possible. The former supposition does not hold in respect of the categories (nor of pure sensible intuition); for, since they are a priori concepts, and therefore independent of experience, the ascription to them of an empirical origin would be a sort of *generatio aequivoca*. There remains, therefore, only the second supposition—a system, as it were, of the *epigenesis* of pure reason—namely, that the categories contain, on the side of the understanding, the grounds of the possibility of all experience in general.   (*CPR* B166–7)

More generally, according to Kant's epigenetic model of the mind, the full meaning content and objective reference of *any* mental representation is satisfactorily explained only by appealing to our innate total human capacity for acquiring cognition of the world, where this capacity is an innate active, multi-faculty, rule-governed, self-guided a priori psychological information-processing system triggered and funded by sensory inputs. Kant calls this total epigenetic capacity the 'faculty of cognition' or *Erkenntnisvermögen* (*CPR* B1).

Kant's theory of our *Erkenntnisvermögen* is also sometimes called his 'transcendental psychology',[42] although this is not Kant's own label. Transcendental psychology shares with contemporary cognitive psychology—and with contemporary cognitive science more generally—a fundamental interest in the innately based human mental processing of information, hence in generative/productive analyses of representations and their contents.[43] But it exceeds contemporary cognitive science in the modal strength and scope of its claims.[44] Kant's transcendental psychology is a non-naturalistic a priori theory of any actual or possible mind possessing a unified system of innate cognitive

---

[42] The precursors of Kant's transcendental psychology can be found in Locke's *Essay*, Hume's *Treatise*, and in J. N. Tetens's *Philosophische Versuche* (1777), although in Kant's opinion the analyses worked out by his predecessors do not ultimately advance beyond 'a physiology of inner sense' (*CPR* A347/B405), or an introspective empirical psychology. See Guyer, 'Psychology and the Transcendental Deduction'; Hatfield, 'Empirical, Rational, and Transcendental Psychology: Psychology as Science and as Philosophy'; and esp. Patricia Kitcher, *Kant's Transcendental Psychology*. During the heyday of linguistic philosophy, Strawson famously disparaged Kant's transcendental psychology and psychological interpretations of Kant more generally; see *The Bounds of Sense*, 16, 32.

[43] See e.g. Neisser's highly influential *Cognitive Psychology*; Sternberg's *Cognitive Psychology*, 6, where the very idea of generative/productive information processing is traced directly back to Kant; and Jackendoff's 'The Problem of Reality', where it is argued that cognitive science entails Kant-style constructivist idealism.

[44] It has been argued that transcendental psychology is compatible with some versions of psychological naturalism. See Brook, *Kant and the Mind*, ch. 1; Hatfield, *The Natural and the Normative*, ch. 7; and Patricia Kitcher, *Kant's Transcendental Psychology*, chs. 1 and 8. This is plausible if—but also only if—one seriously downplays or discounts the role of spontaneity in Kant's model of the mind. See e.g. Hurley, 'Kant on Spontaneity and the Myth of the Giving'.

capacities just like ours—whether that creature happens to be biologically human or not (*CPR* B72).[45]

All the information-processing operations of our *Erkenntnisvermögen* are syntheses. The ultimate source of synthesis—the mind's generative and productive engine—is the power of imagination or *Einbildungskraft* (*CPR* A78/B103). According to Kant, the imagination has the primitive and irreducible property of 'spontaneity'. Spontaneity is 'the mind's power of bringing forth representations from itself' (*CPR* A51/B75); more generally, it is our capacity for creative mental activity that is either strictly underdetermined or else wholly unconditioned by[46] natural or physical causation (*CPR* A448/B476).[47] The spontaneous synthesizing power of the imagination is, in turn, expressed through two different cognitive capacities—receptive sensibility or *Sinnlichkeit* (the faculty of intuitions), and spontaneous understanding or *Verstand* (the faculty of concepts):

Our cognition arises from two fundamental sources in the mind, the first of which is the capacity of receiving representations (the receptivity for impressions (*Eindrücke*)), the second the power of cognizing an object through these representations (spontaneity of concepts). Through the first an object is *given* to us, through the second an object is *thought* in relation to that [given] representation (as a mere determination of the mind). (*CPR* A50/B74)

Synthesis in general . . . is the mere output of the power of imagination . . . To bring this synthesis *to concepts* is a function that belongs to the understanding, and it is through this function of the understanding that we first obtain cognition in the proper sense (*in eigentlicher Bedeutung*). (*CPR* A78/B103)

Kant's explicatively useful contrast between the spontaneous conceptual functions of the understanding and the receptive perceptual functions of sensibility has one quite misleading apparent implication, however. It seems to suggest that the sensibility is wholly passive or non-generative and non-productive. But sensory receptivity is in no way a representational *inertness*, and this is because it is essentially connected with the imagination:

---

[45] Kant's psychology is a species of functionalism (= the thesis that a mind consists in a set of compositionally plastic or multiply realizable organizational structures and patterns of rule-governed activity, not in its actual material substrate). See Brook, *Kant and the Mind*, 12–14; Patricia Kitcher, *Kant's Transcendental Psychology*, 25; and Meerbote, 'Kant's Functionalism'. See also Block (ed.), *Readings in the Philosophy of Psychology*, pt. 3. Kant's functionalism differs sharply from other versions, however, in its direct appeal to spontaneity. Spontaneity, in turn, is a naturalistically intractable feature of the mind; see nn. 46–7 below.

[46] Being strictly underdetermined by experience and being wholly unconditioned by experience are *not* the same. Our a priori cognitive capacities are strictly underdetermined by sensory experience, but still begin *in* experience; by contrast, the acts of our pure practical reason are wholly unconditioned by sensory experience in that they are causally ascribed to a noumenal source (*GMM* Ak. iv. 457; and *CPrR* Ak. v. 29–30). Cognitive spontaneity is a non-empirical property of a *phenomenal* being; non-cognitive moral spontaneity (freedom) is a non-empirical property of a *noumenal* being.

[47] See Pippin, 'Kant on the Spontaneity of Mind'.

Psychologists have hitherto failed to realize that imagination is a necessary ingredient of perception itself. . . . It has been believed that the senses not only supply impressions but also connect them so as to yield mental images (*Bilder*) of objects. For that purpose something more is undoubtedly required—namely, a function for the synthesis of them. (*CPR* A121 n.)

To regard sensibility as wholly passive would be mistakenly to identify it with Locke's model of sense perception—the mind as a sort of conscious black box with a peephole to let in the light, and an impressionable blank tablet on the inside; a mental *camera obscura*.[48] By sharp contrast, for Kant the sensibility and the understanding alike are generative and productive sources: each is a cognitive 'capacity' (*Fähigkeit*) or 'faculty' (*Vermögen*) for spontaneously simplifying and interpreting—for spontaneously informing and transforming—inputs. Hence the most accurate way of characterizing the relationship between sensibility and understanding is in terms of two distinct *levels* of spontaneity of synthesis: lower-level or sensory (receptive) spontaneity; and higher-level or conceptual (discursive) spontaneity.

The several basic products of the generative/productive activity of our *Erkenntnisvermögen* are (serially) intuitions, concepts, and finally judgements:

Besides intuition there is no other mode of cognition than through concepts. The cognition yielded by understanding, or at least by the human understanding, must therefore be by means of concepts, and so is not intuitive but discursive. . . . Concepts are therefore grounded on the spontaneity of thinking, as sensible intuitions are grounded on the receptivity of impressions. Now the only use that the understanding can make of these concepts is to judge by means of them. (*CPR* A68–9/B92–3)

But what sorts of judgements are these? Kant says that sensory experience (*Erfahrung*) of a world of objects is the 'first product' (*erste Produkt*), or primary information-processing achievement, of our mind—in the sense that it is an output that reflects an integration of the contributions of *all* of our distinct cognitive modules or capacities: 'Experience is, beyond all doubt, the first product that our understanding brings forth as it works on the raw material of sensible sensations' (*CPR* A1). And this first product of the faculty of cognition—our sensory experience of the objective world—is also identical with the 'judgement of experience' (*Erfahrungsurteil*):[49]

---

[48] See Locke, *Essay concerning Human Understanding*, bk. II, chs. i–ix, pp. 104–49; see also Alpers, *The Art of Describing: Dutch Art in the 17th Century*, chs. 1–2.

[49] In the *Prolegomena*, Kant claims that judgements of experience result from generative operations on 'judgements of perception' (*Wahrnehmungsurteile*) (*P*. Ak. iv. 298–9)—first-person perceptual reports having at best a subjective validity. This doctrine is notorious, since in the B Deduction Kant explicitly defines a judgement as an *objectively* valid representation (*CPR* B141–2). For this reason I will ignore the *Wahrnehmungsurteile*. But for some attempts to make sense of them, see Allison, *Kant's Transcendental Idealism*, ch. 12; Beck, 'Did the Sage of Königsberg have no Dreams?'; Longuenesse, *Kant and the Capacity to Judge*, ch. 7; and Prauss, *Erscheinung bei Kant*.

Experience consists of judgements.   (*R.* XXXIII E 21—A66; Ak. xxiii. 24)

We must therefore analyse experience in general in order to see what is contained in this product (*Produkt*) of the senses and of the understanding, and how the judgement of experience itself is possible.   (*P.* Ak. iv. 300)

We can appropriately think of judgements of experience as the *focal* output of the generative/productive activity of the mind. And, in relation to this focal output, Kant's overall scheme of the generative/productive operations of our *Erkenntnisvermögen* is this. *First*, there are original inputs or impressions that trigger sensibility and give rise to sensations; *secondly*, these sensations are synthesized apprehensionally and reproductively by the imagination in order to give rise to outputs that both include 'blind' or 'indistinct' empirical intuitions, and also mental images, of spatiotemporally ordered sensory objects, both lacking determinate internal representational structure;[50] *thirdly*, the intuitions and images are further 'recognitionally' synthesized (using empirical schemata) by the understanding, in order to generate empirical concepts as outputs; *fourthly*, complexes of intuitionally funded empirical concepts are synthesized by the imagination (using transcendental schemata) and the understanding (using pure concepts or categories) under the executive power of pure self-consciousness or apperception, in order to generate, as outputs, fully structured judgements of experience, which in turn represent actual or possible determinate objects of experience; and then at last, *fifthly*, higher-order necessary a priori judgements are generated that either express or immediately depend upon the transcendental capacities ingredient in the generation of judgements of experience.

As I have said already, for Kant the various information-processing operations that generate cognitions are all specifications of a single generic processing operation, synthesis: 'By *synthesis* in the most general sense, however, I understand the act of putting different representations together with each other and grasping their manifoldness (*Mannigfaltigkeit*) in one cognition' (*CPR* A77/B102). Synthesis for Kant is the collection of diverse elements of information and their transformation into a single cognition by means of organizing them into a novel structured unity of representational content:

Synthesis of a manifold, however (be it given empirically or a priori) is what first brings forth a cognition. This cognition may, indeed, at first, be raw and confused, and therefore in need of analysis. Yet the synthesis itself is what properly collects the elements for cognition, and unifies them into a certain content. It is to synthesis, therefore, that we must first direct our attention, if we would determine the first origin of our cognition.   (*CPR* A77–8/B103)

---

[50] I am anticipating a little here; I argue for this somewhat controversial point in Sect. 1.4.

In this way, a generative product of synthesis is always of a higher representational type than its elements, in the sense that its internal structure is distinct from, and not wholly determined by, the structures of any of its elements. The human mind thus generates novel contents through synthesis by successively introducing new types of ordering into its lower-level manifolds of elements. And the elements of such manifolds are themselves the reproduced products of syntheses of lower-level manifolds (*CPR* A100–2). The series of syntheses bottoms out in the raw sensory content that is receptively introduced by external triggering and initially processed as empirical intuitions, progresses upwards to empirical conceptualizings of sensory intuitions, centres on contingent judgements of experience, and then finally achieves closure by generating necessary judgements that express or are directly grounded on the non-empirical or a priori conditions for the generation of judgements of experience.

Up and down the series of syntheses, as I have also said, the generative and productive engine of the mind is the power of imagination: 'Synthesis in general ... is the mere output of the power of imagination, a blind but indispensable function of the soul, without which we should have no cognition whatsoever, but of which we are scarcely even conscious' (*CPR* A78/B103). The imagination is blind in the sense that it functions automatically, without being self-consciously willed into action—not in the sense that it is a mere mechanism. The imagination is essentially spontaneous, goal oriented, and vital[51]—in a word, creative. We are 'scarcely even conscious' of it, not because it is *un*conscious and ontologically distinct from or epistemically inaccessible to consciousness,[52] but because, as the engine of synthesis, it is also the very seat or ground of all consciousness[53] and hence properly speaking *pre*conscious.[54]

This raises a crucial point about the imagination. Although all syntheses and all conscious mental activities have their starting points in the capacity for imagination, and although spontaneity is a primitive and irreducible property of the mind, it would nevertheless be a mistake to view the imagination as some sort of noumenal psychological 'fundamental power' (*Grundkraft*) (*CPR* A649/B677). This would be illegitimately to hypostatize the capacity for imagination—just as it is philosophically illegitimate to hypostatize the capacity for self-consciousness or apperception by inferring the existence of an immortal soul (*CPR* A341–66, A381–405/B399–432). There is no valid direct inference from a *fundamental function* of the mind

[51] In Sect. 29 of the *Critique of Judgement* Kant very provocatively says that 'the mind (*das Gemüth*) is itself wholly life (the life principle itself)' (*CJ* Ak. v. 278).

[52] Searle usefully criticizes the very idea of unconscious mind in *Rediscovery of the Mind*, ch. 7.   [53] See Waxman, *Kant's Model of the Mind*, esp. chs. 4–7.

[54] By calling it "preconscious" I mean that it is logically prior to consciousness and is the condition of its possibility; nevertheless, it remains at least indirectly accessible to the conscious mind by means of transcendental reflection (*CPR* A261/B317).

to a *metaphysical substrate* of the mind. At best, one can permissibly use the rational idea of a fundamental mental power as a mere logical fiction to unify philosophical or empirical psychological investigations.

Although, as we have just seen, Kant assigns the fundamental operation of synthesis and even the origins of consciousness itself directly to the functional capacity for imagination, he also treats the imagination more narrowly. Indeed, he carefully distinguishes the imagination from the powers of intuition and understanding, and assigns the imagination its own specialized representational faculty and cognitive function. Let us call this the 'dedicated imagination', in contradistinction to the imagination construed as the mind's generative/productive engine, the source of all synthesis. I will call the latter the 'all-purpose imagination'. What precisely does the dedicated imagination do? As Kant all too tersely puts it:

Imagination is the faculty of representing an object even *without its presence* in intuition. Now since all our intuition is sensible, the imagination, owing to the subjective condition under which alone it can give to the concepts of the understanding a corresponding intuition, belongs to *sensibility*.   (*CPR* B151)

The cognitive powers belonging to *sensibility* (the power of intuitive representations) are divided into *the senses* (*den Sinn*) and *imagination*. Sense is the power of intuiting when the object *is* present; imagination, that of intuiting[55] even when the object is *not* present.   (*A.* Ak. vii. 153)

It is sometimes held by Kant commentators that the dedicated imagination is strictly a function of intuition. But if by 'intuition' we mean human sensory intuition, as Kant normally does (for example, throughout the Transcendental Aesthetic), then the dedicated imagination is more accurately described as being at once quasi-intuitional and quasi-conceptual. In so far as it is sensible in character, the dedicated imagination must be able to operate in conjunction with sensory intuition. But, whereas sensory intuition always depends upon the actual presence of the object, the dedicated imagination can refer to sensory objects in their absence. And, on the other hand, even though the dedicated imagination 'belongs to *sensibility*', yet 'its synthesis is an expression of spontaneity, which is determining and not, like sense, merely determinable' (*CPR* B151–2). This makes the dedicated imagination also quasi-conceptual, since it connects directly with the determination of the form of a sensory representation, rather than with its material presence.

This intuitional/conceptual character of the dedicated imagination in turn corresponds to Kant's important idea that the dedicated imagination has two different sides or faces:

Imagination (*facultas imaginandi*), as a power of intuiting[56] even without the presence of the object, is either *productive* or *reproductive*—that is, either a power of exhibiting

[55] Since Kant *defines* intuition in such a way as to require the actual presence of an object (see Sect. 4.2 below), this is clearly a case of Homer nodding.   [56] See n. 55.

an object originally and so prior to experience (*exhibitio originaria*), or a power of exhibiting it in a derivative way, by bringing back an empirical intuition we previously had (*exhibitio derivata*). (A. Ak. vii. 167)

By virtue of this productive/reproductive duality, the dedicated imagination is able to link together the distinct faculties of conceptual understanding and sensory intuition without being reducible to either:

The more universal the understanding is in its rules, the more perfect it is, but if it wants to consider things *in concreto* then it absolutely cannot do without imagination. (DWL Ak. xxiv. 710)

Experience as such necessarily presupposes the reproducibility of appearances. (*CPR* A101–2)

Generalizing now, we can say that the basic function of the dedicated imagination is to supply representations that mediate between, or fuse, the two fundamentally different and original domains of representational information—sensory intuitional information, and discursive or conceptual information. The reproductive dedicated imagination synthesizes, on the one hand, by streamlining the massive and relatively disorganized concrete informational intake of the senses into simpler formats that store and reproduce only the most salient elements of the sensory data. And, on the other hand, the productive dedicated imagination synthesizes by partially interpreting or partially modelling general concepts and abstract rules of the understanding in terms of original sensible models or 'schemata' (*CPR* A137–42/B176–81). Otherwise put, the reproductive dedicated imagination brings concrete sensory information *up to* concepts, and the productive dedicated imagination brings abstract conceptual information *down to* intuitions.[57] So, by virtue of this Janus-faced dedicated imagination, the *Erkenntnisvermögen* is simultaneously a bottom-up and top-down information-processing capacity, hence a coherently organized multifaceted information-processing capacity.[58]

---

[57] This dual function of dedicated imagination is nicely summarized in one of the *Reflexionen*: 'The act of [productive (RH)] imagination, whereby a concept is given an intuition, is *exhibitio*; the act of [reproductive (RH)] imagination, whereby a concept is made out of an empirical intuition, *comprehensio*' (*R*. 5661; Ak. xviii. 320).

[58] This dual function of the dedicated imagination cannot, in the end, be fully separated from the capacity or faculty for judgement (*Vermögen zu urteilen, Urteilskraft*). Judgement brings together understanding and sensibility, hence also concepts and intuitions. So to judge is to invoke both the productive and reproductive functions of the dedicated imagination. The stupefying passages in which Kant discusses the 'transcendental synthesis of the imagination' (*CPR* A102, A119, B151–2), the 'pure (productive) synthesis of imagination' (*CPR* A118), and the 'transcendental function of imagination' (*CPR* A123) are, I think, best understood as describing the special a priori schematizing function of the productive dedicated imagination that is required to establish the objective validity and applicability of the categories (*CPR* A145–6/B185–6), within the overarching framework of our capacity for judgement. The cognitive centrality of our capacity for judgement will become evident in Sect. 1.4. See also Longuenesse, *Kant and the Capacity to Judge*, esp. pts. 1 (chs. 1–3) and 3 (chs. 8–11).

In relation to this comprehensive, orderly, subspecialized, and yet globally coherent system of information-processing achievements focally aimed at the production of judgements of experience, synthesis is also labelled 'combination' (*Verbindung*). This is in order to emphasize the fact that, no matter how preconscious or tacit it may be, each synthetic act of processing information that is zeroed in on objects of experience is not merely an operation of converting raw elements of information into higher-level, newly ordered complexes of information—not merely a function for mapping relatively unrefined inputs onto increasingly more refined outputs. On the contrary, it is also an act of intelligent unification brought about spontaneously by the overseeing executive or coordinative cognitive power, a single self-conscious, self-representing subject. Kant writes:

Combination (*conjunctio*) of a manifold in general can never come to us through the senses, and cannot, therefore, be already contained in the pure form of sensible intuition; for it is an act (*Actus*) of the spontaneity of the faculty of representation, and, since one must call the latter understanding, in distinction from sensibility, all combination, whether we are conscious of it or not, whether it is a combination of the manifold of intuition or of several concepts, and in the first case either of sensible or non-sensible intuition, is an action of the understanding, which we would designate with the general title *synthesis* in order at the same time to draw attention to the fact that we can represent nothing in the object without having previously combined it ourselves, and that among all representations *combination* is the only one that is not given through objects but can be executed only by the subject itself, since it is an act of its self-activity.   (*CPR* B130)

In this way, combinatory synthesis not only organizes incoming data, or basic information, in order to generate a representation; it also presents it *to* a subject, who can in principle self-ascribe that content according to the form 'I think such-and-such'.

This spontaneous executive power of self-consciousness or self-ascription Kant variously calls 'the original synthetic unity of apperception', 'pure apperception', 'original apperception', the 'transcendental unity of self-consciousness', and the 'I think':

It must be *possible* for the 'I think' to accompany all my representations; for otherwise something would be represented in me that could not be thought at all, and that is equivalent to saying that the representation would be impossible, or at least would be nothing to me. . . . I call it *pure apperception*, to distinguish it from empirical apperception, or, again, *original apperception*, because it is that self-consciousness that, while generating the representation '*I think*' (a representation that must be capable of accompanying all other representations, and that in all consciousness is one and the same), cannot itself be accompanied by any further representation. The unity of this apperception I likewise entitle the *transcendental* unity of self-consciousness in order to indicate the possibility of a priori cognition arising from it. For the manifold representations, which are given in an intuition, would not be one and all *my* representations, if they did not belong to one self-consciousness. As *my* representations (even if I am not conscious of them as such) they must conform to the condition under which they *can* stand together in one universal self-consciousness, because otherwise they would not all without exception belong to me.   (*CPR* B131–2)

We now come to a concept that was not included in the general list of transcendental concepts but that must yet be counted as belonging to that list . . . This is the concept or, if the term be preferred, the judgement, 'I think'. As is easily seen, this is the vehicle (*Vehikel*) of all concepts, and therefore also of transcendental concepts, and so is always included in the conceiving of these latter, and is itself transcendental. But it can have no special title, because it serves only to introduce all our thought, as belonging to consciousness.   (*CPR* A341/B399–400)

The original synthetic unity of apperception is one of two absolutely fundamental explanatory notions in Kant's theory of human cognition. The other is of course the all-purpose imagination—the mind's generative and productive engine, which supplies both the lower-level or receptive spontaneity of sensibility and also the higher-level or discursive spontaneity of the understanding. While the all-purpose imagination accounts for *consciousness*, the original synthetic unity of apperception accounts for *intentionality*.[59] Through the act of referring to some object of experience, via synthetically generated representations, a human mind necessarily also refers to itself—or at least necessarily *can* refer to itself—as the synthesizing subject of those representations. Without the capacity for generating the 'I think', representational content would lack an underlying irreducible unity of conceptualizing and judging, and thus could not represent fully determinate objects. The several distinct generative/ productive capacities, or faculties, required for experiential cognition would then operate without any effective executive coordination.[60] Hence the 'I think' is the '*vehicle* of all concepts' that 'serves to *introduce* all our thought' (ibid.; emphasis added).

    In Section 1.5, I shall say a little more about the nature of the apperceptional 'I think' in the context of Kant's theory of judgement. For the moment, however, we need to ask: what precisely is the *object* of a representation—the 'such-and-such' that the 'I think' thinks? This is the same as to ask: what precisely is the intentional object of the intentional subject of thinking? Kant's answer is this:

[59] See Keller, *Kant and the Demands of Self-Consciousness*, esp. chs. 1–5. Other interpreters argue that the original synthetic unity of apperception effectively accounts only for self-identity. See e.g. Bird, *Kant's Theory of Knowledge*, 120, 136, and Patricia Kitcher, *Kant's Transcendental Psychology*, chs. 4–5.

[60] Brook, in *Kant and the Mind*, esp. 13, 33, 209–212, argues that a 'global representation' will suffice to ground the unity of the mind, without any need to appeal to either a noumenal homunculus or an executive capacity. But a global representation will not suffice to account for the primitive and irreducible object directedness of *Vorstellungen* (BL Ak. xxiv. 40)—i.e. for what Searle calls the mind's 'intrinsic intentionality'; see *Rediscovery of the Mind*, 78–82.

At this point we must make clear to ourselves what we mean by the expression 'an object of representations'. We have stated above that appearances are themselves nothing but sensible representations, which, as such and in themselves, must not be taken as objects capable of existing outside our power of representation. What, then, is to be understood when we speak of an object corresponding (*korrespondieren*) to, and consequently also distinct from, our cognition? It is easily seen that this object must be thought only as something in general = X, since outside our cognition we have nothing that we could set over against this cognition as corresponding to it.   (*CPR* A104)

All our representations are in fact referred by the understanding to some object; and since appearances are nothing but representations, the understanding refers them to *something*, as the object of sensible intuition. But this something, thus conceived, is only the transcendental object; and by that is meant a something = X, of which we cognize, and with the present constitution of our understanding can cognize, nothing whatsoever, but which, as a correlate of the unity of apperception, can serve only for the unity of the manifold in sensible intuition. By means of this unity the understanding combines the manifold into the concept of an object. This transcendental object cannot even be separated from the sensible data, for nothing is then left through which it might be thought. Consequently it is not for cognition an object in itself, but only the representation of appearances under the concept of an object in general —a concept that is determinable through the manifold of these appearances.   (*CPR* A250–1)

An object of a representation for Kant 'must not be taken as . . . capable of existing outside our power of representation'; but at the same time it is represented as an object 'corresponding to, and consequently also distinct from, our cognition'—namely, the 'transcendental object'. These two apparently inconsistent[61] features can be reconciled if we regard the object of a representation *per se* as nothing more than *a generic definite object for a thinking subject*—that is, some X that is 'the F' for some cognizing ego or another. This generic definite object is only a formal place-holder or target for human intentionality in general.

Moreover, the maximal generality of this representation explains why the concept of such an object is the 'supreme concept' of an object (*CPR* A290/B346). In so far as a complex of sensory information is self-consciously taken in—or synthetically appropriated and processed—under concrete empirical conditions as an ordered informational complex, the representation of the generic definite cognitive target subsumes under itself a unitary representation of some determinate corresponding object of experience = A, or = B. This unitary representation results from the application of a necessary conceptual rule to the temporal sequence of sensory inputs given through perceptions:

If we investigate what new characteristic is given to our representations by the *reference to an object* . . . we find that it does nothing beyond making the combination

---

[61] See e.g. Kemp Smith, *Commentary to Kant's 'Critique of Pure Reason'*, 204–22.

of representations necessary in a certain way, and subjecting them to a rule; and conversely that objective meaning (*objektive Bedeutung*) is conferred on our representations only in so far as a certain order in their temporal relations is necessary. (*CPR* A197/B242–3; see also *CPR* A106)

Hence the existence of a particular object that is the actual determinate referent of a representation presupposes the necessary unity of the self-conscious subject who is the formal spontaneous ground of combinatory rule-governed conceptual synthesis directed towards as-yet-unspecified objects:

Now we find that our thought of the reference of all cognition to its object carries with it an element of necessity; the object is viewed as that which prevents our cognitions from being haphazard or arbitrary, and which determines them a priori in some definite fashion, since in so far as they are to refer to an object, they must necessarily agree with one another—that is, must possess the unity that constitutes the concept of an object. But it is clear that, since we have to deal only with the manifold of our representations, and since that X (the object) that corresponds to them is nothing for us—because it is something that has to be distinct from our representations—the unity that the object makes necessary can be nothing else than the formal unity of consciousness in the synthesis of the manifold of representations. (*CPR* A104)

These, then, are the overarching complementary formal transcendental structures of an objective mental representation: (1) the original synthetic unity of apperception—that is, the universal self-representing or self-conscious subject of all representational—but especially conceptual—activity; and, necessarily corresponding to the self-conscious subject of representations, (2) the definite something in general = X, the generic transcendental representational target of a representation, or intentional object. These two generic structures are necessarily implemented, or realized, in every generative/productive act of experiential cognition. The actual output of the synthesizing activities of our *Erkenntnisvermögen*—that is, the representational content—then automatically implies both a concrete representing subject in time and space (the empirical self) and a concrete represented object (the object of experience). Both the empirical subject and the empirical object are reciprocally generated through the very act of synthesis.

1.4. The Elements of Judgement: Intuitions and Concepts

A fundamental feature of Kant's cognitive semantics is a sharp and indeed irreducible distinction between two types of conscious object-directed representation or cognition—intuitions and concepts:

The genus is *representation* in general (*repraesentatio*). Subordinate to it stands representation with consciousness (*Bewußtsein*) (*perceptio*). A perception (*Perception*) that refers solely to the subject as the modification of its state is a sensation (*sensatio*), an objective perception is a cognition (*cognitio*). This is either *intuition* or *concept* (*intuitus vel conceptus*). The former refers immediately to the object and is singular (*einzeln*), the latter is mediate, by means of a characteristic (*Merkmals*) that can be common to several things. (*CPR* A320/B376–7)

As we shall see in Chapters 3 and 4, a clear and distinct understanding of the essential differences between these two types of objective representation will ultimately explicate the essential differences between analytic and synthetic propositions. But what is above all initially puzzling about concepts and intuitions is that, while, according to Kant, the concept/intuition contrast is semantically irreducible, nevertheless they must also be regarded as essentially *complementary*:

Thoughts without content are empty, intuitions without concepts are blind. It is, therefore, just as necessary to make the mind's concepts sensible—that is, to add an object to them in intuition—as to make our intuitions understandable—that is, to bring them under concepts. These two powers, or capacities, cannot exchange their functions. The understanding can intuit nothing, the senses can think nothing. Only from their unification can cognition arise. (*CPR* A51/B75–6)

This apparent hypertension at the heart of Kant's semantics can be relaxed only if we are able to see how intuitions and concepts each contribute separately—as 'the elements of all our cognition' (*CPR* A50/B74)—to a higher-order composite representation: the judgement of experience, or cognition in the focal sense. In this section I will give a preliminary sketch of intuitions and concepts as distinct types of objective representation, and as deriving from distinct representational faculties. Then in the next section I will bring them together in an integrated account of the nature of judgement.

In order to understand intuitions and concepts, we must first make some sense of this notoriously tricky text:

In whatever mode (*Art*) and by whatever means a cognition may refer (*beziehen*) to objects, intuition is that through which it immediately refers (*unmittelbar bezieht*) to them, and to which all thought is mediately directed (*als Mittel abzweckt*). But intuition takes place only in so far as the object is given to us. This in turn is possible at least for us humans only if it affects (*affiziere*) the mind in a certain way (*Weise*). The capacity (receptivity) for receiving representations through the mode in which we are affected by objects is entitled *sensibility*. Objects are therefore given (*gegeben*) to us by means of sensibility, and it alone yields us *intuitions*; they are *thought* (*gedacht*) through the understanding, and from the understanding arise *concepts* (*Begriffe*). But all thought must, either directly (*geradezu* (*directe*)), or indirectly (*im Umschweife* (*indirecte*)), by means of certain characteristics, refer ultimately to [objects given by] intuitions, therefore, in our case, to sensibility, because there is no other way in which objects can be given to us. The effect of an object upon the faculty of representation, in so far as we are affected by it, is *sensation* (*Empfindung*). That intuition that refers to the object through sensation is entitled *empirical*. The undetermined object (*unbestimmte Gegenstand*) of an empirical intuition is entitled *appearance* (*Erscheinung*). That in the appearance that corresponds to sensation I term its *matter* (*Materie*) . . . (*CPR* A19–20/B33–4)

The basic sort of empirical intuition is a singular conscious representation of an object given to us immediately through outer or spatial sensibility and mediately through inner or temporal sensibility. In so far as outer empirical intuitions are the 'intakers' of sensory intake, they express the lowest level of generative/productive activity: sensory receptivity. Viewed on their own, outer empirical intuitions function primarily as sensory ostensions, or bare sensory indicators, of their objects. For example, I can intuit *this* or *that*, something over *here* or over *there*, or something right *now* or just *then*. These ostended objects are appearances, and the conscious representation that constitutes an empirical intuition of an appearance is called a 'perception' (*Wahrnehmung*) (*CPR* B160; see also *R*. 4679; Ak. xvii. 664). Correspondingly, the minimal generative/productive function that underlies outer sense perception is what Kant calls the 'synopsis of the manifold *a priori* through sense' (CPR A94/B127) or the '*pure* synthesis of apprehension' (CPR A98–100/B160).[62]

Conscious synoptic or apprehensional intuitions (i.e. perceptions) are triggered, or initiated, by something beyond the mind—an external input source. The causal process triggering sensibility, deriving from that external input source, is 'affection' (*Affektion*).[63] For the subject, affection is a brute empirical fact. The response of a thinker to the fact of affection always involves 'sensation' (*Empfindung*), which is an internal representational manifold consisting in a temporally successive series of 'qualia', or intensively variable internal changes in the conscious state of the subject (*CPR* A166–76/B207–18). Sensations are not objects of consciousness; instead they are only adverbial qualitative features of consciousness—the flotsam and jetsam in what William James later evocatively calls 'the stream of consciousness'.[64] The stream of consciousness is first and foremost a temporal stream, a successive series of momentary sensational changes in the subject's representational mental state. The series of qualitatively distinct internal changes in time (the series of qualia) is closely connected with the mind's automatic activity of generating mental images (*Bilder*) of the objects given in immediate intuitional

[62] Patricia Kitcher helpfully identifies the implementation of this synoptic or apprehensional function with 'scanning an image'—that is, consciously delineating the contours and boundaries of perceived objects (*Kant's Transcendental Psychology*, 156–7).

[63] Here, of course, lies a notorious puzzle: how can Kant characterize this causal process of affection as deriving from what is wholly mind-independent, without inconsistently having cognition beyond the limits of possible experience? I want to bracket this puzzle for further discussion in Sect. 2.4. For the moment we need only the *fact* of affection.

[64] See James, *Principles of Psychology*, ch. IX.

synopsis or apprehension. In turn, the activity that consists in processing this series of mental images is what Kant calls the 'synthesis of reproduction' (*CPR* A100–2). It seems plausible to regard reproduction as essentially our cognitive capacity for memory.[65]

By contrast to sensations, which are in themselves non-intentional or non-object-directed responses to affection, intuitions of inner sense are singular, immediate cognitions of one's own changing mental states: the unreflective yet still reflexive awarenesses of '*my existence* in time' (*CPR* Bxl n.). Inner sense is in fact our capacity for 'consciousness' (*Bewußtsein*): '(The inner sense) Consciousness is the intuition of its self' (*R.* 5049; Ak. xviii. 72). This is not Cartesian introspection. Kantian inner sense is a capacity for direct access to oneself as a singular flowing temporal subject—as a unique stream of mental life—not for direct access to oneself as a Cartesian 'thinking thing': 'Inner sense, by means of which the mind intuits itself or its inner state, gives . . . no intuition of the soul itself as an object' (*CPR* A22/B37). Otherwise put, inner sense provides us with experience in the sense of *Erlebnis* ('lived experience'), as opposed to experience in the sense of *Erfahrung* ('directed experience'). *Erfahrung* is the sensory cognition of real spatiotemporal material objects, or 'things in space and time' (*Dinge im Raum und der Zeit*) (*CPR* B147).

On the object side, then, given the triggering action of affection, 'sensation is . . . that which indicates (*bezeichnet*) a reality in space and in time, according to whether it is referred to the one or the other mode of sensible intuition' (*CPR* A374). This real thing in space and time is what Kant also calls the '*realitas phaenomenon*' (*CPR* A166) or '*substantia phaenomenon*' (*CPR* A277/B333). The phenomenal reality or substance is represented through 'the matter (the physical element) or content (*Gehalt*), which signifies (*bedeutet*) something that is to be met with in space and time and which therefore contains an existent and corresponds to sensation' (*CPR* A723/B751). In this way, whatever the original source of sensory affection might really be, starting with the sensation as a subjective index of the causal impression, outer intuitions directly pick out macroscopic physical bodies as their efficient triggering spatiotemporal causes:

There are bodies without us, that is, things that, though quite unknown as to what they are in themselves, we yet cognize by the representations that their influence on our sensibility procures us, and that we call 'bodies'. This word means the appearance of that which is uncognized by us but is not therefore less real.   (*P.* Ak. iv. 289)

---

[65] Cognitive psychologists distinguish between different types of memory: short term, long term, semantic (fact memory), episodic (event memory), and procedural (habits or skills). See e.g. Sternberg, *Cognitive Psychology*, chs. 7–8. In the *Anthropology*, Kant distinguishes between 'recall' or *Gedächtnis*, and mere reproduction (*A.* Ak. vii. 182–5). *Gedächtnis* includes long-term, semantic, and episodic memory, whereas mere reproduction includes short-term and procedural memory.

In so far as an intuition is merely apprehensional or synoptic and reproductive, or 'that representation that can be given prior to all thinking' (*CPR* B132),
its content is what I will call 'proto-objective'; and the bare intuition or
perception itself can be correspondingly labelled a 'proto-cognition'. A bare
intuition is only 'proto' and not fully-fledged, because, while my intuitive apprehension of an appearance is immediate and essentially singular, and also falls
under spatiotemporal constraints, yet that apparent object is given to me in
a 'blind' (*CPR* A51/B75) or relatively unarticulated way. It is 'the undetermined object of an empirical intuition'. Thus it is actually represented as
an objective datum, yet my representation of it is still relatively raw or
undeveloped in this sense: my sensory field or manifold with its spatial and
temporal coordinates manifestly includes an occupant, but yields no further
determination of the discriminating characteristics of that occupant. This is
what Kant in 'The Jäsche Logic' calls a 'sensibly clear but indistinct' representation (JL Ak. ix. 33–9): clear, because it delivers an individual sensible
object though intuition; yet indistinct, because it lacks internal differentiation
and resolution. For example, as Kant points out in the *Anthropology*, prelin-
guistic human childhood is characteristically proto-cognitional in character:
'[Early childhood] was the time not of experience, but merely of scattered perceptions, not yet unified under the concept of an object' (*A*. Ak. vii. 127–8).
So too the sensory cognition of non-human animals—for example, an ox—
is said by Kant to be clear yet indistinct (FS Ak. ii. 59), conscious yet not
self-conscious (*PC* Ak. xi. 52), and object directed yet neither conceptual nor
propositional. In this way it is possible to cognize something without also
having a *thought* about it (*CPR* A89–91/B122–3).

   But what more does it take to make an intuition of an object distinct—to
represent a determinate object and not merely a proto-object? What more does
it take to have a thought? Kant's answer is that one must employ an *empirical concept* in order to overcome the indistinctness or blindness of a bare
intuition and make it 'understandable' (*CPR* A51/B75). And that empirical
concept must in turn fall under a pure concept of the understanding.[66] The
use of a categorially conditioned empirical concept tranforms the proto-
cognition into a fully-fledged self-conscious cognition of a determinate sensory
object—that is, into a 'phenomenon' in the strict or technical sense (*CPR*
A248–9). This concept is thereby employed only within the context of 'determining judgement' (*bestimmende Urteilskraft*) (*CJ* Ak. v. 179), which is our
capacity for generating true or false empirical propositions, since 'the only
use that the understanding can make of these concepts is to judge by means
of them' (*CPR* A68/B93). So what we ultimately need to know is just how the

[66] This is well described in one of the *Reflexionen*: 'Every perception must be brought
under a title of the understanding, since otherwise no concept and nothing is thereby thought'
(*R*. 4679; Ak. xvii. 664).

empirical concept manages to function *within a judgement* as the 'determiner' of an otherwise blindly or indistinctly represented intuitional proto-object. But, in order to get a handle on the nature of a judgement, we must first know what an empirical concept is, and also how it is applied to the sensory manifold, to the extent that concepts and sensory manifolds[67] can be characterized in abstraction from the integrated judgement complexes into which a given concept enters.

The clearest and most explicit account of empirical concepts is given in 'The Jäsche Logic'. Here concepts are sharply contrasted with intuitions: 'an intuition is a *singular* (*einzelne*) representation (*repraesentatio singularis*), a concept a universal (*allegemeine*) (*repraesentatio per notas communes*) or reflected (*reflectirte*) representation (*repraesentatio discursiva*)' (JL Ak. ix. 91). For the moment I want to focus on the universality of a concept; later I will come back to its reflected character. By contrast to the singularity of intuitions, a concept is a 'universal or common' (*allgemeinen oder gemeinsamen*) representation—a 'representation of what is common (*gemein*) in several objects' (JL Ak. ix. 91). That is, a concept ranges over many particular objects by virtue of some determinate characteristic or *Merkmal* expressed by that concept: the *Merkmal* corresponds directly to an attribute or property shared by those objects. Every concept is thus itself a freestanding characteristic: 'all our *concepts* are characteristics' (JL Ak. ix. 58). But every characteristic is also a 'partial concept' (JL Ak. ix. 58) or 'a representation *in so far as it can be contained in various ones*' (JL Ak. ix. 91), in the sense that it can enter into other concepts as a constituent part of their intrinsic contents. This double function of the concept is well described in one of the *Reflexionen*: 'The characteristic is, first, considered as a representation in itself, and secondly, considered as belonging as a partial concept to another representation and thereby as ground of cognition of things' (*R.* 2285; Ak. xvi. 299).[68] So, for example, the concept RED ranges over empirically intuited objects that are all instances of red, including the proto-object I have just blindly intuited. Now I see not just an obscure *this X now over there* or *this spatiotemporal thing*, but *this red thing*. The very concept RED that is applied to this red thing also enters as a partial concept into the concept CRIMSON, since to be crimson is to be a certain shade

---

[67] Kant fairly consistently although not very explicitly employs a distinction between (1) the sensory manifold *in* an intuition—the totality of sensory representational content within the phenomenal field of a single apprehension (*CPR* A98–100, B143), and (2) the sensory manifold *of* intuitions—an aggregate of different intuitions reproductively preserved and organized over time according to a conceptual rule (*CPR* A100–2, B161).

[68] In some places—e.g. at JL Ak. ix. 58—Kant says that conceptual characteristics are literally constituents of the things they represent. Given his cognitive or representational idealism, this is of course strictly correct. But it is slightly misleading. Concepts are not numerically identical to the property instances (tropes) or abstract parts that are attributed to the things that fall under the characteristic (e.g. 'this red here', the redness that literally belongs to X), but instead are only *type*-identical.

of red; the concept RED is thereby 'contained in' the concept CRIMSON. And every object to which CRIMSON applies is also an object to which RED applies. Every empirical concept thus is a 'ground of cognition' not only of every object that falls directly under the concept itself, but also of every object that falls under any characteristic in which that concept is contained. In turn, the totality of characteristics contained in a given concept is its intrinsic content or intension.

For Kant, a concept achieves both its universality over objects and its intensional content by virtue of expressing an 'analytic unity of apperception' (*CPR* B133) or 'analytic unity of consciousness' (*CPR* B133 n.), by which he means an overall subjective unity of representation of a higher order than that which is ingredient in any one of the singular representations of objects. The analytic unity of consciousness in turn presupposes the original synthetic unity of self-consciousness or the 'I think', our spontaneous a priori rule-governed capacity for self-representation. So a concept is not merely a representation of a collection of individual objects by means of a shared characteristic, but also 'a representation which is to be thought of as common to *different* representations' (ibid). Kant calls every concept a 'common concept' or *conceptus communis* (*CPR* B133–4 n.) precisely in order to emphasize the essential shareability of content not only across many distinct representations and objects of representation, but also across individual acts of representation. Concepts are at once universal (in relation to represented objects) and intersubjectively accessible (in relation to representing subjects). Thus the '*conceptus communis*' is not only an essentially general content but also a *communicable content*. As he stresses in one of his logic lectures, 'one does not understand a thing until one can communicate it to others' (DWL Ak. xxiv. 781).

An individual object is 'subsumed' under a particular concept by virtue of that object's being intuited or singularly picked out and also at the same time represented as having (tokenizing, instantiating) a property or quality that is type-identical with a characteristic contained in the concept. For example, to use Kant's needlessly complicated example at A137/B176, the empirical concept PLATE (defined, presumably, as ROUND FLAT DISH) contains the characteristic ROUND. A pure geometric circle falls under ROUND just in so far as a pure intuition of that object also represents it as tokenizing or instantiating the very same characteristic of roundness. At the same time, of course, the instance of that concept given in that pure geometric object is a distinct token of that type. A much simpler example of the same subsumptive relationship, however, would be this: a particular rose—say, rose *r*—falls under the concept RED in so far as an empirical intuition of this very *r* also represents *r* as having the attribute or property of being red, which is, of course, type-identical with the characteristic RED. We now have a partial answer to the question of how empirical concepts function as 'determiners' of undetermined objects given in intuition. They determine those objects by subsuming them. The total collection of objects actually subsumed or notionally subsumable under a concept belongs to what Kant calls the 'comprehension' (*Umfang*) of that concept (JL Ak. ix. 95).[69]

Subsumption of an intuited macroscopic physical object under a concept, according to Kant, cannot be managed by concepts alone, but requires a special mediating contribution of the imagination that he calls 'schematism'. In the case of empirical concepts, empirical schemata are in effect what contemporary cognitive psychologists call *prototypes*[70]—Kant calls them 'monograms'—for efficiently sorting through, regimenting, and classifying intuitions in terms of the descriptive specifications of conceptual intensions. Thus, in addition to my concept DOG I can also create in my mind a supplementary rule of the imagination connecting that concept to a set of exemplary images—say, of a four-legged, tail-wagging, barking, fire-hydrant-visiting animal. This prototype effectively mediates my application of DOG to dogs, but does not give a set of necessary or sufficient conditions for belonging to the comprehension of DOG (perhaps some dogs never bark, or visit trees exclusively). Without empirical schemata, conceptual information is far too abstract to be usable in given sensory contexts. So what is needed is a simple scheme for correlating elements of the conceptual content with major elements of the sensory manifold. And in this way the imaginational schema or prototype partially interprets or models the abstract conceptual content in sensory terms:

The concept 'dog' signifies a rule according to which my imagination can delineate the figure of a four-footed animal in a general manner, without limitation to any single determinate shape that experience offers me, or any possible mental image that I can exhibit *in concreto*. . . . The *mental image* is a product of the empirical faculty of productive[71] imagination; the *schema* of sensible concepts, such as of figures in space, is a product and as it were a monogram of pure a priori imagination, through which and in accordance with which the mental images themselves first become possible. These mental images can be connected with the concept only by means of the schema to which they belong. In themselves they are never completely congruent with the concept.   (*CPR* A141–2/B180–1)

---

[69] For Kant, the comprehension of a concept is not restricted to the finite set of actual things subsumed under it by means of intuition, since it also includes the infinite set of possible things specified by the intension. Nor is a comprehension, strictly speaking, exhausted even by the infinite set of possible objects subsumable under the concept; for the comprehension of a given concept C also includes every *concept* more specific than C (which Kant calls 'lower' concepts). See Sect. 3.1 below.

[70] See Smith, 'Concepts and Thought', 25–9. See also Patricia Kitcher, *Kant's Transcendental Psychology*, ch. 8.

[71] The original text says '*empirischen Vermögens der produktiven Einbildungskraft*'. What Kant is stressing here is that all schemata, even empirical schemata, are outputs of the pure productive imagination, our faculty for *synthesis speciosa* or 'figurative synthesis' (*CPR* B151).

By way of an empirical schema, then, a concept can be used by a thinking subject to reduce many diverse items of sensory information to a communicable higher-order content that encodes all the distinct informational bits in a unitary survey. Otherwise put, conceptualization is a projection of a *repeatable pattern* or *rule* onto a sensory manifold:

A concept is always, as regards its form, something general that serves as a rule (*Regel*). The concept of body, for instance, as the unity of the manifold that is thought through it, serves as a rule in our cognition of outer appearances.   (*CPR* A106)

[A rule] is the objective unity of consciousness of the manifold of representations (which consequently is valid in general in this way). (*R.* 5708; Ak. 18, 331)

A given empirical concept thus summarizes or glosses a given sensory manifold by subjecting it to a particular rule. Owing to its generality and commonality, the same summary or gloss can then be applied in different contexts by the same or different thinkers to different sensory manifolds having a tendency to fit into, or under, the same pattern or rule.

Kant calls the basic conceptualizing, pattern-grasping, rule-applying act of the mind the 'synthesis of recognition' (*Synthesis der Rekognition*) (*CPR* A103). He also characterizes this synthesis as the 'logical origin of concepts' or the 'generation of a concept out of given representations' (JL Ak. ix. 93). The generative concept-acquisition process is not simple or one step, but breaks down into three ordered moments or phases: 'comparison' or the discrimination of different qualitative elements; 'reflection' or the unification of the different qualitative elements under a single consciousness; and, finally, 'abstraction' or the suppression of differences among the elements in order to focus solely on partial identities:

To make concepts out of representations one must be able *to compare, to reflect,* and *to abstract,* for these logical operations of the understanding are the essential and universal conditions for generation of every concept whatsoever. I see, e.g., a spruce, a willow, and a linden. By first comparing these objects with one another I note that they are different from one another in regard to the trunk, the branches, the leaves, etc.; but next I reflect on that which they have in common among themselves, trunk, branches, and leaves themselves, and I abstract from the quantity, the figure, etc., of these; thus I acquire a concept of a tree.   (JL Ak. ix. 94–5)

The moment of reflection in concept generation is crucial,[72] since it invokes the standpoint of self-consciousness, and therefore the original synthetic unity of apperception. To synthesize a concept is to link together distinct qualitative or structural elements of simpler sensory representations into a semantically universal, intersubjectively communicable, higher-order, self-consciously unified representation. This representation is a fully objective

---

[72] See Longuenesse, *Kant and the Capacity to Judge,* chs. 5–6.

general content. Kant calls it either a 'rule' or a 'characteristic', depending on whether he is emphasizing the process of imposing patterns on lower-order sensory elements, or instead the internal logico-syntactical structure of the intensional content of the concept. (Indeed, we will see in Section 2.1 how for Kant logical syntax necessarily enters into the constitution of every concept.)

This objective general representation can then be applied to the original affective causal sources of the sensations involved in empirical intuition. By means of the application of a concept to an object delivered by intuitions, the initially indistinct or blind intuitional apprehension of that causal source of affection is replaced by another, more fully structured, representation. In other words the 'undetermined object' or proto-object of empirical intuition and perception (the appearance in the strict or technical sense) is generatively transformed, through the process of concept application—which, as we have seen, involves both the productive and reproductive functions of the dedicated imagination—into the 'determined object' (the phenomenon in the strict or technical sense). Now each completed transformative conceptual application is identified by Kant with an act of *judgement*. So we must now turn to Kant's account of the nature of judgement.

1.5. Kant, Moore, and the Nature of Judgement

As I have stressed, all intuitional and conceptual syntheses for Kant must eventually terminate in judgements, if they are to be determinately objective representations of an empirical world. The 'capacity for judging' (*Vermögen zu urteilen* (*CPR* A69/B94)) or 'faculty of judgement' (*Urteilskraft*) is therefore at the very centre of our *Erkenntnisvermögen*. But what is a judgement? This crucial Kantian conception is two sided. On the one side there is the thinking subject's *cognitive performance* or mental act in generating a judgement, along with that subject's logical attitude in asserting that judgement—what Kant calls a 'holding-to-be-true' or *Fürwahrhalten*; and, on the other side, there is the proposition or truth-bearer, which is the *topic* or content of that generative assertoric attitude:

Judgements are actions of the understanding and of reason.   (BL Ak. xxiv. 844)

The holding of a thing to be true is an occurrence (*Begebenheit*) in the understanding that, though it may rest on objective grounds, requires subjective causes in the mind of the individual who makes the judgement.   (*CPR* A820/B848)

A *judgement* . . . [is] a relation that is *objectively valid*, and so can be adequately distinguished from a relation of these same representations in which there would be only subjective validity, e.g., in accordance with laws of association.   (*CPR* B142)

This 'act/content' contrast should be familiar enough to us from the writings of the early phenomenologists.[73] In its first aspect, a judgement is a mere 'mental phenomenon', a given subject's conscious representational mental act of carrying out a judgement; it is 'an occurrence in the understanding' that 'requires subjective causes in the mind of the individual who makes the judgement', and is governed only by subjective 'laws of association'. In its second aspect, however, a judgement is an 'immanent objectivity' or 'thing' that can be 'held to be true', a thing that can 'rest on objective grounds' and thereby be 'objectively valid'; hence it is a communicable propositional content having a truth value.

This dual-aspect approach to judgement leads directly to a sticky problem. Whereas the act component is strictly subjective, conscious, and private, the content component is supposed to be an objective or public topic of assertoric thought—many different acts of belief can share the same propositional belief content. But if the proposition is actually *generated* in the act in which a propositional attitude occurs, then this seems to assimilate semantic content to an individual consciousness. If a semantic content exists only in the mind of an individual, then it is seemingly individuated *by* that individual thinker, and cannot be communicated; and if it cannot be communicated then it cannot function as a linguistic meaning. Not only that, but if propositions are identified with the mental acts of individual subjects, then seemingly the truth or falsity of judgements is reduced wholly to 'subjective causes in the mind of the individual who makes the judgement', and thereby relativized.

This important line of criticism of Kant's theory of judgement was first clearly spelled out in G. E. Moore's ground-breaking essay, 'The Nature of Judgment'. This paper, a revised version of a part of Moore's Trinity College fellowship dissertation on Kant, has as its official topic a critique of F. H. Bradley's judgement theory; but its real agenda is a thoroughgoing attack on Kant's theory of judgement:

I shall in future use the term 'concept' for what Mr Bradley calls a 'universal meaning'; since the term 'idea' is plainly full of ambiguities, whereas 'concept' and its German equivalent '*Begriff*' have been more nearly appropriated to the use in question. There is, indeed, a great similarity between Kant's description of his '*Begriff*', and Mr Bradley's of his 'logical idea.' For Kant, too, it is the 'analytical unity of consciousness' which *makes* a '*Vorstellung*' or 'idea' into a '*conceptus communis*' or '*gemeinsamer Begriff*' (B133 n).

The idea used in judgment is indeed a 'universal meaning'; but it cannot, for that very reason, be described as part of the content of any psychological idea whatsoever.

When, therefore, I say 'This rose is red', I am not attributing part of the content of my idea to the rose . . . What I mean to assert is nothing about my mental states, but a specific connexion of concepts.

[73] See e.g. Brentano, *Psychology from an Empirical Standpoint*, bk. 2, ch. I; and Husserl, *Logical Investigations*, Investigation V.

It will be apparent how much my theory has in common with Kant's theory of perception. It differs chiefly in . . . refusing to regard the relations in which [concepts (RH)] stand as, in some obscure sense, the work of the mind.[74]

Moore's objection, reduced to its essentials, is that Kant's theory reduces the semantic content of concepts and judgements to an individual's 'analytical unity of consciousness'. Now, as we have seen, the analytical unity of consciousness in a concept according to Kant presupposes the original synthetic unity of apperception; so from the existence of the content of any of my representations it follows (analytically) that that content is a representation belonging to myself, and (synthetically) that it is at least always possible for me to carry out the self-conscious or reflective judgement 'I think such-and-such' in regard to it (*CPR* B131–2). Moore construes this Kantian doctrine as the claim that a judgement is ultimately *nothing but* an assertion about the inner character of the individual judger's mental acts,[75] because the judgement's semantic contents and constituents—especially concepts—are all items produced synthetically within and by a given individual's mind.

According to Moore's own view, by sharp contrast, concepts are wholly mind-independent platonic entities—indeed, they are the essential constituents of reality itself: 'It seems necessary, then, to regard the world as formed of concepts. These are the only objects of knowledge. They cannot be regarded fundamentally as abstractions either from things or from ideas; since both alike can, if anything is to be true of them, be composed of nothing but concepts.'[76] Frege had made a closely related point more than ten years earlier in *Foundations of Arithmetic*, by giving concepts both mind-independent intrinsic generality and also the power of collecting diverse concrete individuals into objectively denumerable sets or classes: 'The concept has a power of collecting *far superior to the unifying power of synthetic apperception*. By means of the latter it would not be possible to join the inhabitants of Germany together into a whole; but we can certainly bring them all under the concept "inhabitant of Germany" and number them.'[77]

---

[74] Moore, 'The Nature of Judgment', 2, 4, 9.

[75] Early Moore's philosophical psychology was heavily influenced by Brentano both positively and negatively; see Moore, 'The Refutation of Idealism', 35–44; Moore, 'The Subject Matter of Psychology'; and n. 73 above. Brentano (at least in the 1880s) held a radically 'adverbial' theory of intentionality according to which mental contents and objects alike are strictly immanent features of mental acts; and Moore ascribed this theory to Kant too. The missing link between Brentano's psychology and Moore's interpretation of Kant is the neo-Kantian psychologist James Ward, who supervised Moore's work towards his fellowship dissertation at Trinity. See Moore, 'An Autobiography', 17–22; and Ward, 'Psychology', esp. 547–48.   [76] Moore, 'The Nature of Judgment', 6.

[77] Frege, *The Foundations of Arithmetic*, 61, emphasis added. For Frege, sets or classes are extensions of concepts.

Moore's doctrines to the effect (i) that a concept is a mind-independent abstract constituent of reality, and (ii) that a judgement is nothing but a 'specific connexion of concepts',[78] when added to Frege's idea (iii) that a concept is a mind-independent determiner of sets or classes, culminate in Russell's Theory of Descriptions of 1905[79]—a theory Frank Ramsey later valorized by dubbing it 'that paradigm of philosophy'.[80] The official aim of the Theory of Descriptions is to give a unified theory of the logical meanings of the words "all", "any", "every", "a", "some", and "the". But perhaps the principal achievement of the theory is that it enables Russell logically to eliminate all singular terms (singular 'denoting phrases') apparently picking out philosophically bothersome, non-existing individuals—for example, 'the present King of France', 'Mr Pickwick', 'the round square', and, worst of all, 'the class of all classes not members of themselves'.

From at least 1900, Russell was fully committed to the view that every well-formed and independently meaningful or categorematic expression stands for something. This is his ' "Fido"-Fido' or denotational theory of meaning. Now the class of all classes not members of themselves is a member of itself if and only if it is *not* a member of itself. This paradox, discovered by Russell in 1901, apparently undermines set theory and thereby also the logicist project of reducing arithmetic to logic via set theory. It devastated Frege when Russell informed him of it in 1902—'Your discovery of the contradiction has surprised me beyond words, and I should like to say, left me thunderstruck'—and bedevilled Russell himself for years.[81]

Given Russell's denotational semantics, however, one way of avoiding this dire result is to prevent the construction of the paradoxical set by eliminating all singular terms that apparently stand for it. The Theory of Descriptions carries out this elimination by treating singular terms as 'incomplete symbols', or syncategorematic parts of wholly general propositions containing only mind-independent concepts and logical constants, including quantifiers. Thus, for example, any phrase of the form 'the F' means that there exists something that is F and for anything else that also happens to be F it is literally identical to the first thing. The appeal to quantification, in turn, enables Russell to eliminate all categorematic terms picking out totalities of objects—especially

---

[78] Since for Moore concepts are the constituents of reality, and judgements are only specific connections of concepts, it follows that all real facts are themselves judgements. No wonder then that, as Keynes wrily reports, Moore once had a nightmare in which he could not distinguish propositions from tables ('My Early Beliefs', 94).

[79] Other versions of the theory of descriptions can be found in Russell's *Introduction to Mathematical Philosophy* (1919), ch. 16, pp. 167–80; and in Whitehead and Russell, *Principia Mathematica to *56* (1910–13/1927), 30–1, 66–71, 173–86.

[80] Ramsey, *The Foundations of Mathematics and Other Essays*, 263.

[81] See Monk, *Bertrand Russell: The Spirit of Solitude*, 142–99 (p. 153 for the famous Frege quotation); Russell, *The Principles of Mathematics*, 79–80, 101–7; Russell, 'Mathematical Logic as Based on the Theory of Types'; and *Principia Mathematica to *56*, 37–65.

terms picking out totalities that include those very terms themselves, hence generating a logical 'vicious circle' in determining the membership of that totality. Quantification avoids vicious circles by systematically reformulating all terms standing for totalities as higher-order logical functions on lower-order constituents of propositions. This, bounded in a nutshell, is the ramified theory of types. But preventing paradox is only Russell's logical means to an ultimately more important philosophical end. Initially at least, Russell believed that, by eliminating all essentially singular or intuitional components and also all totality-collecting or synthesizing components, from the content of propositions, he had finally realized Moore's original goal of a consistently anti-Kantian doctrine of judgement according to which no appeal whatsoever to consciousness, intentionality, or synthesizing subjectivity is required.[82] Obviously, the Theory of Descriptions was designed by Russell to solve some special logico-philosophical puzzles. But in a broader historical sense the complete rejection of Kant's theory of judgement is the true philosophical upshot of the Theory of Descriptions and what stakes its claim as a paradigm of philosophy.

Now how could Kant respond to Moore's objection? An effective response would consist in emphasizing two fundamental points neglected by Moore: (1) that a judgement is *not* merely a 'specific connexion of concepts'—a certain logical concatenation or agglomeration of concepts—but also a higher-order unity imposed on those conceptual representations (and also upon intuitional representations[83]) by a synthesizing subject, and (2) that the self-conscious ground of this higher-order unity—the original synthetic ground, that is, of the analytic unity of consciousness—is *not* in any way restricted to an individual judger's mental states but is on the contrary essentially an a priori cognitive form or function shared by any and every act of judgement within an individual thinker and across all actual and possible human thinkers. Let us now reconstruct these two Kantian points.

---

[82] See Hylton, *Russell, Idealism, and the Emergence of Analytic Philosophy*, ch. 6. Russell's optimism was short lived, however, since he soon realized (*a*) that even the possession of an eliminative analysis of definite descriptive phrases did not altogether obviate the need for psychological acts of acquaintance with concrete individuals where genuine proper names or indexicals were concerned, and (*b*) that he still needed an explanation for the *logical unity* of essentially general propositional complexes. These difficulties eventually drove him to the so-called multiple-relation theory of judgement (*c.*1910), in which—ironically enough—he fully returned to the psychological domain by appealing to multiple acts of acquaintance in order to account for both non-descriptive singular terms and propositional unity. See Russell's 1910 paper, 'On the Nature of Truth and Falsehood'; his 1911 paper, 'Knowledge by Acquaintance and Knowledge by Description'; and his unfinished book from 1913, *Theory of Knowledge*. Wittgenstein's merciless criticism just prior to the First World War convinced Russell that this whole line of thinking was bankrupt. See Lackey, 'Russell's 1913 Map of the Mind'.

[83] See Sects. 4.2–4.3 below.

Like all other types of representation—for example, intuitions and concepts—the judgement is a generative output of the mind. But, unlike intuitions and concepts taken on their own, judgements are representations for which the issue of *truth and falsity* first arises: 'truth and illusion are not in the object, in so far as it is intuited, but in the judgment about it, in so far as it is thought' (*CPR* A293/B350). Here Kant is stressing the difference between a judgement and an empirical intuition. An empirical intuition is an immediate sensory grasp of an object. It cannot be either true or false, strictly speaking, because it only delivers an object of appearances to the mind through the medium of the senses. So it does not thereby produce, by means of the understanding, any *thought* about that object: 'appearances can certainly be given in intuition without functions of the understanding' (*CPR* A90/B122). To say that it lacks a thought is to say that it does not intrinsically involve a concept, for 'thinking is cognition by means of concepts' (*CPR* A69/B94). But concepts taken on their own are not judgements. A concept by virtue of its intensional content represents a set or collection of objects. Merely to assign a set of objects to a concept as its comprehension, however, is not yet to have a thought *about* any of those objects.

According to Kant, even though concepts can be considered on their own, in order to have a *use* a concept must be taken up into a judgement: 'the only use (*Gebrauch*) that the understanding can make of these concepts is to judge by means of them' (*CPR* A68/B93). In turn a concept is used when it is regarded as a general rule that is assertorically applied to something more specific: 'If the understanding in general is explained as the faculty of rules, the power of judgement is the faculty of *subsuming* under rules; that is, of determining whether something stands under a given rule . . . or not' (*CPR* A132/B171).

Let us focus for a moment on the simplest sort of judgement—namely, that in which a concept is applied to a single object given in empirical intuition. Here the concept, considered as itself a characteristic or *Merkmal*, is applied to that object by means of a 'determination' (*Bestimmung*) or 'predicate of a thing' (*CPR* A572/B600), which is a property or attribute instantiated in the object—that is, a property or attribute that is 'tokened' in the object and is also fully type-identical to the concept. For example, let someone make the singular affirmative categorical assertoric judgement (RR), 'This rose is red'. Because the truth or falsity of (RR) depends entirely on experience, it is a posteriori. In so far as the concept or characteristic RED is represented as type-identical with a determination (attribute or property) occurring *in* the object, that intuited object is thereby represented as actually having that determination. In this way, to 'think' an intuited object via a concept in a judgement is immediately to represent something (this rose) *as* something (as determined by having the attribute or property of being red) by means of something (the characteristic RED). Only if the intuited object is conceptually represented as having a determinate attribute or property by means of a characteristic can the issue of truth or falsity arise. We have already seen in Section 1.4 that the process of determining an object in empirical cognition must consist in the generation of an internally articulated (distinct) representation of a sensory object through a unifying recognitional conceptual synthesis of intuitions by means of an empirical schema of the imagination. Now, however, we are in a position to say more about this determining representational process: to synthesize intuitively given sensory content and conceptual content via the imagination, and thereby to generate the distinct representation of an object, is to make a true or false judgement about that very object.

Crucial to Kant's theory of judgement is the idea that the process of object determination has its own sort of form—namely, predicative form. The identification between object determination, making a concept distinct, predication, and judgement is pointed up by Kant as early as 1762 in 'The False Subtlety of the Four Syllogistic Figures':

To compare something as a characteristic with a thing is *to judge*. The thing itself is the subject, the characteristic is the predicate. The comparison is expressed by means of the copula *is* or *are*. When used absolutely, the copula designates the predicate as a characteristic of the subject.   (FS Ak. ii. 47)

The distinctness of a concept does not consist in the fact that that which is a characteristic of the thing is clearly represented, but rather in the fact that it is cognized as a characteristic of the thing. The door is something that does, it is true, belong to the stall and can serve as a characteristic of it. But only the being who forms the judgement: *this door belongs to this stable* has a distinct concept of the building, and that is certainly beyond the powers of animals.   (FS Ak. ii. 59)

According to this gloss, the object itself is the logical subject of the judgement; the logical predicate is the characteristic or partial concept, which is in turn a determination or attribute of the object; and the copula expresses the syncategorematic function of attributing to the logical subject a certain characteristic or determination. In Kant's example, the state of affairs consisting of the door and its property of belonging to the stable is for the first time internally articulated or discriminated through the judgement. An ox in the stall might blindly or indistinctly see the door but will always fail to see it *as* a door. Only through the judgement, and only through predication, can one or another of the discriminable properties of the door explicitly stand forward for a thinking subject. This is to produce a 'clear and distinct' sensible representation of it (JL Ak. ix. 33–9). The distinctness consists precisely in the object's being represented through predication in such a way as to isolate or articulate some part of its internal structure. To determine an object for Kant is, therefore, to generate a clear and distinct representation of that object through a judgement. This pre-Critical account is misleading in three ways, however, each of which is properly sorted out during Kant's mature or Critical period—the period that follows his 'representational turn' of the 1770s.

The first concerns a certain confusion between the object represented and the representation of the object. In Kant's Critical formulations, the logical subject of a judgement is not the object itself but rather an intuition that immediately delivers an individual object as the referent of the subject term.[84] More generally, according to Kant's mature or Critical theory of judgement, the judgement or proposition does not literally contain objects and their determinations or properties but rather only representations *of* objects and their determinations.

Secondly, not only later in the Critical period but even in other passages in 'False Subtlety', Kant emphasizes that judgements can have categorical logical forms that are importantly different from the singular categorical form. In particular, many categorical judgements are general, not singular:

Concepts, however, as predicates of possible judgements, refer to some representation of a still undetermined object. Thus the concept of body means (*bedeutet*) something, e.g., metal, that can be cognized by means of that concept. It is, therefore, a concept solely by virtue of its containing under itself other representations, by means of which it can refer to objects. It is, therefore, the predicate of a possible judgement, e.g., 'Every metal is a body'.   (*CPR* A69/B94; see also FS Ak. ii. 59)

Here Kant stresses that judgement or predication can consist not merely in applying a predicate to an intuited thing, but also in applying a predicate to a predicate. Thus, both the subject and predicate terms of a judgement can be *concepts*—for example, when the judgement is universal or of the form 'Every *F* is *G*'. This holds too in the case of judgements of the form 'Some *F* is *G*'. The crucial point is this. Judgements can, but need not, apply concepts directly to objects—for many judgements involve predicative applications of concepts to concepts. So not only objects but also concepts *themselves* can be discriminated or determined through the judgement. This distinction between concept-to-object predication and concept-to-concept predication, as we will see (Section 3.1), is essential for understanding Kant's theory of analytic propositions.

Thirdly, and closely connected with the last point, in his Critical period Kant also stresses that propositions need not have singular or general categorical form *only*. Rather, they can also be affirmative, negative, or infinite (logical qualities); hypothetical or disjunctive (logical relations); and problematic, assertoric, or apodictic (logical modalities) (*CPR* A70–6/B95–101). It is important to note, however, that, even where the proposition is not categorical in its gross form—I mean its form as specified by the purely logical concept, or logical constant, taking widest scope—Kant still insists that the simplest or 'atomic' judgements contained within it are all categorical and hence take subject/predicate form: 'categorical judgements constitute the *basis* of all

---

[84] See Sect. 4.2.

the remaining ones' (VL Ak. xxiv. 933). According to Kant not all propositions are categorical; nevertheless all propositions are ultimately based on and
generatively derived from categorical propositions. In this strictly generative
sense, categorical predication remains the *Ur*-form of all judgement.[85]

Granting those three important qualifications, then, Kant seems to have held
throughout his philosophical career that all judgements necessarily are, at the
very least, predicative cognitions.[86] But even this does not exhaust the nature
of judgement. Predicative structure is not merely a feature of the logical form
of every judgement but is also the basic form of a determinately objective representation. This is made clear in the following text:

> Since no representation, save when it is an intuition, goes immediately to an object,
> no concept ever refers to an object immediately, but always only to some other rep-
> resentation of it, be that other representation an intuition, or itself already a concept.
> Judgement is, therefore, the mediate cognition of an object, hence the representation
> of a representation of it. In every judgement there is a concept that holds of many
> [representations (RH)], and comprehends under this multiplicity also a given repres-
> entation, which then immediately refers to an object.   (*CPR* A68/B93)

Here, a judgement is not merely an intuitional representation of a single object;
nor is it merely a representation of a concept, or even of several concepts.
Rather, a judgement consists in a representation of the predicative relation
between the intuition of the object and a concept, or *between* two concepts.
If we think of the intuitional element of a judgement as its first level, and the
conceptual element as its second level, then the judgement itself is always a
third-level representation of objects—a representation of the relation between
conceptual (second-level) and intuitional (first-level) representations of

---

[85] Strawson brings out a very similar point in *The Bounds of Sense*, 81–2; *Individuals*,
chs. 5–6; and in *Subject and Predicate in Logic and Grammar*, 3–40.
   The Kant–Strawson view, according to which the operation of categorical predication
is generatively basic for the theory of judgement and hence for logic, can be fruitfully com-
pared and contrasted with Frege's doctrine that it is not the operation of predication but
instead the concept itself (an 'unsaturated' objective function taking individual objects as
arguments and truth values as values) that is basic for judgement and logic. See Frege,
'Function and Concept'. Frege's entity-theoretic approach to predication gets him into big
problems, however. Since he identifies the syncategorematic function of predication with
the concept itself, but categorically distinguishes functions from objects, it turns out to be
impossible to talk about concepts by using singular terms such as "the concept HORSE"—
because that would imply that the concept HORSE is an object, not a function. His struggles
with this puzzle are revealed in 'Concept and Object'.
[86] Longuenesse aptly calls this Kant's 'privileging of predication'; see *Kant and the Capacity
to Judge*, 104. This is not a trivial feature of Kant's view. One could e.g., like the Port Royal
logicians prior to Kant, define a judgement as the mere 'representation of a relation between
two concepts' (*CPR* B140); or, like Brentano, define it as the affirmation or denial of any
object or content of thought (*Psychology from an Empirical Standpoint*, bk. two, ch. VII);
or, like early Russell, define it as a mental act that multiply but extrinsically relates the
parts of a propositional complex. And so on.

objects, or of the relation between two conceptual (second-level) representations. This third representational level corresponds to what I will call the *executive synthesis*—the level at which the overall unity of all the lower-order conceptual and intuitive contents is established. Thus 'a judgment is the representation *of the unity* in the relations of cognitions' (*R*. 3044; Ak. xvi. 629, emphasis added).

In the propositional content of the singular categorical judgement, the executive synthesis corresponds to the relation established by the simple or unqualified copula ('. . . is——'). And in the propositional content of general categorical judgements, the synthesis corresponds to the copula as further modified by quantity ('all . . . are——', 'some . . . are——'). So, pictorially, a categorical judgement for Kant then looks roughly like this:

Level 1: intuition→object ('This')
Level 2: concept→intuition→object ('This rose')
          concepts→concepts ('Red roses')
Level 3: executive synthesis of concepts and intuitions ('This rose is red')
          or of concepts and concepts ('All/some roses are red')

Where the judgement or proposition is not of simple categorical form, the executive synthesis corresponds to the copula as modified by logical constants other than those of mere quantity—for example, by those of quality or modality. But three general points remain the same: (i) the judgement has its own unique sort of third-level form over and above its several constituent representations; (ii) this unique form is always predicative in character; and (iii) predicative form is always represented as a logical modification of the copula.

These points raise in an acute way, however, the question of the source of a judgement's overall unity. What accounts for the third or executive level of representation? What accounts for the synthesizing presence of the copula and its further logical modifications? What binds together the lower-level propositional constituents—none of which on its own takes a truth value even though it represents objects—into an ordered complex that *does* take a truth value? If nothing binds them together, then there is a crucial explanatory gap in Kant's theory of judgement.

It is worth noticing that this logical binding problem also directly afflicts Moore's theory of judgement in 'The Nature of Judgment'; for there Moore defines a judgement as a wholly mind-independent 'specific connexion of concepts', without saying *how* the overall connecting relation between them should be construed. And this leads to a disastrous dilemma. Either the connecting relation is another concept, or else it is not another concept. On the one hand, if the connecting relation is another concept, then that connecting concept Cc belongs as a concept to the set of connected concepts ($C1$, $C2$, $C3$ . . . Cn). If Cc now belongs to the set of connected concepts—hence (Cc, $C1$, $C2$, $C3$ . . . Cn)—then yet another connecting concept Cc^* is needed to relate *Cc* to the other connected concepts, and so the same problem arises again. But, on the other hand, if the connecting relation is not a concept, and so does not belong merely to the set of connected concepts, then the judgement in question is *not* merely a 'specific connexion of concepts' but in fact some other sort of structure altogether.

Now, although Kant obviously was not directly aware of Moore's theory of judgement, nevertheless he addresses this nasty difficulty—sometimes called 'the problem of the unity of the proposition'[87]—quite directly:

> I have never been able to satisfy myself with the explanation that the logicians give of judgement in general. It is, they declare, the representation of a relation between two concepts. . . . I need only point out that the definition does not determine in what the asserted *relation* consists. If, however, I investigate more precisely the relation of given cognitions in every judgement, and distinguish it, as belonging to the understanding, from the relation according to laws of the reproductive imagination, which has only subjective validity, I find that a judgement is nothing but the manner in which given cognitions are brought to the *objective* unity of apperception. This is what is intended by the copula "is". It is employed to distinguish the objective unity of given representations from the subjective. It indicates their relation to original apperception, and its *necessary unity* . . . By that, to be sure, I do not mean to say that these representations *necessarily* belong *to one another* in the empirical intuition, but rather that they belong to one another *in virtue of the necessary unity* of the apperception in the synthesis of intuitions, i.e., according to principles of the objective determination of all representations, in so far as cognition can be acquired by means of these representations—principles that are all derived from the principle of the transcendental unity of apperception.   (*CPR* B140–2; see also *R.* 5923; Ak. xviii. 386)

So Kant grounds the unity of the proposition in transcendental self-consciousness or the original synthetic unity of apperception. It is our spontaneous a priori capacity for applying the representation 'I think such and such' to any manifold of lower-order representational elements in accordance with the basic forms and principles of logic (see Section 2.1), then, that ultimately confers upon those elements the executive synthesis that generates the predicative copula and the logical form of the judgement, and in turn generates a determinate (distinct) representation of an object. This is because the 'such and such' that the 'I think' ascribes to itself is necessarily in the form of a judgement about a determinate object. Thinking is nothing more—and nothing less—than judging that *s* is *P* (*CPR* A81/B106). The 'I think' is not

---

[87] The unity problem—sometimes also called 'Bradley's problem'—certainly was not Moore's alone; in fact, it carried over almost directly into Russell's early theory of judgement, hounding him from *The Principles of Mathematics* right through to his final discarding of that theory in 1913 or 1914 in response to Wittgenstein's criticisms. See Candlish, 'The Unity of the Proposition and Russell's Theories of Judgment'; Hylton, 'The Nature of the Proposition and the Revolt against Idealism'; and Linsky, 'The Problem of the Unity of the Proposition'.

only the 'vehicle of all concepts', but also the vehicle of all judgements, and hence the vehicle of all determinate objective representations.

This finally puts us in a position to address Moore's objection to Kant's theory of judgement—a doubt that must be removed if his project of developing a general cognitive semantics is to be sustained. Who is 'the judging subject'? Is it Peter, Paul, or even Mary? No. It is no one in particular—although, to be sure, every such unification is indeed carried out by a concrete individual thinker—because the underlying unity of a judgement is nothing but an irreducible executive or coordinating rule structure of spontaneous self-consciousness, a rule structure that enters 'anonymously' into all judging processes.

In other words, the rule-governed spontaneous capacity for self-representing synthesis characterizes individual finite sensory thinking or judging subjects at a level of generality that fully abstracts away from individual thinkers and their empirical identities. As Kant argues explicitly and at length in the Paralogisms (*CPR* A341–405/B399–432), original synthetic apperception cannot be validly hypostatized into a noumenal person or spiritual substance—a Cartesian 'thinking thing'. It is not a transcendental homunculus. Transcendental apperception is, instead, only a generic cognitive function—an 'apperception in general = X'—that is necessarily presupposed by every concept and judgement both infrasubjectively and intersubjectively:

Through this I, or He, or It (the thing) which thinks, nothing further is represented than a transcendental subject of the thoughts = X, which is cognized only through the thoughts which are its predicates, and about which, in abstraction, we cannot have any concept whatsoever; because of which we therefore turn in a constant circle, since we must always already avail ourselves of the representation of it at all times in order to judge anything about it.   (*CPR* A346/B404)

Thus pure apperception is strictly anonymous but semantically ubiquitous; necessarily, every act of objectively valid representation implements it. And by the same token every judgement generated by a concrete judging subject is also a semantic content that can be communicated to any other concrete judging subject who implements the very same type of pure apperceptive function. Moore's critical worry about the reduction of the judgement to individual subjects or minds is thereby effectively answered.

1.6. Conclusion

Is Kant's general cognitive semantics now philosophically in the clear? Not quite. Moore's worry about Kant's supposed judgement psychologism only partially expresses a broader master worry: if Kant posits *any* sort of essential connection between meanings (the contents of objective mental representations) and human minds, then the very fact of such a mind dependence will ultimately make all meanings, truth, and knowledge impossible. In the next chapter, we will see that this master worry takes two other specific forms: (1) that Kant is guilty of the fallacy of logical psychologism; and (2) that Kant's thesis of idealism is philosophically unsupportable. It is only by answering these two charges, and especially the latter charge, that this entire family of doubts can be laid to rest. In order to do this, however, we must fully unpack his answer to the most general transcendental question of all, the Semantic Problem: how are objective mental representations—that is, cognitions—possible?

2.

How are Cognitions Possible?

What Kant means in general by synthetic *a priori* propositions is really just that class of propositions our knowledge of the necessity of which could, he supposed, be explained only by mobilizing the entire Copernican resources of the *Critique*, by appealing to the model of 'objects conforming to our modes of representation', i.e., to our sensibility's constitution and the understanding's rules. Since . . . nothing whatever really is, or could be, explained by this model—for it is incoherent—it must be concluded that Kant really has no clear and general conception of the synthetic *a priori* at all.

P. F. Strawson[1]

2.0. Introduction

If I am correct, then the overarching purpose of the first *Critique* is to explain how a mental representation can refer to its object. This is the Semantic Problem. The Semantic Problem leads to the more specific question of how necessary a priori representations can refer to their objects, and finally to the most specific question of how synthetic a priori judgements are possible. This is the Modal Problem. I have argued that the key explanatory notion in Kant's general cognitive semantics is his epigenetic or generative/productive theory of the mind, according to which object-directed representations—including intuitions, concepts, schemata of the imagination, and, most centrally, judgements—are created by the rule-guided application of our innate capacities for spontaneous synthesis to raw sensory intake under the original synthetic unity of apperception. What we need to explore now are the precise conditions under which all cognitive meaning creation is possible.

Broadly speaking, these conditions split into two types: (1) formal or logical conditions; and (2) material conditions, or conditions specially relevant to the objective validity (*objektive Gültigkeit*) and objective reality (*objektive*

---

[1] Strawson, *The Bounds of Sense*, 43.

Realität)—that is, the empirical meaningfulness and actual empirical applicability—of a representation. I discuss these in Sections 2.1 and 2.2. The topic of objective validity leads directly to a discussion of what is clearly the explanatory foundation of all objective mental representations or meanings for Kant: transcendental idealism (Sections 2.3 and 2.4).

That topic requires an anticipatory comment. It is no big secret that Kant's idealism is, and always has been, a fundamental target of analytic criticism. Indeed to an important extent the analytic tradition arises from a radical anti-idealism—directed not only against Kant and the neo-Kantians, but also against Hegel and the British neo-Hegelians—and from its natural accompaniment, an equally radical epistemological and metaphysical realism. These trends are fully expressed in Frege's critique of logical psychologism, and in his function-theoretic and set-theoretic account of the ontology of logic and arithmetic in *Foundations of Arithmetic*; in the platonic atomism of Moore's 'Nature of Judgment' and 'Refutation of Idealism'; and in the rich logicistic development of platonic atomism in Russell's writings after the *Essay on the Foundations of Geometry* (1897) and up to the beginning of the First World War. While the *Tractatus*, logical empiricism, and ordinary language philosophy ultimately turned the analytic tradition decisively away from Frege's metaphysically realistic ontology of logic and arithmetic and from Moore's and Russell's platonic atomism, an official radical anti-idealism remained a non-negotiable point. Indeed, by the 1950s and 1960s, the unqualified rejection of Kant's idealism by analytic philosophers was the conventional wisdom. This hands-off warning on transcendental idealism led to the curious result that even those mid-century analytic philosophers who were the most serious readers of, and borrowers from, the first *Critique*—Wilfrid Sellars and P. F. Strawson are the prime examples—felt compelled either radically to reinterpret Kant's idealism,[2] or else to set it aside as being simply (to use Strawson's strong word) 'incoherent'.

Now Strawson validly infers from his incoherence thesis the conclusion that the ultimate *explanandum* of Kant's idealism—that synthetic a priori propositions not only exist but are also meaningful, necessarily true, and cognizable—is correspondingly vitiated. Yet this line of reasoning cuts two ways. Kant himself, of course, is well aware of how intimately the main elements of his doctrine depend on one another: 'The possibility of synthetic cognition *a priori* . . . was the special problem upon the solution of which the fate of metaphysics rests and upon which my *Critique* (as well as the present *Prolegomena*) entirely hinges. The idealism . . . was only taken up in the doctrine as the sole means of solving the above problem' (*P. Ak.* iv. 377).[3] So,

---

[2] Sellars e.g. reconstrues Kant's noumenon as the submicroscopic, microphysical object of modern physics in *Science and Metaphysics: Variations on Kantian Themes*.

[3] This is slightly misleading. As I mentioned in Ch. 1 n. 20, Kant uses at least two other arguments for idealism in addition to this one.

if Kant's idealism is indeed incoherent, then that fact will obviously vitiate both his general cognitive semantics and in turn his doctrine of the synthetic a priori. But if, on the other hand, Kant's idealism can be shown to be internally consistent and not obviously vulnerable to the most powerful objections against it, then we are entitled to conclude that, to that extent, Kant does in fact have a 'clear and general conception of the synthetic a priori'. It is important to underline the fact that, for our purposes, it need not be demonstrated that Kant's idealism is true. If his idealism can be shown, on at least one interpretation, to be both coherent and resistant to the standard criticisms,[4] and then we also find that we have good independent reasons for accepting his doctrines of analyticity, syntheticity, and the synthetic a priori (Chapters 3–5), then we will have provided more than enough reason *to take transcendental idealism seriously*. A level theoretical playing field is all we need in order to motivate a Kantian re-examination of the historical foundations of analytic philosophy from Frege to Quine. This is because the Frege-to-Quine sequence in the development of the analytic tradition presupposes the very strong assumption that Kant's idealism is *clearly* false.

2.1. The Logical Syntax of the Mind

As I indicated in the Introduction, Wittgenstein's *Tractatus* radically changed the original course of analytic philosophy, by moving it from a predominantly logico-mathematical orientation towards a predominantly logico-linguistic one. Otherwise put, the *Tractatus* turned analytic philosophy away from Frege's and Russell's realistic logical metaphysics, towards an anti-metaphysical logical conventionalism. These assertions capture the root idea behind this big swerve:

5.6. *The limits of my language* mean the limits of my world.
5.61. Logic fills the world: the limits of the world are also its limits.
6.13. Logic is not a theory but a reflexion of the world. Logic is transcendental.[5]

Wittgenstein is saying roughly this. Nothing will count as an intelligible or knowable part of the world—that is, as a possible or actual 'fact' (*Tatsache*)—unless it is represented by truth-valued sentences; but all truth-valued sentences are conditioned a priori by logic; hence 'logic is transcendental'.

---

[4] In Sect. 2.3–2.4 I will argue that, even if Kant sometimes makes the questionable claim that unknowable things-in-themselves exist, he also develops a prima facie consistent and defensible version of transcendental idealism according to which noumenal entities are consistently thinkable but existentially unaffirmable. See Bermudez, 'Scepticism and the Justification of Transcendental Idealism', and Rescher, 'On the Status of "Things-in-Themselves" in Kant's Critical Philosophy'.

[5] Wittgenstein, *Tractatus Logico-Philosophicus*, 149, 169.

According to Wittgenstein, logic does not describe the world—it determines
the very framework of the world. This, as we shall shortly see, is essentially
a Kantian idea. But Wittgenstein also identifies the transcendental logical framework of the world with linguistic structure, the underlying grammar of our
(or, more solipsistically, 'my') language. To borrow Carnap's later formulations in the late 1920s and early 1930s, the 'logical structure (*Aufbau*) of the
world' is ultimately a direct reflection of—and therefore can be discerned a
priori in—'the logical syntax of language'.[6] Or, as Carnap emphatically puts
it in *Philosophy and Logical Syntax*, 'the only proper task of *Philosophy* is *Logical
Analysis*'; but this task is necessarily constrained by the fact of the '*relativity
of all philosophical theses in regard to language*, that is, the need of reference
to one or several particular language systems'.[7]

   This is definitely *not* a Kantian idea. As early as his pre-Critical essay 'The
Only Possible Argument in Support of a Demonstration of the Existence of
God', Kant takes the view that all human languages, owing to their contingent historical and social origins, disguise or distort the underlying logical
structures of the representations they express (OPA Ak. ii. 73). Later, in 'The
Jäsche Logic', he offers the more general thesis that the grammatical form of
any natural language is intelligible precisely to the extent that it accurately
reflects logical form; and logical form in turn operates as a 'universal grammar' for all human languages (JL Ak. ix. 11–13). Moreover, as he puts it elsewhere in his logic lectures, logical form has an even deeper ground:

The form of all our experiences is rational. All experiences have the form of reason,
and without this they will not be experiences.   (BL Ak. xxiv. 236)

Universal logic ought to consider the form of the understanding. Therefore it
abstracts from all speculation and considers the logic of universal human reason.   (VL
Ak. xxiv. 795)

Kant's idea, then, is that all objective experiences have an underlying logical
form or syntax, which he calls the 'logic of universal human reason'. This logic
is transcendental because, 'without this', experiences 'will not be experiences'.
And ultimately he identifies the transcendental logical syntax with a set of pure,
universal, innate, generative/productive rules or formal procedures—the pure
concepts of the understanding. These logically primitive concepts inform all

---

   [6] In the *Aufbau* or *The Logical Structure of the World* (1928), Carnap pursued a logically oriented, constructivist epistemological project that shares as much in common with
contemporary neo-Kantianism and Russell's *Our Knowledge of the External World* (1914)
as it does with the *Tractatus*. See Richardson, *Carnap's Construction of the World*, chs. 1–6.
But by the time of *Logical Syntax of Language* (1934), he had moved decisively away from
neo-Kantianism towards an overtly conventionalist and linguistic construal of his earlier
project, hence much closer to the *Tractatus*. In 1963 Carnap wrote that, 'for me person-
ally, Wittgenstein was perhaps the philosopher who, besides Russell and Frege, had the
greatest influence on my thinking' ('Intellectual Biography', 25).
   [7] Carnap, *Philosophy and Logical Syntax*, 35, 78.

other concepts and judgements, and thereby 'parse' appearances, in a way strictly analogous to that by which a set of grammatical rules parses a natural language:

[The pure concepts] serve, as it were . . . to parse (*buchstabieren*) appearances, so that we may be able to read them as experience. (*P.* Ak. iv. 312)

To search in our ordinary cognition for the concepts that do not rest upon particular experience and yet occur in all cognition from experience, of which they constitute as it were the mere form of connection, presupposes neither greater reflection nor deeper insight than to detect in a language the rules for the actual use of words generally and thus to collect elements for a grammar (in fact both enquiries are very closely related) . . . (*P.* Ak. iv. 322–3)

Now because (according to Kant's thesis of cognitive or representational idealism) all the proper objects of human cognition—the objects of experience—are token-identical with the contents of judgements of experience, it follows that, for Kant, just as for the Tractarian Wittgenstein and Carnap, 'logic fills the world'. According to early Wittgenstein and Carnap, however, logic fills the world because *language* fills the world. In Wittgenstein's view, furthermore, logic is nothing but an ideal reflection of language; in fact, logic is itself an 'ideal language' because it reveals the 'sublime' essence of any natural or ordinary language.[8] But on Kant's picture of things, logic fills the world because in a certain sense the *human mind* fills the world. Indeed language itself is an output of the innate, generative/productive, discursive functions of the human mind: 'all language signifies thought' (*A.* Ak. vii. 192).

Here, however, a major problem confronts us. Kant says explicitly that logic is 'the science that exhaustively presents and strictly proves nothing but the formal rules of all thinking' (*CPR* Bviii–ix) and 'the science of the rules of the understanding' (*CPR* A52/B76). But it seems that, if one takes seriously the revolutionary critique of logical psychologism propounded by Frege and Husserl in the 1880s and 1890s,[9] then a direct consequence of Kant's defining formal logic in terms of the human understanding or reason is that his theory of logic will be psychologistic and therefore wholly unacceptable.[10] Both Wittgenstein and Carnap assume, unquestioningly, the absurdity of any fusion of the logical and the psychological. And, in order to steer well clear of it, they adopt the thesis that logical form is essentially an idealized version of linguistic form—the logical syntax of language. Since language, whatever else it might be, is a public or worldly object, logic is then guaranteed to be thoroughly non-psychological in its nature.

---

[8] See Wittgenstein, *Philosophical Investigations*, sects. 81, 89–92, pp. 38, 42–3.

[9] See Frege, *The Basic Laws of Arithmetic*, 12–25; *The Foundations of Arithmetic*, pp. v–vii, 33–8; 'Logic [1897]', 144–9; 'Review of E. G. Husserl, *Philosophie der Arithmetik I*'; and 'Thoughts', 369; see also Husserl, 'Prolegomena to Pure Logic'.

[10] See e.g. Ayer, *Language, Truth, and Logic*, 49–50; Coffa, *The Semantic Tradition from Kant to Carnap*, 7–21; and Russell, *The Problems of Philosophy*, 87–8.

Now Frege secures precisely the same anti-psychologistic result by the more extreme tactic of making logic depend on a non-physical, non-mental —and explicitly hyper-linguistic—'third realm' of purely logical entities:

Since thoughts are non-mental in nature, it follows that every psychological treatment of logic can only do harm. It is rather the task of this science to purify logic of all that is alien and hence of all that is psychological, and *to free thinking from the fetters of language by pointing up the imperfections of language.* Logic is concerned with the laws of truth . . .[11]

A third realm must be recognized. Anything belonging to this realm has it in common with ideas that it cannot be perceived by the senses, but has it in common with things that it does not need an owner so as to belong to the contents of his consciousness. Thus for example the thought we have expressed in the Pythagorean theorem is timelessly true, true independently of whether anyone takes it to be true. It needs no owner.[12]

Early Moore and early Russell hold (with some interesting variations) the same view. But this Fregean gambit overlooks, with almost breathtaking unconcern, the obvious perils of undergirding logic and arithmetic with a frankly realistic metaphysics: what ontological sense can be made of the inhabitants of the 'third realm'? And how can such non-mental, non-physical entities ever be immediately cognized by us if our model of immediate cognition is sense perception by means of empirical intuition? As Kant points out, empirical intuition requires causal affection; but third-realmers are by hypothesis noumenal, and therefore cannot in any way enter into causal relations in the empirical world. A Fregean epistemology would therefore incoherently require the humanly impossible cognitive faculty of 'intellectual intuition' (*CPR* B72).[13] The linguistic turn in analytic philosophy—taken first by early Wittgenstein, then by the Vienna Circle, and then yet again by Oxford followers of the later Wittgenstein—is a direct consequence of the vigorous Frege–Husserl critique of logical psychologism, *together with* a more silent and implicit but equally thoroughgoing rejection of Frege's, early Moore's, and early Russell's realistic logical metaphysics.

But need one go all the way to 'third-realmism', or equally and oppositely to the linguistic turn, just in order to avoid logical psychologism? It seems clear that, *if* Kant's theory of logic can be shown to be appropriately anti-psychologistic, then it will *not* follow that either platonism or the linguistic turn is required in order to make the fundamental claim that 'logic is transcendental'.

First of all, then, just what is logical psychologism? Pinning down an explicit, universally shared definition, even within the framework of Frege's and Husserl's writings alone, is tricky.[14] Logical psychologism is frequently glossed

---

[11] Frege, 'Logic [1897]', 148–9, emphasis added.   [12] Frege, 'Thoughts', 363.

[13] For a somewhat similar objection to Fregean epistemology and to mathematical platonism more generally, see Benacerraf, 'Mathematical Truth', 671–5.

[14] See Kusch, *Psychologism*, esp. chs. 1, 3, 4–5.

as the thesis that logic is explicable in terms of the human mind. This equates logical psychologism with any mentalistic approach to logic. But, in point of fact, the logical psychologism rejected by Frege and Husserl is the doctrine that logic is fully explicable by means of *empirical (or 'experimental'[15]) psychology*: 'The basic error of Psychologism consists, according to my view, in its obliteration of this fundamental distinction between pure and empirical generality, and in its misinterpretation of the *pure* laws of logic as *empirical* laws of psychology.'[16] Put this way, the real philosophical problem with logical psychologism is reductionism. Psychologism involves the modal reduction of strict necessary laws and truths of logic to contingent generalizations; the epistemic reduction of a priori logical knowledge to a posteriori knowledge; the semantic reduction of universally shareable propositional content to the incommensurable idiosyncrasies of actual individuals, communities, or species; and, finally, as a consequence of the semantic reduction, a corresponding relativistic reduction of objective logical truth to individuals, communities, or species. To repeat, the real problem with logical psychologism is *not* mentalism as such, but instead the reduction of logic to empirical or experimental psychology.

If Kant's theory of logic expresses or entails a version of logical psychologism, then it is certainly unacceptable by the lights of early period and middle period analytic philosophy alike.[17] Indeed, stepping back from both Kant and analytic philosophy for a second, it seems very likely that, if any philosophical thesis is clearly and unequivocally wrong, then logical psychologism is it. So what we need to see is, first, that Kant was fully aware of the unacceptable consequences of logical psychologism, and, secondly, that he incorporates the awareness of these consequences directly into his theory of logic. More emphatically expressed, (1) *Kant is in fact the inventor of logical anti-psychologism*, and (2) *Kant's theory of logic is thoroughly mentalistic but does not in any way imply a reduction of logic to empirical or experimental psychology.*

It is often assumed that (barring anticipations by Bolzano in the 1830s[18]) the philosophers' war against logical psychologism begins in 1884 when Frege issues the then-stunning assertions that 'psychology should not imagine that it can contribute anything whatever to the foundation of arithmetic', that 'a proposition may be thought, and again it may be true; let us never confuse these two things', and that the doctrine that 'concepts sprout in the individual mind like leaves on a tree . . . makes everything subjective, and if

[15] See Boring, *A History of Experimental Psychology*, esp. chs. 12–19.
[16] Husserl, 'A Reply to a Critic of my Refutation of Logical Psychologism', 156.
[17] But not by the lights of Quinean or scientific philosophy. Quine explicitly embraces logical psychologism in 'Epistemology Naturalized'.
[18] See Bolzano, *Theory of Science*, esp. sects. 48 ff., pp. 62–5.

we follow it through to the end, does away with truth'.[19] Yet, an entire century before Frege (not to mention half a century before Bolzano), Kant explicitly recognizes, and just as explicitly eschews, the possibility of logical psychologism in his theory of pure general logic (*CPR* A50–5/B74–9).

'General' (*allgemeinen*) logic is to be contrasted with 'special' (*besondern*) logic. General logic deals with the absolutely necessary and strictly universal laws of thought. Its laws are wholly formal laws of consistency and consequence: the principle of non-contradiction (= no proposition and its negation can be conjointly true, and no predicate and its denial can be conjointly applied to the same object); and the principle of the sufficient ground or logical entailment (= false propositions cannot follow logically from true propositions) (JL Ak. ix. 51–2). Since by virtue of its maximal generality its laws comprehend every possible object of thought, general logic is itself 'topic-neutral'. Special logic, by contrast, is 'topic-sensitive': that is, it deals with the necessary rules of thought in so far as they apply to specific domains of objects, or to some determinate subject matter.

Under the rubric of general logic, in turn, Kant distinguishes sharply between 'pure' (*reine*) or non-empirical general logic and 'applied' (*angewandte*) or empirical general logic:[20]

Logic is the science that exhaustively presents and strictly proves nothing but the formal rules of all thinking (whether this thinking be empirical or a priori, whatever origin or object it may have, and whatever contingent or natural obstacles it may meet in our minds).   (*CPR* Bviii–ix)

In [general logic] we abstract from all empirical conditions under which our understanding is exercised, e.g. from the influence of the senses, the play of imagination, the force of habit, inclination, etc., hence also from the sources of prejudice, indeed in general from all causes from which this or that cognition arise or may be supposed to arise, because these merely concern the understanding under certain circumstances of its application, and experience is required to know these. A *general* but *pure* logic therefore has to do with strictly a priori principles and is a *canon of the understanding* and reason, but only in regard to what is formal in their use, be the content what it may (empirical or transcendental). . . . There are therefore two rules that logicians must always bear in mind, in dealing with pure general logic:

1. As general logic, it abstracts from all intensional content (*Inhalt*) of the cognition of understanding and from all differences in its objects, and deals with nothing but the mere form of thought.

2. As pure logic, it has nothing to do with empirical principles, and does not, as has sometimes been supposed, borrow anything from psychology, which therefore

---

[19] Frege, *The Foundations of Arithmetic*, pp. vi–vii.

[20] The pure (non-empirical) versus 'applied' (empirical) distinction also holds for special logic. A pure special logic is the a priori formal ontology of a domain of objects; and when that domain is maximally large, it is transcendental logic (*CPR* A57/B81–2).

has no influence whatever on the canon of the understanding. Pure logic is a body of demonstrated doctrine, and everything in it must be certain entirely a priori.

What I call applied logic . . . is thus a representation of the understanding and of the rules of its necessary employment *in concreto*—that is, under the accidental subjective conditions that may hinder or help its application, and that are all given only empirically. . . . General and pure logic is related to it as pure morality, which contains merely the necessary laws of a free will in general, is related to the doctrine of virtue proper, which assesses those laws under the hindrances of the feelings, inclinations, and passions to which human beings are more or less subject, and which can never yield a true and proven science, since it requires empirical and psychological principles just as much as applied logic does.   (*CPR* A52–5/B77–9)

Some logicians, to be sure, do presuppose *psychological* principles in logic. But to bring such principles in logic is just as absurd as to derive morals from life. If we were to take principles from psychology, i.e. from observations concerning our understanding, we would merely see *how* thinking does take place and *how* it *is* under various subjective obstacles and conditions; this would lead then to cognition of merely *contingent* laws. In logic, however, the question is not about *contingent* but about *necessary* rules; not how we do think, but how we ought to think. The rules of logic must thus be derived not from the *contingent* but from the *necessary* use of the understanding, which one finds in oneself apart from all psychology.   (JL Ak. ix. 14)

Pure general logic not only expresses the absolutely necessary laws of human thought in so far as they occur independently of all special sorts of objects; it also abstracts away from all specific modes of thinking, particular thought experiences, and particular thinkers. Logical laws are strict norms of human theoretical rationality, and, as such, are always empirically realized by us finite imperfect thinkers only to a certain degree, never fully. The logical 'ought' does not entail the logical 'is'. By contrast, while applied or empirical general logic has to do precisely with those same universal and necessary logical rules or inference patterns, it nevertheless treats them as wholly 'tokenized' or instantiated under concrete, empirical, and idiosyncratic conditions of actual human thinking. Actual human thinkers frequently make errors and commit fallacies. So, under concrete or empirical conditions, logical rules are reduced to merely contingent generalizations inductively abstracted from particular thought events; they only describe how finite human thinkers actually *do* think, not how they *ought to* think if they are to conform to the canons of theoretical rationality. The logical 'is' does not entail the logical 'ought'. In other words, the absolutely necessary a priori normative logical laws are strictly underdetermined by and irreducible to the minds of actual thinkers. Pure general logic is, therefore, strictly underdetermined by and irreducible to the empirical or experimental psychology of logic.

If pure general logic is strictly underdetermined by and irreducible to the empirical psychology of logic, then obviously Kant is no defender of logical psychologism. In fact, Kant is the very first critic of logical psychologism in

the Cartesian or (in the broad sense) modern logical tradition.[21] Closely
connected to this is the fact that Kant's conception of the normativity, pure
apriority, and generality of pure general logic is strikingly similar to Frege's
own emphatically normative, anti-psychologistic, and topic-neutral conception
of logic.[22] In this way, Kant's transcendental philosophy operates entirely under
the assumption that logical psychologism is false. And this holds true *even* when
we explicitly take into account the fact that Kant's general cognitive semantics
involves a non-trivial appeal to the nature of the human mind. Hence Kant
shows us clearly that logical mentalism does not entail logical psychologism.[23]

Let us turn now to the special role of Kant's theory of logic within his
cognitive semantics. One of the central aims of the Transcendental Aesthetic
is to prove that our sensibility has two a priori forms, the pure intuitions of
space and time. These forms are necessarily applicable to all apparent objects
given through empirical intuition, and they thereby are necessary conditions
of all a posteriori and a priori synthetic cognition alike (*CPR* A22/B36; see
also Sections 4.1 and 4.3). In the Introduction to the Transcendental Logic
Kant wants to prove a precisely analogous result for our faculty for generating concepts and judgements, the understanding. He wants to argue that there
exist pure a priori concepts of the understanding that are necessarily applicable to all objects that can be discursively represented. In so far as these a
priori concepts of the understanding are indeed applicable to all discursively
representable objects, they are also 'categories' in a sense broadly akin to
Aristotle's fundamental ontological classifications in his *Categories* and
Metaphysics (*CPR* A80/B105; see also *P*. Ak. iv. 323). It is not always noticed
that this argument—which Kant later labels the 'Metaphysical Deduction' (*CPR*
B159)—in fact has two distinct phases: what I will call (A) the 'Logical
Phase', and (B) the 'Objectual Phase'. The first part of the Metaphysical
Deduction, the Logical Phase, spells out what will count as a pure concept of
the understanding and relates all such concepts directly and necessarily to
pure general logic (*CPR* A66–76/B91–101). The second part, the Objectual
Phase, then ties the set of pure concepts, as derived from pure general logic,
directly and necessarily to intuitions, thoughts, or judgements about 'objects
in general' (*CPR* A77–83/B102–13, A248/B305; see also *P*. Ak. iv. 324).
Subsequently, the Transcendental Deduction of the pure concepts, or categories, builds directly upon the Objectual Phase of the Metaphysical Deduction, by showing that the pure concepts are not merely forms for thought

---

[21] See Easton (ed.), *Logic and the Workings of the Mind: The Logic of Ideas and Faculty
Psychology in Early Modern Philosophy*; Gaukroger, *Cartesian Logic*; and Kneale and
Kneale, *The Development of Logic*, chs. V–XII.

[22] See Frege, 'Logic [1897]', 128, 148–9, and 'Thoughts', 368–9.

[23] A conception of the nature of logic very similar to Kant's—mentalistic but strongly
anti-psychologistic—was also developed in the mid-nineteenth century by Boole in *The
Laws of Thought*.

or judgement about objects in general, but more specifically are a priori conditions of the possibility of cognition of objects of sensory experience (*CPR* A92–4/B124–7, B143, B146–8, B159–61). In other words, the main line of argument in the Transcendental Analytic is a three-step progression: (1) from concepts and judgements, to pure concepts of the understanding interpreted as basic formal functions implicit in pure general logic (= the Logical Phase of the Metaphysical Deduction); (2) from the pure concepts as the basic formal functions implicit in pure general logic, to categories of objects in general (= the Objectual Phase of the Metaphysical Deduction); and finally (3) from categories of objects in general, to categories of objects of sensory experience (= the Transcendental Deduction of the categories).[24]

I leave aside for the moment the Objectual Phase of the Metaphysical Deduction, and the Transcendental Deduction. Both will come into play in the next section. What we need to do now is to expose the rationale for Kant's surprising claim that the basic formal functions of all discursive object-directed representations are derived directly from pure general logic. I will first briefly reconstruct Kant's argument in the Logical Phase. Then secondly I will offer a sketch of a response to a familiar and powerful line of criticism of Kant's argument—that his doctrine of logical form (and thereby his doctrine of pure concepts and categories) is vitiated by his incomplete, inadequate, pre-Fregean conception of logic.[25]

A Partial Reconstruction of the Metaphysical Deduction

In a nutshell, what Kant wants to prove in the Logical Phase of the Metaphysical Deduction is this: assuming that the understanding has pure concepts, just as sensibility has pure forms of intuition, it can be shown that the pure concepts of the understanding—construed as the formal functions of unity implicit in all concepts and thinking whatsoever—are identical to the complete set of formal functions of unity implicit in pure general logic. Or, as he puts it, 'the functions of the understanding can therefore all be found together if we can exhaustively exhibit the functions of unity in judgements' (*CPR* A69/B94). In order to prove that claim, he argues as follows:

(1) Just like sensibility and its pure forms of intuition, the understanding must have its own concepts: they are pure, non-intuitive, and primitive or irreducible; and the roster of such concepts is complete (*CPR* A64–5/B89–90).

(2) Given (1) as an assumption, the problem is: how are we to exhibit the nature and systematic interconnection of such pure concepts (*CPR*

---

[24] Here I am in fundamental agreement with the general lines of the interpretation of the Analytic worked out in detail by Longuenesse in *Kant and the Capacity to Judge.*

[25] See e.g. Kneale and Kneale, *The Development of Logic*, 354–8.

A64–7/B89–91)? The answer is: look to logic as a 'transcendental clue' (*CPR* A67/B92).

(3) All cognition occurs through the synthesis or combination of intuitions and concepts, or of concepts and concepts, and only through such a synthesis (*CPR* A68/B93).

(4) Concepts are 'functions', or rules of spontaneous synthesis, for integrating the various data supplied by intuition into a single representational content (*CPR* A68/B93).

(5) Now the only 'use' (*Gebrauch*), or application, of a concept is to judge by means of it (*CPR* A68–9/B92–3).

(6) Every judgement involves a special third-order or executive (that is, original synthetic apperceptive) function of unity, consisting in a predication-relation between some conceptual representation and another representation—either a concept or an intuition—which in turn refers directly to an object or objects (*CPR* A69/B93–4; see also Section 1.5 and *CPR* B140–2).

(7) Given (5) and (6), it follows that we must 'trace back' (*zurückführen*) all acts of the understanding—that is, acts of conceptualization and thinking—in so far as they refer to objects, to judgements. Thus the understanding is at bottom a capacity for judging (*CPR* A69/B94).

(8) Judgements are inherently subject to formal functions of unity—that is, to the complete set of formal functions implicit in pure general logic, which in turn is the a priori science of the necessary rules of the human understanding and reason without commitment to any special kinds of objects (*CPR* Bvii–ix, A50–5/B74–9, A70–6/B95–101).

(9) Given (1), (7), and (8), the pure concepts of the understanding are identical to the formal functions of unity in judgements, the complete set of formal functions implicit in pure general logic (*CPR* A69/B94).

Kant then proceeds to give what he takes to be a unique and exhaustive list of these logical forms, the 'table of judgements' (*CPR* A70/B95):

I	II
Quantity of Judgements	*Quality*
Universal	Affirmative
Particular	Negative
Singular	Infinite

III	IV
Relation	*Modality*
Categorical	Problematic
Hypothetical	Assertoric
Disjunctive	Apodeictic

The table of judgements is certainly not intended to be a mere summary or trivial reorganization of seventeenth- or eighteenth-century school logics. As early as 1762, Kant argued in 'The False Subtlety of the Four Syllogistic Figures' that the school logics of his day were of limited philosophical use and seriously in need of rethinking (FS Ak. ii. 55–7). Kant's logical revisionism is further indicated by his table's 'four-times-three' organization, which is original to him, and also by the fact that it prominently includes various logical forms ignored or downplayed by seventeenth- and eighteenth-century logicians— for example, singular quantity, and infinite quality. But most importantly of all, the Logical Phase of the Metaphysical Deduction, if sound, guarantees that the pure concepts of the understanding are pure, primitive, universal, formal, conceptual, innate logical functions of the mind. Kant's table is a 'complete table of the moments of thought in general' (*CPR* A71/B96) or a 'transcendental table of all moments of thought in judgements' (*CPR* A73/B98). That is, Kant's table is intended to be *a depth grammar of thought and judgement*— a rational reconstruction of pure general logic from the standpoint of his general cognitive semantics of concepts and judgement—*not* (except incidentally) a contribution to the science of logic as Kant knew it.[26]

Construing the table of judgements as a depth grammar of thought and judgement opens us up to the recognition of one of the key purposes of the list of logical functions. The Logical Phase directly implies that nothing will count as a concept or judgement unless it falls under one or more of the pure concepts, hence under one or more of the headings in the table of judgements. The pure concepts thereby supply rules of well-formedness for all other concepts and unified concept complexes (judgements). They are in this sense metaconcepts. Putative representational contents that do not satisfy these rules, even if they seem superficially to be acceptable concepts or judgements, are ill-formed or nonsensical and hence pseudo-concepts or pseudo-judgements. For example, the doctrine of pure concepts is able to rule out as ill-formed the pseudoconcept THE NOTHING, since the concept of negation is the concept of a primitive logical operation applied to a predicate or judgement, not a concept of some sort of mysterious nihilistic object (*CPR* A290/B347). So too it would immediately rule out (to borrow Carnap's critical parody of Heidegger's metaphysics[27]) the pseudo-judgement 'The Nothing noths', since the very form of a singular categorical judgement requires, in the subject place, a term able to stand for an individual object, and in the predicate place, a concept term able to apply to individual objects. Quite apart from its systematic significance for transcendental philosophy, then, Kant's list of logical forms operates first and

---

[26] See Brandt, *The Table of Judgments: Critique of Pure Reason A67–76; B92–101*, esp. ch. III; Longuenesse, *Kant and the Capacity to Judge*, esp. chs. 1, 4–7; and Reich, *The Completeness of Kant's Table of Judgments*, esp. chs. 1–5.

[27] See Carnap, 'The Elimination of Metaphysics through the Logical Analysis of Language' (1932), 69–73, and Heidegger, 'What is Metaphysics?' (1929).

foremost as an a priori normative doctrine of logical syntax—that is, as a way of ruling out various basic kinds of pseudo-thought, or cognitive nonsense.

A Kantian Reply to a Powerful Objection

Despite this important normative logico-syntactical function, Kant's table of the forms of judgements is notorious. The standard worry is that it reflects an inexhaustive, inadequate, pre-Fregean conception of logic. Without engaging in a detailed evaluative analysis of Kant's logic, however, what could be said by way of a Kantian reply to the standard worry? Two points seem salient.

First, in a historical sense it is of course true that Kant's logical theory is pre-Fregean. And, to the extent that it is a compendium of Aristotelian and Scholastic logic, Kant's logic creaks. Frege's logical theory by sharp contrast is explicitly designed for the theoretical reduction of arithmetic to logic (= Fregean logicism), and essentially includes the special resources required for that purpose: a general theory of functions and in particular a theory of truth functions; a logic of relations; a theory of multiple quantification; a set theory; a fully generalized and formalized deduction theory; and so on. None of these is to be found in Kant's logic. But a contemporary Kantian looking back at both Kant and Frege might well reply: 'Since Frege explicitly holds that all arithmetical truths are logical and analytic, while Kant just as explicitly holds that all arithmetical truths are *non-logical and synthetic*, is it not at the very least question begging to criticize Kant's logic for lacking the special resources required for reducing arithmetic to logic?' The counter-objection expressed by this rhetorical question seems especially cogent in the light of the fact that Fregean logicism itself is far from being unproblematic. Indeed, given the well-known contradiction in the foundations of set theory exposed by Russell's Paradox; given the unclear philosophical status of even such non-paradoxical set theories as the Zermelo–Fraenkel theory;[28] and given Gödel's first incompleteness theorem (roughly, that some true or valid propositions in the logic of *Principia Mathematica* and other similar logical systems such as Frege's, when enriched by the axioms of Peano arithmetic, are demonstrably unprovable—so all such systems are consistent if and only if incomplete[29]), it follows that Frege's logicism is highly questionable. On this way of looking at things, then, the fact that Kant's logic is pre-Fregean need not be regarded as necessarily a deficit. Difficulties in the project of classical logicism have led Quine, for example, to distinguish sharply between two parts of logic: the part that does not contain set theory; and the part that does. And, as Quine points out, Kant's logic quite legitimately belongs to the part that does not.[30] In a closely related way, difficulties in classical logicism have led Alonzo Church

[28] See Fraenkel, 'Set Theory'.
[29] For details, see Boolos and Jeffrey, *Computability and Logic*, esp. chs. 15, 28.
[30] See Quine, 'Carnap and Logical Truth', 389.

and others to distinguish sharply between three parts of logic: (1) a part that is subject to a recursive or mechanical decision procedure for logical truth, (2) a part in which logical truth is undecidable although still provable (hence complete), and (3) a part in which logical truth is unprovable (hence incomplete).[31] Since the logic of truth-functional propositional connectives and quantification into one-place predicates belongs strictly to the first or *decidable* part of logic, one could quite legitimately assign Kant's logical theory to that part alone.[32]

Secondly, it is undoubtedly true that Kant's catalogue of logical forms is not exhaustive. But it follows from this, neither that the forms he has in fact listed are not themselves arguably basic in some way, nor that no such catalogue is possible. Even if Kant's particular table is inexhaustive and shot through with ambiguities, it is still possible that a truly exhaustive, unambiguous table of forms could both exist and be discoverable; and it is also possible that at least some of the forms he does list actually belong to the truly exhaustive, perspicuous list of such forms.

Here it is crucial to see that most of the objections to Kant's list of logical forms are versions of the same worry—that Kant arbitrarily and unjustifiably adopts some particular logical form or another. For example, he apparently pointlessly isolates the affirmative proposition ('It is the case that *s* is *P*') as a distinct logical form. So too he apparently groundlessly distinguishes between negative propositions ('not *Q*') and infinite propositions ('*s* is non-*P*'). And again, seemingly without justification, he regards the hypothetical relational form ('If *P*, then *Q*') as the 'ground-consequence' relation (*CPR* A73/B98).

But are these logical decisions as arbitrary and unjustifiable as they may seem? In the *Tractatus* Wittgenstein targets 'the general form of the proposition' as in some sense *the* fundamental logical notion,[33] and Strawson plausibly glosses this as Wittgenstein's way of pointing up the logically rock-bottom idea of an affirmative atomic subject/predicate proposition.[34] How does this really differ from Kant's privileging of affirmative singular categorical propositions? Again, in *Principia Mathematica* Russell discusses the fundamental topic of ambiguities in the scope of logical operators;[35] and we also know from his distinction between 'primary' and 'secondary' occurrences of expressions that sorting out

---

[31] See Boolos and Jeffrey, *Computability and Logic*, esp. chs. 10, 22, 25; Church, 'A Note on the Entscheidungsproblem'; and Quine, *Methods of Logic*, 213–18.

[32] Although monadic logic is both decidable and analytic in Kant's sense (see Sect. 3.1), not every decidable theory is analytic in Kant's sense—e.g. primitive recursive (quantifier-free) arithmetic is decidable but synthetic. See Van Heijenoort (ed.), *From Frege to Gödel: A Source Book in Mathematical Logic*, 302–3.

[33] Wittgenstein, *Tractatus*, 103, 127, props. 4.5, 5.47.

[34] See Strawson, 'Logical Form and Logical Constants'.

[35] Whitehead and Russell, *Principia Mathematica to *56*, 68–71.

scope ambiguities in the use of negation is a central part of his theory of descriptions.[36] How does this really differ from Kant's distinction between the negation that attaches to the whole proposition and the negation that attaches only to the predicate? Finally, C. I. Lewis in his *Survey of Symbolic Logic* argues vigorously for the logical priority of the strict implication conditional (according to which 'If P then Q' is equivalent with 'Necessarily $(\sim P \lor Q)$') over the Russellian material implication conditional (according to which 'If P then Q' is equivalent with '$\sim P \lor Q$').[37] But, since Kant regards the hypothetical as equivalent to logical consequence (JL Ak. ix. 51–2, 129), and since Lewis also regards strict implication as the expression of logical consequence, then how do their views really differ?

My reading of the standard objection to Kant's list of logical forms is that in virtually every case it implicitly points up the fact that Kant always opts for a less extensional or an outright non-extensional—that is, an intensional—construal of some logical form or another, when a more extensional or strictly extensional construal is available. But suppose we bite the bullet and admit that *Kant's logic is an intensional logic, not an extensional logic.* In an intensional logic, logical forms and semantic contents are not strictly or uniquely determined either by the actual objects in the world to which propositions or their constituents refer, or by an actual-world assignment of truth values to atomic propositions. Intensional logic includes primitive modal concepts, a theory of syntactical and semantic categories, a formal theory of conceptual structure and content, some or another version of the notion of a possible world, and a formal theory of cross-possible-world reference-determination for concepts and propositions.[38] Extensional notions are not by any means ruled out in an intensional logic—but they are treated as abstractions from, or partial reflections of, the more basic intensional forms and contents. If Kant's logic is intensional, then his decisions as to logical forms do not look arbitrary and unjustified any longer but instead seem philosophically well motivated. I will argue in Chapter 3 that the logical doctrine lying behind Kant's theory of analyticity is in fact intensional, and strongly so. If

[36] See Russell, 'On Denoting', 52–3.

[37] Lewis, *A Survey of Symbolic Logic*, ch. V; Whitehead and Russell, *Principia Mathematica to *56*, 94. Lewis's case for strict implication over material implication is closely connected with his neo-Kantian rejection of Royce's neo-Hegelian logic and metaphysics; see Kuklick, *The Rise of American Philosophy*, chs. 20, 28. Russell by contrast derives his extensional conception of the conditional from F. H. Bradley's neo-Hegelian *Principles of Logic*, which defends the doctrine that all logical relations within and between judgements are general, extrinsic, and accidental. See Hylton, *Russell, Idealism, and the Emergence of Analytic Philosophy*, ch. 2.

[38] See e.g. Gamut, *Logic, Language, and Meaning*, vol. ii. The classic texts of modern intensional logic are Lewis, *A Survey of Symbolic Logic* (1918), Lewis and Langford, *Symbolic Logic* (1932/53), Carnap, *Meaning and Necessity* (1947/56), and Strawson, *Introduction to Logical Theory* (1952).

that interpretation is correct, then many of the criticisms of Kant's choices of logical forms are at least significantly blunted. If Kant's logic is intensional, then in order to show that Kant is essentially in error it would have to be shown first that the very idea of an intensional logic is inherently misguided. But this has never been shown. Despite the explicit assumption of extensionality in Frege's logic and in *Principia Mathematica*,[39] and despite Quine's influential attack on the very idea of intensionality (see Section 3.5 below), it is nowadays widely accepted that the intensional approach to logic is a perfectly legitimate competitor to a strictly extensional approach.[40] I conclude that the standard objection to the Logical Phase of the Metaphysical Deduction is a paper tiger—not so very, very devastating after all.

2.2. Objective Validity

Perhaps the most important strategic move that Kant makes in his discussion of logic is to draw a distinction between pure general logic and transcendental logic:

Not every a priori cognition must be called transcendental but only that by means of which we cognize that and how certain representations (intuitions or concepts) are applied entirely a priori or are possible (i.e. the possibility of cognition or its use (*Gebrauch*) a priori). . . . In the expectation, therefore, that there can perhaps be concepts that may be related a priori to objects, not as pure or sensible intuitions, but rather merely as acts of pure thinking—that is, as concepts that are neither of empirical nor of aesthetic origin—we provisionally form for ourselves the idea of a science of pure understanding and of pure cognition of reason, by means of which we think objects entirely a priori. Such a science, which whould determine the origin, the comprehension (*Umfang*), and the objective validity of such cognition, would have to be called *transcendental logic*, because it has to do merely with the laws of the understanding and the reason, but solely as they refer a priori to objects, not, as in the case of general logic, to empirical as well as pure cognitions of reason without distinction. (*CPR* A56–7/B80–2)

As we have seen, pure general logic is the universal, formal, pure a priori science of conceptualization and judgement. It uncovers the complete set of basic logical formal functions of unity; it articulates the laws of consistency and consequence; it is essentially topic-neutral or insensitive to specific objects of cognition; and it is strictly normative and strictly underdetermined by sensory experience. By contrast, transcendental logic is an a priori and yet at the same

---

[39] Both Frege's logic and the logic of *Principia* are not wholly extensional, however, but also second order in that they include quantification over first-order concepts and functions, the admissibility of functions of functions, and (in Frege's case) set theory.

[40] See e.g. Bealer, *Quality and Concept*, and Montague, *Formal Philosophy*.

time 'special' or 'topic-sensitive' logic: it is explicitly concerned with the 'objective validity' of our a priori representations. But what precisely does the factor of objective validity add to pure general logic?

Objective validity is closely connected with the idea of 'objective reality' (*objektive Realität*). Objective validity is the notion that a representation has reference or application to possible objects; objective reality is the somewhat stronger notion that a representation has reference or application to actual, real, or existing objects. And when the relevant representation is a judgement, its objective reality is equivalent to its truth.[41] But more generally objective validity and objective reality, taken together, express the idea that a representation has a determinate and applicable semantic content—that it is *meaningful by virtue of its objective referentiality*. When 'a cognition is to have objective reality—that is, to refer to an object', this is the same as saying that that cognition 'is to acquire meaning and sense (*Bedeutung und Sinn*) in respect to it' (*CPR* A155/B194). Again, '*reference to an object*' is 'objective meaning' (*objektive Bedeutung*) (*CPR* A197/B242–3) and conversely 'all meaning (*Bedeutung*) ... is ... reference to the object' (*CPR* A241/B300). Kant often puts this same crucial point negatively. For a cognition to be 'without objective validity' is for it to be 'senseless and meaningless' (*ohne Sinn und Bedeutung*) (*CPR* A156/B195). For reasons to be spelled out a little later, I will not say that a representation lacking objective validity and hence lacking meaningfulness is strictly speaking nonsensical or absurd, but rather only that it is 'empty' or 'vacuous'.

If objective validity and objective reality constitute the meaningfulness of a representation, and this meaningfulness is the reference or applicability of the representation to a possible or actual object, then obviously everything turns on the question of just what *sort* of object we are talking about. And the answer to that question lies ultimately in the Transcendental Deduction of the pure concepts of the understanding. According to the B Deduction, the categories that govern all meaningful judgements and concepts are valid for all and only the members of a *specially restricted* domain of objects, the objects of possible experience: 'Since experience is cognition by means of connected perceptions, the categories are conditions of the possibility of experience, and are therefore valid a priori for all objects of experience' (*CPR* B161). This necessary restriction of the categories to possible or actual objects of experience, we shall see, supplies us with the fundamental ground of Kant's conception of the meaningfulness of meanings. But, in order to comprehend that general point correctly, we must see how Kant builds up his doctrine of objective validity in several distinct stages.

---

[41] See *CPR* A241–2 n., *CJ* Ak. v. 351, JL Ak. ix. 92, and *MFNS* Ak. iv. 478. See also Allison, *Kant's Transcendental Idealism*, 134–5; Guyer, 'The Transcendental Deduction of the Categories', 125; and Hanna, 'Kant, Truth, and Human Nature'.

According to Kant's theory of pure general logic, no concept or judgement is logically acceptable if it is not syntactically well formed in the sense that it falls definitely under one or more of the pure logical forms of thought. Further, no judgement can be true if it expresses the conjunction of a proposition and its negation (for example, Q and not Q), or the conjunction of a predicate and its denial (for example, s is P and non-P): hence every judgement must be self-consistent. But there is another fundamental constraint on semantic content that derives directly from pure logic—namely, the internal consistency of *particular concepts*. This is brought out in an important footnote in the B edition Preface: 'I can *think* whatever I like, provided only that I do not contradict myself, that is, provided my concept is a possible thought, even if I cannot give any assurance whether or not there is a corresponding object somewhere within the sum total of all possibilities' (*CPR* Bxvii n.). For example, the putative concepts NON-CIRCULAR CIRCLE and SQUARE CIRCLE are each obviously self-inconsistent and cannot form the basis of any thoughts. Moreover, nothing could ever be subsumed under an internally contradictory conceptual intension, since nothing could ever possibly co-instantiate its two characteristics. If a concept is well formed and self-consistent, or if a judgement is logically well formed and contains only well-formed self-consistent concepts, then it is logically acceptable or thinkable.

Now in that same footnote Kant says, or at least implies, that a thinkable concept is to be identified with a particular possibility within 'the sum total of all possibilities'—alluding to a later discussion of this notion in the 'Ideal of Pure Reason' section of the Transcendental Dialectic (*CPR* A573/B601). The sum total of all possibilities is the set of all thinkable concepts taken together with their corresponding logical contradictories. If, on the basis of the sum total of all possibilities, we cognitively construct a multiplicity of mutually exclusive collections of internally consistent and contradiction-proof (that is, thinkable) concepts, then we will have produced an exact Kantian analogue of Leibniz's possible worlds. Every Leibnizian possible world (= a maximal sum of compossible monads) has its equivalent counterpart in a Kantian 'thinkable world' (= a maximal sum of compossible concepts). In this way, Leibniz and Kant are both defenders of possible worlds semantics; but the major difference between them is that, whereas Leibniz's possible worlds are metaphysically real, Kant's possible worlds are merely *transcendentally ideal*, since they are nothing but conceptual constructs—exact reflections of the several parts of our total conceptual repertoire.[42]

Kant also deviates importantly from Leibniz by discriminating between two distinct classes of thinkable worlds. As the footnote from the B edition Preface tells us explicitly, a concept can be thinkable 'even if I cannot give any assurance whether or not there is a corresponding object somewhere within

---

[42] See also Sect. 5.1.

the sum total of all possibilities'. Thus not every thinkable or possible world is a world containing possible objects (aka. 'possibilia'). So, paradoxical as it may at first seem, Kant holds that some strictly speaking *thinkable* concepts describe *im*possibilia: 'Once I have pure concepts of the understanding I can also think objects that are perhaps impossible (*unmöglich*)' (*CPR* A96). It is hard to know just how much the qualifier 'perhaps' (*vielleicht*) weakens the bare assertion that I can think impossible objects. But let us assume that Kant is at least saying that I can think objects that are *in some sense* impossible. What then is he driving at? Here is one way of making sense of it. To modify slightly a famous example used by Chomsky in *Syntactic Structures*, the concept FURIOUSLY SLEEPING GREEN IDEA is a minimally logically acceptable or barely thinkable concept, in the sense that it is both logically well formed and contains no formal contradictions or conceptual self-contradictions. In that sense, it determines what I will call a 'barely possible world', a formally and conceptually consistent set of circumstances. Yet the content is obviously nonsensical, because it violates some purely sortal or semantical-categorial restriction on the meaningfulness of concepts.[43] Unlike Leibniz, then, Kant realizes that the bare syntactical and logical consistency of a conceptual content is not in and of itself sufficient for correlating that content with a possible object. Otherwise put, the Kantian constraints on what will count as a possible world are looser than the constraints on what will count as a possible *object*, since in principle a possible world can correlate with a mere nonsensical congeries of self-consistent well-formed concepts.

So beyond the bare well-formedness and self-consistency of concepts, and beyond the determination of the total class of barely thinkable worlds, there is still the distinct question of whether the thinkable concept can apply to a possible object or not:

For every concept there is requisite, first, the logical form of a concept (of thinking) in general, and, secondly, the possibility of giving it an object to which it is to be referred. In the absence of such object, it has no sense (*keinen Sinn*) and is completely empty of intensional content (*völlig leer an Inhalt*), though it may still contain the logical function for making a concept out of any data that may be presented. (*CPR* A239/B298)

Without reference to a possible object, a concept is non-meaningful or intensionally empty—it cannot be objectively valid or objectively real. So what governs the step from bare thinkability to fully thinkable objects?

The answer, in a nutshell, is that for Kant an object must involve a *synthetic unity* of consistent properties. That means that the several subconcepts that make up the concept of that object must stand in some rule-governed relation to the original synthetic unity of apperception (*CPR* B131–6). When

---

[43] See Husserl, *Logical Investigations*, Investigation IV, for the rediscovery of Kant's distinction between formal or syntactical nonsense and material or semantic nonsense.

a concept has, in addition to its self-consistency and well-formedness, a synthetic unity, then it expresses what Kant calls an 'absolute possibility' (*CPR* A232/B285). In turn, he says of absolute possibility that it 'is valid from every point of view' (*in aller Absicht gültig ist*). To understand this, we must draw explicitly on the Objectual Phase of the Metaphysical Deduction. That phase yields the conclusion that pure concepts of the understanding, as the formal functions of unity in pure general logic, necessarily apply to objects in general or to the transcendental object = *X*. This is the same as saying that they apply to fully thinkable objects. Fully thinkable objects are absolutely possible. Thus the pure concepts of the understanding, regarded on their own, are not only well formed and logically self-consistent—they are also objectively unified or coherent: they specify absolutely logically possible generic objects that consist in synthetic unities of attributes or properties.

The semantic content of the pure concepts or categories, considered on their own, is what Kant calls their 'logical meaning': 'In fact, even after abstraction from every sensible condition, there remains in the pure concepts of the understanding a meaning (*Bedeutung*), but only a logical meaning of the mere unity of representations' (*CPR* A147/B186). But, despite this 'logical meaning of the mere unity of representations', nevertheless 'no object (*Gegenstand*) and thus no meaning is given to [pure concepts] that could yield a cognition[44] of the object (*Objekt*)' (*CPR* A147/B186). In other words, while the pure concepts on their own specify absolutely possible objects in general, they determine no 'real possibility' (*CPR* A244/B302)—that is, no reference or application to a possible concrete spatiotemporal empirical object (*Gegenstand*) or thing (*Sache*): 'The (logical) possibility of a concept is that the concept subsists (*besteht*) in itself; the (real) possibility of a thing (*Sache*) is that an object (*object*) corresponds to the concept' (*R*. 5155; Ak. xviii. 104; see also *CPR* A244–5/B302–3). This concrete thing or object is not just an absolutely possible, fully thinkable object, or object in general, but instead a *cognizable sensory object* (*CPR* Bxvii n.). The B Deduction—especially section 26—shows us that all the cognizable sensory objects simply are, or are at least generatively/productively convertible into, objects of experience. And the Second Analogy of Experience shows us that this conversion occurs via the application of a (causally) necessary rule of time determination to the manifold of subjectively ordered sense perceptions (*CPR* A191–202/B236–47).

Now, according to Kant, were objects in general to be mistakenly treated as objects of cognition, such cognitions would yield only things-in-themselves:

---

[44] Here I adopt Kant's emendation in the *Nachträge*, or marginal corrections to the A edition of the first *Critique* (R: E LXI 28–A147; Ak. xxiii. 46). In the original text it is '*einen Begriff*', which is quite misleading in this particular context, because it fails to respect Kant's sharp B edition distinction between 'cognizing an object' and merely 'thinking an object' (*CPR* Bxxvii n.). Granting this distinction, we *can* think objects in general solely by means of the pure concepts; but we cannot cognize such objects.

'The transcendental use of a concept in any sort of principle consists in its being referred to things *in general and in themselves*' (*CPR* A238/B293). Such objects are, however, totally uncognizable for finite sensory cognizers like us; they could be cognized only by a being with intellectual intuition—a being possessing the power of determinately and immediately grasping individual objects merely by spontaneously thinking them. Such objects are therefore noumena, in the negative sense that we cannot intuit (and therefore cannot properly cognize) them, and also in the positive sense that *only* an intellectual or non-sensory intuition could intuit (and properly cognize) them:

If by a noumenon we understand a thing *in so far as it is not an object of our sensible intuition*, because we abstract from our mode of intuiting (*Anschauungsart*) it, this is a noumenon in the *negative* sense. But if we understand by it an *object of a non-sensible intuition*, then we assume a special mode of intuition, namely intellectual intuition, which, however, is not our own, and of which we cannot comprehend (*nicht einsehen können*) even the possibility. This would be a noumenon in the *positive* sense. (*CPR* B307)

Two things follow immediately from this. First, to advance from the bare thinkability of a concept to its full thinkability, or to advance from a minimally logically acceptable concept to the reference or applicability of that concept to an absolutely logically possible object, is also to invoke the *intuitability* of that object:

If no intuition could be given corresponding to the concept, the concept would still indeed be a thought, so far as its form is concerned, but would be without any object, and no cognition of anything would be possible by means of it. So far as I could know, there would be nothing, and could be nothing, to which my thought could be applied. (*CPR* B146)

We cannot understand anything except that which has something corresponding to our words in intuition. (*CPR* A277/B333)

As long as intuition is lacking, one does not scientifically know (*weiß*) whether one thinks an object through the categories, and whether there can ever be any object that even fits them; and so it is confirmed that the categories are not by themselves *cognitions*, but mere *forms of thought* for making cognitions out of given intuitions. (*CPR* B288)

No concept [can] be admitted to the class of cognitions if its objective reality is not made evident by the possibility of the object's being exhibited (*dargestellt*) in a corresponding intuition. (*PC* Ak. xi. 42)

If a concept lacks all relation to actual or possible intuitions of objects, then it is 'completely empty of intensional content' (*völlig leer an Inhalt*) (*CPR* A239/B298). So the meaningfulness or sense of a conceptual representation lies necessarily in its relation to intuitions. Intuitability in the general or unqualified sense is the accessibility of some individual object to the direct or unmediated grasp of a cognizer.

Secondly, however, the precise *type* of intuitive cognizer must be carefully specified. Is the cognizer divine; is it sensory-but-alien; or is it specifically a creature minded like us? We have seen that that which is absolutely possible is 'valid from *every* point of view'. But the mere intuitability of an object in relation to pure concepts of the understanding is not alone sufficient to determine a concept's objective validity or objective reality in relation to *our* mode of conceptualizing and judging objects. Objective validity is strictly determined by our special spatiotemporally constrained mode of sensory intuition. In principle a mode of intuition might be wholly non-sensible or intellectual, and thereby be totally inaccessible to creatures minded like us. And even if it were not an intellectual intuition but only a sensible one, still it might not be the special sort of sensibility that presupposes time (*this* time, *our* time) and space (*this* space, *our* space) as its unique forms:

The pure concepts of the understanding . . . extend to objects of intuition in general, whether the latter be similar to our own or not, as long as it is sensible and not intellectual. But this further extension of concepts beyond *our* sensible intuition does not get us anywhere. For they are then merely empty concepts of objects, through which we cannot even judge whether they are [really] possible or not. They are mere forms of thought, without objective reality . . . *Our* sensible and empirical intuition alone can provide them with sense and meaning. (*CPR* B148-9)

Even if they were possible, we could still not conceive of and make comprehensible other forms of intuition (than space and time) or other forms of understanding (than the discursive form of thinking, or that of cognition through concepts), and even if we could, they would still not belong to experience, as the sole [type of] cognition in which objects are given to us. (*CPR* A230-1/B283)

If by merely intelligible objects we mean those things that are cognized by us through pure categories,[45] without any schema of sensibility, then things of this sort are impossible. For the condition of the objective use (*Gebrauchs*) of all our concepts of the understanding is merely the mode of our sensible intuition, through which objects are given to us, and, if we abstract from these objects, then the concepts have no reference at all to any sort of object. Indeed, even if one were to assume another sort of intuition than this our sensible one, our functions for thinking would still be without meaning in regard to it. (*CPR* A286/B342)

In this way, for a concept or other type of cognition to be objectively valid is for it to invoke our specifically human type of finite or receptive spatiotemporal sensory intuition of objects. Objective validity or objective reality is thus not merely the empirical meaningfulness or actual applicability of a representational content, but more specifically its *anthropocentric* empirical meaningfulness or actual applicability. Correspondingly, really possible objects are

---

[45] Here again I am interpolating Kant's emendation in the *Nachträge* (R: E CL 46–A286; Ak. xxiii. 49). The original text reads 'are thought through pure categories', which leads to the same misleading impression mentioned in n. 44.

strictly objects for creatures minded like us. This crucial idea—that the full meaningfulness of a semantic content arises only under an explicit transcendental *restriction* (*Einschränkung*) (*CPR* B148) of the content's reference or applicability to objects of possible or actual human sensory experience—is recorded by Kant under the rubric of 'transcendental truth':

All our cognitions . . . lie within the totality of possible experience, and transcendental truth, which precedes all empirical truth and makes it possible, consists in the universal reference to this [totality].   (*CPR* A146/B185)

Only through the fact that these [pure] concepts express a priori the relations of perceptions in every experience does one cognize their objective reality—that is, their transcendental truth.   (*CPR* A221–2/B269)

We are now finally in a position to understand the full text that I have quoted partially already:

For every concept there is requisite, first, the logical form of a concept (of thinking) in general, and, secondly, the possibility of giving it an object to which it is to be referred. In the absence of such an object, it has no sense and is completely empty of intensional content, though it may still contain the logical function for making a concept out of any data that may be presented. Now the object cannot be given to a concept otherwise than in intuition, and even if a pure sensible intuition[46] is possible a priori prior to the object, then even this can acquire its object, thus its objective validity, only through empirical intuition, of which it is the mere form. Thus all concepts and with them all principles, however a priori they may be, nevertheless refer to [objects of] empirical intuitions—that is, to *data* for possible experience. Without this they have no objective validity at all, but are rather a mere play, whether it be with representations of the imagination or of the understanding. . . . Hence it is required that an abstract (*abgesonderten*) concept be *made sensible*, that is, that an object corresponding to it be displayed (*darzulegen*) in intuition, since without this the concept would remain, as we say, without *sense*, that is, without meaning.   (*CPR* A239/B298–9)

This gives us Kant's theory of meaningfulness in a nutshell. He is saying that a concept is objectively valid (empirically meaningful) if and only if (1) the concept is well formed and self-consistent by virtue of pure logical form alone, (2) the concept is internally coherent in that it is synthetically combinable with an intuition of an absolutely possible object under the synthetic unity of apperception, and (3) the concept is combinable *only* with an intuition yielded by our special finite spatiotemporal capacity for the sensory ostension of objects of possible or actual experience.

But here is a point that needs special emphasis. What Kant is *not* saying in this text is that an 'abstract' concept—that is, a concept abstracted away from our sensibility—is nonsensical. It is empty (*leer*) or senseless (*sinnlos*) in that it is lacking in empirical meaningfulness, but not absurd or totally unintelligible.

---

[46] Here too I am following the *Nachträge* (R: E CXVIII 41–A239; Ak. xxiii. 47).

This is because it remains fully thinkable, and therefore logically meaningful in relation to the pure concepts or categories:

The pure categories, without formal conditions of sensibility, have mere transcendental meaning (*bloß transzendentale Bedeutung*), but have not any transcendental use (*keinem transzendentalen Gebrauch*), since this is impossible in itself, for they are lacking all conditions of any use (in judgements)—namely, the formal condition of the subsumption of any ostensible object (*angeblichen Gegenstand*) under these concepts. Since, then (as pure categories merely), they are not supposed to have empirical use, and cannot have transcendental use, they do not have any use at all if they are separated from all sensibility—that is, they cannot be applied to any ostensible object. Rather they are merely the pure form of the use of the understanding in regard to objects in general (*Gegenstände überhaupt*) and of thinking, yet without any sort of object (*Objekt*) being able to be . . .[47] determined through them alone.   (*CPR* A248/B305)

Again, empty concepts cannot be meaningfully applied by us either to noumenal objects or to objects of our sensory intuition, and in that sense they are 'impossible'—that is, impossible to *use*. But purely ornamental jars are still jars; and designs for ideal machines that cannot actually be built are still intelligible designs for machines. Analogously, by virtue of their full thinkability and logical meaningfulness in relation to transcendental apperception and to a possible super-sensible mode of intuition, isolated or empty categorial concepts are still *purely rationally* meaningful. (I am hammering loudly on this point now because it will prove to be of considerable importance in the upcoming discussion of Kant's doctrine of the noumenon in Section 2.4 below.)

Three further points about Kant's anthropocentric theory of meaningfulness must be mentioned. The first is that the notion of objective validity applies not only to concepts or judgements, but also to intuitions. The second is that the notion of objective validity applies not only to *empirical* intuitions, concepts, or judgements, but also to non-empirical or a priori intuitions, concepts, or judgements. Indeed, a transcendental deduction of either pure concepts or pure intuitions consists precisely in showing how those representations are objectively valid (*CPR* A93/B125–6, A155–6/B194–5). Hence a transcendental deduction is always an argument in general cognitive semantics: a proof of the meaningfulness of some a priori representation. In order to handle these two points effectively, an explicit distinction between 'primary objective validity' (POV) and 'secondary objective validity' (SOV)

---

[47] I have elided "*denken*" because it clearly violates Kant's own distinction between thinkability and cognizability—which he invokes in the first half of the sentence. It is just possible that he is using a distinction between an object in general (*Gegenstand überhaupt*), which is thinkable without appeal to our sensory intuition, and a real object (*Objekt*), whose real thinkability would require an appeal to our sensibility. But, if he is, then he has not signalled it adequately.

is needed. Some representations are objectively valid because they apply directly to objects of possible experience; but other representations, despite the fact that they do not apply directly to objects of possible experience, are nevertheless objectively valid because they express formal transcendental conditions for the direct applicability of representations to objects of possible experience. The third and final point is that a complex representation can have objective validity only if each and every one of the representational constituents of which it is synthetically composed is also objectively valid: 'Concepts are for us without sense, and cannot have any meaning, where an object is not given either for them themselves *or at least for the elements of which they consist*' (*CPR* A139/B178, emphasis added).

Taking these three points together puts us in a position to provide a recursive Kantian definition of the objective validity of any representational content. This is the same as spelling out, step by step, what Strawson aptly calls Kant's 'principle of significance'.[48]

Primary Objective Validity (POV)

(1) Any simple representational content has POV if and only if it applies to a possible or actual object of experience by means of our sensory empirical intuition.

(2) Empirical intuitions automatically and trivially have POV by (1).

(3) The pure forms of empirical intuition, the representations of space and time, since they are literally given *in* empirical intuition, automatically have POV by (1) and (2).

[Comment: The POV of a pure intuition does not entail its being a posteriori. Kant also calls the POV of pure or a priori intuitions their 'empirical reality' (*CPR* A27–8/B43–4, A35–6/B52).]

(4) An empirical characteristic or subconcept has POV if and only if it applies to a possible or actual object of experience by means of our sensory empirical intuition. (Specification of (1).)

(5) A complex empirical concept has POV if and only if the conjunction of its constituent characteristics or subconcepts has POV.

[Comment 1: It follows from (5) that self-inconsistent concepts such as NON-CIRCULAR CIRCLE and SQUARE CIRCLE, as well as consistent barely thinkable concepts that are internally incoherent, such as FURIOUSLY

---

[48] Strawson, *The Bounds of Sense*, 16. He later points out that this principle is logically independent of transcendental idealism (ibid. 243). But Stroud persuasively argues that no argument dependent on this principle can be successful against epistemic scepticism *without* transcendental idealism; see 'Transcendental Arguments' and *The Significance of Philosophical Scepticism*, ch. IV.

SLEEPING GREEN IDEA, do not have POV, despite the fact that they contain only characteristics each of which has POV on its own.]

[Comment 2: It follows from (5) that complex concepts applying to empirical objects that are really possible but just happen not to be actual, still have POV; for example, the concept WINGED HORSE has POV.]

(6) An empirical judgement has POV if and only if each of its constituent empirical intuitions and empirical concepts has POV and it organizes the subjective series of perceptions according to a necessary rule of time determination (*CPR* A202/B247).

[Comment: True and false empirical judgements alike have POV (*CPR* A58/B83); hence the POV of an empirical judgement is equivalent with its having a truth value. For example, both 'The president of the USA in 1999 is a male' and 'The president of the USA in 1999 is a female' have POV. Not only that, but even false empirical judgements containing concept terms that apply to no actual empirical objects have POV, so long as each of those concept terms has POV and the relevant judgement organizes perceptions according to a necessary rule of time determination. For example, 'The president of the USA in 1999 is a winged horse' has POV. But empirical judgements containing any concept terms that lack POV thereby lack POV and also lack a truth value. For example, 'The president of the USA in 1999 is a furiously sleeping green idea' lacks POV and is truth valueless.[49]]

(7) An a priori judgement has POV if and only if either (i) it contains or presupposes no pure intuitions and contains no a priori concepts and each of its constituent empirical concepts has POV, or (ii) it contains or presupposes pure intuitions—which have POV by (3)—but does not contain a priori concepts.

[Comment 1: Those analytic (hence also a priori) propositions containing only empirical concepts, such as 'Bachelors are males', have POV. So too those synthetic a priori propositions containing no pure concepts of the understanding, such as '7 + 5 = 12' and—more controversially —Newton's Laws, have POV. The fact that a judgement has POV does not entail its being a posteriori.]

[Comment 2: Not only true, but also false, a priori propositions have POV: for example, 'Bachelors are females' and 'Socrates is

---

[49] Although Kant's topic-neutral pure general logic is strictly bivalent, his topic-sensitive transcendental logic (be it transcendental analytic or dialectic) is not strictly bivalent: it allows for true propositions, false propositions, and semantically empty propositions lacking truth and falsity alike (aka 'truth-value gaps'). This point plays an important role in Kant's theory of synthetic a priori propositions; see Sect. 5.3 below.

mortal and non-mortal' (analytically false)[50] and '7 + 5 = 11' (synthetic a priori false).]

Secondary Objective Validity (SOV)

(8) An a priori concept has SOV if and only if it is a presupposition for the POV of some empirical intuition, empirical concept, or empirical judgement.

[Comment: The pure concepts of the understanding or categories are shown to have SOV by their transcendental deduction. By contrast, pure forms of intuition are shown by their transcendental deduction (*CPR* A87/B119)—the Transcendental Aesthetic—to have POV, not SOV, in relation to empirical intuitions. More generally, a transcendental deduction demonstrates the primary or secondary objective validity of an a priori representational content. Now the Transcendental Deduction of the pure concepts implicitly shows that pure forms of intuition have SOV in relation to judgements of experience; and the Schematism and Analytic of Principles together implicitly show that pure forms of intuition have SOV in relation to transcendental principles and causal laws. Strictly speaking, then, these constitute two extra transcendental deductions of the pure forms of intuition.]

(9) An a priori judgement has SOV if and only if either (i) it contains at least one a priori concept that has SOV, contains no empirical concepts lacking POV, and neither contains nor presupposes the pure forms of intuition, or (ii) it contains at least one a priori concept that has SOV, contains no empirical concepts lacking POV, and contains or presupposes the pure forms of intuition.

[Comment 1: Some analytic propositions have SOV but not POV—for example, 'Every effect has a cause'; and also some synthetic a priori propositions have SOV but not POV—for example, 'Every event has a cause'. More generally, all the transcendental principles including the Axioms of Intuition, the Anticipations of Perception, the Analogies of Experience, and the Postulates of Empirical Thought, have SOV but not POV (*CPR* A157–8/B196–7).]

---

[50] By invoking the principle of non-contradiction Kant is not saying that all self-contradictory judgements are meaningless or that all contradictory pairs of propositions are meaningless. So long as a given proposition meets the conditions for objective validity, then that judgement is meaningful. This allows him to preserve the logical integrity of indirect or *reductio* arguments—'apagogical proofs' (*CPR* A789–97/B817–25)—which, of course, employ contradictions as meaningful premisses. Still, with an eye to his discovery of the Antinomy of Pure Reason, Kant also warns against the indiscriminate use of the *reductio* strategy in philosophy, since (i) a proposition might have the logical form of a contradiction but still be empirically meaningless, and (ii) two propositions can be related through denial as contradictories *or* contraries.

[Comment 2: Not only true a priori propositions but also false a priori propositions have SOV—for example, the denial of the Second Analogy of Experience, 'Some events do not have causes'.]

Objective Validity

(10) Any representational content, whether simple or complex, has objective validity if and only if it has either POV or SOV.

[Comment 1: All true and false propositions alike, whether necessary or contingent, whether a posteriori or a priori, whether analytic or synthetic, and whether they have POV or SOV, are objectively valid (empirically meaningful).]

[Comment 2: All a priori propositions lacking both POV and SOV— for example, some propositions in traditional metaphysics (*CPR* B18) —are truth valueless. So the objective validity of an a priori proposition is also its having a truth value.]

2.3. Transcendental Idealism I: Appearances and Ideality

On Kant's account, the formal condition of the possibility of all cognitions is supplied by the categories or meta-concepts, together with the laws of pure general logic; and the material condition of the possibility of all cognitions is supplied by the factor of objective validity. But pure general logic presupposes the original synthetic unity of apperception, and objective validity presupposes the pure a priori forms of human sensibility, (the representations of) space and time. Now both pure apperception and the pure forms of sensibility are transcendentally ideal—they are generatively/productively innate and mind-dependent. Therefore Kant's theory of objective mental representation or meaning is grounded on the doctrine of transcendental idealism.

Most philosophers in the analytic tradition from Frege to Quine would regard that grounding as scandalous. According to the early analytic philosophers, idealism is either plainly false or logically absurd. Moore in his remarkable paper 'The Refutation of Idealism' writes:

When, therefore, Berkeley supposed that the only thing of which I am directly aware is my own sensations and ideas, he supposed what was false; and when Kant supposed that the objectivity of things in space *consisted* in the fact that they were '*Vorstellungen*' having to one another different relations from those which the same '*Vorstellungen*' have to one another in subjective experience, he supposed what was equally false. I am as directly aware of the existence of material things in space as my own sensations;

and *what* I am aware of with regard to each is exactly the same—namely that in one case the material thing, and in the other case my sensation does really exist.[51]

In a very similar vein, Russell in *The Problems of Philosophy* asserts:

If we say that things known must be in the mind, we are either unduly limiting the mind's power of knowing, or we are uttering a mere tautology. We are uttering a mere tautology if we mean by '*in* the mind' the same as by '*before* the mind', i.e., if we mean merely being apprehended by the mind. But if we mean this, we shall have to admit that what, *in this sense*, is in the mind, may nevertheless be not mental. Thus when we realize the nature of knowledge, Berkeley's argument is seen to be wrong in substance as well as in form, and his grounds for supposing that 'ideas'—i.e., the objects apprehended—must be mental, are found to have no validity whatever.[52]

And, again, Frege in 'Thoughts' offers this characteristically crisp objection to idealism:

A certain idea in my consciousness may be associated with the use of the word 'I'. But then this is one idea among other ideas, and I am its owner as I am the owner of the other ideas. I have an idea of myself, but I am not identical with this idea. What is a content of consciousness, my idea, should be sharply distinguished from what is an object of thought. Therefore the thesis that only what belongs to the content of my consciousness can be the object of my awareness, of my thought, is false.[53]

Frege is telling us that idealism is self-refuting. Idealists say that nothing exists but ideas; but, if ideas exist only *in* minds, then it is automatically false that nothing exists but ideas, since there must also *be* minds in order to contain ('own') those ideas.

These famous criticisms strongly suggest that we could compile a kind of comprehensive worry list about Kant's idealism. So here it is:

(1) Kant's idealism involves the identification of the object of representation with a part of the mental act of representing, which is absurd. (Moore's objection above.)

(2) Kant's idealism is Berkeleyan or phenomenalistic in that it identifies all objects with complexes of sensory ideas inside individual minds, which is absurd. (Russell's objection above.)

(3) Kant's idealism asserts that nothing exists but ideas, which is self-refuting. (Frege's objection above.)

(4) Kant's theory of the ideality of appearances and of space and time implausibly relativizes truth—especially necessary truth in logic and mathematics—to actual human beings. (Russell and perhaps Moore.)[54]

---

[51] Moore, 'The Refutation of Idealism', 44. See also Moore, 'Kant's Idealism'.
[52] Russell, *The Problems of Philosophy*, 42–3.   [53] Frege, 'Thoughts', 366.
[54] See Russell, *The Problems of Philosophy*, 87. Moore verges upon this objection in 'Truth and Falsity', 22. See also Van Cleve, *Problems from Kant*, 37–41.

(5) Kant's theory of the uncognizability of noumena entails Cartesian scepticism about the external, material world. (Moore and Russell.)[55]

(6) Kant's theory of judgement entails the patently false doctrine of logical psychologism. (Moore and Russell.)[56]

(7) Kant's theory of the transcendental ideality of space and time is insufficient for the explanation of the truths of arithmetic and geometry. (Frege for arithmetic; Moore and Russell for both arithmetic and geometry.)[57]

Oddly enough, however, neither Frege, nor Moore, nor Russell seriously[58] recycles the most famous and long-standing objection of all, namely:

(8) Kant's doctrine of 'outer affection'—of the causal source of outer sensory impressions—is internally inconsistent because it applies the category of CAUSE not only to appearances but also to things-in-themselves that are, by Kant's own doctrine of the uncognizability of noumena, inherently beyond the legitimate scope of that category's application.[59]

Clearly, in order to answer the forceful objection stated by Strawson in the epigraph for this chapter, Kant's idealism needs to be shown to be (*a*) internally consistent, and (*b*) resistant to the objections on the worry list. Also it is high time that I fulfil my promise in Chapter 1 to justify my interpretation of Kant's idealism. I have already explicitly dealt with two versions of the sixth charge—that is, Kant's suspected psychologism—in Section 1.5 (judgement psychologism) and Section 2.1 (logical psychologism), and will deal with it briefly yet again when discussing Kant's theory of analyticity in Section 3.1. And I will also grapple with the question of Kant's culpability in regard to the seventh objection—the objection from mathematics—in Chapter 5. Setting those three worries aside for the moment, however, four pressing points must be dealt with immediately.

[55] See Moore, 'Proof of an External World', and Russell, *The Problems of Philosophy*, chs. 1–2 and pp. 85–6.

[56] Moore, 'The Nature of Judgment', 2–3; Russell, *The Problems of Philosophy*, 88–9.

[57] For the criticisms regarding Kant's theory of arithmetic, see Frege, *The Foundations of Arithmetic*, 5–6, 99–102, and Russell, *The Principles of Mathematics*, 158. For the objections regarding Kant's theory of geometry, see Moore, 'Critical Notice of B. A. W. Russell, *An Essay on the Foundations of Geometry*', and Russell, *The Principles of Mathematics*, ch. 52.

The cases of Kant's theories of arithmetic and geometry are importantly asymmetric. Frege *accepts* Kant's theory of geometry; see Sects. 4.1 and 4.4 below. And Russell's 1897 *Essay on the Foundations of Geometry* offers a partial defence of Kant's theory of geometry —as do both Reichenbach's 1920 *Theory of Relativity and A Priori Knowledge* and Carnap's 1922 *Der Raum. Ein Beitrag zur Wissenschaftslehre*. See Sect. 5.6 below.

[58] Russell merely mentions it within parentheses, within a footnote, in *The Problems of Philosophy*, 86 n.

[59] This objection blends two distinct worries expressed respectively by Kant's contemporaries J. S. Beck and F. H. Jacobi. See the correspondence between Beck and Kant in 1791 and 1792 (*PC* Ak. xi. 310–11, 313–16); and also Beiser, *The Fate of Reason*, 124.

First, we must properly understand the meaning of Kant's thesis that all objects are nothing but appearances or phenomena; this corresponds to objections (1)–(3). Secondly, we must explore the precise nature of the ideality or mind dependence that Kant ascribes not only to appearances but also to (the representations of) space and time, to the categories, to logic, and more generally to all the a priori conditions for the possibility of experience; this corresponds to objection 4. Thirdly, we must clarify the nature of the noumenon or thing in itself and the precise meaning of the thesis of the noumenon's uncognizability, which corresponds to objection 5. And, finally, we must face up to the problem of outer affection, which corresponds to objection 8. For convenience, I will deal with the first two objections in the rest of this section, and the second two in the next.

Appearances and the Threat of Subjectivism

On the interpretation of Kant's idealism I am proposing, appearances are of two distinct types: first, they can be the undetermined objects of empirical intuitions ('the undetermined object of an empirical intuition is entitled *appearance*' (*CPR* A20/B34)); and, secondly, they can be the fully determined objects corresponding to true judgements of experience ('that in the appearance that contains the condition of this necessary rule of apprehension is the object' (*CPR* A191/B236)). The first type of appearance is the individual sensory proto-object of an unconceptualized empirical intuition with consciousness, under the pure forms of intuition alone apart from the application of categories (= a blind or indistinct perception). And the second type is an actual empirical state of affairs, or empirical fact—an object of experience—corresponding to a set of conceptualized outer perceptions under the original synthetic unity of apperception and in accordance with the schematized categories, especially those of substance and causality.

The two types of appearances are distinct from one another, but of course not mutually exclusive. This is because it is the basic claim of the Transcendental Deduction in the B edition that necessarily every appearance in the first sense is also generatively/productively convertible into an appearance in the second sense: 'All synthesis, therefore, even that which renders perception possible, is subject to the categories; and, since experience is cognition by means of connected perceptions, the categories are conditions of the possibility of experience, and are therefore valid a priori for all objects of experience' (*CPR* B161). A condition of the possibility of the necessary linkage between the two types of appearance is Kant's thesis that in every case—whether the object of cognition be a sensory proto-object, or a fully determined object of experience— the apparent object of an empirical cognition is identical to the representational content of that cognition. He puts that point—which in Section 1.1 I dubbed Kant's 'cognitive or representational idealism'—this way:

What objects may be in themselves, and apart from all this receptivity of our sensibility, remains completely unknown (*unbekannt*) by us. We are acquainted with nothing but our mode of perceiving them (*unsere Art, sie wahrzunehmen*) . . . With this alone have we any concern. Space and time are its pure forms, and sensation in general its matter (*Materie*) . . . Even if we could bring our intuition to the highest degree of clearness, we should not thereby come any nearer to the constitution of objects in themselves. For in any case we would still completely cognize only our mode of intuition (*unsre Art der Anschauung*), that is, our sensibility . . .   (*CPR* A42–3/B59–60)

External objects (bodies), however, are merely appearances, and are therefore nothing but a mode of my representations (*eine Art meiner Vorstellungen*), whose objects are something only through (*durch*) these representations, but are nothing apart from them.   (*CPR* A370)

You put the matter quite precisely when you say, 'The content of a representation is itself the object; and the activity of the mind whereby the content of a representation is represented is what is meant by "referring it to the object".'   (*PC* Ak. xi. 314)

Now the general thesis expressed in these texts must be carefully distinguished from the claim—vigorously attacked by Moore—that the object of a sensory representation is literally identical to some part of the subject's mental act of perceiving or judging. And, while the immanence of the object in mental acts may indeed be a problem for *Brentano's* theory of intentionality, it is not a problem for *Kant's*.[60] A Kantian 'mode of perceiving' or 'mode of intuition' or a 'mode of my representations' is essentially a *type structure* that inherently can occur, or be realized, in many different mental acts. For example, any number of us can see 'that red thing over there', despite the fact that each of us has her own unique conscious perceptual 'take' on that same thing. The red quality of the thing is not therefore literally immanent in particular sensory consciousnesses, even though *tokens* of it are in fact immanent.

And here is the reason why. A mode of representation always includes 'the representation of the object = X' (*CPR* A105), which, as we have already seen, is at once (*a*) the formal generic objective correlate of the original synthetic unity of apperception or 'I think' underlying all representations, and (*b*) the fully thinkable object of the pure concepts of the understanding even considered apart from the sensible conditions of their objective validity. Since any representation always includes a representation of the generic intentional object = X in relation to the transcendental or non-idiosyncratic 'I think', that representation is not restricted to the particular act of representing. In other words, the content of the representation is not what is literally internal to the individual act of representing; instead, the content is what is generated through the individual act of representing, by using innate rules or protocols of synthesis that are strictly invariant across human cognizers. So, because at bottom all cognitions are directed to the same generic objective target; because

---

[60] See Sect. 1.5.

all cognitions presuppose the same generic irreducible spontaneous sub-jective source (the transcendental 'I think'); and because all cognitions are generated by means of the very same total system of cognitive processing capacit-ies (our *Erkenntnisvermögen*)—for all these reasons, those ways of representing are essentially non-idiosyncratic. Any other empirical realization of the 'I think' in a creature sharing the same kind of perceptual equipment, under roughly the same empirical conditions, would represent the generic target object = X in the very same way. This guarantees that the representational contents generated by my cognitive capacities under particular empirical conditions in particular empirical contexts—which, according to Kant's cognitive or representational idealism, are also the very objects of cognition—are in prin-ciple also able to be generated by yours or anyone else's. So Moore failed to 'refute idealism', because he failed to refute *Kant's* idealism.[61] Just because sensory matter can enter into a particular conscious representation as its con-tent, it does not follow that it is contained inside that consciousness as water is contained inside a bucket. As Kant stresses repeatedly, whether it occurs in a perception or in a judgement, the essential function of sensory content is to indicate or describe a material object (an X) in space *outside* the individual consciousness.

That leaves Russell's and Frege's objections. And here the relevant Kantian reply can be summarized by saying that Kant's idealism is manifestly not a version of Berkeleyan idealism. On one highly uncharitable reading of Berkeley's idealism, his fundamental thesis that 'to be' means the same as 'to be perceived' can be taken to imply that absolutely everything is a sensory idea. Frege, of course, refutes this handily. But, since both Berkeley and Kant hold that minds and ideas are distinct sorts of beings, this refutation fails to apply in either case. As Russell correctly sees, however, Berkeley is indeed a phenomenalist and an immaterialist who reduces all objective or material entities to complexes of sensory ideas existing inside individual finite minds. But objective empirical entities for Kant are essentially intersubjective in char-acter, and exist as material objects in space outside the minds of individuals. Indeed, as Kant's own Refutation of Idealism makes clear, *that* such objects exist in space, and *that* we are directly perceptually aware of them as such, are even conditions of the possibility of empirical self-consciousness (*CPR* B274–9). Kant is therefore—quite unlike Berkeley—an empirical realist about apparent objects: they exist, and are directly perceivable, in space out-side the conscious subject (*CPR* A370–2).

There is also another crucial difference between Kant and Berkeley. In his response to criticisms of the first edition of the first *Critique*, Kant says several times that he is a 'critical' or 'formal' idealist, not a 'visionary' or 'dogmatic'

---

[61] Indeed, Moore's 'Refutation' is important mainly because it influenced Russell. See Baldwin, 'Moore's Rejection of Idealism', 357.

idealist in the Berkeleyan sense (*P.* Ak. iv. 293–4, 375). Kant's terminological fussing appropriately underlines the point that his idealism is driven from above by what I called his 'representational transcendentalism' thesis to the effect that the a priori structures that strictly govern appearances are type-identical with the formal constitutions of our minds. Furthermore, while it is no doubt somewhat inaccurate to say that Berkeley 'declares space, together with all the things to which it is attached as an inseparable condition, to be something that is impossible in itself' (*CPR* 274), nevertheless Kant is quite entitled to the point that, unlike Berkeley, he explicitly refuses to rule out the bare logical possibility that some objects of our thought have a mind-independent ontological status even beyond the limits of human sensibility:

And although certainly there may be[62] entities of the understanding corresponding to the sensible entities, and may even be entities of the understanding to which our sensible faculty of intuition has no reference at all, our concepts of understanding, being mere forms of thought for our sensible intuition, do not reach these in the least. (*CPR* A253/B308–9)

My idealism concerns not the existence of things (*Sachen*) (the doubting of which, however, constitutes idealism in the ordinary sense), since it never came into my head to doubt it; but it concerns the sensible representation of things, to which space and time especially belong. Regarding space and time and, consequently, regarding all appearances in general, I have only shown that they are neither things (but are mere modes of representation) nor are they determinations belonging to things in themselves. (*P.* Ak. iv. 293)

All these *noumena*, together with their sum total, the intelligible world, are nothing but representations of a problem, the object of which is quite possible but the solution, from the nature of the understanding, totally impossible. (*P.* Ak. iv. 316)

My idealism of appearances is the constraining of sensible intuition to mere experience and the prohibition that we do not with intuition overstep the limits of mere appearance to things in themselves. (*R.* 5642; Ak. xviii. 279)

Pure idealism concerns the existence of things outside us. Critical idealism leaves this undecided and asserts only that the form of their intuition is merely in us. (*R.* XXVI E 18–A29; Ak. xxiii. 23)

On Kant's view, then, there can in principle—logically possibly and thinkably—be objective noumena or things in themselves, but he refuses either to doubt or to assert their existence. In this way, their existence is and indeed must be (for reasons we shall see in the next two subsections) problematically thought by us, but they are neither empirically confirmed nor empirically rejected. Kant is thus a metaphysical agnostic about the ontological status of things in themselves, and an epistemological sceptic about knowing those things in themselves. In principle things in themselves can exist (in the thin

---

[62] Here I am significantly deviating from the Kemp Smith and the Guyer–Wood translations, both of which give this phrase an assertoric rather than a subjunctive mood.

or purely logical sense of the concept EXIST), but whether they do or not, and what their intrinsic natures might be, are completely uncognizable and unknowable for all creatures minded like us.

Ideality and the Threat of Relativism

Relativism for our purposes is the thesis that truth or knowledge is strictly determined by the arbitrary decisions of actual human individuals (solipsistic relativism), by the shared consensus of actual communities (communitarian relativism), or by the evolutionary convergence of the human species upon certain shared beliefs (species relativism[63]). Is Kantian idealism a form of relativism? Well, it all depends on how we interpret his notion of ideality or strict mind dependence. While, on the one hand, Kant identifies the objects of representation neither with parts of the conscious act of representing nor with phenomenal complexes inside individual minds, on the other hand there is also no doubt whatsoever that he defends the thesis of the ideality or mind dependence of ordinary empirical objects and of (the representations of) space and time. And, in so far as he holds—according to the conclusion of the B Deduction—that every fully-fledged experience of an object presupposes the pure intuitions of space and time, the categories, the transcendental synthesis of the imagination, and the original synthetic unity of apperception as formal conditions, he thus also more or less explicitly asserts the ideality of all the a priori conditions for the possibility of experience. What is more difficult to gauge, however, is the precise logical strength and scope of this mind dependence. So there is still a genuine worry that Kant's idealism expresses one of the three forms of relativism.

The following texts will help us to evaluate this worry:

Our assertions therefore teach the *empirical reality* of time—that is, its objective validity in respect of all objects that allow of ever being given to the senses. And, since our intuition is always sensible, no object can ever be given to us in experience that does not belong under the condition of time. But, on the contrary, we dispute all claim of time to absolute reality . . . This, then, is what constitutes the *transcendental ideality* of time, according to which it is nothing at all if one abstracts from the subjective conditions of sensible intuition, and cannot be counted either as subsisting or as inhering in the objects in themselves (without their relation to our intuition).   (*CPR* A35–6/B52; and for the corresponding claim about space, see *CPR* A28/B44)

We have therefore wanted to say that all our intuition is nothing but the representation of appearance; that the things we intuit are not in themselves what we intuit them to be, nor are their relations so constituted in themselves as they appear to us; and that, if we remove our own subject or even only the subjective constitution of the senses in general, then the entire constitution and all the relations of objects in space and time, indeed space and time themselves, would vanish. What may be the

---

[63] See e.g. Lorenz, 'Kant's Doctrine of the A Priori in the Light of Contemporary Biology'.

case with objects in themselves and abstracted from all this receptivity of our sensibility remains completely unknown to us. We are acquainted with nothing but our
mode of perceiving them, which is peculiar to us, and which therefore does not necessarily pertain to every being, though to be sure it pertains to every human being.
With this alone have we any concern.   (*CPR* A42/B59–60)

As soon as we take away our subjective constitution, the represented object with the
qualities that sensible intuition attributes to it is nowhere to be found, nor can it be
found, for it is just this subjective constitution that determines its form as appearance.   (*CPR* A44/B62)

I do not say that bodies merely *seem* (*scheinen*) to exist outside me or that my soul
only *seems* to be given in my self-consciousness if I assert that the quality of space
and time, in conformity with which, as condition of their existence, I posit both of
these, lies in my mode of intuition and not in those objects in themselves. It would
be my own fault if I made that which I should count as appearance (*Erscheinung*)
into mere illusion (*Schein*).   (*CPR* B69)

The transcendental object is equally unknown (*unbekannt*) in regard to inner and to
outer intuition. But we are not talking about that, but rather about the empirical object,
which is called an *external* object if it is represented *in space*, and an *inner* object if
it is represented only *in its time relations*; space and time, however, are both to be
encountered only *in us*. . . . The expression *outside us* carries with it an unavoidable
ambiguity, since it sometimes signifies something that, *as thing in itself*, exists distinct
from us, and sometimes something that merely belongs to outer *appearance*.   (*CPR*
A372–3)

In the light of what Kant says here, it is obvious enough that his notion of
ideality does not entail solipsistic relativism. This point can be made in three
ways. First, although Kant says that all appearances, and (the representations
of) space and time, require the human mind as a necessary condition, nevertheless no *particular* human mind is required, but only the constitution of
human sensibility in general. Secondly, appearances are 'in us' without in any
way being illusory or idiosyncratically subjective. This is because the mind
dependence of appearances is perfectly consistent with the empirical reality
of space and time—their objective applicability as pure forms of sensibility
to really possible or actual external empirical objects. Thirdly, consistently with
the second point, the sense in which appearances are 'in us' is purely transcendental. That is, Kant is saying that our cognition is entirely restricted to
the actual and possible objects that are available through the senses. But this
is quite consistent with the thesis that appearances exist objectively in space
outside of us, since the empirical meaningfulness or objective validity of the
prepositional phrase "outside of us" is determined by our spatial form of representation and presupposes the mind dependence of appearances.

What, then, about communitarian and species relativism? This is a slightly
trickier issue. While Kant's thesis of the ideality of appearances and of space
and time is clearly not solipsistic, it nevertheless does lay down a fundamental
existential condition on the actual or possible existence of real empirical objects

and also on the nature of space and time. There can be no empirical objects, and no space and time, without the actual existence of at least *some* human sensory cognizers—that is, without the *fact* of the special formal structure that is our human sensory and discursive constitution. In the Paralogisms chapter in the A edition, Kant puts it this way: 'If I were to take away the thinking subject (*das denkende Subjekt*), the whole corporeal world would have to vanish, as this is nothing other than the appearance in the sensibility of our subject (*unseres Subjekts*) and a mode of its representations' (*CPR* A383). Without 'the thinking subject' or 'our subject'—but notice particularly that he does not say 'without *my individual subject*'—actual human thought or sensory activity could not exist; and, if that were so, then there could not be an actual or possible empirical world, since there could not be any actual application of our generative/productive capacities to sensory content. Just to give it a handy label, let us call this 'the Anthropocentric Condition'.

It is very clearly the case that the Anthropocentric Condition expresses a metaphysically substantive form of idealism, and that therefore Kant's transcendental idealism is not merely a theory of what Henry Allison calls 'epistemic conditions'.[64] Had human cognizers never existed, there could not have been an empirical world nor any (necessary or contingent) truths about it. But precisely what sort of dependence is this? It is certainly not a dependence on human communal consensus. Even more importantly it is not a dependence on human biology—it is not a dependence on the existence of the human species. In principle, according to Kant, our special cognitive constitution could have been realized—and perhaps already is or has been, on other planets[65]— in creatures whose material nature is very different from that of the species *Homo sapiens* (*CPR* B72). In this sense, on Kant's view the property of being human is multiply realizable or compositionally plastic. The mind dependence of the empirical world is thus only a dependence on the existence of the special finite sensory, discursive, and rational cognitive architecture that defines us as minded creatures.

It seems obvious now that the Anthropocentric Condition does not entail relativism. But it does invoke a highly non-trivial form of mind dependence. According to Kant, without the existence of the cognitive constitution of creatures minded like us, there could be no actual world, nor any intuitive or direct mode of access to that world; there could be no way of discursively representing actual objects of experience in that world; there could be no way of intelligibly conceiving or constructing any experientially possible world; and there would even be no way of thinking or constructing logically possible worlds.

---

[64] Allison, *Kant's Transcendental Idealism*, 10–13.

[65] Kant's pre-Critical essay *Universal Natural History and Theory of the Heavens* (1755) contains an appendix entirely devoted to the question of extraterrestrial intelligent life (Ak. i. 349–68). See also Cassirer, *Kant's Life and Thought*, 39–57.

This in turn directly entails that the existence of our cognitive constitution is the essential condition for all strong modality or necessity, be it analytic or synthetic. Otherwise put, Kant is a *modal mentalist*: 'all necessity whatsoever has a transcendental condition as its ground' (*CPR* A106).[66] So, while we human cognizers are certainly not the strictly sufficient condition for the determination of all empirical things—that is, we do not literally create empirical things—and while our actual existence or incarnation in this biological guise is not even a necessary condition of the determination of all empirical things, still the fact of the existence of some creatures minded like us is required as a basic necessary condition by Kant's general cognitive semantics. If creatures minded like us had not existed, then purely logically speaking something might still have existed, but the assertion that it did exist would have been at the very least empirically meaningless and without a truth value. That is, such a thing is only fully thinkable. But even the fully thinkable thought that something might have existed even if we had not already presupposes the cognitive capacities of creatures minded like us (see Sections 2.1 and 2.2).

2.4. Transcendental Idealism II: Noumena and Affection

The Noumenon and Cartesian External World Scepticism

Noumena are said by Kant to be 'things in general and in themselves' (*CPR* A239/B298), 'objects in general and of thinking' (*CPR* A248/B305), or 'beings of the understanding' (*Verstandeswesen*) (*CPR* B306). The noumenon is thus an essentially general, non-relational, non-empirical, thinkable or understandable object of some sort. More precisely, a noumenon is any object that is at least fully thinkable by means of the pure concepts of the understanding under the original synthetic unity of apperception, but that is *not* also empirically intuitable, cognizable (in the narrow sense), or experienceable via our forms of sensible intuition. Noumena are thus trans-sensible or super-sensible objects of representation.

Starting out with this working notion of a noumenon as a thinkable but non-sensory or uncognizable (in the narrow sense) object, Kant then goes on to specify it more precisely. As I have already mentioned in passing, he distinguishes carefully between noumena in the negative and positive senses:

[66] In discussing the Russell–Moore criticism of Kant, Van Cleve remarks that 'I must confess that I have not the slightest idea what nonmodal property might serve to guarantee the presence of necessity in whatever had it' (*Problems from Kant*, 43). Kant's solution to this worry, however, is as clear as a bell: any non-empirical (i.e. spontaneity-based) mental property is necessary and sufficient for the presence of strong modality in whatever instantiates that property.

If by noumenon we mean a thing *in so far as it is not an object of our sensible intuition*, because we abstract away from our mode of intuiting it, this is a noumenon in the *negative* sense. But if we understand by that an *object of a non-sensible intuition*, we thereby presuppose a special type of intuition—namely, intellectual intuition—which, however, is not ours, and the possibility of which we cannot have insight into (*nicht einsehen können*), and this would be the noumenon in the *positive* sense.   (*CPR* B307)

A noumenon in the negative sense is any non-sensible object of our think-ing.[67] By contrast, a noumenon in the positive sense is a noumenon in the negative sense plus a further special property: it is any fully thinkable yet non-sensible object, in so far as it could be cognized by a being possessing a faculty of intellectual intuition, or divine cognition, yet could not be cognized by a being possessing a finite sensory cognitive capacity like ours nor indeed by any sort of sensible cognizer, human or non-human. Positive noumena are— or would be, if they existed—the Really Real beings. More precisely, they would be real natures or real essences, substances that subsisted entirely independ-ently of human minds. The class of positive noumena thus includes God and also all purely intelligible or spiritual entities other than the divine nature —for example, immortal souls, angelic beings, Leibnizian monads, Platonic forms, scholastic essences, and so on. Such entities are represented by what Kant calls 'concepts of reason' or 'ideas of pure reason' (*CPR* A310–38/B366– 96). And, just as pure concepts of the understanding are meta-concepts, or second-order logical concepts for organizing first-order or empirical con-cepts, so ideas of reason are meta-meta-concepts, or third-order concepts whose function is to represent unrestricted extensions of pure concepts (*CPR* A320/B377). Thus concepts of reason 'contain the unconditioned' (*CPR* A311/B367), which is to say that the positive noumena represented by those rational concepts are taken to be absolute, maximal, complete, perfect, or actually infinite.

Members of the class of positive noumena are completely inaccessible to human cognition, since they are super-sensible and cognizable only by means of a totalizing intellectual intuition, which is by hypothesis not possessed by us. Hence we cannot in any way assert or deny the existence of positive noumena; yet we conceive them agnostically and problematically as pure possibilia of the understanding. The concept of the noumenon used in this way serves only to indicate the limits of our cognition, not to determine new objects for our cognition. So for theoretical philosophy the concept of the positive noumenon turns out to have only an exclusionary or negative use:

---

[67] Negative noumena include, among other things, Newtonian or absolute space and time, all non-Euclidean spaces or non-Euclidean spatial entities, and any temporal entity or time structure that involves a deviant time—e.g. non-asymmetric or reversible time, looping time, discontinuous time, multiple or parallel times, etc. More generally, negative noumena fall outside our sensibility. This leaves open the possibility, however, that they are cognitively accessible to alien creatures with different forms of sensibility (*CPR* B72).

Ultimately, however, we have no insight into the possibility of such [positive] noumena, and the domain outside the sphere of appearances is for us empty—that is, we have an understanding that extends farther than [the field of sensibility] *problematically*, but no intuition, indeed not even the concept of a possible intuition, through which objects outside the field of sensibility could be given, and about which the understanding could be employed *assertorically*. The concept of the noumenon is thus merely a *limiting concept* (*Grenzbegriff*), in order to prevent the overextension of sensibility, and therefore only of negative use.   (*CPR* B310–11)

So there is an important distinction to be drawn between (1) the concept of the negative noumenon, and (2) the negative use of the concept of the positive noumenon. The concept of the negative noumenon draws a sharp line between what is strictly speaking humanly sensible and what is super-sensible. The negative—that is, limiting or exclusionary—function of the concept of the positive noumenon, on the other hand, shows us what we cannot cognize, in view of the fact that we are not possessors of an intellectual intuition but instead only of a human sensible intuition. This function is particularly important in philosophical dialectic: the exposure and diagnosis of metaphysical errors and illusions, all of which consist at bottom in confusing appearances and positive noumena (*CPR* A61–2/B85–6, A293–309/B349–66).

   In contrast to the concepts of the negative noumenon and positive noumenon, however, Kant employs a third distinct concept of a non-empirical object as well. This is the by-now familiar concept of the transcendental object = *X*:

Appearances are the only objects that can be given to us immediately, and that in them which refers immediately to the object is called intuition. Now, however, these appearances are not things in themselves, rather themselves only representations, which in turn have their object, which therefore cannot be further intuited by us, and which may therefore be called the non-empirical, i.e. transcendental object = *X*.   (*CPR* A108–9)

The object to which I refer appearance in general is the transcendental object—that is, the completely undetermined thought of something in general. This cannot be entitled the *noumenon*; for I scientifically know (*weiß*) nothing about what it is in itself, and have no concept of it save as merely the object of a sensible intuition in general, which is therefore the same for all appearances.   (*CPR* A253)

From these texts it is clear that the concept of the generic representational object or transcendental object = *X* is not equivalent to either of the two noumenal concepts. As we have seen, the *X* is a basic formal constituent—necessarily correlating with the original synthetic unity of apperception as its generic intentional object—in every representation whatsoever. Hence it plays a necessary role in the representation of appearances and in the representation of noumena alike. Because it is transcendental, the *X* is non-empirical or a priori; and, because it is a necessary condition for the representation of appearances, it automatically has an 'immanent' use (*CPR* A296/B352–3) and therefore is objectively valid. Nevertheless, when abstracted from its immanent use, the representational X also functions beyond the conditions for sensibility as the bare object of 'transcendental affirmation' (*CPR* A574/B602).[68] In the broadest possible sense, according to Kant *to be an object* is *to be represented or representable*. So the representational X occurs even in strictly noumenal representations, or ideas of reason.

Taking into account both concepts of the noumenon, and also the concept of the transcendental object $= X$, we must conclude that it is not the case that Kant is a metaphysical dualist about the phenomenon/noumenon distinction as regards the object of cognition—whether a substance dualist or a property dualist. That is, even given the three different notions of a non-empirical object, on the one hand it does not follow that Kant is committed to the thesis that in the world there are two disjoint classes of real objects such that all the members of the first class are essentially appearances (real-for-us) and all the members of the second class are essentially noumenal and unknowable (real-in-themselves). So Kant is no defender of the Two-Object Theory or Two-World Theory of phenomena and positive noumenal objects traditionally ascribed to him. On the other hand, however, it would also be a mistake to think that Kant is, without qualification, a defender of the Two-Aspect Theory promoted by H. J. Paton, Gerold Prauss, Henry Allison, and many others.[69] According to the Two-Aspect approach, Kant claims that there is one and only one sort of object that actually exists, but two radically distinct ways of considering or describing that very object: the phenomenal way and the noumenal way. It must be admitted, of course, that Kant talks about noumena as 'things in themselves (not considered as appearances)' (*CPR* A256/B312), and also about a 'twofold standpoint' according to which 'the same objects can be considered from two sides, *on the one side*, as objects of the senses and of the understanding for experience, and, *on the other side*, as objects that are merely thought at most for the isolated reason striving to transcend the limits of experience' (*CPR* Bxviii–xix n.). Even more explicitly, Kant suggests that 'our Critique has not erred in teaching that the object should be taken *in a twofold sense*—namely, as appearance and as thing in itself' (*CPR* Bxxvii). And perhaps most explicitly of all, in a letter to Christian Garve on 7 August 1783, he remarks that 'all objects that are given to us can be interpreted in two ways: on the one hand, as appearances; on the other hand, as things in themselves' (*PC* Ak. x. 341 n.). These texts must be taken seriously and not explained away.

Nevertheless, looking charitably at the matter, Kant surely cannot be saying either (*a*) that there is one and only one class of *phenomenal* objects such that

---

[68] Thanks to Robert Greenberg for drawing my attention to this text.

[69] See Allison, *Kant's Transcendental Idealism*, 8; Allison, 'Transcendental Idealism: The "Two Aspect" View'; Paton, *Kant's Metaphysic of Experience*, i. 61; and Prauss, *Kant und das Problem der Dinge an Sich*.

every member of it has the property of being an appearance and also the property of being noumenal, or (*b*) that there is one and only one class of *noumenal* objects such that every member of it has the property of being an appearance and also the property of being noumenal, or even (*c*) that there is one and only one class of *non-phenomenal, non-noumenal* objects such that every member of it has the property of being an appearance and also the property of being noumenal. In the first two cases, since the property of being an appearance (a sensible object) conceptually excludes the property of being a thing-in-itself (a super-sensible or non-sensible object), that would be to define a class of objects by means of a membership criterion requiring the joint possession of contradictory properties. And that is absurd. Moreover, if one takes the third option, then one is also (in addition to the contradiction problem) saddled with a new sort of objective entity altogether, which of course implausibly bloats Kant's ontology.

Now one can avoid both the absurdity and the tendency towards ontological profligacy—as, indeed, both Prauss and Allison explicitly do—by taking Kant's remarks about the phenomenal and noumenal aspects of things to entail only the weaker thesis that there is one and only one class of objects such that every member of it has the two 'converse intentional properties' (to borrow a term coined by Roderick Chisholm) of being taken by us to be phenomenal and also being taken by us to be noumenal—which, of course, are mutually consistent properties. But that strategy still has three problems. First, if all the objects really are phenomenal, and we know that, then why do we also persist in taking the phenomenal objects to be also noumenal? That seems to be simply a false phenomenological description of our ordinary cognition of objects. Secondly, if the object that is taken by us to be phenomenal and that is also taken by us to be noumenal is itself neither strictly phenomenal nor strictly noumenal, then it must be something else altogether; but since we are not told by the Two-Aspect Theory what that something else might be, it would again implausibly bloat Kant's ontology. And, thirdly, the Two-Aspect interpretation cannot make any proper sense of the many texts in which Kant talks quite explicitly about the concept of an ontologically distinct noumenal object, and not merely about ways of considering phenomenal objects as noumena.

So we have reached this impasse: it seems, on the one hand, wrong to interpret Kant as holding unqualifiedly that there are ontologically separate phenomenal and noumenal objects (the Two-Object or Two-World view); and, on the other hand, it also seems equally wrong to interpret him as holding unqualifiedly that there are only empirical objects and two essentially different ways of describing them (the Two-Aspect view). Well then, what *is* Kant saying?

In order to solve this puzzle, we must adopt the standpoint of general cognitive semantics and remember that, for Kant, to be an object is to be literally identical with the communicable content of a representation synthesized by the application of necessary conceptual rules in accordance with the categories and pure forms of intuition under the original synthetic unity of apperception. If we hold that point fixed, then we will be able to construe noumena and phenomena as, correspondingly, two essentially different sorts of objects only in so far as those objects are logically and ontologically parasitic upon two essentially different kinds of *concepts*:

The understanding, when it dubs an object to which it refers a mere phenomenon, at the same time forms, apart from that reference, a representation of an *object in itself*, and hence also represents itself as being able to make *concepts* of such an object, and since the understanding offers nothing other than the categories through which the object [in itself] must at least be able to be thought, it is thereby misled into taking the entirely *undetermined* concept of a being of the understanding (*Verstandeswesen*), as a something in general outside of our sensibility, for a *determinate* concept of an entity that allows of being cognized through the understanding in a certain mode (*auf einige Art erkennen*).   (*CPR* B306–7)

The division of objects into phenomena and noumena and of the world into a world of sense and a world of the understanding is therefore quite inadmissible in the positive sense, *although concepts certainly allow of a division into sensible and intellectual ones*; for one cannot determine any object for [intellectual concepts], and consequently they cannot be put forward as objectively valid. If one abandons the senses, how will one make it conceivable that our categories (which would be the only remaining concepts for noumena) still continue to mean anything at all, since for their reference to any object something more than merely the unity of thinking must be given— namely, a possible intuition, to which they must be applied? Nevertheless if the concept of a noumenon be taken in a merely problematic sense, it remains not only admissible, but even indispensable, as setting limits to sensibility.   (*CPR* A255–6/B311, emphasis added)

Noumenon means (genuinely) at bottom something—namely, the transcendental object of sensible intuition. (This, however, is no real object or given thing, *rather a concept in reference to which appearances have unity*.)   (*R.* 5554; Ak. xviii. 230, emphasis added)

Just to give it a handy name, let us call the view I am proposing the 'Two-Concept Theory' of the noumenon/phenomenon distinction. According to it, what Kant is saying about noumena and phenomena is that there are two essentially different ways of thinking or conceptualizing an object of representations—or a generic transcendental object = *X*—relative to pure concepts of the understanding. The first kind of thinking or conceptualizing is by means of pure concepts alone (the transcendent way), and the second is by means of pure concepts plus our specially restricted sensory capacity (the immanent way). Thus the first kind of conceptualization of the *X* allows us merely to think objects and never to cognize them in the strict sense; and we call all and only such objects 'noumena', whether they be negatively conceived or positively conceived. The second way of conceptualizing the *X*, however, allows us to cognize *appearances* by means of thinking. This is because the second kind of conceptualizing already includes the restrictive a priori or formal and a posteriori or material contributions of pure and empirical intuition. The conceptualizing faculty, or understanding, cannot operate on this formal and material sensible information until it has already been supplied by an independent sensible source. Therefore our understanding is

> an understanding whose whole capacity consists in thinking—that is, in the act of bringing the synthesis of a manifold, given to it from elsewhere in intuition, to the unity of apperception, which therefore *cognizes* nothing at all for itself, but merely combines and orders the material of cognition, the intuition, which must be given to it by the object. (*CPR* B145)

So, through its conceptual determination of independently given sensory content, the second kind of conceptualization provides us with direct access to really possible or actually existent objects, the fully determined appearances or phenomena.

Again, more precisely put, Kant holds that every pure concept of the understanding is such that it can be used either (*a*) merely to think the generic object = X transcendently as a noumenal object, or (*b*) to think the generic object = X immanently as a phenomenally possible or actual object via the sensory data contributed by human intuition. Thus noumenal objects logically possibly can have being (but are completely uncognizable), and phenomenal objects really possibly or actually exist (and are indeed cognizable). This is quite consistent with (*a**) its not being the case that there exist two disjoint classes of real objects, the phenomena and the noumena (= the denial of the Two-Object or Two-World Theory), and also with (*b**) its not being the case that there exists a single class of objects such that every member of it is considered both as phenomenon and as noumenon (= the denial of the Two-Aspect Theory). The Two-Concept Theory retains from the Two-Object Theory the idea that we are compelled by our cognitive constitutions to think (but never cognize in the strict sense) ontologically distinct noumenal objects; yet it also retains from the Two-Aspect Theory the idea that Kant makes only one definite or assertoric ontological commitment. On the Two-Aspect Theory it is in fact unclear just what sort of ontic commitment this will be, but for the Two-Concept Theory it is completely definite: phenomena alone actually exist. On the Two-Concept approach Kant remains consistently and thoroughly agnostic about the existence of noumenal objects,[70] despite their being logically possible and fully thinkable:

---

[70] Kant treats noumenal *objects* and noumenal *subjects* very differently, however. In the third Antinomy, in *Grounding for the Metaphysics of Morals*, sect. III, and in the second *Critique*, ch. I, he argues compellingly for a compatibilist and dualist solution to the free-will/natural-determinism problem. See Adams, 'Things in Themselves', and Wood, 'Kant's Compatibilism'. So Kant is a Two-Concept theorist about noumenal objects and a Two-World theorist about noumenal subjects.

The concept of the noumenon is problematic—that is, it is the representation of a thing of which we can say neither that it is [really or empirically] possible nor that it is impossible, since we are acquainted with no mode (*Art*) of intuition but our own sensible one and no sort of concepts but the categories, neither of which, however, is appropriate to a non-sensible object. (*CPR* A286–7/B343)

The Two-Concept Theory also retains from the Two-Aspect Theory the idea that there are two essentially different *ways* of thinking about objects—as noumena and as phenomena. But, unlike the Two-Aspect Theory, the Two-Concept Theory holds that these ways of thinking about objects are not *properties* of those objects. Finally, the Two-Concept Theory essentially differs from both of the other two theories in holding that the intentional or representational object that persists through noumenal representations and phenomenal representations alike—the transcendental object = X—is no ontologically independent item at all, but rather only a generic cognitive-semantic structure *internal* to the representations used to represent objects.

Question: what is the main philosophical advantage of the Two-Concept Theory, apart from its obvious exegetical value in neatly reconciling many apparently incongruous or even seemingly inconsistent Kantian texts? Answer: above all, it undermines the Moore–Russell objection to the effect that Kant's theory of the noumenon automatically leads to Cartesian external-world scepticism. The huge problem with the Two-Object or Two-World Theory is that, instead of restricting itself to a concept of the noumenon, it posits the existence of a noumenal Really Real object that by hypothesis simply cannot be cognized. This is what Kant calls 'transcendental realism'; and it leads directly down a slippery philosophical slope to 'empirical idealism', 'problematic idealism', or 'sceptical idealism': the Cartesian external-world scepticism spelled out in the first two Meditations (*CPR* B274–5, A369; see also *P*. Ak. iv. 293–4). However, if the positive noumenon is merely a problematic representational projection of an X via a fully thinkable and thinly meaningful concept, then transcendental realism and its evil twin, external-world scepticism, are both completely avoided. If no object is asserted to be transcendently outside cognition, then no object is such that we human knowers must forever try, and miserably fail, to cognize it. Such objects nevertheless logically can exist, and we thereby problematically entertain the notion that they exist; but the crucial agnostic recognition is that we are never in a position to determine whether they actually exist or not. So external-world scepticism never arises as a serious problem for Kant.[71] On the contrary, Kant's metaphysical agnosticism has the entirely

---

[71] Which is not to say that it never arises as an issue. Kant thinks that it is a 'scandal of philosophy and universal human reason' (*CPR* Bxxxix n.) that no one has explicitly refuted Cartesian external world scepticism, and consequently offers just such a refutation in the B edition (*CPR* B274–9; cf. A366–80). See also Hanna, 'The Inner and the Outer: Kant's "Refutation" Reconstructed'.

anti-sceptical function of promoting the stoical acceptance of our epistemically finite human condition, despite our goading natural desires for cognitive self-transcendence.

The Problem of Outer Affection and the Threat of Inconsistency

There is one remaining big worry about Kant's transcendental idealism, and that is the notorious problem of outer affection. Here is the problem in a nutshell:

(1) Outer affection is a causal process of some sort that consists in triggering the sensory responses of our faculty of outer empirical intuition, thereby providing a manifold of sensory content.

(2) The ultimate causal source of outer sensory affection is thought by us to be wholly mind-independent and therefore beyond all sense experience.

(3) In order to explain outer affection Kant must apply the schematized and objectively valid pure concept CAUSE, which applies to empirical objects only, to affection's super-sensible causal source.

(4) Kant commits a howler by attempting to apply the concept of CAUSE beyond the limits of its legitimate sphere of application—that is, beyond all possible experience.

(5) But, if the concept of CAUSE cannot be applied to the source of outer sensory affection, then the existence of the manifold of sensory content simply cannot be accounted for, and Kant's theory of cognition fails.

The problem of outer affection is one of the great unfixed potholes of Kant interpretation.[72] Unlike other more or less serious problems surrounding Kant's doctrines, if this one is allowed to go unrepaired it will surely puncture the tyres of the Transcendental Project. As Jacobi famously noted, if the problem of affection is allowed to stand, then Kant's transcendental idealism is apparently *just plain wrong*. It seems that, without the assumption of a causally affecting thing-in-itself, one cannot enter Kant's system; but with it, one cannot remain inside the system either.[73] In my opinion, on the contrary, it is wrong to think that the problem of outer affection will show the falsity of Kant's idealism. Kant's doctrine of outer affection is perfectly self-consistent.

What I mean is this. Kant can perfectly well accept premisses (1) and (2) in the above argument, but also believe that (4) and (5) do not follow—and indeed are false—*because (3) is false*. The error lies in holding that, just because Kant is committed to the view that we are capable of thinking, and indeed even naturally and philosophically are driven to think, in a problematic sense, a noumenal causal source for outer affection, we are thereby obliged to apply the objectively valid category CAUSE to that thinkable source. On the

[72] See Allison, *Kant's Transcendental Idealism*, 247–54.
[73] See Beiser, *The Fate of Reason*, 124.

contrary, according to Kant, while we can, naturally do, and even must, think or entertain the idea of a noumenal cause, we nevertheless apply the object-ively valid category CAUSE to phenomenal objects only:

Now one can indeed admit that something that *may* be outside us in the transcend-ental sense is the cause (*Ursache*) of our outer intuitions, but this is *not* the object of which we are thinking in the representations of matter and of corporeal things; for these are merely appearances—that is, mere modes of representation (*Vorstel-lungsarten*)—which are always found only in us . . .   (*CPR* A372, emphases added)

The much-discussed question of the community between what thinks and what is extended comes then simply to this: *how outer intuition*—namely, that of space (its filling-in by shape and motion)—*is possible at all in a thinking subject*. But it is impos-sible for any human being to find an answer to this question, and no one will ever fill this gap in our scientific knowledge (*Wissens*), but rather only indicate it through the ascription of outer appearances to a transcendental object that is the cause of this mode (*Art*) of representations, with which, however, we have no acquaintance, nor will we never acquire any [objectively valid] concept of it.   (*CPR* A393)

This crucial point needs further explication. By hypothesis, outer affection is a causal process of some sort that produces outer sensory impressions and triggers our faculty of empirical intuition. Therefore there exists a brute 'fact of affection'; and, by virtue of the principle of sufficient reason—that is, nec-essarily every fact or entity has an explanation in terms of its cause or strict logical ground (*CPR* B112; see also JL Ak. ix. 51)—this brute fact needs to be causally explained. But in saying that, Kant has not yet said *just what sort of causal process he is talking about*. And in fact causal processes can be con-ceived in two irreducibly different ways: (1) as a law-determined 'conditioned' spatiotemporal causal process deriving from an empirical outer physical causal source; or (2) as a spontaneous or free, hence unconditioned, causal process deriving from a non-spatiotemporal or super-sensible causal source (*CPR* A389–94). That is, whatever it is that actually affects us in outer sens-ibility can be conceptualized either (1) as an apparent material object, a 'phenomenal substance' (*substantia phaenomenon* (see *CPR* A277/B333)), or (2) as a noumenal object with mysterious spontaneous causal powers, a purely intelligible substance with the capacity for freedom (*CPR* A358).

Now both concepts can be used in alternative possible explanations of the brute fact of affection *without contradiction*. In this sense, Kant's doctrine of affection is simply the flip side of his famous transcendental solution to the Third Antinomy of freedom and universal natural necessity or determinism (*CPR* A490–7/B518–25, A532–58/B561–86). According to that solution, the very same phenomenal event in nature can be consistently and respectively thought under the two distinct concepts of causation, (1) as naturalistically and efficiently caused ('*n*-caused') by strictly law-governed earlier condi-tioned states of the empirical world, *and* (2) as spontaneously and non-efficiently caused ('*s*-caused') by an unconditioned causal process that operates entirely outside spatiotemporal and sensible constraints.[74] There is no inconsistency in Kant's doctrine of affection, precisely because the two concepts of causation involved are sharply different in meaning. The concept of *n*-causation is thickly meaningful or objectively valid, while the concept of *s*-causation is only thinly meaningful or thinkable and not objectively valid.

To be sure, both concepts do share a single semantic core—that every cause whatsoever is a strictly sufficient reason or ground for its effect, its necessary consequence (*CPR* A112, B112, A200–1/B246; see also JL Ak. ix. 51). But strict sufficiency or grounding leaves quite open the question of *how* the strict sufficiency is to be secured: by means of a naturalistic or efficient, law-governed conditioned empirical cause in time and space; or by means of some non-spatiotemporal, unconditioned, non-efficient, purely intelligible cause? While they share a core of meaning, then, the two causal concepts are also sharply divergent in meaning, because they describe radically different sorts of things. Hence they do not intrinsically contradict one another any more than the concepts CONCRETE OR PHYSICAL CIRCLE and ABSTRACT OR IDEAL CIRCLE intrinsically contradict one another. A contradiction would be possible only if the two concepts were directly predicated of one another, or if one of the concepts was applied to an instance also falling under the other—if one attempted, for example, to apply the concept IDEAL CIRCLE to a dinner plate. Kant commits no fallacy in his doctrine of outer affection, then, because he neither mutually predicates the two causal concepts, nor does he make an attempt to apply one of them to an instance falling under the other. Rather, the two distinct concepts belong respectively to alternative yet distinct causal explanations of the same thing—the fact of affection.

Now since the second or noumenal concept of affection invokes a causal process and a causal source that are by hypothesis wholly uncognizable in the strict sense, such causal notions can play no role whatsoever in a generative/productive explanation of cognition, which begins with the mere phenomenal effects of outer affection—hence with sensory inputs or impressions—and has no reference whatsoever to the inner nature of the causal source of those phenomenal effects. Instead, then, the second or noumenal concept of affection is a concept whose sole employment in the theory of cognition is to play a basic role for noumenal concepts that I have already described—that of an essentially problematic or limiting concept:

---

[74] The psychological spontaneity of the all-purpose imagination, we will remember (Sect. 1.3), implies that its mental acts are strictly underdetermined by sensory inputs—hence a priori—but this does not thereby imply that its acts are wholly unconditioned or non-spatiotemporal. By contrast, the spontaneity of the third Antinomy is an unconditioned or pure spontaneity of the noumenal subject, not the psychological spontaneity of the empirically real human cognizer.

Understanding accordingly limits sensibility without thereby extending its own field, and in warning sensibility that it must not presume to claim applicability to things-in-themselves but only to appearances, it does *think for itself* an object in itself, but only as a transcendental object, which is the cause (*Ursache*) of appearance (thus not itself appearance), and which can be thought neither as magnitude nor as reality nor as substance, etc. (because these concepts always require sensible forms in which they determine an object); it therefore remains *completely unknown* (*völlig unbekannt*) whether such an object is to be encountered within us or outside us, whether it would be at once removed along with sensibility or whether it would remain even if we took sensibility away. If we want to call this object a noumenon for the reason that the representation of it is not sensible, we are free to do so. But, since we cannot apply to it any of our concepts of the understanding, this representation remains empty for us, and serves for nothing other than to designate the limits of our sensible cognition and leave open a space that we can fill in neither through possible experience nor through pure understanding.   (*CPR* A288–9/B344–5, emphasis added)

In interpreting this strictly problematic or agnostic role of the concept of a noumenal cause of affection, however, we must note well that, although the logical place that is left open for a noumenal cause is itself theoretically optional, it is perfectly natural, and even necessary, for us to suppose it. We cannot legitimately assertorically posit or cognize a noumenal cause of outer affection; nevertheless, we quite naturally and automatically form for ourselves a *problematic* concept of such a cause—the idea of unconditioned spontaneous production or freedom. This is in part because outer affection is a brute fact that needs explanation. As we have seen, the notion of an explanation here cuts two ways: one way invokes our understanding alone (naturalistic-causal explanation), and the other invokes our reason as well (rationalistic-causal explanation). Being sensible, discursive human cognizers, we automatically interpret the fact of affection by means of the objectively valid categories and assign it to a phenomenal material causal source. But also being pure rational thinkers, with all the philosophical baggage (some of it perfectly appropriate, some of it excess) that entails, we also quite naturally and automatically suppose that the brute fact of affection can in principle have a purely spontaneous noumenal source. That is, we quite naturally suppose, even over and above its correct physical explanation, that what would be required for a metaphysically complete explanation of affection is an appeal to an ultimate, transcendent, and unconditioned input source for sensibility.

One will wonder, of course, just why our reason leads us—apparently so pointlessly and superfluously—to suppose that the concept of a noumenal cause is philosophically relevant when we already automatically interpret the fact of affection in naturalistic, phenomenal terms. Kant's answer is that we have here a perfect example of our reason's inherent tendency to sublimate the moral impulse. Free or purely spontaneous causation is an a priori presupposition of the moral responsibility that is implicit in all rational human action; and this concept is so centrally important for us that our reason problematically postulates it even in contexts that are not properly practical at all but only theoretical:

I think I perceive that the aim of this natural tendency [towards ideas of pure reason] is to free our concepts from the fetters of experience and from the limits of the mere contemplation of nature so far as at least to open to us a field containing mere objects for the pure understanding that no sensibility can reach, not indeed for the purpose of speculatively occupying ourselves with them (for there we can find no ground to stand on), but in order that practical principles might find some such scope for their necessary expectation and hope and might expand to the universality that reason unavoidably requires from a moral point of view. (P. Ak. iv. 362–3)

Let me now sum up the story I am telling in this subsection. While Kant actually commits no fallacy or inconsistency in his doctrine of affection, he does however leave us with a rather complex five-part doctrine. (1) There exists a primitive cognitive fact—the fact of affection. (2) Applicable to this fact is an objectively valid concept of natural causation, which is in turn applicable only to material objects in space and time, and perfectly suitable for use in scientific causal explanations. (3) But we human beings also have a rational (and ultimately practical) need to try to explain the fact of affection by appeal to a noumenal cause or absolute sufficient ground. (4) In order to attempt to satisfy this rational need, we generate a fully thinkable yet empty or objectively invalid concept of reason that describes a logically possible wholly mind-independent causal source whose inner nature and mode of operation are completely unlike anything we could possibly empirically cognize. (5) This concept has no direct application in theoretical contexts, but on the other hand is essential for our moral thinking and our concept of rational agency.

Even if it is admitted that Kant's theory of affection is internally consistent, however, it may now be thought that Kant has left us with a crucial undischarged arbitrary assumption—or explanatory mystery—in his theory— namely, the very existence of the fact of outer affection: 'In [the B deduction (RH)], however, I still could not abstract from one point—namely, from [the fact (RH)] that the manifold for intuition must already be *given* prior to the synthesis of understanding and independently of it; how [it occurs], however, remains here undetermined' (*CPR* B145). The fact of affection is the fact that we are given sensory content from a source beyond the human mind and therefore cannot generate this content spontaneously. But what sort of fact is this? Certainly it is a *deep* fact about us, not a *comparatively superficial* fact about us. For example, it is a comparatively superficial (albeit very interesting) fact about us that we human beings are constrained to processing information in chunks that have a maximal multiplicity of seven units,

plus or minus two.[75] Nevertheless, we could in principle be much smarter—
by processing information in much larger chunks than we in fact do, and much
faster than we in fact do—and still remain ourselves. The fact of affection, by
sharp contrast, belongs to a special class of crucial constitutive facts or (more
paradoxically expressed) 'transcendental facts' in Kant's general cognitive
semantics, amongst which are 'the fact' (*das Factum*) of the 'reality of the
scientific cognition a priori that we possess, that namely of *pure mathematics*
and *general natural science*' (*CPR* A94/B128); the fact of the irreducible
difference between intuitions (the faculty of sensibility) and concepts (the
faculty of understanding) (*CPR* A67–8/B92–3); the fact that our cognitive
faculty has only two forms of sensibility and twelve discursive categories, no
more and no less (*CPR* B145–6); the fact of the primitive and irreducible psychologically spontaneous synthesizing power of the all-purpose imagination
(*CPR* A78/B103); the fact of 'self-affection' by virtue of which we cognize
ourselves in empirical apperception only as we appear, not as we are (*CPR*
B67–8); and the fact of the original synthetic unity of apperception (*CPR*
A94/B127, A106–7, B131–3). These facts are constitutive or transcendental
facts and not merely accidental or empirical facts, because they determine both
the structure and the scope of our innate generative/productive capacities. Hence
the transcendental facts just mentioned plus the fact of outer affection jointly
have a philosophical force similar to that of the famous 'fact of reason'
(*Factum der Vernunft*) philosophically exploited by Kant in the second
Critique (*CPrR* Ak. v. 56): they determine points at which the otherwise wholly
reasonable demand for further reasons ceases to be reasonable. They are ultimate explanatory starting points, not items in further need of metaphysical
explanation. To ask for a further explanation of a constitutive or transcendental fact would be to ask one question too many. Or, as Kant crisply puts it
in the *Prolegomena*:

How this peculiar property of our sensibility ['according to which it is in its special
way affected by objects that are themselves unknown (*unbekannt*) to it and totally
distinct from those appearances'] is itself possible, or that of our understanding
and of the apperception that is necessarily its basis and also of all thinking, cannot
be further analysed or answered, because it is of them that we are in need for all our
answers and for all our thinking about objects.   (*P.* Ak. iv. 318)

In other words, we cannot without rational incoherence enquire what is behind
constitutive or transcendental facts; and yet at the same time we cannot treat
these facts as explanatory mysteries either. They are the very sources of our
rational ability to explain *anything*. An explanatory mystery is an arbitrary
extrinsic addition to an otherwise coherent body of information. What is

[75] See Miller, 'The Magical Number Seven Plus or Minus Two: Some Limits on our
Capacity for Processing Information'.

partially constitutive of our own nature, however, cannot without self-stultification be regarded as extrinsically imposed.

2.5. Conclusion

The purpose of these first two chapters has been to offer support for my basic interpretive thesis: that Kant's *Critique of Pure Reason* is a treatise in general cognitive semantics. His leading philosophical question is how objective mental representations—more specifically, necessary a priori representations, and most specifically, synthetic a priori judgements—are possible. In precisely this sense Kant's Copernican Revolution introduced the semantic turn into modern philosophy.

Looking backwards from the beginning of the twenty-first century at both the *Critique of Pure Reason* and the historical foundations of analytic philosophy, then, what this very clearly implies is that the debate between Kant and the leading figures of analytic philosophy from Frege to Quine is actually a domestic debate within semantically oriented philosophy. But Kant's transcendental idealism was certainly not regarded as genuine semantics by the leading analytic philosophers—indeed, it was universally regarded as the prime philosophical threat to genuine semantics. According to them, genuine semantics puts up a semi-transparent but wholly impermeable barrier between mind and meaning and also strictly requires the logico-linguistic theory of necessary truth. This important bit of historical irony—that Kant brought about the semantic turn in philosophy yet became the favourite punching bag for the analytic tradition—will be the leading clue for the rest of this book. My thesis is that the main doctrines of the first *Critique* were repeatedly loudly rejected, never actually refuted, and sometimes quietly adopted. Our next task is to look very carefully at what must be in some sense *the* central theme in a tradition that self-consciously styles itself 'analytic': the nature of analyticity.

3.

Analyticity within the Limits of Cognition Alone

Analyticity . . . is a pseudo-concept which philosophy would be better off
without.

W. V. O. Quine[1]

3.0. Introduction

What does the word "analytic" mean in the phrase "analytic philosophy"? Or
putting the same question less telegraphically, what binds the multifarious
intellectual activities of the leading Austro-German and Anglo-American
philosophers from Frege to Quine into a single coherent tradition? One fairly
promising suggestion is that it is these philosophers' root commitment to decompositional or atomistic theorizing—to the method of breaking something down
into its ultimate logical, semantic, psychological, epistemic, or ontological parts.[2]
This does, indeed, capture a good deal of what has actually gone on. Nevertheless, it seems to me that there is a simpler and more illuminating description, one that applies even to those analytic philosophers who on the whole
prefer holistic forms of explanation to atomistic ones (for example, later
Wittgenstein and Quine) or who move back and forth between holistic
strategies and atomistic strategies (for example, early Wittgenstein and Carnap).
My proposal is that, if one were forced to capsulize the analytic tradition from
Frege to Quine in a single sentence or slogan, it would have to be this:

---

[1] Quine, 'Three Grades of Modal Involvement', 171.

[2] See e.g. Hacker, *Wittgenstein's Place in Twentieth-Century Analytic Philosophy*, 3–4;
and Monk, 'What is Analytical Philosophy?', 12. Prime examples of this are Russell's 'On
Denoting' (1905), *Our Knowledge of the External World* (1914), and 'The Philosophy of
Logical Atomism' (1918).

The history of analytic philosophy from Frege to Quine is the history of the rise and fall of the concept of analyticity, whose origins and parameters both lie in Kant's first *Critique*.

In other words, (1) all parts and phases of the analytic tradition from Frege to Quine—however much they may otherwise differ from one another—explicitly exemplify or at least implicitly presuppose a dual concern with semantic issues and with the logico-linguistic theory of necessity; (2) at the centre of these pervasive semantic and logico-linguistico-modal concerns is the concept of an analytic judgement (proposition, statement, sentence, and so on); (3) the origin of that seminal concept is to be found in Kant's *Critique of Pure Reason*; and (4) the thematic development of analytic philosophy from Frege to Quine has been importantly determined by how it has dealt constructively or destructively with Kant's seminal concept.

Here is a thumbnail sketch of the history of analyticity.[3] Kant definitively introduced the concept of an analytic truth in the first *Critique*—although, to be sure, there were important anticipations of it by Locke ('trifling propositions'), Hume ('relations of ideas'), and Leibniz ('*verités de raison*', 'identical propositions', and so on). Kant's conception has seven basic elements. According to it, an analytic truth is a proposition that is (i) necessary, and (ii) a priori, by virtue of either (iii) the containment of its predicate term in its subject term, (iv) the identity of its predicate term with its subject term, or (v) the logical law of non-contradiction together with the fact that its denial always entails a formal contradiction. Further (vi), analyticity itself makes sense only by contradistinction to the notion of a synthetic truth, which in turn comes in two very different flavours—a priori (experience-independent) and a posteriori (experience-dependent). And, finally (vii), all basic truths of philosophy and mathematics are synthetic a priori, not analytic.

With the notable exceptions of some searching critical questions raised by Bolzano in his *Theory of Science* (1837), and Mill's blanket rejection of necessity and apriority in the *System of Logic* (1843), Kant's seven-part doctrine of analyticity remained essentially in place throughout most of the nineteenth century. But in the 1880s and 1890s, the British neo-Hegelians rejected the very idea of a sharp analytic/synthetic distinction. The neo-Hegelians were not only idealists but also thoroughgoing holists about meaning, truth, and belief; and their holism entailed that all propositions are indissolubly analytic in one respect and synthetic in another.[4]

Shortly thereafter, reacting against the neo-Hegelians and Kant alike, the originators of the analytic tradition introduced two root doctrines: (1) that

[3] See esp. Pap, *Semantics and Necessary Truth*, and Proust, *Questions of Form: Logic and the Analytic Proposition from Kant to Carnap*.

[4] See e.g. Bradley, *Principles of Logic*, bk. III, pt. I, ch. vi, pp. 430–54.

there *is* after all a sharp analytic/synthetic distinction, and (2) that Kant's theory of that distinction is unacceptable and therefore must be corrected. This
rejection-and-correction applies not only to Kant's definition of analyticity,
but also to his logic, and to his closely related claims that philosophy and mathematics are synthetic a priori. Broadly speaking, all theories of analyticity in
the analytic tradition from Frege to Quine contain the claim that a proposition (judgement, sentence, statement, and so on) is analytic if and only if it
is true by virtue of the meanings of its terms alone, independently of fact (=
a priori). Despite its catchiness, however, the slogan 'truth by virtue of meaning alone independently of fact' is thoroughly ambiguous—since it does not
tell us precisely what the meaning of the word "meaning" is.[5] In actual practice, then, this gloss has been taken to say that a proposition is analytic if and
only if it is either a truth of elementary logic (that is, first-order polyadic predicate calculus plus identity) or else translatable into a truth of elementary
logic by putting in synonyms for synonyms. This directly indicates the super-
session of Kant's logic by elementary logic. And it indirectly indicates the replacement of Kant's doctrine that the basic truths of philosophy and mathematics
are synthetic a priori, by the successor doctrine that the basic truths of philosophy and mathematics are one-and-all analytic in a purely logico-linguistic
sense. This successor doctrine, in turn, depends directly on the thesis that mathematics is systematically reducible to elementary logic plus something else[6]—
the thesis of logicism.

    The logico-linguistic theory of analyticity held absolute sway until about
1950 or so—and still exerts an enormous residual influence on mainstream
analytic philosophy at the beginning of the twenty-first century.[7] And this is
because it expresses a seemingly stable fusion of Frege's and Carnap's doctrines (see Sections 3.3 and 3.4). Despite its seeming stability, however, the
logico-linguistic theory was vigorously attacked and effectively toppled by
Quine, in four stages: (1) in 1935 in 'Truth by Convention', which featured
the important argument (significantly prefigured, however, by Lewis Carroll
in 1895[8] and Harry Sheffer in 1926[9]) that, in order to apply a conventionalist

---

    [5] Van Cleve correctly points out that this slogan could just as easily cover synthetic a
priori truths as analytic truths; see 'Analyticity, Undeniability, and Truth'.
    [6] Conceptions of what will count as the relevant 'something else' in addition to
elementary logic—Frege's logical definitions and set theory, Russell's theory of types, second-
order logic more generally, modal logic, Carnap's meaning postulates and concept of synonymy, and so on—have, of course, changed significantly over the course of the analytic
tradition. See Sects. 3.3 and 3.4 below.
    [7] See e.g. Boghossian, 'Analyticity Reconsidered', and Harman, 'Analyticity Regained?'
Boghossian argues that an epistemic version of the logico-linguistic theory can be made
to work even if Quine's attack on its metaphysical version is effective; and Harman
defends Quine's blanket rejection of analyticity.
    [8] See Carroll, 'What the Tortoise Said to Achilles'.
    [9] See Sheffer, 'Review of *Principia Mathematica*, Volume I, second edition'.

definition of logical truth, pre-conventional logic must be presupposed; (2) far more influentially and devastatingly in 1951 in 'Two Dogmas of Empiricism', in which he argued that all attempts to account for non-logical analyticity[10] via the concept of synonymy are circular; (3) in 1960 in chapter II of *Word and Object*, where his strategy was to claim that all translational hypotheses concerning non-logical analytical identities across word meanings (whether inter-linguistic, infra-linguistic, or even infra-idiolectic) are based on linguistic behaviour that is underdetermined by sensory evidence and so strictly indeterminate; and finally (4) in 1963 in 'Carnap and Logical Truth', which reprised and recombined the earlier arguments in 'Truth by Convention' and 'Two Dogmas'. Quine's revolutionary second paper was slightly preceded by Morton White's 1950 essay, 'The Analytic and the Synthetic: An Untenable Dualism', which effectively emphasized a Deweyan or pragmatic side of the Quinean critique.

The White–Quine attack directly sponsored many heated discussions of the nature of analyticity and the analytic/synthetic distinction in the 1950s and 1960s.[11] As Quine's radically sceptical conclusions gradually became the conventional wisdom, however, the flow of articles and books on analyticity and syntheticity sharply abated in the 1970s, 1980s, and 1990s and then veered off towards other issues in modal semantics and epistemology.[12] In a forty-year survey article in 1992, Tyler Burge observed that 'no clear reasonable support has been devised for a distinction between truths that depend for their truth on meaning alone and truths that depend for their truth on their meaning together with (perhaps necessary) features of their subject matter'.[13] This concedes complete victory to Quine's critique;[14] and, somewhat more ironically, it returns the analytic tradition full circle to something very like the preanalytic, holistic standpoint of the neo-Hegelians.

It should be clear enough even from this quick sketch that the changing theoretical status and shifting implications of the post-Kantian concept of an

[10] It has sometimes been noted that Quine's attack on the analytic/synthetic distinction leaves purely logical analyticity untouched. See e.g. Boghossian, 'Analyticity Reconsidered', 389 n. 15. I will come back to this important point in Sect. 3.5.

[11] For collections of seminal papers and bibliographies up to 1970, see Harris and Severens (eds.), *Analyticity: Selected Readings*; Sleigh (ed.), *Necessary Truth*; and Sumner and Woods (eds.), *Necessary Truth*. Apart from Quine's and White's papers, see esp. Bennett, 'Analytic–Synthetic'; Gewirth, 'The Distinction between Analytic and Synthetic Truths'; Katz, 'Analyticity and Contradiction in Natural Language'; Grice and Strawson, 'In Defense of a Dogma'; Katz, 'Some Remarks on Quine on Analyticity'; Mates, 'Analytic Sentences'; and Putnam, 'The Analytic and the Synthetic'. But by far the best overall treatment is Pap's 1958 *Semantics and Necessary Truth*.

[12] See e.g. Hanson and Hunter (eds.), *Return of the A Priori*, and Moser (ed.), *A Priori Knowledge*.   [13] Burge, 'Philosophy of Language and Mind: 1950–1990', 9–10.

[14] Of course, not everyone accepts Quine's views; for notable dissent, see Bonjour, *In Defense of Pure Reason*, ch. 3; Katz, *Cogitations*, chs. IV–VI, XIII; and Katz, *The Metaphysics of Meaning*, ch. 5.

analytic truth are effective indicators of the development of analytic philosophy from Frege to Quine. The first or logicistic phase of analytic philosophy
gets properly underway with Frege's deduction-oriented alternative to Kant's
theory of analyticity; the second or linguistic phase is determined by Carnap's
Tractatus-inspired, conventionalistic reinterpretation of Frege's doctrine;[15]
and the third or scientific phase is the direct result of Quine's radically holistic,
behaviouristic, and (to a slightly lesser extent) pragmatic attack on the very
idea of an analytic truth.

Now within the three-phased framework of the analytic tradition up
to Quine—not too surprisingly—Kant's theory of analyticity has been the
direct critical target of logicists, linguistic philosophers, and Quineans alike.[16]
Following suit, Kant scholars have generally been rather uneasy about it
too.[17] The main objections to it boil down to these: (*a*) that Kant employs,
incoherently, several logically independent or even inconsistent criteria of analyticity; (*b*) that his theory is narrowly restricted to judgements or propositions of subject/predicate form; (*c*) that his central appeal to the notion of
conceptual containment is metaphorical at best and unintelligible at worst;
(*d*) that all the criteria of analyticity offered by Kant are psychologistic in character; and, last but certainly not least, (*e*) that Kant's theory fails to explain
the data of analyticity in a way consistent with the major developments in
the analytic tradition from Frege to Quine—Frege's logico-deductive theory
of analyticity, Carnap's logico-linguistico-conventionalist theory of analyticity, and Quine's attack on the analytic/synthetic distinction. These objections
have combined to provide what no doubt seems to most contemporary
philosophers a critical juggernaut. Indeed looked at *that* way, any serious reconsideration of Kant's theory of analyticity at this point in the analytic tradition is bound to seem anachronistic at best and irrelevant at worst.

Nevertheless I believe that seriously reconsidering Kant's theory of analyticity is neither anachronistic nor irrelevant. I will argue that, while Kant does
indeed employ several distinct formulations of his doctrine of analyticity, his
use of these formulations is not after all incoherent, because each merely brings
out a different aspect of a single, internally consistent, defensible Kantian
theory. His theory, moreover, does not actually require a restriction to

[15] The idea that analyticity (or necessity, or apriority) is determined by language
conventions was a shared credo of ideal language philosophers and ordinary language
philosophers alike, whatever their other differences. See e.g. Waismann, *The Principles of
Linguistic Philosophy*.

[16] See e.g. Ayer, *Language, Truth, and Logic*, 77–8; Frege, *The Foundations of Arithmetic*,
99–101; and Quine, 'Two Dogmas of Empiricism', 20–1.

[17] Paton e.g. laconically remarks that 'Kant's theory is not so simple as it looks, and the
nature of analytic *judgement*s is not altogether clear'; see *Kant's Metaphysic of Experience*,
i. 86. See also Allison, *Kant's Transcendental Idealism*, 74–5; Beck, 'Can Kant's Synthetic
Judgments be Made Analytic?', 232–5; and Bennett, *Kant's Analytic*, 4–8.

subject/predicate propositions. And, far from being merely metaphorical or unintelligible, his appeal to the notion of conceptual containment implies a highly sophisticated and highly original theory of conceptual form[18] and conceptual content.[19] Similarly, appearances notwithstanding, Kant's account of analyticity is not psychologistic in any unacceptable sense. Finally, the three central competing accounts of analyticity in the analytic tradition—the positive theories of Frege and Carnap, and Quine's radical scepticism—all fail either to give a plausible and coherent account of analyticity or to undermine Kant's theory.

The proper point of access to the correct interpretation of Kant's theory of analyticity, it seems to me, is the assumption that the first *Critique* is a treatise in general cognitive semantics. If we assume that the concept of analyticity is merely one central notion within the general theory of objective mental representation—that analyticity is possible only within the limits of cognition alone—then everything falls into place. As we just saw, the history of analyticity from Frege to Quine began with the double rejection of the Kantian and neo-Hegelian doctrines, gradually fixed upon the logico-linguistic conception of analyticity, and ended in radical scepticism. The road not taken in this history was a serious defence of the Kantian or cognitivist option. So that is the road I will explore here.

These preliminaries were necessary in order to provide the rationale for my argument strategy. In Section 3.1 I unpack Kant's cognitivist theory of analyticity, with special concentration on his three formulations in terms of the notions of containment, identity, and contradiction. In Section 3.2 I describe Kant's response to the charge of psychologism. I then critically examine Frege's and Carnap's theories in relation to Kant's in Sections 3.3 and 3.4. And finally in Section 3.5 I rehearse Quine's objections to the concept of analyticity and offer a Kantian rebuttal.

3.1. Kant's Cognitivist Theory of Analyticity

It is useful to begin by simply listing some of the propositions said by Kant to be analytic:

---

[18] All logical form is conceptual form, but not all conceptual form is captured by elementary logic. See Sects. 2.1 and 3.1.3.

[19] Kant made two original discoveries about the content of concepts. The first is that the content of a concept has a structural dimension called the 'intension' (*Inhalt*), which introduces a subpropositional level of logical form into the concept itself; and the second is that this content also includes a dimension of cross-possible-worlds reference called the 'comprehension' (*Umfang*), which is irreducible to either actual extension or singular reference. See Sects. 3.1.1, 3.1.2, and 4.2 below.

All bodies are extended.   (*CPR* A7/B11)

a = a, the whole is equal to itself.   (*CPR* B17)

a + b > a, i.e. the whole is greater than its part.   (*CPR* B17)

No predicate attaches to a thing that contradicts [that predicate].   (*CPR* A151/B190)

No unlearned man is learned.   (*CPR* A153/B192)

In everything manifold of which I am conscious I am identical with myself.   (*CPR* B408)

Gold is a yellow metal.   (*P.* Ak. iv. 267)[20]

Every body is divisible.   (OD Ak. viii. 229)

Man is man.   (JL Ak. ix. 111)

These judgements and infinitely many others are the raw data for Kant's theory of analyticity. As he sees it, all cognizers minded like us (which of course includes all linguistically competent cognizers) share the prima facie insight that these propositions and indefinitely many others like them are possessed of the salient property of being analytic. What that salient property is is gradually specified by looking at how such propositions are actually used in our judgement activities, and also at how we would use them across a broad range of thought experiments. Then against the backdrop of Kant's general cognitive semantics, it is wholly reasonable to assume that an epigenetic explanation can be given of this salient property. For this reason, Kant explicitly uses the primitive notion of combinatory synthesis in order to explain the nature of analyticity (*CPR* B130–1). It may seem paradoxical to employ the notion of synthesis in order to explain analyticity, but the whiff of paradox evaporates when we realize two things. First, as we have seen in Chapter 1, for Kant the notion of combinatory synthesis implies an imagination-driven spontaneous pure-apperception-governed, generative and productive mental processing that is perfectly neutral as between the creation of analytic judgements, on the one hand, and of synthetic judgements, on the other. Secondly, Kant's explanatory appeal to combinatory synthesis in fact avoids the pitfall of circularity in explanation, since it avoids the question-begging strategy of attempting to give an analytic definition of analyticity. Indeed, the very possibility of an analytic definition is part of what needs to be explained by the theory of analyticity.

As I have already mentioned, Kant's theory of analyticity employs three distinct formulations of the nature of an analytic truth—in terms of containment, identity, and contradiction. I propose to develop Kant's overall theory

---

[20] The analyticity of this proposition has been challenged by scientific essentialists; see e.g. Kripke, *Naming and Necessity*, 39 and 123 n. 63. See also Hanna, 'A Kantian Critique of Scientific Essentialism'.

by working through each formulation in turn. And there is a progressive method in my pedantic madness. I will argue, first, that each of the first two formulations solves some problems, yet leaves others untreated; and, secondly, that the last formulation, working in tandem with the other two, solves (or at least suitably finesses) all of the outstanding dificulties.

One last point in this connection. For simplicity, in what follows I will adopt Kant's procedure of focusing almost exclusively on affirmative analytic truths (for example, 'Bachelors are unmarried males'). But this focus implies no special constraints on the overall account. For Kant also explicitly countenances negative analytic truth (for example, 'There are no female bachelors'), negative analytic falsity (for example, 'Bachelors are not males'), and affirmative analytic falsity (for example, 'Bachelors are females').[21] Kant's idea is that, if an adequate theory can be developed for affirmative analytic truth, then its extension to the other three types will be fairly trivial.[22]

3.1.1. Analyticity and Containment

The best-known version of Kant's doctrine of analyticity is found in the following passage:

In all judgements in which the relation of a subject to the predicate is thought . . . this relation is possible in two different ways. Either the predicate B belongs to the subject A, as something that is (covertly) contained in this concept A [*in diesem Begriffe A (versteckter Weise) enthalten ist*]; or B lies wholly outside the concept A, although it does indeed stand in connection with it. In the first case I entitle the judgement analytic, in the other synthetic.   (*CPR* A6–7/B10–11)

A few pages later, in the course of explicating synthetic a priori judgements, Kant also remarks that analytic and synthetic a priori judgements alike are 'apodeictic' in that in them 'we are required to join in thought a certain predicate to a given concept, and this necessity is inherent in the concepts themselves' (*CPR* B17).

Now what Kant seems to be driving at in these texts is this:

(CONTAINMENT-1) A subject/predicate proposition is analytic if it is necessary by virtue of the predicate concept's being contained in the subject concept.

Three features of CONTAINMENT-1 stand out immediately. First, the concept of necessity plays a distinctive and ineliminable role. Analytic judgements are apodeictic, and every apodeictic judgement 'expresses logical necessity' (*CPR* A76/B101). Since for Kant there are both analytically and synthetically

---

[21] See Marc-Wogau, 'Kants Lehre vom analytischen Urteil', 142–4.
[22] See n. 75 for this trivial extension of the theory.

necessary propositions, the general concept of necessity is independent of that of analyticity and can therefore be used in the latter's explication.[23] Many theorists of analyticity—especially logical empiricists, but it is an almost universally shared assumption in the analytic tradition after the 1930s—reject the very idea of synthetic necessity.[24] Such theorists must therefore in effect identify the analyticity of a proposition with its necessity,[25] and cannot without circularity explain analyticity in terms of necessary truth. But this is not Kant's problem. Secondly, as many critics of Kant have noticed, CONTAINMENT-1 does not attempt to give a criterion for the analyticity of any proposition whatsoever, but states only that the proposed condition holds for propositions of categorical or subject/predicate form. And, thirdly, whereas a superficial reading of the text at A6–7/B10–11 above might lead one to think that Kant states that a proposition is analytic if and only if its predicate concept is contained in its subject concept, the text actually says instead that a subject/predicate proposition is analytic *if* it is necessary and its predicate concept is contained in its subject concept. So the text lays down a sufficient condition for the analyticity of a proposition, but not a necessary condition.

Most obviously, however, CONTAINMENT-1 leaves interpreters with the apparently unexplicated notion of containment. Critics have often complained that Kant gives no way of explicating conceptual containment other than by appealing to a strained analogy with spatial containment. According to them—and their main spokesman is Frege—Kant crudely holds that an analytic proposition involves 'simply taking out of the box again what we have just put into it'; again, Kant thinks that concepts are contained in other concepts merely 'as beams are contained in a house'.[26] But this complaint is superficial. In the Transcendental Aesthetic, for example, Kant explicitly and sharply distinguishes the conceptual mode of containment from the spatial mode (*CPR* A25/B39–40). So, even if there is a high-level analogy between conceptual and spatial containment (that is, both involve whole–part relations), Kant certainly does not conflate them.

If conceptual containment is not spatial or quasi-spatial, then what sort of containment is it? An oversimplified although strictly correct answer is: the sort of containment peculiar to concepts. In turn, a more sophisticated answer is: Kantian conceptual containment is irreducibly intensional

---

[23] I assume here without further argument that the necessity of an analytic proposition is equivalent to its truth in all possible worlds. This is, of course, Leibnizian or metaphysical necessity. See Sects. 5.1–5.3 for a justification of this assumption, and a discussion of other kinds of necessity.   [24] See Sect. 5.0 for details.

[25] See Beck, 'On the Meta-Semantics of the Problem of the Synthetic A Priori', 94–5. Others have been led to the opposite extreme of logically *detaching* analyticity from necessary truth. See e.g. Katz, 'Analyticity, Necessity, and the Epistemology of Semantics', and Van Cleve, 'Analyticity, Undeniability, and Truth'.

[26] Frege, *The Foundations of Arithmetic*, 101.

containment.[27] And the most sophisticated answer of all is: Kantian conceptual containment is either irreducibly intensional *structural* containment (that is, containment by virtue of embedding subpropositional infraconceptual logical forms) or irreducibly intensional *comprehensional* containment (that is, containment by virtue of sharing cross-possible-worlds extensions).[28] We can bring out these points by comparing, contrasting, and relating the two notions of (1) a concept's being contained in (*enthalten in*) another concept, and of (2) a concept's being contained under (*enthalten unter*) another (JL Ak. ix. 140) (*R.* 2896, 2902, 3043; Ak. xvi. 565, 567, 629). The two distinct dimensions of conceptual 'containment-in' and conceptual 'containment-under' are as important as they are easily overlooked.[29] In order to understand them, we shall have to delve again (see Section 1.4), but this time even more deeply, into Kant's theory of concepts.

The main outlines of Kant's cognitive semantics of concepts can be recovered from these texts:

Every concept must be thought as a representation that is contained in an infinite collection (*Menge*) of different possible representations (as their common characteristic). (*CPR* A25/B40; see also JL Ak. ix. 91)

A concept is always, as regards its form, something universal that serves as a rule. The concept of body, for instance, serves as the rule in our cognition of outer appearances by means of the unity of the manifold that is thought through it. . . . In the case of the perception of something outside of us, the concept of body *necessitates* the representation of extension, and with it [the representations] of impenetrability, shape, etc. (*CPR* A106, emphasis added)

All combination, whether we are conscious of it or not, whether it is a combination of the manifold of intuition or of several concepts, and in the first case either of sensible or non-sensible intuition, is an action of the understanding, which we would designate with the general title *synthesis* . . . Among all representations *combination* is the only one that is not given through objects but can be executed only by the subject itself, since it is an act of its self-activity. It will be easily observed that this action must originally be unitary and equipollent for all combination, and that the dissolution [*Auflösung*], namely *analysis* [*Analysis*], which appears to be its opposite, yet always presupposes it, for where the understanding has not previously combined anything, neither can it dissolve anything, since only *through* [*the understanding*] can something have been given to the power of representation as combined. (*CPR* B130)

An objective perception is cognition (*cognitio*). This is either *intuition* or *concept* . . . The former refers immediately to the object and is singular, the latter refers to it

---

[27] See Beck, 'Remarks on the Distinction between Analytic and Synthetic', 100, and Katz, 'The New Intensionalism', 700.

[28] At this point in my account obviously the parenthetical glosses remain to be explicated. I include them here only to indicate the multifaceted character of Kant's theory of concepts.

[29] The two dimensions are nicely highlighted by Friedman, *Kant and the Exact Sciences*, 67.

mediately by means of a characteristic that several things have in common.   (*CPR* A320/B377)

[The logical essence] includes nothing further than the cognition of all the predicates in regard to which an object is determined *through its concept* . . . If we wish to determine, for example, the logical essence of body, then we do not necessarily have to seek for the data for this in nature; we may direct our reflection to the characteristics that, as essential points (*constitutivae rationes*), originally constitute the basic concept of the thing. For the logical essence is nothing but *the first basic concept of all the necessary characteristics of a thing* (*esse conceptus*).   (JL Ak. ix. 61)

The origin of concepts as to *mere form* rests on reflection and on abstraction from the difference among things that are indicated (*bezeichnet*) by a certain representation. And thus arises the question: *which acts of the understanding constitute a concept?* or, what is the same, *which are involved in the generation of a concept out of given representations?*   (JL Ak. ix. 93)

Every concept, *as partial concept*, is contained in the representation of things; as *ground of cognition, that is, as characteristic*, these things are contained under it. In the former respect, every concept has an *intension* (*Inhalt*), in the other, a *comprehension* (*Umfang*).   (JL Ak. ix. 95)

As one says of a *ground* in general that it contains the *consequence* itself, so one can also say of a concept that as *ground of cognition* it contains all those things under itself from which it has been abstracted—for example, the concept of metal contains under itself gold, silver, copper, and so on. For since every concept, as a universally valid representation, contains that which is common to several representations of various things, all these things, which are to this extent contained under it, can be represented through it. . . . The more things that can be represented through a concept, the greater its sphere (*Sphäre*). Thus the concept *body*, for example, has a greater comprehension than the concept *metal*.   (JL Ak. ix. 96)

Here are the main points. (1) A concept is an objective mental representation that is essentially general, and not singular like an intuition. (2) A concept has both (*a*) an intension made up of partial concepts or characteristics, and (*b*) a sphere or comprehension. The intension is an ordered set of descriptive features; and the sphere or comprehension includes whatever meets the intension's descriptive criteria. (3) A concept's partial concepts or characteristics are contained in its intension. (4) By contrast, contained under that intension are (*a*) every concept more specific than that concept (this is what Kant sometimes calls the concept's '*sphaera notionis*' (BL Ak. xxiv. 240) or *notional* comprehension), and (*b*) the set of all actual or possible things satisfying the intension's descriptive criteria (this is what I will call a concept's *objectual* comprehension). (5) Every concept is the result of a specific generative mental operation, or a rule-governed act of synthesis deriving from the understanding, applied to a finite set of characteristics, each of which is originally abstracted from perceptual indicative representations of objects. (6) This generative procedure of the understanding, encoded in the form of a rule, when taken together with the relevant set of constituent characteristics, makes up the logical or conceptual essence—or what I also call the 'conceptual microstructure'[30]—of that empirical concept. (7) The constituent characteristics of a conceptual microstructure are *necessary* parts of that concept.

To say that a concept has a microstructure that constitutes it is to say that it incorporates its own infra-conceptual 'architecture': 'Human reason is by nature architectonic—that is, it considers all cognitions as belonging to a possible system . . .' (*CPR* A474/B502). The 'possible system' in the case of a single concept is its subpropositional unity of characteristics organized under transcendental logico-categorial rules. In particular, the characteristics embedded in a concept's logical essence are either 'coordinate' or else 'subordinate' with respect to one another (JL Ak. ix. 59). This is to say that the characteristics embedded within the internal structure of a concept are either horizontally or vertically related in a logical sense.

Characteristics are horizontally related or coordinate when they express some semantically coherent and partially overlapping but logically independent[31] pair of concepts within a total set of such concepts (say, RED and ROSE). The limits of coordination are reached when two concepts exclude one another either (i) through sortal incoherence (as with GREEN and IDEA), or (ii) through their being mutually contradictory (as with ROUND and SQUARE, or RED and NON-RED), or (iii) through their being intensively distinct determinates under a single qualitative determinable (as with RED and GREEN, in relation to COLOUR).[32]

By contrast, a characteristic $c1$ is vertically related or subordinate to a characteristic $c2$ (say, $c1$ = ROSE and $c2$ = FLOWER) when $c2$ is related by species inclusion to characteristic $c1$: $c2$ is a necessary condition of $c1$, and of some coordinates of $c1$ as well. Otherwise put, $c1$ is contained under $c2$, but $c2$ is not contained under $c1$. Since in this way $c1$ is subordinate to $c2$, but $c2$ is not subordinate to $c1$, then $c2$ is 'wider' (superordinate) and $c1$ is 'narrower' in the sense that $c2$ is less specific and more generic than $c1$.

The horizontal and vertical structural relations of characteristics do not fully exhaust the scope of the notion of conceptual microstruture, however. In 'The Jäsche Logic', in his reply to Eberhard, and again in a letter to Reinhold, Kant also indicates that some of the characteristics within a given conceptual essence are more basic than others (JL Ak. ix. 60–1; see also OD Ak. viii. 229 and *PC* Ak. xi. 34–5). For example, he claims that the concept TRIANGLE

---

[30] For a similar idea of subpropositional, infra-conceptual structure, although in a purely linguistic framework, see Katz, *Semantic Theory*.

[31] Coordination is not strictly required for the inclusion of characteristics in a given conceptual microstructure, however, but only for the inclusion of characteristics in an analytic definition. Analytic definitions require non-redundancy as between characteristics (JL Ak. ix. 144–5).

[32] See Prior, 'Determinables, Determinates, and Determinants', and Searle, 'Determinables and Determinates'.

immediately contains the characteristic THREE SIDED as a part of its analytic definition, which in turn immediately entails THREE ANGLED by containment-in (*CPR* A303/B359); but THREE ANGLED does not itself automatically yield THREE SIDED. Similarly, the concept BODY immediately contains EXTENDED as a part of its analytic definition, which in turn immediately entails DIVIS-IBLE by containment-in; but again, DIVISIBLE does not alone yield EXTENDED. Not every part of a concept's essence is part of its analytic definition. More precisely, a characteristic is 'primitive' (*primitive*) or 'constitutive' (*konstitut-ive*) in relation to a given conceptual essence if and only if it belongs to that essence as a part of the concept's definition, and is immediately contained in no other characteristics belonging to that essence. The non-primitive, medi-ately entailed, or non-definitional characteristics within a given conceptual essence are called 'attributes'.[33]

For convenience, I will continue to represent concepts and subconceptual characteristics in small capital letters; and I will also represent the conceptual microstructure of a given empirical concept—say, BACHELOR—as an ordered conjunction of constitutive or attributive characteristics enclosed between angled brackets, for example:

BACHELOR = <ADULT + UNMARRIED + MALE>.

In this connection Kant helpfully provides us with several indications of the microstructure of the empirical concept BODY (*CPR* A20–1/B35, A106):

BODY = <EXTENDED + DIVISIBLE + HAS A SHAPE + IMPENETRABLE + COLOURED + SUBSTANTIAL + ENTERS INTO DYNAMICAL RELATIONS + . . . etc.>.

Each of these characteristics specifies a categorially sorted, horizontally and vertically ordered, necessary feature of empirical bodies, even if (as in the case of EXTENDED and DIVISIBLE) some characteristics are more primitive than others. Kant calls characteristics that have these properties 'analytic character-istics' (JL Ak. ix. 59; see also *R.* 2290; Ak. xvi. 301). By contrast, the predicate HEAVY is merely an inessential or 'synthetic' characteristic associated with the concept BODY, and does not belong to its conceptual microstructure (*CPR* B11).[34] The distinction between synthetic and analytic characteristics is closely related to the important distinction between a 'determination'

---

[33] Thus attributes are not synthetic characteristics but instead secondarily embedded analytic characteristics; and this is the nub of Kant's reply to Eberhard, a Leibnizian critic of Kant's theory. See Allison, *The Kant–Eberhard Controversy*, 46–75, and Beck, 'Analytic and Synthetic Judgments before Kant', 95–100.

[34] As a student of Newton, Kant of course knew that heaviness or weight is a function of gravitational attraction, which is in turn a function of the sizes of bodies and their dis-tances from one another; hence one need only conceive of a body situated outside any gravitational field, or placed equidistantly between two or more identical gravitational sources, in order logically to imagine a weightless body. 'All bodies are heavy' is therefore neither analytic nor necessary.

(*Bestimmung*), a 'determining predicate', or a 'real predicate' (*reales Prädikat*), on the one hand, and a merely 'logical predicate' (*CPR* A598–9/B626–7), on the other. A predicate (= a concept or partial concept) is a determination or real predicate just in case predicating it of a subject concept adds to or supplements the semantic content of the subject concept by changing its semantic structure and narrowing the set of things to which it applies; by contrast, a predicate is merely logical just in case predicating it of a subject concept neither changes the semantic structure of that concept nor narrows the set of things to which the concept applies. Strictly speaking, only analytic, logical characteristics can be really contained in any concept; synthetic, real characteristics merely 'belong to it' (*zu ihm gehören*) (*CPR* A718/746).[35]

In this connection, Lewis White Beck aptly points out that the distinction between analytic and synthetic characteristics invokes a

tacit distinction between two types of concepts, one being a concept of a highly refined analytical or abstractive unity, subject to strict definition, the other being a looser complex of representations, more or less loosely held together and expandable through the accretion of new experience or subject to restriction in content.[36]

Beck's good point is in need of some slight rewording, for it seems to suggest that the two types of concepts are exclusive of one another. In fact, however, the analytic-concept/synthetic-concept difference is a relative distinction applying to all concepts, pure or empirical: every concept is analytic in one way[37] and synthetic in another. Its analytic aspect comprises its conceptual essence, whereas its synthetic aspect yields a complement of conceptually non-essential features or accidents.

Kant also discusses the analytic versus synthetic characteristics distinction under the somewhat misleading rubric of 'given' (*gegebene*) versus 'made' (*gemachte*) concepts (JL Ak. ix. 93, 141–2, and VL Ak. xxiv. 914–15). What is misleading is the impression it leaves that analytic or given concepts are somehow primitively unmade and original to the mind, like Cartesian or Leibnizian innate ideas. Yet the given concept is a generative cognitive product every bit as much as the made or synthetic concept; it differs from the made concept only in the semantic ground of its cognitive production, and consequently in its form and content. Made concepts depend crucially on intuition and its a priori figurative synthesis (*synthesis speciosa*) (*CPR* B151) in the dedicated productive imagination (see Sections 1.3 and 1.4). By contrast, the ultimate generative ground of given concepts is an intellectual synthesis (*synthesis intellectualis*) of understanding, which is directly expressed in the

[35] See also Allison, 'The Originality of Kant's Distinction between Analytic and Synthetic Judgements', 331–2, 337–41.
[36] Beck, 'Can Kant's Synthetic Judgements be made Analytic?', 234.
[37] This is even true of the pure concepts of the understanding. Although logically basic, they are also at least partially decomposable (*CPR* A82–3/B108–9).

pure general logical forms of judgement under the original synthetic unity of apperception (*CPR* B151–2).

The theory of the intellectual generation of concepts is the key to Kant's theory of analyticity, since it explains the notion of a conceptual microstructure or essence—and, as Arthur Pap correctly remarks, 'to clarify Kant's concept of analyticity is the same as to clarify the expression "essence of a concept"'.[38] One crucial connection between the theory of conceptual essences and analyticity is this. To carry out an analytic predication is, in a great many[39] cases, merely to assert the result of a 'decomposition' (*Zergliederung*) (*CPR* A5/B9)[40] of a conceptual essence. This is because the cognitive operation of decomposition is the precise inverse of intellectual concept generation and thereby consists in systematically revealing a conceptual microstructure—in breaking down the essence of a concept into at least some (and in the ideal or limiting case, all) of its ordered constituent analytic characteristics.[41] It is important to emphasize, however, that a given decomposition need not be complete. It is not normally possible for finite thinkers like us to carry out the exhaustive exposure of the essence of a concept. Hence a decomposition of a concept may legitimately reflect any part of its conceptual essence, up to the point at which it is sufficiently articulated for the theoretical purposes of the thinker (VL Ak. xxiv. 916).

On the basis of conceptual decomposition, an analytic proposition is automatically framed or frameable:[42]

If I say, for instance, 'All bodies are extended', then this is an analytic judgement. For I do not need to go beyond the concept that I combine with the word "bodies",[43] in order to find that extension is connected with [that concept], but rather I need only to decompose that concept—that is, become conscious to myself of the manifold (*Mannigfaltigen*) that I always think in it—in order to encounter this predicate therein; it is therefore an analytic judgement.   (*CPR* A7/B11)[44]

---

[38] Pap, *Semantics and Necessary Truth*, 32.

[39] But not in all cases. See Sects. 3.1.2 and 3.1.3 for examples of analytic propositions whose truth is based on concept identity or the principle of non-contradiction, but not strictly on containment-in.

[40] Kant also calls this operation 'development' (*Entwickelung*) (JL Ak. ix. 111) or 'expounding' (*Exponieren*) (JL Ak. ix. 142).

[41] Kant distinguishes carefully between decomposition and 'exposition' (*Exposition, Erörterung*) (*CPR* A729/757 and JL Ak. ix. 141–3). Decomposition breaks down concepts into their analytic characteristics only; exposition breaks down concepts into their analytic characteristics *together with* their synthetic characteristics. Thus an exposition is 'the clear, though not necessarily exhaustive, presentation of what belongs to [i.e. not merely what is *contained in*] a concept' (*CPR* A23/B38).

[42] Longuenesse's discussion of conceptual content very usefully focuses on how the decompositional structure of concepts supports analytic proofs, especially syllogistic ones; see *Kant and the Capacity to Judge*, 50.

[43] Here I am following the A edition instead of the B.

[44] This formulation has often been regarded as unacceptably psychologistic. I will argue in Sect. 3.2 that it is not.

Analytic predication is the two-step operation of first detaching, by means of decomposition, any partial concept contained in the conceptual essence, and then secondly ascribing that essential conceptual part, or analytic characteristic, to the whole conceptual essence. In this way, analytic predication is the paradigm case of 'concept-to-concept' predication.[45] To illustrate this, Kant gives us a more explicit description of the semantic structure of 'All bodies are extended': 'An example of an *analytic* proposition is, to everything *x*, to which the concept of body $(a + b)$ belongs, belongs also *extension* (b)' (JL Ak. ix. 111). Following up on Kant's interesting idea that propositions and concepts can be pictured or diagrammed in language, and using the representational conventions for concepts that I adopted above, we can then schematically represent the proposition (BE) 'All bodies are extended' as:

[(All *x*) (BODY*x* = < . . . etc. + EXTENDED*x*> pred EXTENDED*x*)].

In this symbolism, the outermost square brackets enclose a propositional content. The symbol "(All *x*) (. . . *x* . . .)" is a universal quantifier. (Later, I will similarly use "(Some *x*) (. . . *x* . . .)" to represent a particular quantifier.) Concept words, as before, are in small capital letters. The bound variable *x* ranges over the comprehension of the concept denoted by the concept word to which *x* is appended. The identity sign stands for identity of concepts. Also, as before, angled brackets enclose the decompositional content of a concept, the several constituent characteristics of which are joined by "+". And "pred" stands for an operator on concepts that predicates the concept denoted by the concept word on the right-hand side of "pred", of the concept denoted by the concept word on the left-hand side of "pred". The whole expression thus means the proposition to the effect that the concept of being extended is predicated of the concept of being a body, which in turn contains (along with other subconcepts) the concept of being extended as an essential decompositional part.

In this way, the linguistic schema of (BE) clearly and distinctly displays the containment-in relation between subject concept and predicate concept, since the predicate concept EXTENDED is revealed through predication to be essentially included as a member of the complex of characteristics making up the conceptual microstructure of the subject concept BODY. Analytic predication based on containment-in is thus—to borrow an apt Quinean term—'essential predication'.[46] Each analytic proposition that is true by virtue of containment-in is *necessarily* true, because what it says is that its predicate term belongs to the conceptual manifold of a subject term that contains this very predicate term as an intrinsic or essential part.

There is more, however, to the containment theory of analyticity than the relation of containment-in. Containment-in involves the necessary relation

---

[45] See Sect. 1.5 for the distinction between concept-to-concept predication and concept-to-object predication. [46] Quine, 'Carnap and Logical Truth', 128.

between conceptual wholes and their essential parts. But the partial concepts or characteristics included in the conceptual microstructure also necessarily bear reference relations to objects. This object relatedness is what I represented just above as the bound variable x assigned to concept terms in the schema of the proposition (BE). The bound variable for concept terms is closely related to, but still in one important way distinct from, the transcendental object = X. As the generic transcendental object of representation, the transcendental object = X is the Kantian *variable of representation*, ranging over merely thinkable (noumenal) and experienceable objects alike. But, as we saw in Section 2.2, Kant's doctrine of objective validity entails that, in order to be fully meaningful or possessed of a truth value, a representation must have application to some possible or actual objects of human experience. Hence the bound variable for concept terms, or the Kantian *variable of quantification* as it occurs in objectively valid propositions, has an ontic commitment[47] satisfying the requirement that the relevant concepts and propositions have application to objects of possible experience. It should be noted particularly that it does not follow from this that the variable of quantification necessarily ranges *only* over objects of possible experience; rather it follows that it necessarily ranges *at least* over objects of possible experience. The total universe of discursive cognition must therefore contain objects of possible experience; but not every possible world within that total universe has to contain nothing but objects of possible experience.

This is closely connected with an important and unusual feature of Kant's theory of concepts, which has been mentioned in passing already. The characteristic or partial concept functions as a ground of cognition when it determines both the set of objective representations partially constituted by a given characteristic, and also the set of actual or possible objects represented by those representations. Now those characteristic-constituted objective representations are themselves concepts. Therefore the comprehension of a given concept will always include not just the actual or possible objects instantiating the concept (which I called the 'objectual comprehension') but also every concept that is more specific than the given concept (which I called the 'notional comprehension').[48] The total set of concepts, ordered in relations of higher/lower and coordination, form a conceptual 'series' (JL Ak. ix. 96–100). In this series,

---

[47] See Quine, 'On What There Is', and *Word and Object*, 238–43. Ontic commitment is how bound variables of quantification range in an unmediated way over domains of objects.

[48] Friedman holds that the comprehension or *Umfang* of a Kantian concept is made up solely of other concepts; see *Kant and the Exact Sciences*, 68, 307. Nevertheless Kant states explicitly (JL Ak. ix. 95–6) that a concept has a comprehension in so far as 'things are contained under it' (*Dinge unter ihm enthalten*), and that a concept's comprehension is increased 'the more the things that stand under a concept and can be thought through it' (*je mehr Dinge unter ihm stehen und durch ihn gedacht werden können*). See also BL Ak. xxiv. 239. A Kantian comprehension is a hybrid intensional entity.

higher concepts are contained in lower concepts, while lower concepts are contained under higher concepts, as Kant explicitly points out: 'The lower concept is not contained *in* the higher, for it contains *more* in itself than does the higher; it is contained *under* it, however, because the higher contains the ground of cognition of the lower' (JL Ak. ix. 98).

For simplicity's sake, I will focus mainly on the part of the comprehension of a concept that is made up solely of objects. This objectual comprehension is, in effect, the result of treating the concept's intension as a function mapping from possible worlds into corresponding indefinitely large sets of possible objects. For readers of Frege, this general idea should be very familiar. Frege famously argued in 1892 that linguistic meaning has two distinct aspects, 'sense' (*Sinn*) and 'Meaning' (*Bedeutung*); that sense is the 'mode of givenness' (*Art des Gegebenseins*) of the Meaning; that Meaning is the reference or extension of an expression (what it stands for), which can remain the same across two or more expressions while the sense or mode of givenness varies; that sense uniquely determines Meaning; and that an expression can have a sense even if it has no actually existing Meaning.[49] The Kantian doctrine of containment-under, when restricted to all the possible objects represented by a concept, is equivalent to the doctrine that sense uniquely determines Meaning. Conceptual *Inhalt* (intension) uniquely determines conceptual *Umfang* (objectual comprehension).[50]

Why should we fuss about objectual comprehensions anyway? Well, quite apart from the analytical decomposition of a concept, there is another Kantian route to analyticity—one that relies exclusively on containment-under. To show this, one need only describe how the objectual comprehension of the subject concept in an analytic proposition relates to the objectual comprehension of the predicate concept. The predicate concept is contained in the subject concept only if either the comprehension of the subject concept falls within the total comprehension of the predicate concept, or (in the symmetrical case) the comprehensions of the two concepts are entirely shared. Since concepts, as intensions, uniquely determine objectual comprehensions, it will follow immediately that every possible thing that exemplifies all of the constituent characteristics of the subject concept must also exemplify the predicate concept. This is because in an analytic proposition true by containment-in, the predicate concept simply *is* one of the constituent characteristics of the subject concept. So, if the predicate is contained in the subject, then necessarily every member of the objectual comprehension of the subject is contained under the predicate.

[49] See Frege, 'On Sense and Meaning' and 'Comments on Sense and Meaning'. See also Dummett, 'Frege's Distinction between Sense and Reference', and Carl, *Frege's Theory of Sense and Reference*.

[50] See C. I. Lewis's 'The Modes of Meaning', where Lewis argues that Frege erred in thinking that sense uniquely determines the actual-world extensions of general terms; instead, sense uniquely determines only their cross-possible-worlds extensions, or comprehensions.

Whenever the comprehension of a concept $C1$ and the comprehension of a concept $C2$ are wholly shared, then $C1$ and $C2$ are in Kant's terminology 'convertible' concepts (JL Ak. ix. 98). As we have seen already, whenever the comprehension of a concept $C1$ falls entirely within the comprehension of a concept $C2$, but not conversely, then concept $C1$ is the lower concept and $C2$ is the higher concept. So, in an analytic proposition in which the predicate concept is contained in the subject concept, then either the subject concept and the predicate concept are convertible, or else the subject concept is subordinated (as lower or narrower concept) to the predicate concept (as higher or wider concept). For convenience, let us call the relation between two concepts such that they are either convertible or else the first is contained under the second, 'comprehensional overlap'. With this idea in hand, we are now in a position to give a more refined version of Kant's containment formulation:

> (CONTAINMENT-2) A subject/predicate proposition is analytic if it is necessary by virtue of (1) the predicate concept's being contained in the subject concept, and (2) the subject concept's and the predicate concept's being related by comprehensional overlap.

This version, it will be noted, has two clauses: it thus expresses the conjunction of the two notions of containment-in and containment-under. On Kant's account, therefore, the necessary proposition that bodies are extended is analytic precisely because the subconcept or characteristic EXTENDED can be detached by decomposition from, and essentially predicated of, the microstructure of the complex concept BODY; and also because the comprehension of BODY falls entirely within the comprehension of EXTENDED.

It should be obvious by now that Kant's containment formulation of analyticity is neither vague nor based on any specious analogy with spatial containment; on the contrary, it gives a clear, systematic, strongly intensional, and cognitivist account of analyticity. This is reflected in Kant's appeals (i) to the basic distinction between conceptual intension and comprehension, (ii) to the idea of synthetically generated conceptual essences or microstructures, (iii) to the thesis that comprehensions include not only actual but possible objects of cognition, and especially (iv) to the notion of strongly modal or essential connections between whole and partial concepts on the one hand, and between overlapping comprehensions on the other. The containment-in relation, which is sufficient for analyticity, depends directly on the conceptual microstructure of the subject term. And secondly, equally sufficient for analyticity, the partial or complete containment-under relation between the objectual comprehensions of terms depends directly on the Kantian doctrine that *Inhalt* uniquely determines *Umfang*. Nevertheless, CONTAINMENT-2 presents certain difficulties. Let us look briefly at two of them.

The first problem arises in connection with necessary propositions such as (TT) 'Triangulars are trilaterals', which I will understand to mean: 'All three-angled closed rectilinear plane figures are three-sided closed rectilinear plane figures'—reserving the word "triangle" for the expression of the concept TRIANGLE, which contains both THREE ANGLED and THREE SIDED as analytic characteristics. One might easily think that for Kant such a proposition as (TT) would be synthetic;[51] but in fact he regards it as definitely analytic[52] in the sense that the concepts THREE-ANGLED CLOSED RECTILINEAR PLANE FIGURE and THREE-SIDED CLOSED RECTILINEAR PLANE FIGURE are essentially linked by virtue of their conceptual content alone:

Give a philosopher the concept of a triangle, and let him try to find out in his own way how the sum of its angles might be related to a right angle. He has nothing but the concept of a figure enclosed by three straight lines, and *in it* the concept of equally many angles. Now he may reflect on this concept as long as he wants, yet he will never produce anything new. He can analyse and make distinct the concept of a straight line or of an angle or of the number three, but he can never arrive at any properties that do not already lie in these concepts.   (*CPR* A716/B744, emphasis added)

In the case of the triangle the three angles are just as necessary and indispensable as the three sides.   (BL Ak. xxiv. 115; see also JL Ak. ix. 60–1 and *R.* 3220; Ak. xvi. 718)

According to CONTAINMENT-2, the proposition that triangulars are trilaterals is analytic, because the subject concept and the predicate concept have the same comprehensions and so are related by comprehensional overlap. But the problem is that the two concepts have different conceptual microstructures: one contains THREE ANGLED, the other THREE SIDED. Now according to Kant's distinction between constitutive characteristics and attributes, although the three-sidedness of a triangle immediately analytically entails its three-angledness by containment-in, the converse is not the case. And, quite apart from Kant, it seems obvious that the concepts of being angled and being sided are not contained in one another. So in 'Triangulars are trilaterals' the predicate term will fail to be contained in the subject term, as apparently required by the containment theory. Hence it appears that 'Triangulars are trilaterals' is both analytic and non-analytic.[53]

A second problem with CONTAINMENT-2 lies in Kant's (putative) assumption that all analytic propositions are of categorical or subject/predicate

---

[51] It is important to remember that, although Kant holds that 'mathematical judgements, without exception, are synthetic' (*CPR* B14), nevertheless 'a few principles presupposed by the geometrician are actually analytic' because they are 'links in the chain of method' (*CPR* B16–17). He gives as instances of the latter such propositions as 'a = a' and '(a + b) > a'; but analytic definitions of geometric concepts would be included as well.

[52] See Marc-Wogau, 'Kants Lehre vom analytischen Urteil', 151–2, and Beck, 'Analytic and Synthetic Judgments before Kant', 91 n. 42.

[53] It might be thought that this problem arises only for mathematical propositions. But precisely the same phenomenon of analyticity without containment-in is present in such non-mathematical propositions as 'Divisible bodies are extended bodies', 'Truth is the contradictory of falsity', etc.

form. But, so the objection goes, quite clearly there are many propositions that are analytic but not of subject/predicate form. This is especially evident in the case of logical truths—for example, 'If Socrates is mortal, then Socrates is mortal'. Logical truths are true by virtue of their logical form alone. Or to use a more philosophically pregnant formulation deriving from Bolzano and Quine,[54] logical truths are propositions that come out true under *every* possible uniform reinterpretation of their non-logical constants. Most, if not all, logical truths fall outside the boundaries drawn by CONTAINMENT-2, because they are not categorical propositions (even if they include subparts that are of subject/predicate form). Propositions of this type will include any logical truth taking the form of a conditional, a biconditional, a disjunction (for example, the law of excluded middle), or a negation (for example, the law of non-contradiction).

Now one might think that Kant has a simple response open to him. He could simply insist that logical truths are not analytic truths in his sense. Unfortunately for this dodge, however, Kant also holds that all the truths of logic—that is, all the truths of what he regarded as logic—are analytically true (*CPR* A59–60/B83–4, A151–2/B190–1). Taking up another even more desperate line of response, he could try to translate all logical truths into subject/predicate form. But, despite Kant's notorious fondness for Aristotelian–Scholastic logic, he obviously does not feel himself driven to this reductive extremity, since he both explicitly chides those logicians who forget in their definitions of 'judgement' that not all judgements are categorical (*CPR* B141 n.), and also insists that hypothetical and disjunctive propositions are irreducible in form to categorical propositions (JL Ak. ix. 105). Hence Kant is apparently caught in a gross inconsistency. By virtue of his logical theory, all logical truths must be analytic; but, by virtue of CONTAINMENT-2, most logical truths would seem not to be analytic.

Unless Kant can solve these two problems—that is, how to account for categorical analytic truths not falling under the criterion of containment-in, and how to account for non-categorical analytic truths—his theory of analyticity is in serious trouble. So should we abandon his theory? Not yet. There is an obvious strategy for solving the two problems: simply expand the scope of the theory beyond CONTAINMENT-2. My claim will be that Kant quite explicitly does this. On the one hand, this interpretation adequately motivates the otherwise seemingly redundant and therefore puzzling appeals that Kant makes to other formulations of analyticity. And, on the other hand, this theory expansion is perfectly legitimate given the fact, noted at the beginning of this section, that the containment theory clearly provides only a sufficient condition of analyticity, not a necessary condition. The way is then open for Kant

---

[54] See Bar-Hillel, 'Bolzano's Definition of Analytic Propositions'; Bolzano, *Theory of Science*, sect. 148, pp. 191–3; Quine, 'Truth by Convention', 79–81; and Sect. 3.5 below.

to propose, over and above the containment formulation and by virtue of his other formulations, a super-theory of analyticity that captures not only all the analytic propositions true by virtue of CONTAINMENT-2, but also all other analytic propositions of any logical form whatsoever. In Sections 3.1.2 and 3.1.3 I will argue that Kant's identity and contradiction formulations jointly supply this super-theory.

3.1.2. Analyticity and Identity

In the first *Critique*, in tandem with his containment formulation, Kant supplies another formulation that explicitly invokes the notion of identity (*Identität*). And in 'The Jäsche Logic' a formulation in terms of identity is even given as the primary description of the nature of an analytic proposition. Here are those two texts:

Analytic judgments are . . . those in which the connection of the predicate with the subject is thought through identity . . . If I say, for instance, 'All bodies are extended,' then this is an analytic judgement.   (*CPR* A7/B10–11)

Propositions whose certainty rests on *identity* of concepts (of the predicate with the notion of the subject) are called *analytic* propositions.   (JL Ak. ix. 111)

The main idea here seems straightforward, and we can give an initial formulation of Kant's identity doctrine as follows:

(IDENTITY-1) A subject/predicate proposition is analytic if it is necessary by virtue of its predicate concept's being identical with its subject concept.

Two things are worth noticing right away. First, as in the case of the containment theory, Kant restricts IDENTITY-1 to subject/predicate propositions. Secondly, again as in the case of the containment theory, he states that a subject/predicate proposition is analytic if—but he does not say "only if"—it is necessary[55] because its predicate concept is identical with its subject concept. So he is providing here merely another sufficient condition for analyticity and not a necessary condition. Even with these qualifications, however, the precise sense in which the two concepts in a categorical analytic proposition are identical does not at all lie on the surface of the texts, but needs to be spelled out carefully, via two points of clarification.

First, we must understand that the relevant notion of identity for Kant is not objectual or numerical identity—the purely extensional notion of a sheer coincidence between a thing and itself. Nor is it—as in Frege's mature logic—the partially intensional notion of a sheer coincidence between a thing and itself, mediated by the senses of the same or of different names of that

---

[55] More precisely, what he says is that its 'certainty' (*Gewißheit*) rests on identity. And, according to Kant, objective certainty entails necessity (*CPR* A2; see also JL Ak. ix. 66).

thing.[56] It is instead the fully intensional notion of an identity relation between two conceptual contents. This becomes manifest when we recognize that for Kant the non-logical constants in instantiations of the logical law of identity—which Kant expresses as '$a = a$' (*CPR* B17)—do not stand directly for things at all but instead only for concepts. This is epitomized in Kant's favourite example of an instance of the law of identity, (MM) 'Man is man' (JL Ak. ix. 111),[57] which is clearly an assertion of conceptual identity, not objectual identity.

Secondly, on a superficial reading, one might think that Kant's identity theory admits as analytic only such simple identity propositions as (MM), in which the subject concept of the identity proposition just *is* the predicate concept. But it is clear from the passages quoted above that propositions such as (BE) 'Bodies are extended' are meant to be included under IDENTITY-1. Indeed, Kant distinguishes carefully in 'The Jäsche Logic' between 'tautological' analytic propositions such as (MM) and analytic propositions such as (BE), which are 'identical *implicite*' (JL Ak. ix. 111). Tautological analytic propositions are those for which the identity of concepts is wholly explicit in the logical surface grammar of the proposition, whereas implicitly identical propositions are those for which conceptual identity depends on the decompositional structure of the subject concept.[58] Here we can see that the predicate concept of (BE) is implicitly identical with the subject concept simply by being identical with some microstructural conceptual *part* of the subject concept.

---

[56] See Frege, 'On Sense and Meaning', 157–8, 176–7.

[57] Actually, it is misleading to talk about 'the' law of identity for Kant. He not only recognizes that there are several different 'identity concepts' (*R.* 5726; Ak. xviii. 337–8), but also that there is a fundamental difference between the analytic law of identity (identity of concepts) and the synthetic law of identity (identity of objects). Identity propositions involving singular terms for objects must include empirical or pure intuition. The concept of synthetic identity comprehends the identity of actual empirical individuals (*CPR* A263–4/B319–20), equality relations in arithmetic, and congruence relations in geometry. Leibniz's identity laws (i.e. the identity of indiscernibles, and the indiscernibility of identicals), as laws of objectual identity, are synthetic for Kant, not analytic, since they always implicitly invoke spatiotemporal factors—or what Kant in his early treatise 'A New Elucidation of the First Principles of Metaphysical Cognition' (1755) calls 'external properties' (NE Ak. i. 409).

[58] In an essay written in 1791 but for various reasons not published until 1804, *What Real Progress has Metaphysics made in Germany since the Time of Leibniz and Wolff?*, Kant says that tautologically identical propositions are not genuinely analytic (*RP* Ak. xx. 322). This apparent turnaround can be discounted when we remember that the rhetorical strategy of this essay is to distinguish Kant's own views from those of Leibniz and Wolff as sharply as possible; hence anything in his doctrine of analyticity that even suggested the Leibnizian reduction of all true propositions to tautological identities would be naturally downplayed.

This of course raises the crucial question of the criterion of identity for concepts.[59] And that in turn involves a Kantian doctrine whose proper formulation is again somewhat disguised by the texts quoted above. According to Kant, there are in fact two distinct criteria of identity for concepts—or, correspondingly, two distinct types or levels of concept identity. One identity criterion appeals to the notion of a concept's objective reference across all logically possible sets of circumstances. In this sense, two concepts are identical just in case they are 'convertible' or have mutually shared comprehensions (JL Ak. ix. 98). More precisely put, let us say that a concept $C1$ and a concept $C2$ are 'comprehensionally identical' (*c*-identical) if and only if every logically possible object falling under $C1$ falls under $C2$, and conversely. Any two *c*-identical concepts will thus occur in true strongly modal biconditional propositions of the form,

$$\text{(Necessarily) (All } x) \ (C1x \text{ if and only if } C2x).$$

The rationale for isolating *c*-identity as the first criterion of Kantian conceptual identity is manifest when we look more closely at the different sorts of analytic proposition. *C*-identity obviously obtains in cases of propositions in which a complex predicate term is used to give an analytic definition (JL Ak. ix. 141) of a subject term—as in 'Bachelors are unmarried adult males'; for here the definitionally related concepts BACHELOR and UNMARRIED ADULT MALE could hardly fail to occur in a true strongly modal biconditional. So too *c*-identity manifestly obtains in tautological propositions such as (MM). But, most importantly for our purposes, *c*-identity also obtains in propositions such as (TT) 'Triangulars are trilaterals'. The members of the concept pair THREE-ANGLED CLOSED RECTILINEAR PLANE FIGURE and THREE-SIDED CLOSED RECTILINEAR PLANE FIGURE share comprehensions, and occur in a true strongly modal biconditional, despite the fact that they are not quite microstructurally the same. Kant's criterion of *c*-identity is thus relatively rough-grained—it identifies concepts strictly by virtue of their convertibility and does not discriminate between concepts that share comprehensions but do not share exactly the same conceptual microstructure.

But not all conceptual identity is rough-grained. When two concepts, in addition to being *c*-identical, also share the same set of partial concepts or characteristics, ordered in the same way, I shall say that they are 'microstructurally identical' or '*m*-identical'. More precisely, two concepts are *m*-identical if and only if they decompose to exactly the same conceptual microstructure under

---

[59] Pap correctly observes that 'the problem of philosophical semantics which is implicit in Kant's statement about the relation of subject and predicate in analytic judgments is simply the problem of what a suitable criterion of *identity* (total or partial) *of concepts* might be'; see *Semantics and Necessary Truth*, 30–1. This problem is still unsolved; see Fodor, *Concepts: Where Cognitive Science Went Wrong*, esp. chs. 1–4, and Peacocke, *A Study of Concepts*, esp. ch. 1.

the inverses of their concept-generating operations. For example, in the proposition 'Bachelors are unmarried adult males', the concepts BACHELOR and UNMARRIED ADULT MALE are not only c-identical but also m-identical because the proposition expresses an analytic definition. The subject concept decomposes to its conceptual microstructure, and, since the predicate concept of an analytic definition just *is* that microstructure, it redundantly decomposes to itself. Other examples—this time non-definitional ones—include 'Dogs are canines' and 'Furze is gorse'. Thus the criterion of m-identity gives us the second level or type of Kantian conceptual identity.

Question: why is the bi-level or multigrade[60] character of Kant's theory of conceptual identity philosophically important? Answer: not only does it set his theory of identity decisively apart from those of Leibniz and Frege, but also from a systematic point of view it gives his theory of analyticity an enriched explanatory power.

We can recognize one of its virtues simply by looking back at Kant's containment formulation. IDENTITY-1 implicitly extends the scope of analyticity from necessary truths involving m-identical concepts to necessary truths involving only c-identical concepts as well. That is, either sort of conceptual identity will suffice for analyticity. According to CONTAINMENT-2, an analytic proposition is a necessary subject/predicate proposition if the predicate concept is a part of the microstructure of the subject concept, and the subject concept and predicate concept are related by comprehensional overlap. This is a conjunctive criterion that excludes 'Triangulars are trilaterals'; by sharp contrast, IDENTITY-1 is a disjunctive criterion that includes it. So 'Triangulars are trilaterals' is analytic by virtue of comprehensional overlap alone, even though it is not analytic by virtue of the predicate concept's being contained in the subject concept. This shows us that intensional containment relations are of two distinct sorts: a concept $C2$ can be a part of the microstructure of a concept $C1$ (containment-in); or two concepts $C1$ and $C2$ can be related by comprehensional overlap even when there is no structural containment of the predicate concept in the subject concept (containment-under). And this frees Kant not only from the 'Triangulars are trilaterals' problem, but also from a more general objection, originally made by Hilary Putnam, that Kantian or concept-based theories of analyticity are over-narrowly restricted to 'one-criterion' conceptual terms.[61] The notion of comprehensional overlap constitutes a second identity criterion for every concept term, a criterion importantly distinct from the more familiar identity criterion that appeals solely to its conceptual microstructure.

And here is a second systematic virtue. Kant's multigrade theory of conceptual identity does not appeal to any specific logical operations within

---

[60] For a unigrade theory, see Bealer, *Quality and Concept*, 184–5.

[61] See Putnam, 'The Analytic and the Synthetic'.

propositions, *including categorical predication*, but instead appeals only to intrinsic connections within or between concepts. This implies, however, that analytic conceptual identity relations can in principle be found even in propositions that are not of categorical form. This is part of what Kant means by his often-unnoticed observation in the *Prolegomena* that the analytic/synthetic distinction is not based on the logical form (*logischen Form*) of propositions, but rather has to do with their intension (*Inhalte*) only (*P.* Ak. iv. 266). Thus, despite misleading appearances, Kant's focus on categorical propositions in his theory of analyticity is only an expository convenience, but not a necessary or substantive feature of the theory.[62] In view of this fact, we can reach a more comprehensive version of Kant's identity theory (the formulation IDENTITY-1 'really wants to be') merely by dropping the restriction to subject/predicate propositions:

> (IDENTITY-2) A proposition is analytic if it is necessary by virtue of identical concepts occurring within its propositional content.

According to IDENTITY-2, then, a proposition is analytic if (providing of course it is necessary[63]) it involves truth-determining comprehensional or microstructural identities of concepts in its content, no matter which logical form the proposition happens to take. As we have seen in Section 1.5, Kant grants a certain primacy to the subject/predicate structure in his theory of judgement by treating it as generatively basic. But his theory of analyticity, construed in terms of his identity formulation, does not entail that every analytic truth be categorical in its gross logical or grammatical form.[64]

3.1.3. Analyticity and Contradiction

As we have just seen, the theory of analyticity lying behind Kant's IDENTITY-2 formulation usefully avoids any restriction of analyticity to propositions of categorical form. Yet an even more fundamental issue remains unclarified— namely, the relationship of analyticity to logic itself. How can Kant's theory, even in its logically comprehensive or as it were decategoricalized version, IDENTITY-2, be brought into connection with the idea of a logical truth?

---

[62] See Allison, *The Kant–Eberhard Controversy*, 56.

[63] This qualification is especially important here, since it effectively rules out contingent propositions containing *c*-identical or *m*-identical concepts, such as 'Bodies are extended and the moon is made of green cheese'.

[64] This also gets around a problem noted by Katz: that Kant's criterion of analyticity apparently does not account for analytic truths containing polyadic or relational predicates, e.g., 'Smith marries those he weds'; see *The Metaphysics of Meaning*, 192. Here I need only repeat the point made in the text: Kant's theory of analyticity is based on the intensional structure and comprehensional content of concepts occurring within a given proposition, not on the gross logical form of the proposition.

In the light of this question, I have been saving what is apparently the most troublesome of Kant's formulations for the last. This is because, in this formulation Kant seems to offer a wholly new version of his doctrine of analyticity without any special regard either for the containment formulation or for the identity formulation. And what is worse, this third formulation seems to exclude most of the analytic propositions captured by CONTAINMENT-2 and IDENTITY-2.

Here is what Kant writes:

> Now the proposition that no predicate attaches to a thing that contradicts [that predicate] is called the principle of contradiction, and is a general though merely negative criterion of all truth, but for that reason it belongs only to logic ... But one can also make a positive use of it—that is, not merely to dispel falsehood and error (in so far as it rests on contradiction), but also to cognize truth. For, *if the judgement is analytic*, whether affirmative or negative, its truth must always be able to be adequately cognized in accordance with the principle of contradiction. For the contrary (*Widerspiel*) of that which as a concept already lies and is thought in the cognition of the object is always correctly denied, while the concept itself must necessarily be affirmed of it, since its opposite (*Gegenteil*) would contradict the object. *The principle of contradiction* must therefore be recognized by us as being the universal and completely sufficient *principle of all analytic cognition*.   (*CPR* A151/B190–1; see also *CPR* A598/B626, and *P*. Ak. iv. 267)

Now a first and obvious gloss of this text can be given as follows:

(CONTRADICTION-1) A subject/predicate proposition is analytic if and only if it is necessary by virtue of the fact that the denial of the attribution of its predicate to its subject results in a contradiction.

That is, unlike the other formulations we have looked at, CONTRADICTION-1 is clearly intended to supply both necessary and sufficient conditions for analyticity. But what, more precisely, is it saying?

Its sense can be revealed when we ask ourselves just what Kant means by 'contradiction' (*Widerspruch*). If an analytic proposition is necessarily true, then the proposition resulting from the denial of the attribution of its predicate to its subject—a contradiction—must be necessarily false. Moreover, Kant himself describes the law of non-contradiction as 'the proposition that no predicate attaches to a thing that contradicts [that predicate]'. This would seem to be best expressible as

(For all predicates P) (All x) $\sim (Px \ \& \sim Px)$.

If so, that implies that for Kant every particular contradiction will take the form '$Px \ \& \sim Px$'. Thus what Kant seems to be saying is that a proposition is analytic if and only if it is a necessary subject/predicate proposition because the denial of the attribution of its predicate to its subject results in a proposition that is necessarily false and takes the form '$Px \ \& \sim Px$'. But this interpretation of his contradiction theory is obviously too narrow. According to Kant, as I have mentioned already, all logical truths are analytic. And because

Kant clearly recognizes that there are non-subject/predicate propositions treated by logical theory (*CPR* A70/B95), he must also recognize that there will be non-subject/predicate analytic logical truths. Then, since 'the principle of contradiction must therefore be recognized by us as being the universal and completely sufficient principle of all analytic cognition', and since 'the nature of an analytic proposition is thereby clearly expressed' (*CPR* A153/B193), it follows that Kant must also hold that the principle of contradiction applies far more widely than merely to subject/predicate propositions whose denials result in a proposition of the categorical form 'Px & $\sim Px$'.

Given these considerations, I think that we will more accurately represent Kant's contradiction formulation if we understand it to be saying the following:

> (CONTRADICTION-2) A proposition is analytic if and only if it is necessary by virtue of the fact that its denial deductively entails[65] a contradiction of the form 'Px & $\sim Px$'.

According to this formulation, it is not absolutely required that the attribution of a predicate be denied in order to apply the principle of contradiction to a given proposition, but only that the whole proposition (of whatever logical form) be denied. Moreover, according to CONTRADICTION-2, it is not required that the contradiction that results from the denial of the relevant proposition actually take the categorical form 'Px & $\sim Px$', but only that it deductively entail a contradiction of that form.[66] In other words, CONTRADICTION-2 says that the immediate logical result of the denial of the relevant proposition need only be a formal contradiction, not specifically a formal categorical contradiction. Then via deductive entailment, since any proposition whatsoever deductively follows from a formal contradiction, the denial of the relevant proposition still—ultimately—logically results in the categorical contradiction.

CONTRADICTION-2 more faithfully reflects Kant's intentions than does CONTRADICTION-1. Now there is a unique class of propositions, each of which

---

[65] Logical entailment is strict implication, or Kant's logical 'ground-consequence' relation: i.e. it is not possible for the premises to be true and the conclusion false. By the narrower notion of 'deductive entailment', however, I mean the following:

> A proposition Q is deductively entailed by a set of propositions {$P1$, $P2$, . . . Pn} if and only if Q is logically entailed by {$P1$, $P2$, $P3$, . . . Pn} and Q can also be derived from {$P1$, $P2$ . . . Pn} by means of logical inference rules alone.

Kant's most explicit account of deductive entailment is given in the third section of 'The Jäsche Logic', 'Of Inferences' (JL Ak. ix. 114–31). Deductive entailment is narrower than analytic entailment, because some arguments that are analytically valid are not also valid by the inference rules alone.

[66] It follows by successive applications of the truth-functional rules of conjunction elimination ('from P & $\sim P$, derive P'), disjunction addition ('from P, derive P v Q'), conjunction elimination again ('from P & $\sim P$, derive $\sim P$'), and disjunctive syllogism ('from $\sim P$ and P v Q, derive Q').

is such that its denial is necessarily false and deductively entails a proposition of the form 'Px & $\sim Px$', and that of course is the class of the truths of deductive predicate logic. Since Kant knew only Aristotelian–Scholastic syllogistic logic, however, his deductive predicate logic extends only as far as monadic logic— first-order predicate logic with quantification into one-place predicates exclusively.[67] Let us call the logical truths of monadic logic 'classical logical truths'. So what CONTRADICTION-2 says is that all and only classical logical truths are analytic.[68]

But, even if CONTRADICTION-2 articulates a more faithful version of Kant's contradiction formulation, it still seems to fall into the problem mentioned at the beginning of this subsection. That is, most propositions that are analytic according to CONTAINMENT-2 and IDENTITY-2 are not such that their denials (deductively) result in propositions that are formally contradictory. For example, the denial of the analytic proposition (BE) 'Bodies are extended'— namely 'Some bodies are not extended'—is not a formal contradiction. Nor, indeed, is the denial of (TT) 'Triangulars are trilaterals' formally contradictory. So does Kant's theory of analyticity at last suffer shipwreck here? Has he produced a second and distinct theory of analyticity that effectively excludes

---

[67] Monadic logic is consistent (it contains no contradictions), complete (all the logically true sentences are theorems or provable sentences), sound (all the theorems are logically true), and decidable (it has a recursive or mechanical test for logical truth). To be sure, classical or monadic logic is very limited; but on the other hand, it has one striking theoretical advantage over modern or polyadic logic, which allows quantification into two-place predicates or higher: polyadic logic is undecidable. See Boolos and Jeffrey, *Computability and Logic*, ch. 25, esp. 250–1. Polyadicity increases the explanatory power of logic in the sense that it explains more intuitively valid inferences than monadicity does. But at the same time it decreases logic's structural simplicity (since there is no recursive decision procedure), universality or comprehensiveness (since it makes special ontological assumptions), and uncontrovertibility (since it fails in empty domains).

[68] This raises an extremely important but also extremely thorny set of issues. Because Kant identifies predicate logic with monadic logic, he leaves himself wide open to the charge of having had, A. P. Hazen puts it, 'a terrifyingly narrow-minded, and mathematically trivial, conception of the province of logic' (see his 'Logic and Analyticity', 92). In turn, Kant's notorious conception of the province of logic has profound implications for his theory of pure intuition in particular and his philosophy of mathematics more generally, as both Michael Friedman and Jaakko Hintikka have clearly (if somewhat differently) recognized: see Friedman, *Kant and Exact Sciences*, chs. 1–2, esp. 63–95, 121; Hintikka, 'Are Logical Truths Analytic?'; and Hintikka, *Logic, Language Games, and Information*. It seems to me that at least five distinct but tightly intertwined leading questions can be posed in this connection: (1) what is the nature of logic?; (2) what is the nature of pure mathematics?; (3) if there really is an analytic/synthetic distinction, how does it apply to logic?; (4) if there really is an analytic/synthetic distinction, how does it apply to pure mathematics?; (5) how do Kant's particular conceptions of logic, pure mathematics, analyticity, and syntheticity bear upon correct answers to the other four questions? Unfortunately I cannot even begin to deal adequately with these issues here; but I hope to tackle at least some of them elsewhere.

the theory adumbrated in the containment formulation and identity formulation? No and no again. While Kant is certainly guilty of unclear exposition, his contradiction formulation is not actually inconsistent with the other formulations. And the trick of recognizing the real meaning of the contradiction formulation lies, I believe, in seeing the following two points.

First, as I have already pointed out in Section 2.1, Kant identifies the logical constants with the pure concepts of the understanding (*CPR* A76–80/ B102–5; see also *P*. Ak. iv. 304–5, 324). More generally, pure concepts have an intension or meaning (*Bedeutung*) that is 'purely logical' (*CPR* A147/B186) in the sense that they express 'the functions of unity in judgements' (*CPR* A69/B94). In this way, the concepts that determine classical logical truths, all of which are pure concepts of the understanding, are strictly syncategorematic logical meanings or intensions. That is, they do not independently determine objects or comprehensions, but instead systematically determine logical relations between those semantic contents that *do* independently determine objects—the categorematic meanings. Moreover, since they are both syncategorematic and logically basic, pure concepts are dependent meanings and yet also strictly invariant meanings. Although they may be partially analysed, their meanings fully reveal themselves only in the context of whole judgements (negation, the copula, monadic propositional quantities) or whole judgement complexes (disjunction, conjunction,[69] conditionalization); but, at the same time, these meanings remain fixed under every possible uniform reinterpretation of the categorematic terms or non-logical constants in judgements. Hence a classical logical truth is *also* a necessary proposition true strictly by virtue of its conceptual meanings alone. What distinguishes classical logical truths from the other sorts of analytic truths is merely that, while analytic truths by containment, or by identity, are based on conceptual form and content intrinsic to the non-logical or categorematic constants in propositions, classical logical truths are analytic by virtue of the deepest level of conceptual content—the logical truth functions, or rather those pure concepts of the understanding expressing the truth-functional logical constants.[70] In other words, instead of reducing all analytic truths to logical truths, as Frege and Carnap propose,[71] Kant in fact brings (at least all classical) logical truths under his broader conception of analytic truth according to which a judgement is analytic if and only if it is necessarily true by virtue of intrinsic conceptual interconnections alone.

---

[69] Kant's logic does not contain a primitive judgement form for conjunction, but conjunction is definable in terms of disjunction and negation.

[70] The analyticity of truth-functional logical truths can in fact be directly and mechanically tested by means of truth tables, although Kant did not know this—since it was not discovered until 1921 by E. L. Post and Wittgenstein. See Kneale and Kneale, *The Development of Logic*, 532.   [71] See Sects. 3.3 and 3.4.

Secondly, and consistently with the first point, it is clear that Kant's appeal to the principle of contradiction is not meant to be restricted merely to the logical forms of whole propositions, but must be understood to apply equally to conceptual microstructures. Look again closely at Kant's own words as he describes how the contradiction criterion is to be applied:

For, *if the judgment is analytic*, whether affirmative or negative, its truth must always be able to be adequately cognized in accordance with the principle of contradiction. For the contrary of that which *as a concept already lies and is thought in the cognition of the object* is always correctly denied, while the concept itself must necessarily be affirmed of it, since its opposite would contradict the object.   (*CPR* A151/B190–1; second emphasis added)

All analytic judgements depend wholly on the principle of contradiction . . . For the predicate of an affirmative analytic judgement is *already thought in the concept of the subject,* of which it cannot be denied without contradiction.   (*P.* Ak. iv. 267; emphasis added)

Kant's idea here is that what is negated in the denial of an analytic proposition is (at least sometimes) a concept $C2$ that is contained in or thought in a whole complex concept $C1$ and therefore necessarily belongs to the conceptual microstructure of $C1$. So, for instance, in the denial of (BE)—'It is not the case that all bodies are extended' or equivalently 'Some bodies are non-extended'—what is ultimately negated is the predicate concept EXTENDED.[72] But this would be to negate a concept that stands in a necessary identity relation to a concept already assumed to belong—as a subpart—to the original complex concept, BODY. That is, the denial of the predicate concept generates an instance of a violation of Kant's conceptual law of identity within the structure of the whole proposition.[73]

In this way, following our conventions for representing the structures of concepts and propositions, and letting "non-" stand for the operation of concept negation, the decomposition of the denial of (BE) comes out as:

$$[(\text{Some } x)\ (\text{BODY}x = <\ldots \text{etc.} + \text{EXTENDED}x>\ \text{pred non-EXTENDED}x)].$$

---

[72] As we saw in Sect. 2.1, Kant allows negation to attach either to whole propositions (wide-scope negation) or to concepts (narrow-scope negation). And he also believes that the sort of negation that attaches to concepts alone is of a subtly different logical type from that which attaches to whole propositions (*CPR* A71–2/B97).

[73] In many places Kant makes it clear that he takes the law of non-contradiction and the law of conceptual identity to be interchangeable; see e.g. JL Ak. ix. 52 and OD Ak. viii. 229. Given Kant's other views, this equivalence is plausible. If conceptual identity is essentially a relation between intensional contents (see Section 3.1.2 above), and if negation can take either wide scope or narrow scope (see n. 72), then the way is wide open to viewing a contradiction as the assertion either of the identity of a concept C and its (narrow-scope) negation non-C, or of a proposition P and its (wide-scope) negation not-P. So Kant's law of non-contradiction is simply the denial of the possibility of identifying a concept or proposition with its negation.

But this is formally self-contradictory at the level of conceptual micro-structure, by virtue of including something of the form '*C*, non-*C*'. Thus the contradiction theory applies not merely to gross logical form but also to microstructural conceptual form. With an eye to using this point, and just to fix terminology, let us call any propositional structure containing something of the form '*C*, non-*C*' a *microstructural contradiction between concepts*, or, more simply, an '*m*-contradiction between concepts'. Then we should reformulate CONTRADICTION-2 to read:

> (CONTRADICTION-3) A proposition is analytic if and only if it is necessary either because its denial deductively entails a contradiction of the form '*Px* & ~ *Px*' or else because its denial results in an *m*-contradiction between concepts.

Of course, the great advantage of CONTRADICTION-3 over CONTRADICTION-2 is that it captures not only all classical logical truths, but also all analytic propositions falling under CONTAINMENT-1 (and of course also CONTAINMENT-2, since it is equivalent with CONTAINMENT-1). Obviously every necessary proposition that is such that its predicate concept is contained in its subject concept is also such that the denial of its predicate concept results in an *m*-contradiction between concepts. Kant in several places strongly supports this interpretation of the contradiction theory by simply running together the CONTAINMENT-1 and CONTRADICTION-3 formulations. For example, in his reply to Eberhard he writes:

In the proposition *every body is divisible* the predicate is an attribute ... [that] can be derived as a necessary consequence from an essential part of the concept of the subject—namely, extension. It is, however, an attribute that is represented as belonging to the concept of body according to the principle of contradiction. Thus, the proposition itself ... is analytic.   (OD Ak. viii. 229; see also *CPR* B11–12)

Taking this text together with the other ones given earlier in this subsection, it is manifest that CONTRADICTION-3 is intended by Kant to be a first attempt at a super-theory of analyticity in the sense that (*a*) it incorporates CONTAINMENT-1, (*b*) it comprehends all classical logical truths, and (*c*) it aims to provide both necessary and sufficient conditions for the analyticity of a proposition.

But one medium-sized fly remains in the ointment. Although, as we have just seen, CONTRADICTION-3 manages to capture not only all classical logical truths but also all the analytic propositions falling under CONTAINMENT-1, we may well wonder whether it accounts for all analytic propositions falling under IDENTITY-2. There exist, as we have seen, some subject/predicate propositions—for example, our old friend (TT) 'Triangulars are trilaterals'— that fall outside CONTAINMENT-1 and are captured only by IDENTITY-2. And unfortunately it appears that CONTRADICTION-3 does not apply to (TT); for its negation does not generate either a formal logical contradiction or an *m*-contradiction of concepts.

What to do now? An important clue, I think, lies ready-to-hand in Kant's crucial idea that concepts may be identical in two distinct ways: by virtue of their sharing the same conceptual microstructure under the inverses of their concept-building operations (*m*-identity), or by virtue of their sharing comprehensions even if the concepts fail to share conceptual microstructure (*c*-identity). Now, just as two *c*-identical concepts (say, TRIANGULAR and TRILATERAL) may nevertheless not be *m*-identical, so two concepts may be intensionally opposed or contradictory without strictly realizing the form of an *m*-contradiction of concepts. In other words, just as for Kant there is a purely comprehensional criterion for the identity of concepts (*c*-identity), so too there is for him a purely comprehensional notion of conceptual contradiction (let us call it '*c*-contradiction of concepts').

This crucial point can be approached in two steps. First, we can go back and redescribe the contradiction found in the denial of a proposition such as 'Bodies are extended' purely in terms of the comprehensions of its concepts alone, rather than in terms of the formal properties of its conceptual microstructure. As we will remember from CONTAINMENT-1, Kant's fundamental idea of containment-in is that an analytic proposition is one in which the predicate concept is predicated of the very subject concept of which it is an essential part. And we saw that this entails that the comprehension of the subject concept falls within that of the predicate concept, although not necessarily conversely. Kant's terminology for this, again, is that the lower or narrower subject concept is contained under the higher or wider predicate concept. Now, if the predicate concept is negated, then every concept contained under that concept, including the subject concept, will also be negated: 'What . . . contradicts higher concepts also . . . contradicts all lower concepts that are contained under those higher ones' (JL Ak. ix. 98). Moreover, given the fact that for Kant lower concepts themselves actually belong to the comprehensions of higher concepts (see Section 3.1.1), the negation of the predicate concept also entails the negation of the comprehension of the subject concept: 'Whatever universally . . . contradicts a concept also . . . contradicts every particular (*allem Besondern*) that is contained under it' (CPR A280–1 /B337). In other words, negating the predicate of an analytic judgement implies that every member of the comprehension of the predicate concept will be logically subtracted from the comprehension of the subject concept (see also JL Ak. ix. 103). But, since by hypothesis the comprehension of the subject concept falls within that of the predicate concept, that will be logically to subtract every member of the comprehension of the subject concept; and that result is patently absurd, since it is assumed by Kant from the start that the subject concept in every objectively valid (empirically meaningful, truth-valued) affirmative proposition has a non-empty comprehension, because every such concept is also automatically objectively valid (see Section 2.2). Just to fix terminology again, let us say that whenever a concept C1 has its entire comprehension logically subtracted by predicating a concept C2 of C1, then C2 'comprehensionally contradicts' (or 'c-contradicts') C1.

Secondly, we can take this idea of c-contradiction and extend it. As we have seen, Kant holds that two concepts are convertible just in case they share the same comprehension. But what about two concepts (say, CIRCLE and SQUARE) that are, in effect, contra-convertible because they share no possible entity whatsoever in common in their comprehensions? Clearly, asserting contra-convertible concepts of one another (as in 'Circles are squares') will amount to the same as mutually subtracting the entirety of each concept's comprehension. But such a dual assertion will be necessarily false, because each of the assertions involves a c-contradiction. So let us call any two concepts that are contra-convertible in this way 'mutually c-contradictory concepts'.

We are now in a position to use this purely comprehensional notion of contradiction to liberate Kant's theory of analyticity from its last major difficulty. Although (TT)'s negation—'Some triangulars are non-trilaterals—is neither formally contradictory nor contains an *m*-contradiction of concepts, it does contain a mutual *c*-contradiction between the concepts THREE-ANGLED CLOSED RECTILINEAR PLANE FIGURE and NON-THREE-SIDED CLOSED RECTILINEAR PLANE FIGURE. Thus we have found a perfectly intelligible way in which the denials of subject/predicate analytic propositions not containing *m*-identical concepts, and also the denials of non-categorical analytic propositions, will necessarily lead to contradictions. So I will now rewrite the contradiction formulation, incorporating what we have just learned:

(CONTRADICTION-4) A proposition is analytic if and only if it is necessary either because (1) its denial deductively entails a contradiction of the form 'Px & $\sim Px$' or else because (2) its denial leads to either an *m*-contradiction between concepts or a *c*-contradiction between concepts.

The many and shining theoretical virtues of CONTRADICTION-4 should be evident. Falling within its scope are all analytic propositions of subject/predicate form that are true either by containment or by identity; as well as all non-categorical non-logically analytic propositions that are true by identity; and also all classical logical truths. With CONTRADICTION-4, then, we have reached our goal—a plausibly complete[74] and internally coherent

---

[74] By 'plausibly complete' in this context I mean only that Kant's theory of analyticity plausibly captures all of the propositions belonging to the set of raw data for his theory, as selected by prima facie or pre-theoretical insight. I do not mean that it captures all of the propositions held by other philosophers to be analytic.

Kantian cognitivist theory of analyticity.[75] And we have not, I think, strayed at any point either from the letter of Kant's texts, or from the philosophical motivations and argumentation supporting the several formulations of his theory.

To summarize the argument so far, then. On Kant's account, an analytic proposition is a proposition that is necessary by virtue of its conceptual form (= its gross logical form) or content (which includes both conceptual microstructure and comprehension) alone. That is, it is either necessary by virtue of the logical meaning of pure concepts of the understanding, which express the classical or truth-functional logical constants; or it is necessary by virtue of complete or partial identities of conceptual microstructure between non-logical concepts; or else it is necessary by virtue of relations of comprehensional overlap between non-logical concepts. What CONTRADICTION-4 brings out is that the negation of an analytic proposition will invariably lead to the violation of some necessary infra-conceptual or inter-conceptual relation grounded in a concept's logical essence. Kant's theory of analyticity thus relies upon his conceptual essentialism, which in turn is a result of his epigenetic or generative/productive theory of concepts. Moreover, to express a true analytic proposition for Kant is to bring forth 'real a priori cognition' (*CPR* A6/B10), because every such proposition exposes some necessary fact within the constitutive non-empirical architecture of our total repertoire of objectively valid concepts.

So that is Kant's cognitivist theory of analyticity. Now we must submit it to the rational test of fire by looking closely at the main criticisms of it, at its leading competition, and at the sceptics.

3.2. But is it Psychologistic?

A recurring theme in criticism of Kant's theory of analyticity is the charge that Kant's theory is psychologistic and therefore unacceptable. Even such a staunch defender of Kant as Lewis White Beck unhappily remarks that 'it is

---

[75] We are now in a position to extend Kant's theory of analyticity from (1) true affirmative analytic propositions to (2) true negative analytic propositions, (3) false affirmative analytic propositions, and (4) false negative analytic propositions. The respective definitions are as follows (I'll assume that double negation always cancels out). (1) A true affirmative analytic proposition is a proposition containing no negation operators that is necessary because either (*a*) its denial deductively entails a contradiction of the form 'Px & $\sim Px$' or else (*b*) its denial leads to either an *m*-contradiction of concepts or a *c*-contradiction of concepts. (2) A true negative analytic proposition is a proposition containing negation operators that is otherwise defined in the same way as a true affirmative analytic proposition. (3) A false affirmative analytic proposition is a proposition not containing negation operators whose denial is a true negative analytic proposition. (4) A false negative analytic proposition is a proposition containing negation operators whose denial is a true affirmative analytic proposition.

clear that Kant was not free from a psychologizing, introspective tendency in his decisions on what is analytic'.[76]

This, of course, is merely a specification of the blanket charge of psychologism laid against Kant's cognitive semantics. But the charge is not the less serious for being part of a general pattern of such worries. To be sure, we have already seen in Sections 1.5 and 2.1 that Kant is an opponent of judgement psychologism and logical psychologism alike, and that he anticipates by a century the famous anti-psychologistic arguments given by Frege and Husserl. Given these facts, together with his doctrine that all classical logical truths are analytic, is it likely that Kant would adopt a psychologistic doctrine of analytic propositions? Of course not. So all I need to do here is show how his anti-psychologism actually carries over into his theory of analyticity. The bridging notion, it turns out, is a sharp and important distinction between subjective (or phenomenological) and objective (or semantic) elements of representations.

The nub of Kant's idea is that, over and above a concept's or judgement's representational content, there is also a corresponding purely subjective consciousness—in inner sense—of the thinking subject: '*I* as intelligence and *thinking* subject cognize my self as object that is *thought*, in so far as I am also given to myself in intuition, only, like other phenomena, not as I am for the understanding but rather as I appear to myself . . .' (*CPR* B155). In other words, according to Kant every act of thought or judgement has its own special sort of conscious qualia.[77] This in turn leads him to hold that it is quite possible to possess and even use a given concept, without being explicitly aware of its form or content: 'No doubt the concept of "right" that is used by the common-sense understanding (*gesunde Verstand*) contains the very same things that the subtlest speculation can develop out of it, though in its ordinary and practical use we are not conscious (*bewuß*) of these manifold representations in these thoughts' (*CPR* A43/B61). Thus what is semantically contained in the concept—its 'manifold representations'—may be quite hidden from the subjectively conscious mental acts, states, or processes in which that concept occurs. Therefore the intensional contents of concepts are not determined or individuated by a given thinker's consciousness of those concepts, even for thinkers who quite competently employ those very concepts in theoretical cognition or practical life.[78]

---

[76] Beck, 'Can Kant's Synthetic Judgments be made Analytic?', 233.

[77] Searle has recently rediscovered this important idea, which he calls the 'aspectual shape' of intentional states; see *Rediscovery of the Mind*, 155.

[78] Revealingly and somewhat inconsistently—given his overall thesis that Kant's theory of concepts and judgements is psychologistic—in his gloss on this text Coffa remarks that 'there is no way to avoid the conclusion that [Kant] was tacitly endorsing a distinction between the mental acts in which concepts are involved and those concepts themselves' (see *The Semantic Tradition from Kant to Carnap*, 12).

Now there is much that can and should be said about Kant's extremely interesting doctrine of the phenomenology of conceptual consciousness.[79] At the moment, however, the crucial point is the fact that the mode-of-consciousness of a concept and its semantic content vary independently of one another. Kant says that phenomenological differences in representational consciousness are registered in varying degrees of 'clarity' (*Klarheit*) and 'distinctness' (*Deutlichkeit*), and are to be sharply contrasted with differences in the intensional contents of representations: 'The difference between an indistinct and distinct representation is merely logical and does not concern the intension' (*CPR* A43/B60–1). Now obviously, if the distinctness or indistinctness of consciousness does not concern the intensional content of a representation, then it does not concern its comprehensional component either, since the comprehension of a concept could not be changed without also changing the intension. What may prevent one's properly understanding this text is simply that Kant uses "logical" here in a slightly unusual way. In this context it means roughly 'a predicate relevant to subjectively conscious mental acts, states, or processes alone, whose application to those mental postures does not modify the intensional content of any concept occurring in them'. This use, however, is perfectly consistent with the general Kantian notion of a logical predicate as one that does not change the intension or comprehension of any concept to which it is applied (see Section 3.1.1 above).

These points enable us to give a proper interpretation of the following text, which is almost invariably brought forward in support of the claim that Kant's theory of analyticity is psychologistic:

One could also call [analytic propositions] *explicative judgments* . . . since through the predicate they add nothing to the concept of the subject, but merely decompose it into those constituent concepts that were already thought in it (although confusedly) . . . If I say, for instance, 'All bodies are extended', then this is an analytic judgement. For I do not need to go beyond the concept that I combine with the word "bodies",[80] in order to find that extension is connected with [that concept], but rather I need only to decompose that concept—that is, become conscious to myself of the manifold that I always think in it, in order to encounter this predicate therein; it is therefore an analytic judgement.   (*CPR* A7/B11; see also *P.* Ak. iv. 266–7)

Here what Kant seems to be saying is that the criterion of analyticity is purely psychological in character: a proposition is analytic if and only if the mental act of judgement adds no new phenomenological content to the subject concept, because it merely brings forward, through concept decomposition and predication, what is already implicitly 'thought' in that concept. Now we know already that for Kant the conscious activity of making clear or making distinct is logically independent of the representational content of concepts. In

---

[79] See e.g. Hanna, 'How Do We Know Necessary Truths? Kant's Answer'.
[80] See n. 43.

particular, then, (*a*) it is quite possible to *increase* clarity or distinctness even though the proposition is analytic (hence non-addition of phenomenological content is not necessary for analyticity), and (*b*) it is also quite possible to *fail to increase* clarity or distinctness even though the proposition is synthetic (hence non-addition of phenomenological content is not sufficient for analyticity).

As regards the first or (*a*) sort of case, Kant remarks:

> *Decomposition* of the concepts we already have of objects. . . . supplies us with a collection (*Menge*) of cognitions, which, while nothing but explications or elucidations of what has already been thought in our concepts (though still in a confused manner), are, *at least as regards their form (Form), valued as new insights. But so far as matter or intension (die Materie, oder dem Inhalte) is concerned, they do not extend the concepts that we possess, but only take them apart.*   (*CPR* A6/B9, second emphasis added)

In other words, a proposition can be analytic, as revealed through decomposition and analytic predication, and yet still be grasped in a conscious act, state, or process that supplies new insights (*neuen Einsichten*) or greater clarity and distinctness in the phenomenological dimension of the cognition.

And, as regards the second or (*b*) sort of case, Kant points out that synthetic propositions, every bit as much as analytic ones, are accessible to conscious acts, states, or processes that involve greater or lesser degrees of clarity and distinctness. The dimension of clarity and distinctness, as it applies to consciousness of synthetic propositions, is part of what Kant calls the 'aesthetic perfection' of cognition, as opposed to its 'logical perfection' (JL Ak. ix. 35–9). The aesthetic clarity and distinctness of a cognition is its sensible intensive quality, and expresses the thinker's consciousness of the way in which objects are represented through empirical or pure intuition. But, just as in the case of conceptual consciousness, this has no automatic implications for the semantic contents of propositions of which the thinker is conscious. So an intuitive consciousness could easily be quite obscure (*dunkel*), hence relatively devoid of aesthetic clarity or distinctness, and yet still be directed to a synthetic proposition, even to a synthetic a priori proposition. Good examples would be a child's fuzzy grasp of '$7 + 5 = 12$' in the early stages of learning arithmetic, and the similarly fuzzy grasp by even expert adult arithmeticians— prior to actual calculation—of sums involving large numbers (*CPR* B16; see also *P.* Ak. iv. 269).

The conclusion we must draw from all of this is that Kant's doctrine of analyticity not only reflects the sharp contrast between pure general logic and the empirical psychology of logic, but is also appropriately sensitive to a fundamental distinction between two irreducibly different sides of every objective representation or cognition—the phenomenological or subjectively conscious aspect, and the semantic or objective aspect. But the relation of this point to the historiography of post-Kantian criticism of Kant is equally important. Bolzano—in what he took to be a critique of Kant—employed precisely this Kantian distinction throughout his *Theory of Science* under the rubric of the contrast between subjective representations (or 'representations in us') and objective representations (or 'representations in themselves'). Nevertheless, it did not really receive its proper recognition until Frege independently reintroduced it in *Foundations of Arithmetic*:

> A representation (*Vorstellung*) in the subjective sense is what is governed by the psychological laws of association; it is of a sensible, pictorial character. A representation in the objective sense belongs to logic and is in principle non-sensible, although the word that means an objective representation is often accompanied by a subjective representation, which nevertheless is not its meaning. Subjective representations are often demonstrably different in different men, objective representations are the same for all. Objective representations can be divided into objects and concepts. I shall myself, to avoid confusion, use "representation" only in the subjective sense. It is because Kant associated both meanings with the word that his doctrine assumed such a very subjective, idealist colouration (*subjective, idealistiche Färbung*) and his true view (*wahren Meinung*) was made so difficult to discover.[81]

Here Frege not only uses Kantian terminology to introduce his distinction between 'representations in the objective sense' (= meanings or semantic contents[82]) and 'representations in the subjective sense' (= that which belongs strictly to the subjective consciousness of representational mental acts, states, or processes), but he explicitly claims that he is penetrating beyond the mere 'colouration' of the Kantian doctrine to get at Kant's 'true view' in doing so. Therefore, far from accusing Kant of the serious crime of psychologism, Frege himself actually *exonerates* Kant of it—charging him only with the misdemeanour of misleading advertising.

How then did the 'psychologism' label come to attach itself to Kant's theory of analyticity? That is, how did Kant's distinction between the phenomenological and semantic contents of an objective mental representation come to be disregarded, despite the fact that Frege even explicitly attributes it to him? The simplest answer is that Kant was a convenient surrogate for a widespread tendency towards psychologism in late-nineteenth-century philosophy. In order to reject the whole camp of psychologicists, then, the founders of the analytic tradition after Frege—Moore and Russell—discovered that it best served their immediate purposes to attack Kant. A slightly subtler answer points up the fact that for various non-philosophical reasons Frege's critique of psychologism, which was in fact almost entirely directed at Mill and his contemporary German followers, was far less well known to

---

[81] Frege, *The Foundations of Arithmetic*, 37 n. 1, translation modified slightly.

[82] Frege's undifferentiated notion of 'representations in the objective sense' in *Foundations* later folds out into the sense versus Meaning (reference) distinction. See Dummett, *Frege: Philosophy of Mathematics*, 66–7, and Frege, *The Basic Laws of Arithmetic*, 6–7.

contemporary European philosophers than Husserl's more comprehensive and extremely influential 'Prolegomena to Pure Logic'[83]—and Husserl pointedly ascribes a version of psychologism to Kant: 'even transcendental psychology *also* is psychology.'[84] The subtlest answer of all, however, is that, in order to preserve its own healthy self-development as an ongoing anti-Kantian revolution, the analytic tradition from Frege to Quine was internally driven to forget—that is, ignore, suppress, or downplay—any troublesome substantive doctrinal similarities or continuities there might actually be between Kant and Frege. This thought will be further developed in Chapter 4.

We should now turn, however, to an area in which there actually is a genuine substantive disagreement between Kant and Frege: Frege's theory of analytic propositions.

3.3. Frege, Analyticity, and Kant

Frege's theory of analyticity, as spelled out all too briefly in *The Foundations of Arithmetic*, is motivated by what I will call 'moderate logicism'.[85] Moderate logicism is the conjunction of two claims: (1) that all truths of arithmetic are logical truths, and (2) that all arithmetical concepts are expressible in purely logical terms. Frege argues for claim (1) by way of arguing for the two subclaims (1*a*) that all truths of arithmetic are analytic[86] and (1*b*) that all analytic truths are logical truths. In turn, Frege holds that his two-step argument for claim (1) suffices to establish claim (2). If he is right about (1*a*), then Kant is wrong in thinking that all truths of arithmetic are synthetic a priori truths. If he is right about (1*b*), then Kant is wrong that only some analytic truths are (classical) logical truths. And if he is right that his two-step argument for (1) suffices to establish (2), then Kant is wrong that the concept NUMBER presupposes the pure intuition of time (*P*. Ak. iv. 283).

According to Frege, the analyticity of a proposition is not in any way a psychological matter, in the sense of inherently belonging either to the consciousness

---

[83] See Kusch, *Psychologism*, 203–10.

[84] Husserl, 'Prolegomena to Pure Logic', 122 n.

[85] By contrast, what I call 'strong logicism' is the view defended by Russell, Carnap, and the logical empiricists: all mathematical truths whatsoever—including all truths of arithmetic and geometry—are logical truths, and all mathematical concepts are expressible in purely logical terms. The weakest logicism of all is the thesis that arithmetic or geometry and mathematics more generally *presupposes* logic, but it is neither the case that all mathematical truths are logical truths nor that all mathematical concepts are expressible in purely logical terms. Even Kant is a weak logicist.

[86] This is not an inevitable feature of logicism. It is possible to hold that all truths of arithmetic are logical truths while still holding that they are both synthetic a priori. Indeed, Russell held just such a view from 1900 to 1912; see Ch. 5 n. 4 below.

(*Bewußtsein*) of a thinker, or to the mental acts or processes in which an assertoric propositional attitude or belief (*Führwahrhalten*, 'holding to be true')
is formed. Instead, a proposition is analytic if and only if it is provable from
general logical laws together with logical definitions:

> When a proposition is called . . . analytic in my sense, this is not a judgement about
> the conditions, psychological, physiological, and physical, that have made it possible
> to form the content of the proposition in our consciousness; nor is it a judgement
> about the way in which some other man has come, perhaps erroneously, to believe
> it true; rather it is a judgement about the ultimate ground upon which rests the
> justification for holding it to be true . . . The problem becomes, in fact, that of finding
> the proof of the proposition, and of following it up right back to the primitive truths.
> If, in carrying out this process, we come only on general logical laws and on
> definitions, then the truth is an analytic one, bearing in mind that we must take account
> also of all propositions upon which the admissibility of any of the definitions depends.[87]

Especially to be noted here are Frege's three leading ideas: (1) that the analyticity of a proposition depends entirely upon its logical provability—more
precisely, that this proof is the ultimate objective ground of the epistemic
justification for belief in the proposition; (2) that every strict logical derivation begins with primitive or unprovable true premises that are general logical laws; and (3) that, in addition to general logical laws, logical definitions
are also admissible as premises for the derivations (along with any other propositions upon which the definitions logically depend).

The fundamental element of Frege's account is his notion of a 'logical
definition'. None of the really interesting and informative analytic truths—
paradigmatically, those of arithmetic—are accessible by means of derivations
from general logical laws alone, but in fact they also require logical definitions
as premises. Indeed, it is precisely the addition of 'fruitful' logical definitions
to general logical laws that makes Frege's analytic propositions grow out of
those definitions 'as plants are contained in their seeds, not as beams are contained in a house'.[88] Unfortunately for Frege, however, the notion of a logical
definition is deeply problematic.

In order to count as seed premises in logical proofs, logical definitions must
be either themselves primitive and unprovable, or else provable from other
premises. But, since the analyticity of a proposition is defined strictly in terms
of its provability from logical laws and logical definitions, it follows, on the
one hand, that if Fregean logical definitions are primitive and unprovable then
those definitions cannot themselves be analytic,[89] and, on the other hand, that

---

[87] Frege, *The Foundations of Arithmetic*, 3–4.   [88] Ibid. 101.

[89] Strictly speaking, even general logical laws are not analytic by Frege's criterion of analyticity, unless he allows their self-provability to cohabit with their unprovability. But, although
this latter option is consistent with his other views, he actually says nothing that suggests
that he had it in mind.

if Fregean definitions are analytic and provable then they must be derivable from general logical laws plus further logical definitions. The latter option clearly leads to a vicious regress.

Rejecting the regress, then, the Fregean logical definitions that ultimately ground analyticity must be primitive and unprovable from general logical laws, and so cannot themselves be analytic. Now, if the logical definitions are not analytic, then they must either be synthetic, or else primitive unprovable truths of some other sort. If they are synthetic, then, by Frege's own account, they must be 'not of a general logical nature, but belong to the sphere of some special science'.[90] And this of course would rule them out as premisses for the purely logical derivations of analytic propositions. Therefore Frege's only remaining option for admitting logical definitions as seed premisses in logical proofs is to hold that such definitions are primitive unprovable truths of a third *sui generis* sort—neither strictly analytic nor strictly synthetic.

What, however, could this third sort of primitive truth be? In *Basic Laws of Arithmetic* and the late unpublished essay 'Logic in Mathematics'—taking a linguistic standpoint on the issue—Frege states that definitions are explications of simple signs in terms of complex signs; and that a fundamental constraint on any definition is that the definiens must preserve not only the reference but also the sense of the definiendum.[91] Nevertheless, according to Frege, it is important to distinguish between (i) a definition constructed by 'arbitrary fiat', which although 'a definition in the proper sense' is merely part of the apparatus of constructing formal systems,[92] and (ii) an 'analytic definition', which records the correct analysis of the sense of a sequence of signs having a long-established use.[93] Only the latter adds new axioms to a logical or mathematical system. According to Michael Dummett, Frege also implicitly adopts a second constraint on analytic definition: 'nothing should be defined in terms of that to which it is conceptually prior.'[94] This is to say that a definition is not acceptable unless it employs, in the definiens, only concepts that are conceptually prior to those in the definiendum. In short, the definiens cannot presuppose the definiendum.

Summarizing now, we can say that, according to Frege, a logical (or analytic) definition is a primitive and unprovable axiomatic truth that is neither strictly analytic (= derived from general unprovable laws of logic plus logical definitions) nor synthetic (= derived from the principles of a special science), but that nevertheless (i) preserves identity in the meanings of signs, (ii)

[90] Frege, *The Foundations of Arithmetic*, 4.

[91] See Frege, *The Basic Laws of Arithmetic*, 82, 90, and 'Logic in Mathematics [Spring 1914]', 208.

[92] It is likely that Carnap derived his own stipulative theory of analytic 'explication' primarily from this Fregean doctrine; see Resnik, 'Frege and Analytic Philosophy: Facts and Speculations', 97–8.   [93] Frege, 'Logic in Mathematics [Spring 1914]', 210–11.

[94] Dummett, *Frege: Philosophy of Mathematics*, 33.

preserves the conceptual priority of definiens over definiendum, and (iii) is the result of a correct logical analysis. Strikingly, however, as regards those three adequacy conditions, there seems on the face of it to be very little that would allow us to differentiate Fregean definitions of this sort from *Kantian* analytic definitions (JL Ak. ix. 140–2). According to Kant, analytic definitions arise 'through decomposition of concepts given a priori or a posteriori' (JL Ak. ix. 122). In other words, such definitions are unpackings of the conceptual microstructures of concepts—not complete unpackings, but only those that display 'a sufficiently distinct and precise concept' (JL Ak. ix. 141). So they are the results of correct analyses. Moreover, according to the first two of Kant's 'principal requirements of definition', such definitions must preserve identity in the comprehension and in the intension of the definiens and the definiendum alike; and the preservation of conceptual priority is included under the third requirement that states that the definition 'must not be *tautological* —that is, the characteristics of the *definitum* must, as *grounds of its cognition*, be different from itself' (JL Ak. ix. 144). So the parallelism is perfect. If Fregean logical definitions are equivalent to Kantian analytic definitions, then in effect Frege's theory of analyticity is that a proposition is analytic (in his sense) if and only if it is logically derivable from general logical laws together with analytic truths (in one of Kant's senses of analyticity). But that would hardly represent an *advance* over Kant's theory of analyticity, however; it would rather covertly presuppose it.

On the other hand, it might be supposed with some justification that, despite Frege's official doctrine of definition, Fregean definitions in actual logical practice are *not* Kantian analytic definitions. This appears very likely in view of Frege's explicit complaints about Kantian definitions in *Foundations of Arithmetic*:

[Kant] seems to think of concepts as defined by giving a simple list of characteristics in no particular order; but, of all ways of forming concepts, that is one of the least fruitful. If we look through the definitions given in the course of this book, we shall scarcely find one that is of this description. The same is true of the really fruitful definitions in mathematics, such as that of the continuity of a function. What we find in these is not a simple list of characteristics; every element in the definition is intimately, I might almost say organically, connected with the others.

What we shall be able to infer from [the definition] cannot be inspected in advance; here we are not simply taking out of the box what we have just put into it. The conclusions we draw from it extend our knowledge, and ought therefore, on Kant's view, to be regarded as synthetic; and yet they can be proved by purely logical means and are thus analytic. The truth is that they are contained in the definitions, but as plants are contained in their seeds, not as beams are contained in a house.[95]

---

[95] Frege, *The Foundations of Arithmetic*, 100–1.

One point can be dispensed with immediately. Frege's claim that Kantian concepts consist of a 'simple list of characteristics in no particular order' is misinformed. As we have seen, all Kantian concepts possess logical essences or conceptual microstructures consisting of systematically well-ordered or well-synthesized complexes of characteristics bearing categorially governed relations of coordination, subordination, and relative primitiveness to one another.

The second point is subtler. The critical reader would certainly want to put this question to Frege: 'Just *how* can logical definitions be such that their parts are "organically connected" and also such that they contain all their logical consequences as "plants are contained in their seeds"?' Frege does in fact give three very famous examples of definitions in *Foundations*: a definition of direction in terms of parallel lines; a definition of cardinal numbers in terms of sets of sets and equinumerosity relations; and a definition of *X*'s following in the series of natural numbers after *Y* (that is, the ancestral relation).[96] Let us focus briefly on the first two definitions.

The first definition is of course contextual in that it defines a given term not by assigning it an independent sense but rather by stating an equivalence between sentences in which that term occurs; and both definitions employ the strategy of identity criteria—according to which a given term is defined by specifying a set of properties such that something is denoted by that term just in case it satisfies those very properties.[97] But just how contextual or identity-criterial definitions are specially related to their logical consequences is not so obvious.

Something that does seem quite obvious, however, is the fact that such definitions presuppose more basic items in terms of which contextualization or identification can occur—for example, straight lines in the case of the definition of direction, and sets or enumerable concept extensions in the case of the definition of number. This raises the deep question as to whether the presupposed items are themselves purely logical in character. And it is very significant that, by Frege's own reckoning, the notion of a straight line is *not* purely logical but instead based on Kantian pure intuition: 'Everything geometrical must be given originally in intuition. But now I ask whether anyone has the intuition of the direction of a straight line. Of a straight line, certainly . . .'[98] So the first paradigm case of a definition is not a purely logical definition, but instead is synthetic because it reflects first principles of a special non-logical science—geometry. But what about the fundamental notion of a class? Is it purely logical, as it seems on the face of it (and as Frege explicitly assumes in both *Foundations of Arithmetic* and *Basic Laws of Arithmetic*), or is it instead somehow based on Kantian pure intuition too?

---

[96] Ibid. 73–94.
[97] See Dummett, *Frege: The Philosophy of Mathematics*, chs. 9–14.
[98] Frege, *The Foundations of Arithmetic*, 75.

Obviously that hard question cannot be decided here. Nevertheless, after many years of attempting to assimilate and solve Russell's paradox, Frege proposed in 1924–5 that the concept of number requires pure temporal and spatial intuition in the Kantian sense.[99] This is usually regarded as an old man's act of philosophical desperation. But one could *also* interpret it as a way of constraining ground-level class membership to fully determinate objects—that is, to concrete or actual spatiotemporal objects. This in turn has the same logical force as a well-founded or non-paradoxical set theory—only without the controversial axioms required by, say, the Zermelo–Fraenkel theory.[100] If Frege implicitly assumed this in *Foundations of Arithmetic* and *Basic Laws of Arithmetic*, that might explain why he failed to see Russell's Paradox. So one might argue that the non-paradoxical set theory that Frege *thought* he was working with in *Foundations* and *Basic Laws* implicitly presupposes Kantian pure intuition, and that he finally realized this clearly and distinctly in 1924–5.

In any case, to get back to analyticity again, Frege makes the intriguing remark that Kant did 'seem to have some inkling' of the wider sense of analyticity he (Frege) has in mind; and then, in the corresponding footnote, he glosses a passage at B14 of the first *Critique* by remarking that Kant 'says that a synthetic proposition can only be seen to be true by the law of contradiction, if another synthetic proposition is presupposed'.[101] To the naked philosophical eye, this certainly suggests that Frege thinks of his definitions—the really interesting and fruitful ones like those of direction, number, and the ancestral relation—as all synthetic in Kant's sense, even if all the logical consequences of those definitions are held by Frege to be analytic because deducible from those definitions plus the laws of logic. But then, unfortunately, by Frege's own account, those definitions would be 'not of a general logical nature', and the proofs in question would thus no longer be purely logical, as required in the original characterization of analyticity.

In this way we have come full circle, and are no closer to understanding Frege's notion of a logical definition. So I am compelled to agree with what Paul Benacerraf has remarked in this connection: 'It seems clear that definitions for Frege are not a number of things we might have thought they might be. But it remains unclear what he thinks they are. This makes his notion of analyticity correspondingly unclear, or at least unspecified.'[102] If Frege's notion of analyticity is ultimately unclear or unspecified, then, of course, so long as—as I have argued in the last two sections—Kant's notion is internally coherent and not psychologistic, it follows that Frege's theory of analyticity certainly

---

[99] See Frege, 'A New Attempt at a Foundation for Arithmetic', 279. See also Sects. 4.1 and 4.4 below.   [100] See Potter, *Sets: An Introduction*, ch. 1.
[101] Frege, *The Foundations of Arithmetic*, 100–1 and 101 n. 1.
[102] See Benacerraf, 'Frege: The Last Logicist', 31.

cannot justifiably be used either to reject or to replace Kant's theory. The first giant step in the history of analyticity from Frege to Quine was therefore a false step.

3.4. Carnap, Analyticity, and Kant

Now what about the second giant step? As we have seen, the main problem in Frege's theory of analyticity lies in his notion of a logical definition. Suppose, however, that someone possessed of a powerful philosophical intellect were to endorse the project of logicism and also Frege's critique of Kant's theory of analyticity—and also were to be fully informed about Russell's paradox, Gödel's incompleteness theorems, and Tarski's hierarchy-of-languages solution to the Liar Paradox?[103] It seems very likely that such a person, seeing the weak points in Frege's theory, and knowing the basic difficulties in the project of logicism, would accept the Fregean idea that all and only analytic propositions are logical truths, but would also try to fix up Frege's problematic appeal to logical definitions (especially the definition of number) as primitive unprovable premisses in the derivations of analyticities. This, in essence, is the strategy adopted by Carnap in his logico-semantic writings after *The Logical Syntax of Language*, which culminated in 1947 with *Meaning and Necessity*.

Carnap's official and rather syncretic aim in this book is to systematize the basic ideas of both Fregean–Russellian and Tarskian[104] semantics while combining that with a further development of C. I. Lewis's insight that the extensional (albeit second-order) logic and denotational semantics of *Principia Mathematica* badly need to be enriched and extended by (1) the addition of primitive modal concepts (especially the strict implication conditional) and (2) an intensional semantics.[105] Lying behind that official aim, however, is the wider project of logical empiricism, which can for our purposes in this section[106] be conveniently packaged as the conjunction of two doctrines:

(1) *The Semantic Doctrine.* All fully meaningful theoretical propositions are to be exhaustively categorized as either (*a*) analytic, necessary, and true

---

[103] See Carnap, *The Logical Syntax of Language*, esp. sects. 58–60d.

[104] See Tarski, 'The Concept of Truth in Formalized Languages'.

[105] See Lewis, 'The Modes of Meaning'; Lewis, *A Survey of Symbolic Logic*, ch. V; and Lewis and Langford, *Symbolic Logic*, esp. ch. VI, sect. 4, and app. II. Interestingly, in *The Logical Syntax of Language*, sect. 71, Carnap vigorously rejects the very idea of an intensional logic: '*A special logic of meaning is superfluous*; "non-formal logic" is a *contradictio in adjecto. Logic is syntax*' (p. 259). It seems that what prompted Carnap's intensional turn over the next decade or so was the general failure of his theory of logical and mathematical truth in *Logical Syntax*; see Friedman, *Reconsidering Logical Positivism*, chs. 7 and 9.

[106] See also Ch. 5 n. 10.

by virtue of meaning alone, or else (*b*) synthetic, contingent, and true by virtue of meaning together with empirical facts. So a proposition is fully meaningful (or has cognitive significance) just in case it is deducible either from the general semantic rules of a language (= an analytic proposition) or from specific rules for the sensory verification of beliefs (= a synthetic proposition).

(2) *The Epistemic Doctrine.* All and only analytic propositions are knowable a priori or independently of experience, and all and only synthetic propositions are knowable a posteriori or in and through sensory experience. To know an analytic proposition is to institute or follow a linguistic convention; and to know a synthetic proposition is to establish its justification in terms of foundational sensory evidence.

From the Semantic Doctrine it follows that there are no synthetic necessary truths, and from the Epistemic Doctrine it follows that there is no synthetic a priori knowledge. Not only traditional metaphysics, but also more importantly Kant's transcendental philosophy, are impossible. Logical empiricism in this minimal sense strongly circumscribes and channels the content of *Meaning and Necessity*.

At the very heart of Carnap's modal semantics is an 'explication'—that is, a stipulative constructive analysis or logical reconstruction—of Kant's notion of analytic truth, in terms of what he calls '*L*-truth'.[107] According to Carnap, a sentence is *L*-true (logically true) in a given language if and only if it is true by virtue of the semantical rules of that language alone, without any appeal to worldly facts. This is what he calls *L*-truth's 'Convention'.[108] Semantical rules determine, or at least constrain, the interpretations of all the logical (syncategorematic) and non-logical (categorematic) terms in the language. Now, every distinct, complete, logically consistent assignment of meanings (intensions and extensions) to the atomic sentences of the language determines a 'state description', or the linguistic analogue of a Leibnizian or logically possible world. A sentence true by virtue of the semantical rules of the language alone is true not just in some state descriptions, but in all state descriptions; it is, therefore, necessarily true, or true in every logically possible world. This is what Carnap calls *L*-truth's 'Definition'.[109]

Pre-theoretically, the domain of analyticity for Carnap is the set of sentences true by virtue of the meanings of their constituent terms alone. Oddly enough, however, in the first edition of *Meaning and Necessity* he does not carefully distinguish between (1) those *L*-truths that are true by virtue of the semantical rules for the logical constants alone (for example, "Fido is black or not black"), and (2) other *L*-truths that are not true *merely* by virtue of the rules for the logical constants (for example, "If Jack is a bachelor, then he

---

[107] Carnap, *Meaning and Necessity*, 8.   [108] Ibid. 10.   [109] Ibid. 9–11.

is not married"). Following Carnap's own turn of phrase, let us call sentences of type (1) 'narrow analytic truths', and those of type (2) 'wide analytic truths'. Narrow analytic truths include at least all the truth-functional tautologies and the valid sentences of first-order predicate logic with identity; by contrast, into the class of wide analytic truths fall all the truths of mathematics, Locke's trifling propositions, and more generally all the propositions true by virtue of Kant's IDENTITY-2 formulation.

The obvious problem for Carnap here (pointedly pointed up by Quine in 'Two Dogmas of Empiricism' and again in 'Carnap and Logical Truth') is that, while it is clear enough how narrow analytic truths are *L*-true—that is, some of them are truth-functional tautologies and the rest are deducible from the laws of elementary logic that govern polyadic quantification—it remains rather mysterious how the wide analytic truths are *L*-true. The strategy of systematic translation of wide analytic truths into the narrow class of *L*-truths by means of replacing synonyms by synonyms clearly does not work, as Quine shows, since it necessarily relies on an ambiguous and unexplicated notion of synonymy. And, in using the notion of a semantical rule to generate a list of those sentences or statements *S* that are analytic for a given language *L*, Carnap is merely pushing back the locus of explication to the unexplicated concept of a semantical rule: 'Once we seek to explain "*S* is analytic for *L*" generally for variable "*L*" . . . the explanation "true according to the semantical rules of *L*" is unavailing; for the relative term "semantical rule of" is as much in need of clarification, at least, as "analytic for".'[110] In a famous appendix added to the second or 1956 edition of *Meaning and Necessity*, Carnap offers the ingenious device of 'meaning postulates' as a rejoinder to Quine and as a way out of the problem.[111] His idea is to add to the semantical rules of the language an indefinitely large set of formal sentences representing such intuitively analytic English sentences as "Bachelors are unmarried"—for example, "$(x) (Bx \rightarrow \sim Mx)$". As he puts it: 'If logical relations (e.g., logical implication or incompatibility) hold between the primitive predicates of a system, then the explication of analyticity requires that postulates for all such relations are laid down.'[112] In other words, meaning postulates are supplementary axioms of the formal language for extending the logical reach of the semantical rules. Using the postulates together with the original semantical rules, all narrow and wide analytic sentences can be logically derived as theorems, hence as additional *L*-truths.

Thus Carnap. The big problems here from a Kantian point of view are two, and I will dub them, respectively, 'the selection problem' and 'the modal slide'.

---

[110] Quine, 'Two Dogmas of Empiricism', 34.
[111] Carnap, *Meaning and Necessity*, 222–9.   [112] Ibid. 224.

The Selection Problem

Clearly, the class of meaning postulates coincides with just that class of axioms needed to derive all the wide analytic truths as *L*-truths. That is, they function just like Frege's logical definitions were supposed to, in providing primitive and unprovable premisses for the derivation of all analytic truths that cannot be derived from the logical laws alone. But according to Carnap the class of meaning postulates is selected wholly pre-theoretically, sometimes by appealing to untutored semantic intuition, but ultimately by stipulation. So meaning postulates are definitions by personal or group decision (that is, by convention). He writes:

Suppose that the author of a system wishes the predicates "*B*" and "*M*" to designate the properties Bachelor and Married respectively. How does he know that these properties are incompatible and that therefore he has to lay down postulate P1 [i.e. "(x) $(Bx \rightarrow \sim Mx)$"]? This is not a matter of knowledge, but of decision. His knowledge or belief that the English words "bachelor" and "married" are always or usually understood in such a way that they are incompatible may influence his decision, if he has the intention to reflect in his system some of the meaning relations of English words. In this particular case, the influence would be relatively clear, *but in other cases it would be much less so.*[113]

Now what, we may ask, is the sufficient reason for Carnap's selecting just *that* class of meaning postulates to be stipulated? Either there is another semantical theory behind the theory of meaning postulates, grounding the selection of just *those* meaning postulates by linking their semantic contents up explicitly with the class of wide analytic truths, or else there is no such theory. If there is such a theory, then it must be made explicit. But Carnap never spells out such a theory, for obvious reasons, since it would amount to giving just the sort of theory about the nature of logical definition that Frege was unable to give.

   If, on the other hand, there is no such theory, but all is left to arbitrary or pragmatically based choice, then in fact any grammatically well-formed sentence (other than a narrow analytic falsehood) can in principle count as a meaning postulate. As Carnap points out, the formal sentence "(x) $(Rx \rightarrow Blx)$" (translating the English sentence "All ravens are black") can be adopted as a meaning postulate as easily as "(x) $(Bx \rightarrow \sim Mx)$";[114] but "All ravens are black" clearly does not reflect 'some of the meaning relations of English words', since it is obviously empirically known and contingent. But this directly implies that any contingent sentence in English—presumably even false ones—can in principle be logically derived as *L*-true.[115] Moreover, and perhaps most ironically given Carnap's attack on metaphysical nonsense in his earlier theory of

---

[113] Carnap, *Meaning and Necessity*, 224–5, emphasis added.   [114] Ibid. 225.
[115] See also Pap, *Semantics and Necessary Truth*, 411.

logical syntax,[116] any well-formed logically consistent yet sortally corrupt 'pseudo-proposition' such as 'All green ideas sleep furiously' is at least minimally acceptable as a meaning postulate,[117] thus giving rise to all sorts of analytic pseudo-propositions such as 'If Jack is a green idea, then Jack sleeps furiously.' But all this leads to a logical overproduction problem of epic proportions. For Carnap, a sentence is *L*-true or analytic just in case it is either a truth of first-order logic with identity or else any other sentence we like so long as it is formally consistent with the narrow analytic truths. And that makes the notion of a wide analytic proposition virtually vacuous.

The problem here, in a nutshell, is that the free creation of a concept, or the stipulative adoption of a proposition, guarantees neither empirical meaningfulness nor truth. This point is stressed by Kant. He explicitly allows for what he calls 'arbitrarily invented concepts', which then automatically and trivially support definitions; but 'I cannot, however, say that I have thereby defined a genuine object (*wahren Gegenstand*)' (*CPR* A729/B757). And as for stipulation:

> It seems strange that [Meier[118]] speaks of arbitrary truth. For because I say it, something is not yet true; instead truth must lie in the object. It is better for us to say *arbitrary propositions*, then. These are propositions where I will that something be so, propositions that actually rest on my will. They are commands of my reason . . . (VL Ak. xxiv. 892)

In other words, one should never confuse a decision to act as though a proposition were true, for some special purpose of one's own, with truth. Stipulative definitions are in fact a special subspecies of what Kant in the *Grounding for the Metaphysics of Morals* calls 'imperatives of skill' (*GMM* Ak. iv. 415); hence they are 'commands of my reason', not truth-bearing claims. So, while I *ought* to adopt such and such a meaning postulate if I *want* to be permitted to *call* a certain proposition *P* 'analytic' in a certain language *L* (that is, the means suffices for the logical end that I desire), that goes no distance whatsoever towards showing that *P actually is* analytic, or true in all possible state descriptions.

The Modal Slide

This brings us to the second difficulty. The class of *L*-truths is explicitly intended by Carnap to be coextensive with the class of analytic truths, which in turn

---

[116] See Carnap, *The Logical Syntax of Language*, sects. 72–81.

[117] Meaning postulates are semantical rules that determine the meanings of predicate expressions. Hence, so long as meaning postulates violate no rules of formation or transformation in elementary logic, they are not subject to the charge of meaninglessness. For, as Carnap himself points out, they need not be laid down with any faithfulness whatsoever to meaning relations in natural language.

[118] G. F. Meier was the author of the textbook on which Kant's logic lectures are based.

is supposed to be coextensive with the class of necessary truths. Necessary truths are true in every state description or logically possible world. As we have seen, the addition of meaning postulates enriches the class of L-truths so as to include, in principle, any logically consistent sentence. This means that many intuitively non-necessary sentences—including all sentences of English now intuitively regarded as contingent truths, contingent falsehoods, or grammatically well-formed nonsense—can count as analytic, hence necessary, hence true in all state descriptions or possible worlds.

Carnap points out in 'Meaning Postulates' that to say that a sentence is L-true by means of meaning postulates is to say that it is strictly implied by the set of meaning postulates—hence its L-truth is relative to the set of meaning postulates in the sense that the derived sentence holds in all the state descriptions or possible worlds in which the set of meaning postulates holds.[119] In the section entitled 'My Conception of Semantics' in a retrospective volume on his philosophy, Carnap admits that meaning postulates effectively carve out a set of admissible models (that is, a specially designated set of state descriptions or possible worlds) from the total set of models, for the truth evaluation of wide analytic sentences (which he there calls 'A-true sentences').[120] Now A-true sentences are not true in every model, but instead are true only in every admissible model. Yet Carnap adopts as a basic definition in 'Meaning Postulates' the thesis that every sentence which is L-true relative to the set of the meaning postulates is L-true, *period*, in the language enriched by the set of postulates.[121]

This of course leads to the manifestly paradoxical conclusion that although all L-true sentences are true in every logically possible world, in fact not all L-true sentences are true in every logically possible world. That is, although all L-true sentences are (with the addition of meaning postulates) indeed logically derivable from semantical rules, in fact not all L-true sentences are true in every possible state description. The L-true sentences that are derivable only from meaning postulates are strictly speaking true only in every state description that satisfies the conditions of the relevant postulates. To be sure, the material conditional that takes the conjunction of the relevant meaning postulates as an antecedent and the relevant wide analytic truth as a consequent is satisfied even in worlds in which the relevant postulates are not satisfied. But that is not the same as to say that the consequent of the conditional is satisfied in those worlds. Thus we can discern an unexpected semantical gap between Carnap's original Convention of L-truth and his original Definition of L-truth.

What has gone wrong here? I think that Carnap has unconsciously changed the very meaning of "L-true", by sliding from his original notion of

---

[119] Carnap, *Meaning and Necessity*, 225–6.
[120] See Carnap, 'Replies and Systematic Expositions', 901.
[121] Carnap, *Meaning and Necessity*, 226.

L-truth as *logical derivability from the empty set of premisses* (which holds of narrow analytic truths only) to an extended notion of *L*-truth as *logical derivability from a non-empty, conventionally stipulated set of premisses* (which holds of narrow and wide analytic truths alike). But the maximally strong modal property of the first kind of *L*-truth—that is, truth in all logically possible worlds—does not in fact carry over to the second kind of *L*-truth, which determines truth only in all admissible worlds.

I shall come back to this fundamental issue of the nature of strong modality or necessity in Chapter 5; for the moment we need note only that Carnap must face up to the unhappy consequences of the attempt to cram all necessary truths whatsoever under the single umbrella of analyticity. An obvious alternative would be to admit, adopting Kant's Pitchfork (see Section 1.2), that there is after all more than one kind of necessary truth. But a far more breathtaking alternative would be to give up the concept of analyticity altogether. For all intents and purposes, that is Quine's radically sceptical way out.[122]

3.5. Quine, Analyticity, and Kant

I argued in the last two sections that neither Frege's logico-definitional theory of analyticity nor Carnap's logico-linguistico-stipulative-definitional theory is adequate to the philosophical task of providing a coherent and plausible account of analyticity. Even if Kant's theory of analyticity were not at this point to be deemed superior to the other two, at the very least it should be quite obvious by now that the Fregean and Carnapian theories differ quite substantially from Kant's. Certainly neither of them could now be taken with a straight face to provide a proper explication or reconstruction of *Kant's* doctrine of analyticity. In this way it is not altogether charitable, although of course strategically expedient, for Quine to claim in 'Two Dogmas of Empiricism' that 'Kant's intent, evident more from the use he makes of the notion of analyticity than from his definition of it, can be restated thus: a statement is analytic when it is true by virtue of meanings alone and independently of fact'.[123] Thus in Quine's version of the history of analyticity, Kant becomes Immanuel

---

[122] I hedge my assertion here a little by saying 'for all intents and purposes', because it is not quite correct to say that Quine gives up talking about analyticity altogether. Having rejected the traditional concept of analyticity, he then goes on to develop an account of what he calls 'stimulus analyticity'. A sentence is stimulus analytic for a speaker if and only if she would assent to it (or refuse to assent to anything) under every sensory stimulation; see *Word and Object*, 55, 60–7. But this is a purely deflationary—or, as Quine pithily puts it, a 'strictly vegetarian imitation' (p. 67)—of the traditional concept of analyticity.

[123] Quine, 'Two Dogmas of Empiricism', 21.

von Frege–Carnap. Jerrold Katz remarks drily and quite accurately of this passage that 'Quine's "restatement" of Kant's intent subverts it rather than conforms to it.'[124]

In this section I want to sketch the rudiments of Quine's critique of the Fregean–Carnapian (or logico-linguistic) doctrine of analyticity—which is, of course, the centrepiece of his attack on the analytic/synthetic distinction— with an eye to how Kant could in turn provide a critical response to it. Given the false assimilation of Kant's theory to the Fregean and Carnapian theories, however, the applicability of Quine's critique to Kant's case is bound to be somewhat oblique. Arguments devastating for Frege's or Carnap's theory cannot by any means be automatically carried over to Kant's. Yet it is almost universally assumed by philosophers in the analytic tradition after Quine, I think, that the Quinean arguments *are* automatically and directly applicable to Kant.[125] So long as we keep firmly in mind from the start that this assumption is wrong, however, things will go much more smoothly.

In his brilliant 1935 paper 'Truth by Convention', Quine takes a first crack at the concept of analyticity by showing that logical truth cannot be adequately explained by the notion of stipulative semantical rules or conventions. In a nutshell, the reason is that preconventional logic itself is already presupposed in the application of conventions; therefore such conventions cannot be plausibly taken to supply a non-circular explanation of the nature of a logical truth.[126] Fifteen years later Quine radically expands and extends this critical argument in 'Two Dogmas of Empiricism'. The dogma centrally under attack is the very idea of a conceptually sharp and philosophically well- motivated distinction between analytic and synthetic truths. Quine's stategy is to focus on analyticity, reasoning that, if the concept of analyticity can be undermined (in the sense that every attempt to give a complete or adequate analysis of it must fail in principle), the sharp theoretical line between it and syntheticity will simply disappear.

A fundamental metaphilosophical problem with Quine's strategy in 'Two Dogmas', first pointed up by H. P. Grice and P. F. Strawson,[127] is the obvi- ously dodgy assumption that, *unless* the concept of analyticity can itself be analytically defined, it is of no philosophical use whatsoever. This problem has two components. First, Quine's assumption presupposes that the only admis- sible form of philosophical analysis is that of a non-circular, reductive ana- lytic definition. On the one hand, however, Grice and Strawson themselves offer the alternative method of non-reductive, holistic (that is, non-viciously

[124] Katz, *Cogitations*, 57.

[125] See e.g. Philip Kitcher, 'How Kant almost Wrote "Two Dogmas of Empiricism". (And Why He Didn't)'.   [126] Quine, 'Truth by Convention', 104.

[127] Grice and Strawson, 'In Defense of a Dogma', 148–52.

circular) version of conceptual analysis.[128] And, on the other hand, according to Kant, analytical method in philosophy is primarily oriented towards a non-definitional, non-reductive strategy of transcendental proofs for synthetic a priori propositions (*CPR* A782–90/B810–18). So, unless Quine can show that both non-reductive, holistic conceptual analysis and Kantian transcendental proof are false or pointless philosophical methods, he is not entitled to his exclusionary presupposition. Secondly, Quine's assumption implies that concepts are of no philosophical significance prior to their definitive analysis. But this seems to be contradicted by the very methodology of the analysis of concepts, which must always start out with some concepts already in use as relatively unanalysed primitives, in order to analyse others in terms of them. As Kant puts it, 'if we could not make any use of a concept until we had defined it, then all philosophizing would be in a bad way' (*CPR* A731/B759 n.).

Setting aside the metaphilosophical problems, however, what is Quine's actual argument? He begins by articulating the standard gloss on analyticity as the truth of a sentence by virtue of meanings alone independently of fact, and then immediately proceeds to discard intensional meanings themselves, on the grounds that they cannot be used in any acceptable philosophical explanation of analyticity.[129] Then he distinguishes between two kinds of analytic truth: (1) the truths of first-order predicate logic with identity (= the narrow Carnapian analyticities of Section 3.4), and (2) analytic sentences that are not truths of the first class, but that can be translated into truths of that class by systematically replacing synonyms by synonyms (= the wide Carnapian analyticities).[130] Thus the manifestly analytic sentence "No bachelor is married" is transformable into the narrow analytic truth "No unmarried man is married" simply by replacing "bachelor" by its synonym, "unmarried man". This elegant device not only captures the nub of Carnap's theory of analytic truths as *L*-truths but also implicitly incorporates Frege's view that analytic truths are those propositions either derivable from general logical laws alone or else from general logical laws together with logical definitions. Sentences of the first or narrow class of analyticities are derivable from the empty set of premisses with the use of logical inference rules alone. And each sentence of the second or wide class functions as a premiss, which, under the assumption that all synonymy transformations are valid or truth-preserving, has as a logical consequence that it itself is provable from logical laws alone. So sentences of the wide class of analyticities are, with the addition of the notion of synonymy, the functional equivalents of Frege's logical definitions.[131]

---

[128] The Grice–Strawson doctrine of analyticity ('In Defense of a Dogma', 150–1) has two serious problems, however. First, in its appeal to the distinction 'between not believing something and not understanding something' (p. 151), it is every bit as deflationary as Quine's own successor notion of stimulus analyticity in *Word and Object*. And, secondly, it fails to distinguish between analytic falsity and nonsense.

[129] Quine, 'Two Dogmas of Empiricism', 20–2.   [130] Ibid. 22–4.

[131] See Quine, 'Truth by Convention', 87 and n.

Leaving aside analytic truths of the narrow class (although these will prove to be of importance for us later), Quine focuses on analytic sentences of the wide class. He considers, case by case, several attempts to give a clear and determinate account of synonymy (via the notions of definition, intechange-ability, and semantical rules), and finds them individually and collectively wanting by reason of circularity.[132] He concludes that, in the absence of a non-circular account of synonymy, 'a boundary between analytic and synthetic state-ments simply has not been found. That there is such a distinction to be drawn at all is an unempirical dogma of empiricists, a metaphysical article of faith.'[133] These fine, ringing words announce the end of logical empiricism as a serious philosophical programme—to be replaced, of course, by Quine's own post-empiricist doctrine of holistic, behaviouristic, quasi-pragmatic scientific naturalism.[134] But what precisely is the impact of Quine's attack upon Kant's theory, and what could Kant say in response?

The first thing to say is merely an embellishment upon what I have stressed already—namely, that, since Kant's doctrine of analyticity is neither Frege's nor Carnap's, Quine's critique is simply not directly applicable to Kant's theory. More precisely, Kant's theory does not hold that analytic propositions are true by virtue of meanings alone in Carnap's (or Frege's) sense—that is, true by virtue of semantical rules (or logical laws plus logical definitions) alone. The total class of Kantian analytic propositions is not captured by determin-ing the set of those propositions that are logical truths of elementary logic or else transformable into logical truths of that sort by replacing synonyms with synonyms. This is because—just to take the most obvious reasons—(1) Kant's conception of logical truth is such that many of Frege's or Carnap's logical truths are synthetic, not analytic; (2) Kant's theory of non-logical analyticity appeals to intrinsic relations of conceptual microstructure and com-prehension, not to extrinsic synonymy relations between words; and (3) Kant's

---

[132] Quine, 'Two Dogmas of Empiricism', 24–37. Katz finds a crucial gap in Quine's argument here in the appeal to an inadequate methodology for linguistics—Quine's use of 'substitution criteria' or 'interchangeability' as the central tool of linguistic explanation (*Cogitations*, 28–32).   [133] Quine, 'Two Dogmas of Empiricism', 37.

[134] For the purposes of telling a clear philosophical story I am sharply emphasizing the semantic differences between Carnap's logical empiricism and Quine's post-empiricism, as Quine himself does in 'Two Dogmas'. Nevertheless it is arguable that a suitably broad comparison of Carnap's and Quine's epistemological views would show them to be very similar in content and ultimately divergent only in overall emphasis; see George, 'On Washing the Fur without Wetting it: Quine, Carnap, and Analyticity'. On George's reading, roughly, Carnap holds that analyticity and the a priori are radically epistemically autonomous from empirical facts and scientific methods of enquiry, while Quine holds that analyticity and the a priori are radically epistemically irrelevant to empirical facts and scientific methods of enquiry. What I like about this reading is that it brings out the plausible thought that the step from the radical autonomy of the a priori to the radical irrelevance of the a priori is a short one indeed.

multigrade theory of conceptual identity allows for analytic truths to involve comprehensional identities of concepts alone. So, for Kant, being a proposition of elementary logic (or a substitution instance of one) is not sufficient for analyticity, and synonymy is not a necessary condition of analyticity. Synonymy, as Quine rightly points out, is the key to the Frege–Carnap theory of analyticity—but Kant does not make any sort of appeal to synonymy.[135] So Quine's attack on the Frege–Carnap theory, even if completely sound, will obviously fail to undermine Kant's theory.

The second thing to say is that the only part of Quine's argument in 'Two Dogmas' that really is directly relevant to Kant's theory is his all-too-rapid opening move of throwing intensions in the theoretical dustbin. As we have seen, Kant's theory is strongly intensional and cognitivist. So to trash, with sufficient justification, the very notion of an intension would indeed undermine Kant's theory. In 'Two Dogmas', however, Quine's critique of intensions restricts itself to some tossaway witticisms ('The Aristotelian notion of essence was the forerunner, no doubt, of the modern notion of intension or meaning' and 'Meaning is what essence becomes when it is divorced from the object of reference and wedded to the word'[136]) and to the more substantive assertion that intensions are nothing but 'obscure intermediary entities' between words and their reference. But that latter assertion is not backed up in 'Two Dogmas'; for that we must turn to more detailed argumentation provided by him elsewhere.

Now Quine gives us two references in the footnote corresponding to the 'obscure intermediary entity' passage: to 'On What There Is', and to 'Meaning in Linguistics'. But in fact the *locus classicus* of Quine's attack on intensions is to be found in the crucial chapter VI of *Word and Object*, 'The Flight from Intension'. Quine's flight here—that is, his radical extensionalism—is motivated by the leading idea that semantics can be theoretically reduced to a judicious combination of logical theory, behavioural linguistics, and the theory of reference. Were this reduction to be fully successful, then it would indeed be the case that 'the explanatory value of special and irreducible intermediary entities called meanings is surely illusory'.[137] But is Quine's reduction strategy successful? This is what we must now consider.

Close inspection of Quine's argument shows us that a prior condition of reduction is being able to make a prima facie case for elimination. Intensions must be shown by him to be at worst strictly mythical and at best theoretically otiose. Quine's eliminative argument in turn has two parts. First, he asserts that intensions are at bottom nothing but wholly private psychological entities—mere ideas endowed with the highly non-naturalistic or even occult

---

[135] Indeed, Kant is himself explicitly sceptical about the possibility of exact synonyms (DWL Ak. xxiv. 783).   [136] Quine, 'Two Dogmas of Empiricism', 22.

[137] Quine, 'On What There Is', 12.

property of intentionality.[138] For Quine the 'idea of ideas in the mind'[139]—indeed, mentalism (= the doctrine that human beings and other creatures have ontically irreducible conscious and intentional acts, states, or processes) more generally—is nothing but a philosophical fiction.[140] Secondly, he argues for the thesis that intensions are not in any case actually required for the explanations of any semantic facts.[141] Quine's strategy here is to show that, for every case in which intensions might seem to be in the domain of discourse of semantic theory, a functionally equivalent device not presupposing intensions—a purely extensional eliminative paraphrase—can be developed in its place.

Taking up the first pro-elimination argument, Kant could immediately respond by pointing up the fact that his conceptual intensions are not subjectivistically psychological, even if they are necessarily generated by and realized in individual mental acts, states, or processes. As we have seen, for Kant there is a crucial distinction to be made between the transcendentally grounded, intersubjectively valid semantic content of a representation, and the phenomenological features of the subject who generates that representational content; this captures the nub of Frege's later distinction between objective ideas and subjective ideas. Indeed, Quine can make the charge of the necessary solipsism of intensions even remotely plausible only by narrowing his gaze to the traditional or Lockean theory of meaning (= meanings are nothing but ideas inside the minds of individual thinkers[142]), looked at through Carnapian lenses (= meanings are to be viewed under the aspect of 'methodological solipsism'[143]), thereby again not altogether charitably (but of course also expediently) ignoring the patent fact of non-solipsistic, non-psychologistic theories of intensions.[144] And finally, as far as mentalism itself is concerned, Quine frankly admits that he has no decisive arguments against it and just chooses anti-mentalism.[145]

This leaves the second pro-elimination argument, and here Quine is on firmer ground. He points out that intensions have been taken by their proponents

---

[138] See Quine, 'The Problem of Meaning in Linguistics', 47–8, and *Word and Object*, 216–21, 264–6.   [139] Quine, 'On What There Is', 9.

[140] See Quine, 'On Mental Entities', and Quine, 'Mind and Verbal Dispositions'.

[141] Quine, *Word and Object*, 191–232.

[142] See Hanna, 'How Ideas Became Meanings: Locke and the Foundations of Semantic Theory'.

[143] For a similar move, see Putnam, 'The Meaning of "Meaning"', 218–22. Methodological solipsism is a psychologistic strategy used by Carnap in the *Aufbau* for the logical construction of ordinary empirical cognition from 'elementary experiences'.

[144] Frege's theory of meaning is an obvious counter-example, since it allows for mind-independent fine-grained intensions—senses or *Sinne*. Indeed, one of the many small puzzles of 'Two Dogmas of Empiricism' is how Quine can consistently reject intensions altogether and yet still accept Frege's distinction between sense and reference (p. 21).

[145] Quine, *Word and Object*, 221.

to fill six important explanatory roles. First, intensions are used to explain how words and sentences are meaningful in the first place, by providing special entities for words and sentences to signify. Secondly, intensions function as truth vehicles, or as what remains eternally true or false across varying circumstances of the utterance of sentences. Thirdly, intensions explain how words or sentences can have the same meaning within the same language or across different languages, by remaining identical or constant under inscriptional, syntactical, and even terminological variations. Fourthly, intensions provide objects to which to attribute the modal properties expressed by sentences about possibility or necessity. Fifthly, intensions provide objects for sentences about propositional attitudes such as belief-that-*P* and doubt-that-*P*. Sixthly, intensions function as the direct objects of philosophical analysis. But for each semantical function, according to Quine, a functionally equivalent extensional substitute can be devised.

More specifically, acccording to Quine, the meaningfulness of words and sentences can be construed as nothing but the construction of 'significant sequences' of phonemes.[146] A sentence's being a truth vehicle can be explained in terms of 'eternal sentences', or sentences explicitly describing all relevant contextual details of their utterance.[147] Sameness of meaning can be explained as linguistic synonymy under strictly behavioural conditions and within the constraints of the fact of universal (that is, cross-language, infra-language, cross-idiomatic, and even infra-idiomatic) translational indeterminacy.[148] The interdefinable modal terms "necessarily" and "possibly" can be treated as metalinguistic predicates applying to names of logically true or logically consistent sentences; or, alternatively, whole sentences governed by one or other of the modal predicates can be treated as interdefinable with some specially designated logically true or consistent sentence.[149] The objects of propositional attitudes can be taken to be merely the sentences assented to by speakers; or else all "believes-that" constructions can be treated as primitive 'fused' predicates ("believes-that-*P*", "believes-that-*Q*", and so on) susceptible to the same sort of translational indeterminacy that afflicts the 'stimulus synonymy' of predicates more generally.[150] And, lastly, the substantive assumption of underlying intensional objects for philosophical analysis can be replaced by the purely procedural notion of a 'canonical notation'—the apparatus of first-order predicate logic construed as an all-purpose paraphrastic or definitional tool.[151] There are many semantical jobs to be done, but intensional entities need not apply.

Just for the sake of argument, let us grant Quine that explicit talk about intensional entities in these six cases can be translated without theoretical

---

[146] Quine, 'The Problem of Meaning in Linguistics', 49–56, and *Word and Object*, 195.

[147] Quine, *Word and Object*, 191–4, 206–9, 226–7.   [148] See n. 162.

[149] See Quine, 'Reference and Modality', and Quine, *Word and Object*, 195–200.

[150] Quine, *Word and Object*, 211–21.   [151] Ibid., ch. V, and pp. 226–32.

remainder into talk about purely extensional or naturalistically kosher sorts of things. The claim I would like to challenge directly here is the blanket thesis that intensions are never required in semantic explanation. And what I want to focus on is a fundamental notion left conspicuously unreduced by Quine in 'Two Dogmas' and elsewhere: that of a logical truth.[152] This is particularly important, since it directly and essentially presupposes the canonical notation so central to Quine's austere semantics. Logical truths are, in effect, sentences true by virtue of the rules of the canonical notation alone.

In 'Truth by Convention', Quine defines a truth of logic as a true sentence in which only the logical constants occur 'essentially'.[153] In other words, a logical truth is a sentence that remains true under absolutely every distinct uniform assignment of values to its non-logical constants. But for slight differences in terminology, this account is preserved intact in Quine's later writings as well.[154] I will leave aside the admittedly hard question of how to formulate a criterion for selecting the logical constants,[155] and ask the more direct question: 'what *is* an "essential occurrence" of an expression?'

Quine says that an expression occurs essentially in a statement just in case every other expression occurs 'vacuously' in that statement—just in case 'its replacement therein by any and every other grammatically admissible expression leaves the truth or falsehood of the statement unchanged'.[156] So an essentially occurring expression is a subexpression of a sentence that holds its semantic function and interpretation fixed under absolutely every uniform variation of the interpretations of the other subexpressions. It belongs, as Quine puts it, to the 'skeleton of symbolic make-up',[157] or deep logical form, of the sentence. But—and here is the Kantian critical point—whatever holds its interpretation invariant in this way *must* be an intension. Only an intension could consist in the lawlike or strict determination of semantic values across all consistent arrangements of things, corresponding to the varying interpretations of the non-logical expressions. What Quine is really saying, then, is that a logical constant holds its interpretation fixed in *all possible worlds*. So Quine's notion of an essential occurrence is an uneliminated and unreduced intensional notion embedded in the core of logic, and thus the very idea of

---

[152] In the argument that follows in the next few paragraphs, I exploit the general strategy of criticism sketched by Strawson in 'Propositions, Concepts, and Logical Truths'. Strawson argues that Quine's definition of a logical truth covertly involves an appeal to irreducibly intensional notions. Whereas Strawson focuses on the role of non-logical constants in logical truths, however, I focus on the role of the logical constants.

[153] Quine, 'Truth by Convention', 80.

[154] See Quine, 'Two Dogmas of Empiricism', 22–3; Quine, *Methods of Logic*, 4; and Quine, *Philosophy of Logic*, 47–60.

[155] See Quine, *Word and Object*, 57–61. See also Pap, *Semantics and Necessary Truth*, 133–43; Tarski, 'On the Concept of Logical Consequence', 418–19; and Warmbrod, 'Logical Constants'.   [156] Quine, 'Truth by Convention', 80.

[157] Ibid.

logical truth presupposes intensions. Ironically enough, then, Quine's logical truths are true by virtue of intensions alone.[158]

What Quine calls 'essentially occurring expressions' are, in effect, a special subclass of what Kant calls the 'logical functions of all possible judgements' (*CPR* A79/B105), which in turn correlate directly with the categories, or pure concepts of the understanding. Indeed, Quine himself explicitly speaks in *Word and Object* of the fundamental components of the canonical notation—predication, universal quantification, and the truth functions—as conveying 'a philosophical doctrine of categories'.[159] This is not a slip of the pen. He also says that 'the quest of a simplest clearest overall theory of canonical notation is not to be distinguished from a quest of ultimate categories, a limning of the most general traits of reality'.[160] And even more tantalizingly, he remarks in a later essay that, when the device of quantification is viewed purely relativistically, 'both truth and ontology may in a suddenly rather clear and even tolerant sense be said to belong to transcendental metaphysics'.[161] These passages suggest a very strong internal connection between Quine's 'quest of a simplest overall theory of canonical notation' and Kant's Metaphysical Deduction of the pure concepts of the understanding. Quine's canonical notation is, in effect, a relativized transcendental logic.

For both Kant and Quine, then, logical truths are true by virtue of categorial concepts alone. So Quine has by no means flown from intensions altogether; he has simply narrowed the class of philosophically acceptable intensions. If he then turns around and successfully reduces non-logical intensions to other sorts of items, using logical devices and the canonical notation, then at best he has shown only that the former sorts of intensions are definable in terms of a privileged or categorial sort of intensions and some other non-intensional things. But then, why not simply admit that intensions

---

[158] Quine's own official position on this crucial issue has taken various twists and turns. In 'Two Dogmas of Empiricism', 22, 43, he begins by admitting that logical truths are genuinely analytic, but ends by asserting that even logical truths are revisable. In 'Carnap and Logical Truth', 107–11, he says that the linguistic theory of logical truth is perfectly acceptable for the truths of elementary logic, although not acceptable for those logical truths involving set theory. In *Word and Object*, 57–61, he argues that the truth-functional logical constants escape translational indeterminacy, but then also says in a footnote (p. 65 n. 3) that he does not 'embrace the analyticity of the truths of logic as an antecedently intelligible doctrine' because of Tarskian worries about selecting criteria for logical constancy. And in *Philosophy of Logic*, he claims (1) that anyone who seriously denied a law of logic like the principle of non-contradiction would have to change the very meanings of the logical constants (p. 81); (2) that 'logic is true by virtue of language only as, vacuously, it is true by virtue of anything and everything' (p. 97); but nevertheless finally (3) that 'logic is in principle no less open to revision than quantum mechanics or the theory of relativity' (p. 100). I doubt that all these claims can be made consistent with one another. See also the 'Concluding Un-Quinean Postscript' below.

[159] Quine, *Word and Object*, 228.   [160] Ibid. 161.

[161] Quine, 'Ontological Relativity', 68.

are essential to semantic explanations right across the board? Why covertly accept one kind of intension—the logical constants of elementary logic—while officially banning the others? The truth is that Quine's flight from intensions never really happened. You cannot flee from your own getaway vehicle.

3.6. Conclusion

I have argued that Kant's cognitivist theory of analyticity stands up well against internal and external criticism of Kant's doctrine; against competing views on analyticity; and against Quine's radically sceptical attack on the very idea of analyticity.[162] Since Kant's theory of analyticity does stand up well, then analyticity in his sense can function as a solid left-hand term of the much-battered analytic/synthetic distinction. So we may now turn our attention to the right-hand term, syntheticity.

This chapter also has a broader Kantian moral that might be summarized as follows. All creatures minded like us are compelled to think via concepts. Otherwise put, concepts are cognitively indispensable because they are the proper outputs of the natural activation of the discursive side of our psychological constitution. Since concepts are cognitively indispensable, philosophy must admit the legitimacy of the concept CONCEPT. But the concept CONCEPT leads directly to the idea of a conceptually necessary truth—the analytic proposition. The function of an analytic truth is to express intrinsic features of the form and content of the several concepts included within our total conceptual repertoire. Therefore we must admit the legitimacy of the concept of analyticity. Analyticity is a genuine concept which philosophy is better off *with*.

---

[162] Dummett has argued that Quine's later attack on the analytic/synthetic distinction from the indeterminacy of translation in *Word and Object*, ch. II, is an independent and important argument; see 'The Significance of Quine's Indeterminacy Thesis (1973)'. But on the contrary it seems to me (1) that the indeterminacy argument begs the question by assuming Quine's holism, behaviourism, and fallibilism—which jointly presuppose the rejection of the analytic/synthetic distinction; and (2) that the indeterminacy thesis fails in any case because it inconsistently appeals to the fact that we can intuitively fix fine-grained differences between intensions of predicates in order to show that sensory stimulations and behavioural dispositions underdetermine precisely those fine-grained intuitive differences. See also Katz, *The Metaphysics of Meaning*, ch. 5.

4.

The Significance of Syntheticity

I consider Kant did great service in drawing the distinction between synthetic and analytic judgments.

Gottlob Frege[1]

4.0. Introduction

Nearly all discussions of the analytic/synthetic distinction reflect an important bias—what for lack of a better term I will call the 'privileging of the analytic'. This privileging of the analytic entails a corresponding underprivileging of the synthetic. For instance, on the standard gloss of analyticity, according to which a proposition is analytic when it is true by virtue of meanings and independently of fact, one can derive by negation only the thesis that a proposition is synthetic if and only if it is true not by virtue of meanings, or not independently of fact—or, of course, both. But the standard gloss offers no good explanation of how a proposition could ever be true by virtue of something other than meanings, or of what it is for the content of a proposition to be fact-dependent.

The Kantian picture of these matters is very different. As I have argued, Kant's general aim in the first *Critique* is to explain how objective mental representations and their meanings (that is, their intersubjectively accessible object-specifying contents) are possible; more specifically how necessary a priori objective mental representations are possible; and most specifically how synthetic a priori propositions are possible. Without a well-worked-out doctrine of syntheticity, then, Kant's programme would fall short of its own goal. So—given its privileging of the analytic and underprivileging of the synthetic—while the analytic tradition from Frege to Quine generally treats syntheticity as a mere adjunct of the concept of analyticity, for Kant the concept of syntheticity is instead the dog that wags the tail of analyticity. I mean that the

[1] Frege, *The Foundations of Arithmetic*, 101.

general cognitive semantics of synthetic truth inherently constrains and negatively determines the cognitive semantics of analytic truth. And, as we shall
see, this implies that for Kant the cognitive semantics of *intuitions* inherently
constrains and negatively determines the cognitive semantics of *concepts*.

Given this important difference in philosophical orientation, it seems self-
evident that an adequate investigation into Kant's theory of syntheticity in
relation to the analytic tradition up to Quine must begin with the full recognition of a text (partially quoted as this chapter's epigraph) found near the
end of Frege's *Foundations of Arithmetic*:

I consider Kant did great service in drawing the distinction between synthetic and
analytic judgements. In calling the truths of geometry synthetic and a priori, he revealed
their true nature. And this is still worth repeating, since even today it is often not
recognized. If Kant was wrong about arithmetic, that does not seriously detract, in
my opinion, from the value of his work. His point was that there are such things as
synthetic judgements a priori; whether they are to be found in geometry only, or in
arithmetic as well, is of less importance.[2]

Now it is undeniably true that, as Michael Dummett puts it, 'analytical
philosophy is post-Fregean philosophy'.[3] Frege's anti-psychologism and his
logicism—in particular, his logical definition of the concept of a number and
his new non-Kantian conception of an analytic truth—initiate and repeatedly
motivate the analytic tradition, whether by acceptance, modification, or rejection. But we can plainly see that in this crucial text Frege also emphatically
endorses Kant's theory of syntheticity, by way of endorsing his conception of
geometric propositions: 'in calling the truths of geometry synthetic and a
priori, he revealed their true nature.' In fact Frege never takes back this
endorsement, and at several stages in his later career he explicitly reaffirms it.[4]
Yet it is frequently asserted by historians of the analytic tradition that Kant's
doctrines and Frege's doctrines are as different as oil and water.[5] This idea is
perhaps most vigorously expressed by Dummett, who asserts that 'it was almost
certainly a historical necessity that the revolution which made the theory of
meaning the foundation of philosophy should be accomplished by someone
like Frege who had for idealism not an iota of sympathy',[6] and again that 'Frege

    [2] Frege, *The Foundations of Arithmetic*, 101–2.
    [3] Dummett, 'Can Analytical Philosophy be Systematic, and Ought it to Be?', 441.
    [4] See Frege's letter to Hilbert in 1899, in *Philosophical and Mathematical Correspondence*,
100; his 1903 paper, 'On the Foundations of Geometry', 22–6; and his unfinished MSS,
'A New Attempt at a Foundation for Arithmetic' and 'Sources of Knowledge of Mathematics
and the Mathematical Natural Sciences', both written in 1924–5.
    [5] See e.g. Coffa, *The Semantic Tradition from Kant to Carnap*, 62–82.
    [6] Dummett, *Frege: Philosophy of Language*, 684. Dummett's influential interpretation
of Frege has been challenged by Sluga in *Gottlob Frege*, esp. chs. I–II; see also 'Frege: The
Early Years'. Sluga very usefully situates Frege's doctrines in relation to the neo-Kantian
idealistic tradition deriving from Lotze; but he overstates his case somewhat by insisting

overtly discusses Kant's views almost exclusively to disagree with them'.[7] What explains this interpretive blind spot? What explains this tendency in the historiography of analytic philosophy to play down or even suppress Frege's acceptance of Kant's theory of syntheticity?

Well, is it not rather like the normally unseen gap every human being has in the middle of her visual field, which is tacitly filled in by the mind/brain in order to preserve the representational integrity of visual perception? Taken this way, the obvious reason for overlooking any deep Kant–Frege connections lies simply in the natural felt need of any genuine intellectual tradition for a sense of historical integrity. Hence there must appear to be a smooth intellectual continuity between the earlier stages of the analytic tradition and its later stages. Since the parameters of debate in the analytic tradition are set by the central focus on semantics, by the project of reducing mathematics to logic, by the impossibility of the synthetic a priori, and by the acceptance or sceptical rejection of some version of the logico-linguistic theory of necessary truth, then what is bound to seem of paramount importance when considering the historical relationship between Frege and Kant is Frege's rejection of Kant's theories of arithmetic and analyticity.

Nevertheless, this highly selective way of looking backwards suppresses a stubborn and possibly uncomfortable fact about the historical foundations of analytic philosophy: that Frege's rejection of Kant's theories of arithmetic and analyticity are seamlessly coupled with an equal and seemingly opposite endorsement of Kant's thoroughly anti-logicist and anti-logical-empiricist doctrines of syntheticity, geometry, and (especially) intuition.[8] But, if one plays up Frege's logicism to the exclusion of Frege's intuitionism, then a crucial dimension of the actual Fregean origins of analytic philosophy will go unacknowledged.

My goal in this chapter is to work out an interpretation of Kant's theory of syntheticity with an eye to exposing this dimension. More precisely, I want to sketch the basics of Kant's theory of syntheticity in relation to Frege's theory, and, in the course of so doing, offer good historical and philosophical

that Frege is a transcendental idealist. In many respects Frege's epistemology is closer to Cartesian rationalism, as Carl urges in *Frege's Theory of Sense and Reference*. Yet Carl also goes too far in asserting that Frege is not in any sense a platonist, and that his epistemological aims always dominate over his logico-semantic aims. Frege *is* in some respects a platonist, as Burge effectively argues in 'Frege on Knowing the Third Realm'. And Frege's concern with epistemology is indeed essentially complementary to and coordinated with his overall logical and semantic aims, not dominant over them. The fact is that Frege's view is *sui generis*. He simultaneously incorporates Kantian, rationalistic, and platonic doctrines into a single highly original doctrine, and he simultaneously pursues epistemological and logico-semantic aims.

[7] Dummett, *Frege: Philosophy of Mathematics*, 2.

[8] In 'Frege and Kant on Geometry', 243–4, 254, Dummett concedes that Frege's theory of syntheticity is equivalent to Kant's—yet denies that this commits Frege to intuitionism. But see Sect. 4.4 below.

reasons for challenging the vigorous anti-intuitionism that generally characterizes the analytic tradition after Frege and right up to Quine. This time my
argument has three stages. First, in Section 4.1, I claim that, according to both
Kant and Frege, a proposition is synthetic just in case its meaning and truth[9]
(whether necessary or contingent) strictly depend upon intuition. An added
bonus of this doctrine of syntheticity is that it leads to a new, negative
characterization of an analytic proposition as a proposition that is necessarily
true *without* strict dependence on intuition. And it also points up another
deep affinity between Kant and Frege—the thesis that the logico-semantic
and epistemic-cognitive domains are essentially complementary. Secondly, the
rudiments of Kant's all-important doctrine of intuition are spelled out in Sections
4.2 and 4.3. I argue that, in sharp contrast with a Kantian concept, a Kantian
intuition is a non-descriptive, sensibility-related, singular representation that
incorporates a relation either to actual empirical individuals (via empirical
intuition), or to the a priori structures of space and time that in turn govern
all actual and possible sense experience of the empirical natural world (via
pure intuition). Thirdly and finally, in Section 4.4 I argue that, despite some
appearances to the contrary, Frege's theory of intuition is not only a necessary part of his semantics but also equivalent to Kant's.

Sections 4.2–4.4 emphasize what I take to be the most important feature
of both syntheticity and intuition: 'essential indexicality'.[10] A representation
(or a term within another representation) is indexical just in case its semantic
content is based (at least in part) on subject-centred and contextual—that
is, actual or existential, environmental, spatiotemporal, or worldly—factors;
and a term is *essentially* indexical just in case it is indexical and cannot
be replaced without loss of meaning by any conceptual, descriptive, or
otherwise non-subject-centred and non-context-dependent term. If I am right,
then Kantian and Fregean intuitions alike introduce essentially indexical
elements into the contents of all synthetic propositions and thereby determine
their semantic and modal characters.

4.1. Frege, Kant, and Syntheticity

As I mentioned in Section 3.3, the driving force behind all of Frege's work in
logic, mathematics, and philosophy is his logicism, according to which all truths
of arithmetic are analytic logical truths, and all arithmetical concepts are expressible in purely logical terms. Frege's doctrine of analyticity is that a proposition

---

[9] I adopt here the same simplifying assumption as in Ch. 3, by focusing on true propositions only.
[10] I borrow the useful phrase "essential indexicality" from Perry; see 'The Problem of
the Essential Indexical'.

is analytic if and only if it is rigorously deducible from one or both of two special classes of primitive or unprovable truths—general logical laws and logical definitions (plus whatever is presupposed by the definitions):

The problem [of properly drawing the analytic/synthetic distinction (RH)] becomes, in fact, that of finding the proof of the proposition, and of following it right back to the primitive truths. If, in carrying our this process, we come only on general logical laws and on definitions, then the truth is an analytic one, bearing in mind that we must take account also of all propositions upon which the admissibility of any of the definitions depends.[11]

Now the fundamental problem with Frege's doctrine, we will remember, is that he cannot ultimately make clear sense of the crucial notion of a logical definition. This renders Frege's doctrine of analyticity, to use Benacerraf's pithy phrase, 'correspondingly unclear, or at least unspecified'. But, backing away from analyticity now, this naturally leads us to further questions. What about Frege's views on the analytic proposition's silent partner, the synthetic proposition? Are they also 'unclear' or 'unspecified'?

Frege holds that a proposition is synthetic if and only if it is derivable only by using, as premises, primitive or unprovable truths of a non-logical nature:

If, however, it is impossible to give the proof without making use of truths which are not of a general logical nature, but belong to the sphere of some special science, then the proposition is a synthetic one. For a [synthetic] truth to be a posteriori, it must be impossible to construct a proof of it without including an appeal to facts, i.e., to truths which cannot be proved and are not general, since they contain assertions about determinate objects. But if, on the contrary, its proof can be derived exclusively from general laws, which themselves neither need nor admit of proof, then the [synthetic or analytic] truth is a priori.[12]

In order to understand this doctrine, we need to know just what it is for a primitive or unprovably true proposition to 'belong to the sphere of some special science'. A special science, it turns out, can be as abstract and general as geometry, or as concrete and factual as any form of enquiry that includes empirical propositions as assumptions—which is to say that, for Frege, primitive truths of a special science can be either a priori or a posteriori. That is clear enough. But the appeal to special science may seem to be every bit as troublesome as Frege's appeal to logical definitions. If, as it first appears, a special science is simply any science other than logic or arithmetic, then it looks suspiciously as if the synthetic is merely the non-analytic. And in that case the theory of syntheticity too depends entirely, although negatively, upon the thoroughly vexed notion of a logical definition.

Here, however, it proves very useful to look more closely again at Frege's general remarks about the analytic/synthetic distinction:

[11] Frege, *The Foundations of Arithmetic*, 4.
[12] Ibid., translation modified slightly.

It not uncommonly happens that we first discover the content of a proposition, and only later give the rigorous proof of it, on other and more difficult lines; and often this same proof also reveals more precisely the conditions restricting the validity of the original proposition. In general, therefore, the question of how we arrive at the content of a judgement should be kept distinct from the other question, Whence do we derive the justification for its assertion? Now these distinctions between a priori and a posteriori, synthetic and analytic concern, as I see it, not [how we arrive at] the content of the judgement but [whence we derive] the justification for making the judgement. Where there is no such justification, the possibility of drawing the distinction vanishes. . . . When a proposition is called a posteriori or analytic in my sense, this is not a judgement about the conditions, psychological, physiological and physical, which have made it possible to form the content of the judgement in our consciousness; nor is it a judgement about the way in which some other man has come, perhaps erroneously, to believe it true; rather, it is a judgement about the ultimate ground upon which rests the justification for holding it to be true.[13]

The crucial thing to notice is Frege's sharp distinction between (1) the purely subjective and/or psychological elements of cognition on the one hand—consciousness (*Bewußtsein*) and the mental or physiological processes by which belief or holding-to-be-true (*Fürwahrhalten*) comes about—and (2) the non-subjective, non-psychological epistemic element of justification (*Berechtigung*) on the other. Justification has to do with the objective ultimate ground (*tiefsten Grunde*) for belief in a proposition. Broadly speaking, we can say that for Frege belief in a proposition Q is ultimately grounded if and only if there is a set of true propositions $P1, P2, P3, \ldots Pn$, from which Q is logically provable, and all of the Pi are primitive or unprovably true. The existence of a logical justification for a proposition thus fully determines that proposition's semantic character.

In this way, Frege's semantics of propositions in *Foundations* is objectively proof based or deduction based.[14] This can be seen clearly in his brief remarks about the nature of logical proof. In the long text quoted just above, he makes the pregnant remark that 'the rigorous proof' of a proposition 'reveals more precisely the conditions restricting the validity of the original proposition'. Later in *Foundations* he points out that, on his view, every arithmetical truth 'would contain concentrated within it a whole series of deductions for further use, and the use of it would be that we need no longer make the deductions one by one, but can express (*aussprechen*) simultaneously the result of the whole series'.[15] And, most famously of all, he thinks of all analytic propositions as in a certain special sense contained in the set of general logical laws

---

[13] Frege, *The Foundations of Arithmetic*, 3. The bracketed material I have added for clarification is controversial; I offer a rationale for it in the next few paragraphs.

[14] Indeed, this is Frege's view throughout all his logicist writings, as Burge points out in 'Frege on Knowing the Foundation', 306–15.

[15] Frege, *The Foundations of Arithmetic*, 24.

and logical definitions from which they are logically provable: 'The truth is that they are contained in the definitions, but as plants are contained in their seeds, not as beams are contained in a house. Often we need several definitions for the proof of some proposition, which consequently is not contained in any one of them alone, yet does follow purely logically from all of them together.'[16] In other words, Frege's view in *Foundations* is that the semantic content of any true non-primitive or derived proposition wholly incorporates and expresses some objective truth-guaranteeing derivation or proof of that proposition. So the content of the derived proposition is provably contained in the set of its premises. These derivations are not the immediate or automatic outcomes of general logical laws, or even usually of general logical laws plus a single logical definition, but instead follow organically from complexes of laws and definitions (together, of course, with other propositions upon which the introduction of a definition depends). The truth conditions of a proposition are thus fully determined by its objective proof conditions, in the sense that the necessary and sufficient condition of a non-primitive proposition Q's being true is the existence of a rigorous logical proof of Q from a set of primitive or unprovable true premises plus other assumptions needed for the introduction of definitions.

It is not my intention here to work out Frege's proof-based semantics of propositions, interesting though that might be for its own sake. The point I am making is that Frege's analytic/synthetic distinction can be plausibly understood to turn entirely on the way in which the justification of a belief is ultimately grounded, which in turn depends on the type of logical proof of that proposition—which in turn depends on the type of primitive or unprovable true premises of that proof. Since each such proof does indeed go back to primitive or unprovable starting points, the only way of discriminating between them lies in the differing epistemic or cognitive modes of access to those starting points. So what semantically distinguishes the analytic and synthetic types of propositions is given in the mode of epistemic or cognitive access to the different types of primitive or unprovable propositions upon which justified beliefs in the derived propositions are ultimately grounded.

This epistemically or cognitively oriented semantic picture of Frege's analytic/synthetic distinction is confirmed in his closely related appeal to what he calls the three 'sources of knowledge'.[17] These are: (1) thinking or conceptualizing (the logical source); (2) pure spatial intuition (the geometrical source); and (3) sense perception. This crucial doctrine of the three sources of knowledge appears in Frege's writings throughout his career, showing up

---

[16] Ibid. 101.

[17] Here I use "knowledge" to translate "*Erkenntnis*" rather than "cognition", because Frege—unlike Kant—does seem to assume that every *Erkenntnis* is true, and because the standard translations of Frege's works usually use "knowledge".

in correspondence or manuscripts in 1882, 1899, and 1924–5.[18] Most importantly, in these texts, Frege explicitly characterizes the three fundamentally different sorts of propositions (analytic a priori, synthetic a priori, synthetic a posteriori) by direct appeal to the three knowledge-sources. The two triads line up in the following way:

Epistemic-Cognitive		*Logico-Semantic*
the logical source	<---------------->	analytic a priori
the geometrical source	<---------------->	synthetic a priori
sense perception	<---------------->	synthetic a posteriori.

The fundamental idea here, again, is that the three different sources of knowledge severally supply immediate veridical access to the relevantly different sorts of primitive or unprovable premises required as starting points for the proofs that in turn supply ultimate objective grounds for justified beliefs in the relevantly different sorts of propositions.[19] The logical source gives access to the absolutely general logical laws and logical definitions needed as primitive premises for the derivation of analytic propositions in pure logic or arithmetic. Correspondingly, the geometric source gives access to the general spatial axioms or postulates required as primitive premises for deductions of synthetic a priori propositions in geometry. And, finally, sense perception gives access to the fully factual or empirical primitive premises needed in inductive or quasi-deductive derivations of synthetic a posteriori propositions in the natural sciences.

It is striking, and I think in a sense essential, that Frege never even raises the questions of how such sources of knowledge are themselves possible, or how they can be invulnerable to sceptical worries. He assumes without argument that our capacities for exploiting the three sources of cognition are also sources of knowledge—that they are perfectly reliable and truth-tracking. Is this a blatant case of begging the question? No. A better explanation is that, while Frege is fully aware of the existence of sceptical problems, his appeal to epistemic or cognitive notions is first and foremost simply a smooth methodological conduit to the logical and semantic distinctions he wants to make. Conversely, his basic logical and semantic distinctions are, as we have seen, also directly cashed out in epistemic-cognitive terms. For Frege, then, epistemic-cognitive factors are always directly complementary to and essentially coordinated with logico-semantic factors. Neither domain, in the end, dominates over the other. This direct interplay of the logico-semantic and the

---

[18] See Frege's letters to Marty in 1882 and Hilbert in 1899, both in *Philosophical and Mathematical Correspondence*, 37, 100; and also 'A New Attempt at a Foundation for Arithmetic' and 'Sources of Knowledge of Mathematics and the Mathematical Natural Sciences'.

[19] See also De Pierris, 'Frege and Kant on a Priori Knowledge', 296, and Burge, 'Frege on Knowing the Foundation'.

epistemic-cognitive is, of course, Kantian to the core; the only salient difference between Kant and Frege here is that Kant also goes on to raise deeper transcendental-idealist questions about the conditions of the possibility of the various sources of knowledge.

Let us focus on the two epistemic sources that are correlated with the two classes of synthetic proposition. What sorts of knowledge are these, and how do they determine the semantic character of syntheticity? In a letter to Anton Marty in 1882, and then later in *Foundations* in 1884, Frege quite explicitly lays out his views on the nature of syntheticity:

I regard it as one of Kant's great merits to have recognized the propositions of geometry as synthetic judgments, but I cannot allow him the same in the case of arithmetic. The cases are anyway quite different. The field of geometry is the field of possible spatial intuition; arithmetic recognizes no such limitation. . . . The area of the enumerable is as wide as that of conceptual thought, and a source of cognition more restricted in scope, like spatial intuition or sense perception, would not suffice to guarantee the general validity of arithmetical propositions.[20]

We shall do well in general not to overestimate the extent to which arithmetic is akin to geometry. . . . One geometrical point, considered by itself, cannot be distinguished in any way from any other; the same applies to lines and planes. Only when several points, or planes, or lines, are included together in a single intuition, do we distinguish them. In geometry, therefore, it is quite intelligible that general propositions should be derived from intuition; the points or lines which we intuit are not really particular at all, which is what enables them to stand as representatives of the whole of their kind. . . . Empirical propositions hold good of what is physically or psychologically actual (*Wirklichkeit*), the truths of geometry govern all that is spatially intuitable, whether real or product of our fancy. The wildest visions of delirium, the boldest visions of legend and poetry, where animals speak and stars stand still, where men are turned to stone and trees turn into men, where the drowning men haul themselves up out of swamps by their own topknots—all these remain, so long as they remain intuitable, still subject to the axioms of geometry. Conceptual thought alone after a fashion shakes off this yoke, when it assumes, say, a space of four dimensions or positive curvature. To study such conceptions is not useless by any means; but it is to leave the ground of intuition entirely behind. If we do make use of intuition even here, as an aid, it is still the same old intuition of Euclidean space, the only one whose structures we can intuit. For purposes of conceptual thought we can always assume the contrary of some one or another of the geometrical axioms, without involving ourselves in any contradictions, when we proceed to our deductions, despite the conflict between our assumptions and our intuition. The fact that this is possible shows that the axioms of geometry are independent of one another and of the primitive laws of logic and consequently are synthetic.[21]

---

[20] Frege, *Philosophical and Mathematical Correspondence*, 100.

[21] Frege, *The Foundations of Arithmetic*, 19–21. See also Frege's letter to Hilbert, in *Philosophical and Mathematical Correspondence*, 37, and 'On the Foundations of Geometry'. Frege, like Kant, holds that non-Euclidean geometry is thinkable but not cognizable (in the narrow sense); see Sects. 5.4–5.5 below.

Several extremely important claims are crammed into these texts. First, a synthetic proposition is true if and only if it is directly related—by way of a source of knowledge that gives access to the primitive, unprovable premisses of the proof and that justifies belief in that proposition—either to sense perception (in the case of empirical propositions) or to spatial intuition (in the case of geometric propositions). Secondly, arithmetical propositions—a special class of analytic propositions—are by contrast true if and only if directly related by their epistemic grounds to the enumerable (the platonic domain of numbers), which is coextensive with the field of conceptual thought governed solely by the primitive laws of logic. Now numbers for Frege are sets or classes of equinumerous classes, and classes are in turn extensions of concepts;[22] hence all arithmetical cognition is conceptual cognition. Thirdly, a common feature shared by sense perception and spatial intuition is that each is a source of knowledge more restricted in scope than the conceptual-logical thinking that grounds analytic arithmetical propositions. This restrictedness derives from the brute contingency of the objects of perception (as 'actual' (*wirklich*) or spatially real) and of Euclidean space (as only one among the many conceptually possible types of space). Fourthly, while sense perception and spatial intuition share the common feature of their restrictedness, they differ in that (*a*) sense perception relates the proposition to 'what is physically or psychologically actual'—the empirical world, and that (*b*) spatial intuition relates the proposition to 'all that is spatially intuitable, whether actual or product of our fancy'. Thus sense perception relates to empirical or a posteriori facts containing concrete empirical objects or mental states, while spatial intuition relates to general and non-empirical or a priori features of actual Euclidean space.[23] In other words, all true empirical propositions are synthetic, contingent, and a posteriori by virtue of their relation to sensory perception or introspection of real individuals; by contrast, true geometric propositions are synthetic, necessary, and a priori because they are related via pure spatial intuition to whatever must obtain in all and only the possible spatially intuitable (= Euclidean) worlds. Fifthly and finally, the denial of a synthetic proposition —be it contingent and a posteriori, or necessary and a priori—is always logically and conceptually consistent. In the case of true geometric propositions, this means that, despite their apriority and necessity, nevertheless there still are coherently conceivable non-Euclidean spatial frameworks in which those propositions do not hold.[24]

[22] Frege, *The Foundations of Arithmetic*, 79–81.

[23] Elsewhere Frege explicitly locates the a posteriori/a priori distinction in the contrast between empirical particularity and non-empirical generality, as they are found in the primitive or unprovable premisses of the proof of the relevant asserted proposition (*The Foundations of Arithmetic*, 4). So both arithmetical and geometric truths are a priori, but in essentially different ways.

[24] Frege spells out a criterion for the mutual logical independence and consistent deniability of Euclidean geometric axioms in 'On the Foundations of Geometry', 107–11.

These points jointly bring us up to this salient fact: Frege's theory of syntheticity (leaving aside the obvious disagreement over arithmetic) falls fully within the framework of Kant's theory of syntheticity.[25] In two crucial passages in the first *Critique*, Kant writes:

In synthetic judgements I must have besides the concept of the subject something else (*X*) on which the understanding depends in cognizing a predicate that does not lie in that concept (*in jenem Begriffe nicht liegt*), nevertheless as belonging to it (*dazu gehörig*). (*CPR* A8)

In synthetic judgements . . . I have to go beyond the given concept in order to consider in relation to [that concept] something altogether different from what was thought in it, a relation that is consequently never one either of identity or of contradiction, and one such that neither the truth nor the falsity of the judgement can be seen in the judgement itself. If it is thus granted that we must advance beyond a given concept in order to compare it synthetically with another, then a third something is necessary in which alone the synthesis of the two concepts can originate. But what now is this third something that is to be the medium of all synthetic judgements? (*CPR* A154–5/B193–4)

The obvious points in these texts are that (1) a judgement or proposition is synthetic when, instead of depending for its truth solely on what is contained in a given concept, it advances beyond the intension of that concept and establishes a novel connection with another concept; (2) something 'altogether different' from a conceptual content or intension, a semantic '(*X*)', makes this novel conceptual connection possible; and (3), in virtue of its not being based on an analytically or conceptually necessary connection, the synthetic proposition can always be denied without logical or analytic contradiction. Moreover, (4) in synthetically advancing beyond the given concept and in relating it to another concept that is not contained in the first, the semantic content of the original concept is 'amplified' in the special sense that its intensional structure is augmented while its comprehension is narrowed (*CPR* A7/B11).[26]

In Kant's pre-Critical reflections on the analytic/synthetic distinction—for example, in his account of the difference between metaphysical and mathematical cognition in the Prize Essay of 1764—he concentrated solely on the first point. That is, he concentrated solely on the advance beyond the content or intension of a given concept to its predicative combination with a distinct concept. But he eventually came to realize that this actually undermines the analytic/synthetic distinction. This is because all propositions, whether analytic or synthetic, are generated by the combinatory synthesis of concepts under the original synthetic unity of apperception (see Sections 1.3–1.5). So, if one were then to consider the new complex concept generated by the novel conceptual

---

[25] See also Philip Kitcher, 'Frege's Epistemology'.
[26] This is the same as adding a determining predicate, real predicate, or synthetic characteristic (as opposed to a merely logical predicate or analytic characteristic) to the given concept. See Sect. 3.1.

connection as itself a given concept, then although a proposition was by hypothesis synthetic, the conceptual connection making up its content would paradoxically come out analytic: 'If one were to have the whole concept, whereby the notions of the subject and predicate are *compartes*, then the synthetic judgement would change itself into an analytic judgement. The question then arises of the extent to which this is arbitrary' (*R.* 3928; Ak. xvii. 350).

To prevent this collapse into paradox and arbitrariness, Kant therefore turns in the Critical period to another ground of syntheticity. This ground solely concerns the nature of the semantic content of the proposition, not its mode of generation (nor, for that matter, its logical form): 'Whatever be their origin (*Ursprung*) or their logical form, there is a distinction in judgements, as to their intension (*Inhalte*), according to which they are merely *explicative*, adding nothing to the intension of the cognition, or *ampliative*, increasing the given cognition: the former may be called *analytic*, the latter *synthetic*, judgements' (*P.* Ak. iv. 267). For some reason, however, when Kant initially introduces the analytic/synthetic distinction in the Introduction to the first *Critique*, he is unaccustomedly coy about explicitly revealing the nature of this ground. But later in the Doctrine of Method he is not so oblique: 'If one is to judge synthetically in regard to a concept, then one must go beyond this concept, and indeed go to the intuition in which it is given' (*CPR* A721/B749; see also *R.* 4674; Ak. xvii. 644–5). The same point is later put even more emphatically in a letter to K. L. Reinhold in 1789, and yet again in the long polemical essay directed against Eberhard in 1790:

This principle [of syntheticity (RH)] is completely unambiguously presented in the whole *Critique*, from the chapter on the schematism on, though not in a specific formula. It is: *All synthetic judgements of theoretical cognition are possible only through the relating of a given concept to an intuition.* If the synthetic judgement is an experiential judgement, the intuition must be empirical; if the judgement is a priori synthetic, there must be a pure intuition to ground it.   (*PC* Ak. xi. 38)

It was not merely a verbal quibble, but a step in the advance of cognition, when the *Critique* first made known the distinction between judgements that rest entirely on the principle of identity or contradiction, and those that require another principle through the label 'analytic' in contradistinction to 'synthetic' judgements. For the notion of synthesis clearly indicates that something outside the given concept must be added as a substrate that makes it possible to go beyond the concept with my predicate. Thus, the investigation is directed to the possibility of a synthesis of representations with regard to cognition in general, which must soon lead to the recognition of intuition as an indispensable condition for cognition, and pure intuition for a priori cognition.   (*OD* Ak. viii. 245)

Thus for Kant the determining factor of syntheticity is the *intuition dependence* of a proposition. A true proposition is synthetic if and only if it is consistently deniable (hence not logically or conceptually necessary) and its meaning and truth strictly require a connection with an intuition—an empirical intuition in the case of synthetic a posteriori propositions, and a pure intuition in the case of synthetic a priori propositions.[27] Now an empirical intuition picks out a sense-given individual in the actual empirical world, and a pure intuition immediately represents some unique structural whole that governs not only the actual empirical world, but also any possible world of human sense experience (*CPR* A19–21/B33–5, B160–1 n.).[28] And, according to Kant in the Transcendental Aesthetic, there are only two such unique formal wholes, (the representations of) space and time. So the intuition dependence of syntheticity is the strict semantic dependence of a proposition either on the existence of particular empirical objects or on the 'reality' (*Realität*) (*CPR* A28/B44, A35/B52) of total space and time—as given in human empirical or pure intuition respectively.

A side-benefit of this account of syntheticity is that it puts analyticity in a new light. We have seen in Chapter 3 that a proposition is analytic for Kant if and only if it is necessary and its necessity depends entirely on the resources of its conceptual form and content—whether those resources be syncategorematic and based on pure concepts of the understanding alone, categorematic and based on conceptual microstructures alone, or categorematic and based on conceptual comprehensions alone. In none of these cases is there any necessary semantic appeal to particular individuals or to any special actual or possible states of affairs:

An analytic [assertion (*Behauptung*)] carries the understanding no further, and since it is concerned only with what is already thought in the concept, it leaves it undecided whether this concept has in itself any reference to objects, or only signifies the unity of thought in general (which completely abstracts from the mode in which an object may be given); it is enough for [the understanding] to know scientifically (*wissen*) what lies in its concept; [the understanding] is indifferent as to what the concept may apply to. (*CPR* A258–9/B314)

In so far as the understanding in relation to any analytic proposition is indifferent as to what the concept may apply to, that proposition is strictly

---

[27] This interpretation of Kant's doctrine of syntheticity promotes what Gram calls Kant's 'implicit theory' of syntheticity in *Kant, Ontology, and the A Priori*, 15–82; my reading differs from his only in assigning this theory to Kant as his official or explicit theory. See also Allison, *The Kant–Eberhard Controversy*, 55, 61–3, 103; Allison, *Kant's Transcendental Idealism*, 73–8; Allison, 'The Originality of Kant's Distinction between Analytic and Synthetic Judgements'; and Allison, 'Transcendental Schematism and the Problem of the Synthetic A Priori'.

[28] In Sects. 4.3 and 5.1 I will argue that for pure intuition to pick out space and time as unique structural wholes is also to presuppose the transcendental figurative synthesis of the imagination, the original synthetic unity of apperception, the categories, and the schematism of the categories—in short, all the a priori conditions required for the possibility of experience. Hence synthetic a priori truths invoke not merely the pure forms of intuition, but also what Kant calls 'the *formal intuition* [that] gives unity of the representation' (*CPR* B160 n.).

topic-neutral.[29] Thus Kantian analyticity, which we defined positively in Chapter 3 as propositional necessity by virtue of intrinsic connections within conceptual form and content, can now be defined negatively as topic-neutral propositional necessity—a necessity that, just because it is intrinsically conceptual or non-intuitional, does not presuppose any special ontological furniture.

It should be manifest by now that Kant's empirical intuition corresponds directly to Fregean sense perception, and that Kant's pure intuition of space corresponds directly to Fregean spatial intuition. Further, both Kant and Frege are committed to the two-part view that (*a*) the denials of synthetic propositions are logically and conceptually possible and (*b*) synthetic propositions are semantically derivable only from either empirical or pure intuition in so far as these are considered to be 'sources of knowledge' for the ultimate grounds of the justification of beliefs in propositions of those types. Therefore (always, of course, setting aside the disagreement about the nature of arithmetic), the Kantian and Fregean doctrines of syntheticity are equivalent.

Now, of course, to establish that Kant's and Frege's theories of syntheticity are equivalent is not by any means yet to reveal the full nature of the shared doctrine. The core of similarity, we can see already, is a joint appeal to human sensible intuition and to its special role in the semantic constitution of synthetic propositions. But it is often asserted—or at least often assumed—that the very appeal to intuition, whether in a Kantian or Fregean framework, 'implies that the ground of synthetic judgments does not lie in semantics'.[30] So what I need to show is that the Kantian and Fregean theory of intuition is in fact a legitimately semantic doctrine, even if it is one that is explicitly routed through the theory of cognition. And that can be done only by first unpacking Kant's, and then secondly Frege's, theories of intuition.

4.2. What an Intuition Is

What is an intuition? In philosophical (as opposed to everyday) English, "intuition" has traditionally meant either (1) the unmediated grasp of abstract objects (platonic intuition), (2) a non-inferential, infallible, purely rational grasp of necessary truths (Cartesian intuition), or (3) a prima facie compelling non-inferential judgement that is not based on empirical evidence and that is, if true at all, then necessarily true.[31] Kant's *Anschauung* is in some ways similar

---

[29] For Kant, however, the topic neutrality of an analytic truth does not imply its irrelevance to empirical reality. See Sects. 2.2, 5.0, and 5.1.

[30] Coffa, *The Semantic Tradition from Kant to Carnap*, 21.

[31] Kant discusses this third conception under the rubrics of 'insight' (*Einsicht*) and 'rational certainty' (JL Ak. ix. 65–6). For more recent versions, see Bealer, 'The Incoherence of Empiricism', 100–4; Bonjour, *In Defense of Pure Reason*, ch. 4; and Kripke, *Naming and Necessity*, 34–9, 99–105, 108–9.

to these notions, but also crucially different.[32] The rudiments of his doctrine can be found in the following texts:

In whatever mode (*Art*) and by whatever means a cognition may refer (*beziehen*) to objects, intuition is that through which it immediately refers (*unmittelbar bezieht*) to them, and to which all thought is mediately directed (*als Mittel abzweckt*). But intuition takes place only in so far as the object is given to us. This in turn is possible at least for us humans only if it affects (*affiziere*) the mind in a certain way (*Weise*). The capacity (receptivity) for receiving representations through the mode in which we are affected by objects is entitled *sensibility*. Objects are therefore given (*gegeben*) to us by means of sensibility, and it alone yields us *intuitions*; they are *thought* (*gedacht*) through the understanding, and from the understanding arise *concepts* (*Begriffe*). But all thought must, either directly (*geradezu* (*directe*)), or indirectly (*im Umschweife* (*indirecte*)), by means of certain characteristics, refer ultimately to [objects given by] intuitions, therefore, in our case, to sensibility, because there is no other way in which objects can be given to us. (*CPR* A19/B33)

Our nature is so constituted that our *intuition* can never be other than *sensible*— that is, it contains only the mode (*Art*) in which we are affected by objects. (*CPR* A51/B75)

That representation that can be given prior to all thinking is called *intuition*. (*CPR* B132)

Sensible intuition is either pure intuition (space and time) or empirical intuition of that which, through sensation, is immediately represented as actual (*wirklich*) in space and time. (*CPR* B146–7)

[Intuition (RH)] refers immediately (*bezieht sich unmittelbar*) to the object and is singular (*einzeln*). (*CPR* A320/B377)

An intuition is a singular representation. (JL Ak. ix. 91)

An intuition is such a representation as would immediately depend upon the presence (*Gegenwart*) of the object. Hence it seems impossible to intuit anything a priori originally, because intuition would in that event have to take place without a formerly (*vorher*) or currently present (*jetzt gegenwärtigen*) object to refer to, and hence could not be intuition. (*P.* Ak. iv. 281–2)

At least five quite distinct things are said about intuition here. First, intuition refers immediately to an object. Secondly, this immediate reference to an object must always be sensible in that it presupposes the mode in which we are affected by objects. Thirdly, an intuition is such that it can be given prior to all thinking. Fourthly, an intuition is a strictly singular representation of an object. And, finally, an intuition is a representation that would immediately depend upon the presence of the object, where this dependence will consist in the intuition's having either a formerly or currently present object to refer to. This

---

[32] Kant is very careful to use two different terms—"*Anschauung*" and "*Einsicht*"—for the two quite different notions of (i) the direct singular cognition of an object and (ii) the non-inferential prima facie compelling non-empirical cognition of a necessary proposition, respectively. Parsons comes close to recapturing this difference in his distinction between 'intuition-of' and 'intuition-that'; see 'Mathematical Intuition'.

last feature would seem to be the same as what Kant expresses by claiming that 'intuition takes place only in so far as the object is given to us'. Summarizing now, the five necessary features of a Kantian intuition are: (A) immediacy; (B) relatedness to sensibility; (C) priority to thought; (D) singularity; and (E) object dependence. Unfortunately, just what any of these features amounts to, what it implies, and how they jointly interrelate, are by no means self-evident; and to complicate matters further, the five features have often been conflated—and some of them have been altogether overlooked— in scholarly interpretations of Kant's doctrine.[33] This unclarity and lack of interpretive consensus, taken together with the fact that Kant's theory of syntheticity hinges on his theory of intuition, dictate that we had better look closely at each of the aspects in turn.

Immediacy

The immediacy of an intuition is best understood by contrast with the mediated character of concepts. Objectively valid concepts and intuitions are both intrinsically related to objects of possible experience in that they 'refer' (*beziehen*) to them, but 'no concept ever refers to an object immediately' (*CPR* A68/B93). Only an intuition can immediately refer to an object: 'In whatever mode and by whatever means a mode of cognition may refer to objects, intuition is that through which it immediately refers to them' (*CPR* A19/B33). This contrast supplies an important distinction between two very different sorts of objective reference—mediate and immediate—corresponding precisely to the distinction between concepts and intuitions. On the one hand, we will remember, a concept is a representation whose intension contains in itself an ordered complex of subconcepts or characteristics, which in turn collectively and uniquely determine a comprehension of possible objects contained under that concept. The objects exemplify the attributes expressed by the conceptual characteristics. On the other hand, however, and in sharp contrast to the containment-under relation between a concept and its comprehension, that concept can under certain special circumstances function so that it 'indicates (*bezeichnet*) an object of experience' (*CPR* A8/B12) and 'directly (*geradezu* (*directe*)) . . . refer[s] ultimately to [objects given by] intuitions' (*CPR* A19/B33). A concept indicates an object only when it cannot automatically bring the object under itself through its conceptual characteristics alone; this is to say that it must appeal directly to the intuition, and so get *onto* the object without a detour through intensions and attributes—without going 'indirectly,

[33] See e.g. Falkenstein, 'Kant's Account of Intuition'; Hintikka, 'On Kant's Notion of Intuition (*Anschauung*)'; Howell, 'Intuition, Synthesis, and Individuation in the *Critique of Pure Reason*'; Meerbote, 'Kant on Intuitivity'; Parsons, 'Kant's Philosophy of Arithmetic'; Parsons, 'The Transcendental Aesthetic', 63–6; Thompson, 'Singular Terms and Intuitions in Kant's Epistemology'; and Wilson, 'Kant on Intuition'.

by means of certain characteristics'. An intuition is thus immediate precisely because it is non-descriptively referential. So the Kantian distinction between conceptual (mediate) reference and intuitive (immediate) reference is most accurately construed as the difference between, on the one hand, indirect or description-determined reference to an object, and, on the other, direct or non-description-determined reference to an object. More plainly put, intuitional reference is *direct reference*.[34]

Intuitional immediacy in the Kantian sense, moreover, must not be confused with Cartesian immediacy, according to which a thinking subject is infallibly and self-consciously confronted by an essentially inner object—in Cartesian terms, by an object whose 'formal reality' is wholly mental. In early analytic philosophy, the paradigm of Cartesian immediacy is the relation that obtains between a conscious, intentional mind and its purely phenomenal or subjective direct object—a 'sense datum'.[35] But Kantian empirical intuitions never have purely phenomenal or subjective direct objects. This is for two reasons: (*a*) intuitions of outer sense pick out phenomenally given, causally efficacious objects in empirically real space (see Section 1.4); and (*b*) although intuitions of inner sense do indeed pick out the subject herself and her temporal stream of sensory consciousness (*CPR* A33–4/B49–51, B152–6), that stream of consciousness is nevertheless necessarily ascribed to 'the permanent' or 'the persistent' (*das Beharrliche*)—that is, to some temporarily or perhaps even sempiternally enduring material substance in space (*CPR* Bxxxix–xli n., B174–9). Whether a Kantian empirical intuition is outer or inner, then, its object is never a mere sense datum.[36] And, since empirical intuitions can be combined with unclear or indistinct consciousness, no epistemic certainty need be involved (JL Ak. ix. 33–8). Further, pure intuitions represent total space and total time, the two unique structural frameworks shared by all actual and possible empirical objects and human perceivers (see Section 4.3). For all these reasons, then, Kant's doctrine of intuition is in no way burdened with Cartesian subjectivism.

[34] I use this label in its contemporary sense, according to which a singular term is directly referential if and only if it introduces an object into the truth conditions of propositions containing that term, thereby partially determining the content of those propositions, without thereby also introducing any descriptive content into the truth conditions and without any necessary mediation by descriptions. See esp. Kaplan, 'Demonstratives: An Essay on the Semantics, Logic, Metaphysics, and Epistemology of Demonstratives and Other Indexicals'; Kripke, *Naming and Necessity*, 24–97; Marcus, 'Modalities and Intensional Languages'; and Perry, 'The Problem of the Essential Indexical'. The close similarity between Kant's theory of intuition and direct reference theory has also been noted by Burge, 'Belief *De Re*', 362; Burge, 'Sinning against Frege', 430–1; Howell, 'Intuition, Synthesis, and Individuation in the *Critique of Pure Reason*'; and Howell, 'Kant's First *Critique* Theory of the Transcendental Object', 108–9.

[35] See Moore, 'The Refutation of Idealism'; Moore, *Selected Writings*, 45–58; and Russell, *The Problems of Philosophy*, chs. I–IV.

[36] This is controversial, however. For the other side of the story, see Falkenstein, *Kant's Intuitionism*, and Waxman, *Kant's Model of the Mind*.

Relatedness to Sensibility

Although, as we have just seen, Kantian empirical intuitions do not pick out sense data, nevertheless all (finite, human) intuition is inherently sensible. The force of this claim comes from Kant's explicit comparison of our sensible intuition with a capacity for intellectual intuition. Intellectual intuition is (or at least would be, if it ever actually existed) a mode of cognition that 'is one through which the existence of the object of intuition is itself given (and that, so far as we can judge, can belong only to the primordial being)' (*CPR* B72). For the intellectually intuitive thinker—God—merely to think it, is to make it so; to conceptualize an object is thereby to intuit that very object. Our sensory intuition, by sharp contrast, is the lot of finite cognizers whose intuition must be receptive to empirical objects that externally and independently trigger and fund the operations of their faculties for sense and thought: '[Our mode of intuition] is dependent upon the existence (*Dasein*) of the object, and is therefore possible only in so far as the subject's faculty of representation is affected (*affiziert*) by that [object]' (*CPR* B72). In other words, a human cognizer cannot stand in an intuitive relation to an object unless that relation somehow involves both the fact of affection (see Section 2.4) and a determinate rule-governed efficiently causal connection between that object, his bodily organs of sense, and his faculty of sensibility (*CPR* B275–9). Yet, while all human intuition must in one way or another involve externally triggered, causally implicated, existentially grounded sensory experiences, it does not follow that every intuition must itself be a sensory experience of this sort. As the Transcendental Aesthetic demonstrates at length and in depth, empirical sensory intuitions have unique fundamental subjective forms, (the representations of) space and time (see Section 4.3). As unique, fundamental, formal, and yet also subjective, (the representations of) space and time are the necessary conditions of all possible empirical intuitions given in outer and inner sense respectively (*CPR* A22–4/B37–9, A30–1/B46). Now space and time can—and, in order for pure mathematics to be possible, space and time must (see Section 5.3)—be cognizable in such a way that they can be given without any sensory features whatsoever. Indeed, they are representable as infinite given wholes from which the empirical representation of any and every object of appearance can be reflectively subtracted (*CPR* A24–5/B39–40, A31–2/B47–8). So all intuition for Kant is indeed sensible in that it is necessarily related to the faculty of sensibility and its causally grounded ordinary sensory operations; but not every intuition is itself a causally grounded empirical intuition: some intuitions are pure a priori.

Priority to Thought

By way of its essential connection with sensibility, intuition can of course be contrasted with thought, the cognitive function of conceptualization: 'Objects are *given* to us by means of sensibility, and it alone yields us *intuitions*; they are *thought* through the understanding, and from the understanding arise *concepts*' (*CPR* A19/B33). Kant holds that intuitions are in an important sense prior to thought and its concepts. This is not a temporal priority, but instead a logical and generative/productive priority. How does this priority show itself? Kant explicitly claims that it is possible to intuit an object without invoking or presupposing conceptualization. He says that 'objects can indeed appear to us without necessarily having to be related to functions of the understanding' (*CPR* A89/B122), that 'appearances can certainly be given in intuition without functions of the understanding' (*CPR* A90/B122), and again that

appearances might very well be so constituted that the understanding would not find them in accordance with the conditions of its unity, and everything would then be in such confusion that, for instance, in the series of appearances nothing would present itself that would yield a rule of synthesis and so correspond to the concept of cause and effect, so that this concept would be entirely empty, null, and meaningless. Appearances would none the less present objects to our intuition, since intuition by no means requires the functions of thought.   (*CPR* A90–1/B122–32; see also B145)

For systematic reasons having to do with the overall soundness of the Transcendental Deduction, Kant here is particularly worried about a special sceptical problem that the existence of unconceptualized intuitions and undetermined appearances poses for it: what if those undetermined appearances were also in principle undetermin*able* by means of concepts?[37] He believes that he can answer that worry. But that answer does not remove the patent possibility of intuitions without concepts. For this reason, intuitions are said to make up a distinct species of objective perception, or cognition, over against concepts (*CPR* A320/B376–7). This is not to say that intuitions are always or even usually cognitively generated apart from concepts, but rather only that they can be and sometimes are.

Let us call an intuition that exhibits this sort of cognitive autonomy from concepts 'concept-independent'. Question: what is a concept-independent intuition like, according to Kant? Answer: in having such an intuition, one is perceptually affected by an object either (1) without thereby conceptualizing it *as* an object; or (2) without conceptualizing it as an object of any *specific* sort; or (3) without *correctly* conceptualizing it as an object of any specific sort; or, finally, (4) without being able to conceptualize *anything* at all. The four cases are each subtly different from one another.

In the first sort of case, perceptual objects can show up within one's perceptual field, but without being consciously noticed or focused upon. For example, I am visually aware of a farmhouse occurring within a bucolic country scene; every part of my visual field is perceptually filled in, but much of it simply falls outside my cone of conscious attention, which by hypothesis is

---

[37] See also Patricia Kitcher, *Kant's Transcendental Psychology*, ch. 6.

directed to the farmhouse. In such cases, according to Kant, my perceptual monitoring of the perceptual objects falling outside the properly illuminated area of the cone of attention—in the example, my monitoring of those parts of my visual field other than the perceived farmhouse itself—is phenomenologically obscure, which is to say that, although my visual perception is conscious, it has a relatively low degree of sensory intensity and is therefore phenomenologically neither clear nor distinct (*CPR* B414–15, and *A*. Ak. vii. 135–7).

In the second sort of case, the object does indeed show up in the conscious attentive focus of the subject's perceptual field (so the perception is phenomenologically clear and non-obscure), yet the object is not sorted or articulated under any specific descriptive classification. In one brief and slightly chauvinistic passage in 'The Jäsche Logic' Kant describes a so-called savage who sees a house but not *as* a house, and compares him to the civilized European house-dweller who looks at the same object: 'with the one it is *mere intuition*, with the other it is *intuition* and *concept* at the same time' (JL Ak. ix. 33). The civilized cognizer recognizes the house as a house, by descriptively articulating its various parts (roof, door, windows, and so on) within a total representational *Gestalt*. The uncivilized cognizer, by contrast, is aware only of a large unlabelled, unarticulated object in the focus of perception. Setting aside the chauvinism, we can see the important cognitive point Kant is making. Such a perceptual consciousness is clear but indistinct.

The third sort of case involves both perceptual clarity and perceptual distinctness, but under an incorrect set of conceptual descriptions; hence the clarity and distinctness are misdirected and bogus. For example, I see what I take to be a bent stick in water while in fact it is a straight stick—and perhaps it is not even a stick but instead a piece of thin rusty pipe; and perhaps it is not even water but actually gin. In other words, I am directly perceptually aware of an object, but incorrectly describe it under every consciously occurrent concept in my repertoire. Kant deals with this sort of case under the rubric of 'empirical (e.g. optical) illusion' (*CPR* A293–5/B350–2). Here the senses are functioning properly and indeed supply direct perceptual access to an object, but conceptualization and judgement are in error and therefore do not themselves correctly determine the cognitive reference.

The fourth and last sort of case—the most extreme and unusual—involves the possibility of a short-term disruption or long-term breakdown of our conceptual abilities. In a passage I quoted a few paragraphs above, Kant speculates that

everything would then be in such confusion that, for instance, in the series of appearances nothing would present itself that would yield a rule of synthesis and so correspond to the concept of cause and effect, so that this concept would be entirely empty, null, and meaningless. Appearances would none the less present objects to our intuition, since intuition by no means requires the functions of thought. (*CPR* A90–1/B122–32)

What Kant is touching on here is the possibility of situations—whether through brain injury, seizure, or insanity; or less drastically through temporarily unfavourable conditions such as diverted attention, fatigue, or the consumption of too much alcohol—in which the mind's discursive representational functions are in a state of dysfunction or agnosia, so that there is a selective disintegration of our otherwise tightly unified cognitive processing capacities. Contemporary neuropsychology provides a rich range of examples of the former, drastic sort of case;[38] and, given what Kant says in the passage just quoted, together with his 1764 'Essay on the Maladies of the Mind' (Ak. ii. 257–71), and also what he says in sections 45–53 of the *Anthropology* under the rubric 'Of the Weaknesses and Illnesses of the Soul with respect to its Cognitive Power' (*A*. Ak. vii. 202–20), he appears to have been well aware of at least the general profile of such abnormal cognitive phenomena. The salient point is that during temporary or long-term cognitive breakdown, or during periods of reduced cognitive efficiency, it is in principle possible for appearances to present objects to our intuition without our being able in any way to determine them by means of sensory concepts. Objects could then be perceptually tracked by us in space and time in the sense that they were both apprehended in intuition and reproduced in the imagination, but without any descriptive determination whatsoever. In short, our cognition of these objects would lack a synthesis of recognition. Since intuitions under these adverse conditions are non-discursive, they count as 'blind' intuitions (*CPR* A51/B75). Indeed, in empirical support of Kant's view there appear to be some literally blind intuitions. These are found in the cognitively extreme but fascinating phenomenon of 'blindsight', in which subjects sincerely report having no visual sensory qualia whatsoever yet are able to guess and fix the locations and orientations of objects in the blind domain at levels significantly higher than chance.[39]

Kant also discusses concept-independent intuition in a somewhat different but equally noteworthy context. The disinterested feeling of pleasure in response to beautiful objects, as Kant describes it in the third *Critique*, is another instance of strictly intuitional, or non-discursive, perceptual awareness.[40] In pure aesthetic experience, 'the cognitive powers brought into play by this [beautiful] representation are . . . engaged in free play, since no definite concept restricts them to a particular rule of cognition' (*CJ* Ak. v. 217). This point exploits the fact that the bottom-up syntheses of apprehension and reproduction are cognitively detachable from the top-down conceptual processing with which they are normally combined in the production of empirical cognition (*CPR* A103–10). Or, as Kant puts it explicitly: 'If pleasure is connected with the mere

---

[38] See e.g. Sacks, *The Man who Mistook his Wife for a Hat.*
[39] See Weiskrantz, *Blindsight.*
[40] See Guyer, *Kant and the Experience of Freedom*, 10, 219.

apprehension (*apprehensio*) of the form of an object of intuition, apart from any reference it may have to a concept for the purpose of determinate cognition, this does not make the representation referable to the object, but solely to the subject' (*CJ* Ak. v. 189). All talk of the syntheses of apprehension or reproduction of course invokes the dedicated imagination (see Section 1.3); so it appears very likely that Kant sees a direct connection between concept-independent cognizing in aesthetic contexts and the specifically non-intellectual or figurative synthesis, the *synthesis speciosa* (*CPR* B150–2). The dedicated imagination can introduce non-conceptual forms into sensory processing in such a way that it generates a strictly lower-level synthetic unity of representational consciousness without carrying out a combinatory or higher-level synthesis under the original synthetic unity of apperception—hence without invoking any empirical concepts or any categories.

Various cases and types of concept-independent intuition are therefore surprisingly common in Kant's writings. Despite the textual and other evidence just presented, however, it must still be admitted that the concept-independence thesis is controversial both inside and outside the circle of Kant studies. Empirical intuitions, it is often vigorously counter-asserted, are strictly complementary to concepts and so cannot even in principle refer to objects independently of the discursive functions of the mind. We can call this 'the concept-dependence thesis'.[41] There is in fact considerable prima facie textual support for this thesis. Kant explicitly argues that 'neither [the power of thinking nor that of intuition] is to be preferred to the other' because 'only through their unification can cognition arise' (*CPR* A51/B75–6). Even more pointedly, he claims in the same passage that 'intuitions without concepts are blind'. In the A edition Transcendental Deduction he says that 'intuition without thought' is 'never cognition, and would therefore be as good as nothing for us' (*CPR* A111). And, as the B edition Transcendental Deduction explicitly states, there cannot be conscious empirical intuitions or perceptions of objects of experience that do not also presuppose concepts, judgements, the original synthetic unity of apperception, and the categories (*CPR* B143, B159–61). One might easily be tempted to conclude from these texts that concept-independent intuitions are impossible, and that the many texts that do seem to imply concept independence are errors—perhaps, as the famous Hans Vaihinger–Kemp Smith 'patchwork thesis' implies, unassimilated danglers from earlier manuscripts.

But it seems to me quite possible to reconcile the concept-independence thesis with the concept-dependence thesis without having to resort to accusing

---

[41] See e.g. Allison, *Kant's Transcendental Idealism*, 68. See also McDowell, 'Having the World in View: Sellars, Kant, and Intentionality', 451–70, 475; and McDowell, *Mind and World*, 3–65, 162–74. For arguments against the concept-dependence thesis, however, see Evans, *Varieties of Reference*, ch. 6; Hanna, 'Direct Reference, Direct Perception, and the Cognitive Theory of Demonstratives'; and Martin, 'Perception, Concepts, and Memory'.

Kant of widespread error or compositional incoherence. A good clue towards such a reconciliation lies in a marginal comment made by Kant on a letter from Beck dated 11 November 1791: 'To make a concept, by means of intuition, into a cognition of an object, is indeed the work of judgement; *but the reference of an intuition in general is not*' (PC Ak. xi. 310–11, emphasis added). In other words, my proposal is that what Kant is arguing in the texts I used to support the concept-dependence thesis is not that intuitions, *per se*, are necessarily dependent on concepts, but rather that, just in so far as fully formed judgements of experience are concerned, intuitions are necessarily complementary to and dependent upon concepts. But otherwise, intuitions are neither complementary to nor dependent upon concepts. So strictly in the context of judgements of experience (or cognitions in the narrow sense) do intuitions presuppose concepts, because in that special context intuitions must be brought under concepts for the purpose of making assertions about fully determined empirical objects. But in all cognitive contexts that are not essentially discursive or propositional, and in which the corresponding objects of intuition are not also represented in a strictly predicative or attributive way, then intuitions are concept-independent. Construed this way, the thesis of the concept-independence of intuition is perfectly consistent with the famous slogan about blind intuitions and empty thoughts, and the corresponding doctrine of intuition–concept complementarity. Blind intuitions are not non-intuitions or non-cognitions but instead only obscure, or else clear-but-indistinct, cognitions via apprehension and/or reproduction alone—that is, proto-cognitions (see Section 1.4). The existence of proto-cognitions is perfectly consistent with the existence of empirical cognitions in the full or judgemental sense, since, according to Kant's doctrine of the three syntheses of apprehension, reproduction, and recognition, empirical cognitions in the full or judgemental sense are always discursive generative transformations *of* proto-cognitions.

Singularity

Just as the immediacy of intuition-based (= non-descriptive, direct) reference makes sense only by comparison with the mediated character of concept-based (= descriptive, indirect) reference, so too the singularity of intuition can be understood only by comparison with the generality of concepts. A concept is a 'universal (*repraesentatio per notas communes*) or reflected representation (*repraesentatio discursiva*)' (JL Ak. ix. 91). This implies that, whereas a concept contains the abstracted ('reflected') representation of an attribute—or set of attributes—shared by infinitely many actual or possible empirical objects, by contrast an intuition picks out one and only one object. In other words, Kant's sharp distinction between concept-based or description-determined reference, and intuition-based or direct reference, is also a fundamental distinction between irreducibly general reference—that is, concept instanti-ation, or the 'subsumption of an object under a concept' (*CPR* A137/B176, A247/B304)—and irreducibly singular reference.

From a cognitive-semantic point of view, this also raises the deep and difficult issue of the relationship between Kantian intuitions and what Carnap later dubs 'individual concepts'.[42] Unfortunately, to complicate matters, the very idea of an individual concept—that is, of an intension whose function is to deter-mine, strictly by means of description, one and only one object—is deeply ambiguous as between (1) individual concepts that pick out one and only one object in the actual world or in an arbitrarily chosen possible world, but that can nevertheless pick out different particular objects in different possible worlds; and (2) individual concepts that pick out the self-same particular object in every possible world.[43] Let us call the first sort of individual concept an 'accid-entally individual concept' (AIC), and the second an 'essentially individual concept' (EIC). The EIC corresponds closely to Leibniz's 'complete indi-vidual notion' or 'haecceity'.[44] The Leibnizian doctrine, in a nutshell, is that an individual concept expresses a sum of attributes that determines the intrinsic or metaphysical identity of a substantial individual or monad—that is, it expresses a sum of attributes the possession of which is necessary and sufficient for being that individual. The notion of an AIC, by contrast, closely corresponds to Russell's notion of a definite description.[45] As I mentioned in Section 1.5, definite descriptions are expressions of the form 'the *F*', treated by Russell as incomplete symbols or syncategorematic expressions saying—in

[42] Carnap, *Meaning and Necessity*, 41–2.

[43] This distinction between the two types of individual concept corresponds closely to Kripke's distinction between accidental and rigid designators; see *Naming and Necessity*, 48 and 59 n. 22. The only difference is that for Kripke not all rigid designators express intensions that are descriptive or conceptual in character, since he holds that some rigid designators are directly referential or non-descriptive—e.g. ordinary proper names.

[44] See Leibniz, 'Discourse on Metaphysics', sects. 8–9, 13, pp. 40–1, 44–6.

[45] See Sect. 1.5. There is in fact an important historical connection between Leibniz's theory of complete individual notions and Russell's Theory of Descriptions. 'On Denoting' was originally published in 1905 and thereby superseded the theory of 'denoting concepts' developed in the 1903 *Principles of Mathematics*. But in his earlier book of 1900, *A Critical Exposition of the Philosophy of Leibniz*, 48–50, Russell radicalized Leibniz's version of the traditional doctrine of the logical and real subject by arguing that Leibniz is unjustified in assuming that a substance has a nature distinct from the logical sum of predicates making up its complete individual notion. As Russell sees it, an individual substance is reducible to the logical sum of its predicates. This neatly paves the way for the Theory of Descriptions by (*a*) allowing for the elimination of terms apparently referring to indi-vidual substances, and by (*b*) taking the sets of attributes that logically replace substance terms to be only contingently applicable to whatever instantiates them. For more on the Russell–Leibniz connection, see Hylton, *Russell, Idealism, and the Emergence of Analytic Philosophy*, 152–66. For us, what all this means is that Kant's various criticisms of the Leibnizian conception of a complete individual notion are at least indirectly, by Russell's own admission, also criticisms of Russell's Theory of Descriptions.

context—that there exists something that is *F* and anything else that is also *F* is literally identical to the first thing. This general proposition, in turn, can be treated as a contextually defined concept satisfied by one and only one thing if satisfied by anything at all.[46] So, while a Leibnizian EIC expresses the intrinsic identity of an individual across all possible worlds, the Russellian AIC expresses only a contingent identification of an individual in a given possible world.

Now the really hard question in this connection is this: does Kant accept the existence of EICs? If Kant does accept their existence, then there will be the possibility of eliminating all intuitions in favour of EICs. For by hypothesis the EIC plays the same semantic role as the intuition—namely, to pick out a single individual rigidly—across all possible sets of circumstances. So every Kantian proposition having apparent intuitive or direct reference to an individual would be convertible or translatable into a corresponding strictly conceptual complex, containing only EICs in the places for the intuitional terms. Just to give it a handy label, let us call this 'Leibnizian Eliminationism'. Leibnizian Eliminationism is strong enough to yield both G. E. Moore's radical conceptualist elimination of all intuitions and indexical elements from judgements in 'The Nature of Judgment'[47] and also Quine's equally radically conceptualist elimination of singular terms in *Word and Object*.[48] The crucial point, however, is that, if Leibnizian Eliminationism is possible, then the cognitive-semantic function of intuitions, which Kant otherwise takes to be irreducible and irreplaceable, is in fact theoretically otiose.

By way of resolving this complex issue, I will defend three claims. (I) For Kant there really are no such things as EICs, and consequently there is no possibility whatsoever of Leibnizian Eliminationism.[49] (II) Still, Kant *does* accept the existence of at least some individual concepts. (III) Nevertheless, all such individual concepts are only accidentally individual concepts (AICs); moreover, Kant's acceptance of the existence of AICs does not imply the possibility of semantically eliminating intuitions, because the application of those concepts to objects is always logically parasitic upon the existence of intuitions. The conjunction of the separate arguments for these three theses can be regarded

[46] See Whitehead and Russell, *Principia Mathematica to *56*, 66–71.

[47] In 'The Nature of Judgment', Moore says that his theory of judgement differs from Kant's 'chiefly in substituting for sensations, as the data of knowledge, concepts' (p. 9), and also that 'from our description of judgment, there must, then, disappear all reference either to our mind or to the world' (p. 18).

[48] Quine, *Word and Object*, 176–86. Thompson advocates applying Quine's strategy to virtually all Kantian singular terms; see 'Singular Terms and Intuitions in Kant's Epistemology', 334–5.

[49] This is the sense in which I strongly agree with Coffa's assertion that 'Kant concluded that the idea of an individual concept is a *contradiction in adjecto*'; see *The Semantic Tradition from Kant to Carnap*, 375.

as providing a cumulative Kantian case[50] against the very idea of individual concepts as fundamental devices of cognitive-semantic individuation or essentially singular reference—and in favour of the thesis that only intuitions and other functionally equivalent directly referential terms can serve as such devices. For convenience, however, I will go through the arguments for each claim separately.

Arguments for (I). Kant remarks in the first *Critique* that setting aside the possibility of a direct, intellectually intuitive, and in effect divine insight into the natures of things as they are in themselves, 'a thing can never be represented *through mere concepts*' (*CPR* A284/B340), and again in 'The Jäsche Logic' that, 'since individual things, or individuals, are thoroughly determinate, there can be thoroughly determinate cognitions only as *intuitions*, but not *as concepts*' (JL Ak. ix. 99). These texts state quite unambiguously that no concept alone, but only an intuition (or a cognition that is combined with an intuition), can determinately represent a particular real object. And in the *Critique of Judgement* he expresses the same point in terms of a basic contrast between cognitive universals and particulars: 'In cognition by means of understanding the particular is not determined by the universal. Therefore the particular cannot be derived from the universal alone' (*CJ* Ak. v. 406–7). The view that there really are reference-determining individual concepts is, as I have mentioned already, historically derived from Leibniz's striking idea that there exist complete individual notions or EICs that express the essences of particular monads. But, as these Kantian texts indicate, in an important sense the whole point of the Kantian notion of an intuition is to *avoid* the Leibnizian idea that the grasp of concepts alone ever explains the cognition of real individuals: 'a thing can never be represented *through mere concepts*'. Kant's view is that concepts can at best uniquely determine an indefinitely large range of possible objects sharing the same attributes (notional counterparts), but cannot by themselves individuate any actual individual object. For that, intuition is required. As a consequence, Kant's theory of intuitional reference is profoundly at odds with the general semantic and metaphysical thrust of Leibnizian Eliminationism.

Moreover, if Kant really had intended to accept EICs as replacements for intuitional terms, then he would have of necessity fallen headlong into what might be called 'Leibniz's Trap'. By this I mean the doctrine that all true propositions, including singular empirical propositions, are analytic by virtue of the containment of the predicate in the subject.[51] If a singular proposition is true,

---

[50] Kant did not himself, unfortunately, make this case as explicitly as he should have. See Gram, 'The Crisis of Syntheticity: The Kant–Eberhard Controversy', 170, and Hanna, 'Kant's Theory of Empirical Judgment and Modern Semantics'.

[51] For a clear statement of Leibniz's view that all propositional truth is truth-by-conceptual-containment, see 'On Freedom', 96–7.

and its subject term expresses a concept used to determine the individual subject of predication, then necessarily the predicate concept that is correctly asserted of the subject is also contained in the conceptual microstructure of the subject concept. But, if the predicate concept is contained in the subject concept, then the proposition is analytic, and Leibniz's Trap snaps tightly shut. Now Kant obviously does not hold the absurd view that ordinary true empirical singular judgements are analytic; for him, such judgements are strictly synthetic a posteriori (*CPR* A7/B12).

Arguments for (II). While Kant rejects EICs and Leibnizian Eliminationism —and so avoids being caught in Leibniz's Trap—he also accepts the existence of some individual concepts. This can be seen in two ways. First, he explicitly allows for the possibility of singular judgements—judgements employing singular terms as their logical subjects—and then assimilates them to universal judgements when they occur as minor premises in categorical syllogisms: 'Logicians rightly say that in the use (*Gebrauch*) of judgements in syllogisms singular judgements can be treated like universal ones' (*CPR* A71/B96; see also JL Ak. ix. 102 and BL Ak. xxiv. 275–6). This implies that the subject term of the minor premiss in a categorical syllogism—say, the term "Socrates" in the simple syllogism

> All humans are mortal.   [= All Hs are Ms.]
> Socrates is human.   [= All Ss are Hs.]
> Therefore, Socrates is mortal. [= Therefore, all Ss are Ms.]

logically functions as a general term rather than as a non-conceptual referring term. But since the term retains its original logical role as a singular term, the concept expressed by it could only be an individual concept. And, in the second place, Kant does in several texts speak explicitly of 'conceptu singulari' or singular concepts 'through which we think a singular subject', such as 'the earth' or 'Julius Caesar' (*R.* 2392; Ak. xvi. 342; see also DWL Ak. xxiv. 755–6 and VL Ak. xxiv. 910–11).

Arguments for (III). Kant's acceptance of the existence of some singular or individual concepts must be carefully qualified, however. While it is true that he does explicitly assimilate singular judgements to universal judgements for the purpose of logically analysing the categorical syllogism, he immediately adds the following rider: 'If, on the contrary, we compare a singular judgement with a universally valid one, merely as cognition, with respect to quantity, then the [singular judgement] relates to the [universal judgement (RH)] as unity to infinity, and is therefore in itself essentially different from the [universal judgement]' (*CPR* A71/B96). In other words, even if singular judgements can be treated like universal judgements, in order to use them for the special logical purpose of displaying the validity of categorical syllogisms, it does not follow that singular judgements are semantically reducible to universal judgements. In fact, they are 'essentially different'. And this difference, I want to argue, consists precisely in the fact that, outside the context of categorical syllogisms, in their application to actual empirical objects, the singular concepts in singular judgements must necessarily include intuitions as supplementary semantic devices for genuine singular reference.

Kant's explicit distinction between universal concepts, particular concepts, and singular concepts clearly implies that some singular or individual concepts exist. But he also writes that 'it is a mere tautology to speak of universal or common concepts—a mistake that is grounded in an incorrect division of concepts into *universal, particular*, and *singular*. Concepts themselves cannot be so divided, but only *their use* (*Gebrauch*)' (JL Ak. ix. 91).

Since all concepts are by their nature universal or general, it is only in their use that they have a singular interpretation: 'the use of a *conceptus* can be *singularis*' (VL Ak. xxiv. 908). If there really were individual concepts in the strong sense of Leibniz's complete individual notions, they would be 'lowest concepts'; but in fact 'there is no lowest concept (*conceptus infimus*) or lowest species, under which no other could be contained, because such a one cannot possibly be determined' (JL Ak. ix. 97). Then two sentences later Kant offers what I take to be the clinching remark that 'only comparatively for use (*Gebrauch*) are there lowest concepts, which have attained this significance, as it were, through convention (*Konvention*)' (see also VL Ak. xxiv. 911).

Now Kant's conventional use of an individual concept to apply to an individual—which he also calls a 'concrete use' of a concept (JL Ak. ix. 100)—seems to be for all intents and purposes an anticipation of what Kripke calls the 'reference-fixing' use of a definite description.[52] The reference-fixing use of a definitive description conveys a package of contextually identifying but non-semantic properties of the referent. That is, it conveys properties of the referent that are epistemically salient in a given context for the speaker or her listeners, but are neither strictly necessary nor sufficient for semantically determining the reference of the singular term. If this interpretation is correct, then singular concepts for Kant are at best AICs having a merely reference-fixing function. This is because, while (*a*) singular concepts are certainly associated with empirical intuitional acts of reference in empirical judgements, and while (*b*) they contingently apply to the relevant object of reference in a given empirical context, nevertheless (*c*) they play no deep semantic role in determining that singular reference. And this construal conforms very nicely to Kant's pointed remark that, if we consider singular concepts apart from their conventional, concrete use, we realize that 'they have no comprehension at all' (*CPR* A71/B96; see also BL Ak. xxiv. 240 and JL Ak. ix. 102). Manley Thompson glosses this remark as the doctrine that a Kantian singular concept

---

[52] See Kripke, *Naming and Necessity*, 54–60.

'applies to at most one object'.[53] This is, of course, true of EICs and AICs alike; but it is also pretty plainly *not* what Kant has actually said. He has said that singular concepts do not have any comprehension, which is to say that they do not uniquely determine a reference.

For all these reasons, we are now in a position to recognize that for Kant *only* intuitions (and their functional equivalents) are genuine singular terms: '*Repraesentatio singularis*—has an *intuitum*, indicates it immediately, but is at bottom not a *conceptus*. For example, Socrates is not a *conceptus*' (DWL Ak. xxiv. 754). According to Kant, then, there are no essentially individual concepts or EICs; and while there are indeed some accidentally individual concepts or AICs, such concepts apply to objects only by means of conventional, concrete use in empirical judgements and therefore are semantically parasitic upon intuitions.[54] And this brings out the even deeper point that for Kant, in sharp contrast to early Moore's theory of judgement, Russell's Theory of Descriptions, Carnap's semantics, Quine's name eliminationism, and 'descriptivism' more generally,[55] to make a genuine singular reference to an individual is never merely to assert that some set of concepts or descriptions is uniquely instantiated—or even to assert this (as it so happens in that particular context, relative to some speaker's or speakers' set of beliefs) correctly. On the contrary, a certain cognitive *rapport* with the individual object is required, and only an intuition (or what functions just like an intuition) can supply this.

Object Dependence

Can we say more about the nature of this cognitive *rapport*? Yes. Kant wants to say that the object dependence of an intuition is bound up with the fact that the very constitution of our sensory intuition presupposes existing or actual[56] objects: 'our mode of intuition is dependent upon the existence (*Dasein*) of

[53] Thompson, 'Singular Terms and Intuitions in Kant's Epistemology', 318.

[54] In at least one place, Kant identifies intuitions and singular concepts: 'the representations of immediate experience are all *conceptus singulares*, for they represent individual things' (BL Ak. xxiv. 257). This I think reflects Kant's confusing occasional tendency to use the term "concept" in a broad and non-technical way to mean simply 'representation'; see n. 61 below.   [55] See McCulloch, *The Game of the Name*, chs. 2, 3, 7.

[56] On the concept of existence, see *CPR* A597–602/625–30; see also OPA Ak. ii. 73, and R. 6276; Ak. xviii. 543. EXISTS for Kant is a second-order or categorial concept—that is, a predicate of ordinary (i.e. first-order) concepts. It says of any such first-order concept that that first-order concept is instantiated. Furthermore, the schematized category of existence, which Kant identifies with 'actuality' (*Wirklichkeit*), expresses the determinate occurrence of a sensory object—i.e. its location in a fixed set of causal and spatiotemporal relations (*CPR* A145/B184, A218/B265–6). Thus the objectively valid concept EXISTS says of any concept to which it is applied, that that concept has actual instances in the empirical world. Since 'in the *mere concept* of a thing no mark of its existence is to be found' (*CPR* A225/B272), and since 'the perception that supplies the content to the concept is the sole mark of actuality' (*CPR* A225/B273), according to Kant all objectively valid existential judgements are synthetic and not analytic (*CPR* A598/B626).

the object' (*CPR* B72). Indeed, our sensory intuition is the very criterion of an object's existence: 'we cognize the existence of things through sensation' (*R.* 3761; Ak. xvii. 286). In other words, an intuition is essentially relational and existential. It is relational in the sense that its structure is dyadic—it always contains places for both an intuiting subject and an intuited object. And it is existential in the sense that the place for the intuited object is always filled—there are no such things as non-referring empirical intuitions. A representation that has sensory content but is non-referential would be imaginational, not strictly intuitional. The dedicated imagination 'is the faculty of representing an object even *without its presence* in intuition' (*auch* ohne dessen Gegenwart *in der Aschauung*) (*CPR* B151), and this can happen when the object does not exist in any sense at all.[57]

Now, although Kant holds that every intuition is existential, he is not committed to the thesis that the object of intuition must occur in the very same moment or at the very same place as the act of intuiting. He distinguishes explicitly between 'direct' and 'indirect' intuition (*CPR* A116), by which he intends a contrast between cases in which the object of intuition is spatially or temporally local, and cases in which it is spatially or temporally distant. In this way intuition can be, as it were, either directly directly referential or indirectly directly referential. Local, present objects of intuition are received through the synthesis of apprehension. Immediately past objects are directly intuitable through the synthesis of reproduction. And spatially distant or even temporally future empirical objects are indirectly intuitable by means of the mediation of causal rules for the 'progressive' synthesis of perceptions (*CPR* A225–6/B272–4 and A411/B438). Hence for Kant there is both direct reference at-a-distance and direct reference to-the-future.[58] So long as the object is caught up appropriately in the total causal-law-governed spatiotemporal nexus of dynamical empirical nature, in relation to the intuiting subject, then it is accessible to empirical intuition. Now this total nexus is what Kant calls the 'context of experience as a whole' (*CPR* A601/B629). In so far as the object is directly or indirectly accessible to outer intuition, that object can thereby be said to be existent in the strong sense that it is literally a part of 'actuality' (*Wirklichkeit*) or the actual world as a whole (*CPR* A218/B265–6, A225/B272–3). Thus every intuition is not only existentially dependent on particular objects but also existentially dependent on the entire actual world.

In the light of these five defining features of intuition, I conclude that a Kantian intuition is an essential indexical. It has indexicality because it is

---

[57] This is shown by the cases of hallucinations and illusory dreams ('phantoms of the brain') that are sensory and imaginational, but for which actual objects are lacking (see e.g. *CPR* A201–2/B247, B278, A376). In general, however, our capacity for imagination presupposes that we have had some veridical outer perceptions (*CPR* B276–7 n.).

[58] See also Hanna, 'Extending Direct Reference'.

a direct, sense-related, thought-prior, representationally singular, object-dependent semantical term that is necessarily bound up with the stubbornly actual, given empirical conditions under which our capacity for sensibility is triggered into (lower-level) spontaneous activity, and also with our pure forms of sensibility, the intuitional representations of space and time, the two empirically real, unique, formal, holistic, pure a priori conditions of all possible sensible experience (*CPR* A28/B34, A35/B52). Indeed for these reasons Kantian intuition is triply indexical. It is dependent (i) on the unique cognitive constitution of our human sensibility, (ii) on the material dynamical context of the actual physical world, and also (iii) on the formal mathematical context of total space and total time (*CPR* A160/B199). Further, a Kantian intuition has *essential* indexicality because it cannot be semantically replaced by, or even have its semantic function mimicked by, any purely descriptive term or conceptual complex, without an inevitable loss of meaning. The sensible side of our cognitive constitution cannot be reduced to the discursive side.

Now it may well seem to the critical reader that there are still two important gaps in Kant's account. How can he show that our sensory intuition is not merely empirical but also pure? And how can he show that our pure intuition must involve the representations of space and time only, and not a representation of something else instead? To fill in these apparent gaps we must look directly at Kant's theory of pure intuition.

4.3. Pure Intuition

Kant's theory of pure intuition is worked out mainly in the Transcendental Aesthetic. Unfortunately, however, in one crucial respect the Aesthetic is deeply ambiguous. W. H. Walsh puts his finger directly on the problem: 'an immediate difficulty about the whole question [in the Transcendental Aesthetic] is whether Kant is discussing space and time or the ideas of space and time'.[59] This reflects an ambiguity in Kant's thinking about space and time that goes as far back as his Inaugural Dissertation of 1770, 'On the Form and Principles of the Sensible and Intelligible World': is he arguing that the *representations* of space and time are the a priori forms of human intuition; or is he arguing instead that space and time *themselves*[60] are the a priori forms of intuition? The two options are, of course, ultimately merged in the thesis of the transcendental ideality of space and time. This thesis asserts the identification of space and time themselves with our a priori representations of

---

[59] Walsh, *Kant's Criticism of Metaphysics*, 17.

[60] I mean space and time considered as objects of our representation, not space and time considered as objects in themselves.

space and time (*CPR* A28/B44, A36/B52). One cannot deny that Kant is committed to the ideality thesis. But it is possible to assign a relative priority to the two options. My overall cognitive-semantic approach to interpreting the first *Critique* implies a general priority of representational questions over metaphysical or epistemological questions. Therefore in this section I will develop the idea that the Aesthetic is primarily an investigation into the a priori features of the so-called concepts—that is, the pure intuitional representations —of space and time,[61] and only secondarily an enquiry into 'the question of the ontological status of space and time'.[62]

Kant's theory of pure intuition is grounded on his theory of empirical intuition (*CPR* A20/B34), and in this way avoids any hint of platonism. We have already seen in Section 1.4 that empirical intuitions are singular sensory representations directly picking out appearances. Appearances, in turn, are either undetermined or determined. Whether undetermined or determined, however, the object of empirical intuition or appearance is always a phenomenal physical thing to which we automatically assign a naturalistic causal role: it affects us in sensibility. Affection gives rise to sensation, the modification of a subject's conscious mental state in direct response to affection, and the matter of a sensation is its qualitative representational content. By contrast, the matter of an *appearance* is the affecting material object that corresponds to our conscious sensations and their object-directed qualitative contents. But appearances not only have a matter; they also possess form: 'I call that in the appearance that corresponds to sensation its *matter*, but that which makes [it possible] that the manifold of appearance be ordered in certain relations, I term the *form* of appearance (*Form der Erscheinung*)' (*CPR* A20/B34). The *Form der Erscheinung* specifies in advance the manner in which appearances are to be intuited. The form of empirical intuition, which is the form of appearance, is thus an overarching structure or framework obtaining implicitly within the representational content of every possible empirical intuition.

---

[61] Unfortunately Kant's use of the term "*Begriff*" in the Aesthetic is very misleading. He explicitly discusses the 'concepts' of space and time. But a central conclusion of his argument is that neither the representation of space nor the representation of time is a 'discursive' representation or 'general concept'; instead, both are intuitions (*CPR* A24–5/B39, A31/B47). So in order—charitably—to avoid the absurdity of Kant's arguing that the concept of space is not a concept (not to mention the lesser crime of redundancy in the expression "general concept", *allgemeiner Begriff*), we must read all his references to the 'concepts' of space and time in the Aesthetic (with two exceptions mentioned below) as invoking a broad and non-technical meaning of "*Begriff*" that is essentially the same as that of "*Vorstellung*" or "representation". So, for clarity, I will consistently use the term "representation" wherever the broad and non-technical sense of "concept" is intended by Kant. The only exceptions to this in the Aesthetic are passages at A25 and A25/B39 where he explicitly refers to the *general concept* of space. But the general concept of space is semantically parasitic on the pure intuition of space.

[62] Allison, *Kant's Transcendental Idealism*, 81.

Now, says Kant, it is possible to make a *Form der Erscheinung* into an explicit object of cognition by means of a two-step procedure of transcendental reflective abstraction.[63] He gives a specific example of this, in the case of the representation of an ordinary empirical object or material body. First, prescind from 'everything the understanding thinks about it' (*CPR* A20/B35) —that is, imaginatively remove all non-empirical or empirical conceptual characteristics from the representation of the body. This is to '*isolate* sensibility' (*CPR* A22/B36). Secondly, abstract away from 'what belongs to sensation, impenetrability, hardness, colour, etc.' (*CPR* A20/B35)—that is, imaginatively remove both the subjective psychological response to external empirical intuition (conscious sensation) and all the objective qualitative contents that are given through it. This is to 'detach from it everything that belongs to sensation' (*CPR* A22/B36). The reflective residue is 'pure intuition and the mere form of appearances, which is all that sensibility can yield a priori' (*CPR* A22/B36). This residue then becomes itself an immediate target of intuition, although it is obviously not an empirical object. According to Kant, the immediate non-empirical formal targets of reflected intuition are the representations of space and time.

If an appeal to reflective abstraction were the *only* way of proving the existence of a form of intuition, however, then Kant would be in trouble. This is because, while reflective abstraction is, plausibly, a capacity possessed by every thinker like us, it is actually realized only occasionally. But forms of intuition are supposed to obtain at least implicitly in each and every actual or possible sensory experience. So can we say something more incisive about the nature of a Kantian form of intuition in its relation to empirical intuitions?

Here I think that a linguistic analogy is very helpful. In Section 4.2 we saw that empirical intuitions function as directly referential singular terms, whether on their own or in judgements. This implies, among other things, that empirical intuitions cannot be semantically assimilated to Russellian definite descriptions or Carnapian individual concepts. But there is a further question as to whether the semantic role of empirical intuitions can be assimilated to that of proper names. At least one consideration strongly suggests that they cannot be so assimilated. Kripke has plausibly argued that every ordinary proper name is a special sort of rigid designator.[64] Translated out of Kripkean jargon, this means that a proper name is a term that refers to the same entity in every context of utterance of tokens of that term and in every possible set of circumstances in which that entity exists. But an empirical intuition picks out any individual object that happens to be the causal source of

---

[63] Paton correctly points out that Kant employs two quite different conceptions of abstraction: one for empirical concepts, i.e. empirical reflection (JL Ak. ix. 93–5); and one for isolating a priori representations, i.e. transcendental reflection (*CPR* A260–1/B316–17). See *Kant's Metaphysic of Experience*, i. 126.

[64] See Kripke, *Naming and Necessity*, 48.

sensation in the local spatiotemporal environment of the receptive subject. Thus the reference of empirical intuition can vary from empirical context to empirical context. Otherwise put, the empirical intuition is directly referential, but is not the special sort of rigid designator a proper name is. In fact, the correct linguistic correlate of the empirical intuition is the *demonstrative*—"this" or "that"[65]—and not the proper name.

Now it is plausible to hold that demonstrative words do not express complete concepts or descriptions that alone uniquely determine their reference, but instead express special semantic rules that necessarily guide or govern the determination of reference by means of sense perception in particular contexts of utterance. David Kaplan calls these semantic rules 'characters';[66] for example, the character of "this" or "that" would be, very roughly, '*x* is the perceptual object at which the speaker is now pointing'. Upon a closer examination of the character of a demonstrative, we can readily see that spatial and temporal factors are fundamental, in the sense that the rule that governs demonstrative reference immediately implies a formal framework of egocentric spatial and temporal coordinates.[67] Imagine for a moment a speaker who correctly uses a demonstrative. To say that the perceptual object is that 'at which the speaker is now pointing' is to say that the speaker places the object in a dynamically structured space whose coordinates must make reference to herself. As Kant argues in his seminal 1768 essay,[68] 'Concerning the Ultimate Ground of the Differentiation of Directions in Space', to locate an object spatially is necessarily to give that object a position in a subject-centred phenomenological space defined by the three-dimensional orientational axes of the perceiver's own body: up/down, right/left, and in front/behind (DS Ak. ii. 378–9). Further, to say that the perceptual object is that 'at which the speaker is now pointing' is to say that the speaker locates the object simultaneously to herself in a dynamical framework relatively to the autobiographical temporal framework of her own stream of consciousness: her sentient existence and life history (*CPR* B257,

---

[65] Demonstratives are sometimes said to be 'impure' indexicals because they require supplementation by a further act—e.g. an act of perception, or of pointing—in order to be applied, whereas ordinary pure indexicals like "I" do not require such supplementation but rather only need to be uttered in a context. The close connection between demonstratives and empirical intuitions has been urged, e.g., by Howell in 'Intuition, Synthesis, and Individuation in the *Critique of Pure Reason*'.

[66] See Kaplan, 'Demonstratives', 505. Technically, characters are functions from contexts, i.e. speakers and space-time locales, into contents, i.e. intensions that uniquely determine cross-possible-worlds extensions.

[67] See also Evans, *The Varieties of Reference*, ch. 6.

[68] 'Seminal', because it sponsored, in 1769, Kant's first major step towards the transcendental idealism of the Critical philosophy by suggesting the brilliant idea—worked out in the 1770 Inaugural Dissertation—that space is a necessary form of our sensibility. He says in one of the better-known *Reflexionen* that 'the year '69 gave me great light' (*R.* 5037; Ak. xviii. 69).

A213/B260, B275–6).[69] The representations of space and time are therefore accurately labelled 'forms of intuition' because they are formal necessary conditions of the possibility of subject-centred demonstrative reference in empirical intuition.[70]

Kant also says that the representations of space and time are 'forms of sensibility'. And the argument for this claim is in fact subtly logically distinct from that which I just used to show that the representations of space and time are forms of intuition.[71] More precisely, the argument concerning forms of sensibility depends upon certain primitive phenomenological features of all empirical intuitions:

By means of outer sense (a property of our mind) we represent to ourselves objects as outside us, and all without exception as in space. In space their shape, magnitude, and relation to one another is determined, or determinable. Inner sense, by means of which the mind intuits itself, or its inner state, yields indeed no intuition of the soul itself as an object; but it is nevertheless a determinate form, under which the intuition of its inner state is alone possible, so that everything that belongs to inner determinations is represented in relations of time. (*CPR* A22–3/B37)

Thus Kant holds that there are just two sorts of objects of empirical intuition— external objects, and aspects of one's own inner mental life. Outer sense, our receptive access to external objects, is directly associated with the representation of space; and inner sense, our receptivity to ourselves, is directly associated with the representation of time. In this way, the contents of our representations of space and time cannot be divorced from their phenomenological functions. We must think of outer sense as providing us with a perceptual field that is intrinsically differentiated by the systematic contributions of the five traditional sense modalities, together with an intermodal capacity for bodily movement and orientation in space (OT Ak. viii. 134–5). My outer sense thereby provides access to objects either contiguous with or beyond my body. The several outer sense modalities (touch, smell, sight, hearing, kinaesthesia, and so on) differentiate this outer field into several closely coordinated subfields of outer sensation—a tactile subfield, an olfactory subfield, a visual subfield, an auditory subfield, and so on (A. Ak. vii. 153–61). Each of these subfields is sensitive to causal affection via the relevant bodily organs associated with

---

[69] See also Longuenesse, *Kant and the Capacity to Judge*, 387–93, and Campbell, *Past, Space, and Self*, ch. 4.   [70] See also Strawson, *The Bounds of Sense*, 48–9.

[71] As Kemp Smith points out in his *Commentary to Kant's 'Critique of Pure Reason'*, 115, the proof that the representations of space and time are forms of intuition is not on its own sufficient to show that they are also forms of sensibility. Given only the appeal to the semantic argument from the conditions of the possibility of perceptual demonstration, one might still consistently take the view that the spatial and temporal structures contained in empirical intuition are concepts contributed by the understanding, not intuitions contributed by our sensibility.

experiences of that sort. By contrast, inner sense is at once more narrow and yet more dense than outer sense; it is essentially a direct mode of access to an ego-field, or Jamesian stream of consciousness, a swarm of momentary or recurring empirical mental activities, feelings, and desires, all of which are attributed directly to a single vital temporally enduring subject (*A*. Ak. vii. 161).

The union of all the sensory fields and subfields in inner and outer sense, together with their sensory contents, is what Kant calls the sensory 'manifold' (*Mannigfaltiges*) (*CPR* A99). But the fundamental difference between the two distinct domains of the sensory manifold is grounded on the central fact of the perceiver's own body, as the phenomenological border and two-way gate between the inner and the outer. When someone touches, smells, sees, tastes, or hears something, she automatically represents it relatively to her bodily organs of sense in a causally structured space extending locally and even infinitely out beyond her own body; the nature of the functioning of these senses is such that they have efficient causal sources that are discriminable although distant (*CPR* A213/B260). But, on the other hand, when she introspects, she automatically represents the target of introspection—an aspect of the empirical ego—as a sensory quality in time realized somewhere within her own human body. Spatial and temporal representation cannot for Kant be ultimately detached from the stubborn fact of human embodiment.

In this connection we must also briefly consider what Jonathan Bennett calls a 'queer remark'[72] of Kant's: 'time cannot be outwardly intuited, any more than space can be intuited as something in us' (*CPR* A23/B37). Here he appears to be saying that the representations of time and space essentially exclude one another. But in fact Kant is not saying that at all. The representations of time and space cannot essentially exclude one another, just as inner sense and outer sense cannot essentially exclude one other. He states explicitly that (the representation of) time is the 'mediate condition of outer appearances' (*CPR* A34/B50–1), which is to say that the perception of objects in space necessarily implements temporal form: 'all appearances whatsoever—that is, all objects of the senses—are in time, and necessarily stand in time relations' (*CPR* A34/B50–1). Indeed, the very possibility of representing the motion of material objects in space presupposes the representation of time (*CPR* B48–9). Correspondingly, for Kant we always represent our own inner mental states and acts in direct relation to space. I can introspectively pick myself out in empirical apperception only because there is 'something in another region of space from that in which I find myself' (*CPR* A23/B38). Moreover, in the B edition's crucial Refutation of Idealism in the Postulates of Empirical Thought, Kant argues that 'inner experience is itself only mediate, and possible only through outer experience' (*CPR* B277). This doctrine is extended in the General Note on the System of Principles, where he explicitly asserts

---

[72] Bennett, *Kant's Analytic*, 15.

that the objective reality of the schematized categories requires the representation of space (*CPR* B291). And even the pure intuition of time, it seems, is possible only in so far as the imagination can create a spatial analogue or schema of time by mentally drawing a line in space (*CPR* A33/B50, B154, B292). So Kant holds the two-part doctrine (1) that the representation of time is the immediate condition of inner sense and the mediate condition of outer sense, and (2) that the representation of space is the immediate condition of outer sense and the mediate condition of inner sense. The representations of space and time are in this way strictly complementary to one another.[73] In the light of this fact, it seems clear that what Kant is driving at in the text at A23/B37 is simply this key semantic point: that the representations of time and space have semantic integrity and therefore their contents cannot be directly translated into one another. The difference between earlier and later events cannot be immediately or originally represented using such purely spatial notions as the pairs 'up/down', 'right/left', and 'in front/behind'. Nor can the differences among the members of a set of distinct spatial points be cashed out immediately or originally in purely temporal terms—earlier and later points might well be the same point in space, and the mere relation of contemporaneity does not discriminate spatial differences. The representations of space and of time are strictly complementary but not wholly commensurable.

So far, what Kant has argued is that empirical intuitions have formal features over and above the contributions of the understanding and the sensory awareness of empirical objects; that the necessary forms of all empirical intuitions are the representations of space and time; that the representations of space and time are also the necessary forms of outer sense and inner sense respectively; and that the representations of space and time are complementary, although not intertranslatable. But there is significantly more to say about the nature of these representations. One basic task of Kant's argument in the Transcendental Aesthetic is to show that both the representations of space and of time are a priori representations. And another is to show that they are not merely the forms of empirical intuition, but themselves pure intuitions.

Kant says that by a 'metaphysical exposition' of a representation he means a partial analysis of that representation's content, with an eye to teasing out just those features that are a priori. The Metaphysical Expositions of the representations of space and time are, therefore, specifically devoted to demonstrating their apriority. Now according to Kant's account in the Introduction, apriority involves a representation's being '*absolutely* independent of all experience' (*CPR* B3), together with its necessity and strict universality (*CPR* B3–4).[74]

---

[73] It is true, however, that in some places Kant appears to say that the representation of time is more basic than that of space. He says that 'time is the formal a priori condition of all appearances in general' and that 'space, as the pure form of all outer intuitions, is limited as an a priori condition merely to outer intuitions' (*CPR* A34/B50).

[74] See Sect. 5.2.

In the Introduction, Kant applies the notion of apriority only to propositions or judgements. But he also notes in passing that non-propositional representations too can in an important sense be a priori: 'an a priori origin is manifest in some concepts, no less than in judgements' (*CPR* B5). Strictly speaking, then, non-propositional representations cannot be necessarily and universally true; but they can function as necessary and universal conditions for other sorts of representations. It is this modal property that Kant ascribes to the forms of intuition when he remarks that, 'if sensibility were found to contain a priori representations, which constitute the condition under which objects are given to us, it will belong to transcendental philosophy' (*CPR* A15/B29–30), and later unconditionally that 'space is a necessary a priori representation, which is the ground of all outer intuitions' (*CPR* A24/B38) as well as that 'time is a necessary representation that grounds all intuitions' (*CPR* A31/B46).

With regard to the experience-independence feature, however, Kant writes that 'I call all representations pure (in the transcendental sense) in which nothing is to be encountered that belongs to sensation' (*CPR* A20/B34). Pure representations, that is, do not contain any sensory content. Obviously the purity of a content directly entails its apriority in the sense of experience independence. But following the lead of our earlier analysis of objective validity (Section 2.2), we should not read this as implying that pure intuitions involve no *relations* whatsoever to sensory content. Indeed, Kant points out explicitly that 'time, as the formal condition of the possibility of alterations, is indeed objectively prior to [that possibility (RH)], yet subjectively, however, in actual consciousness, the representation of time, like every other, is given only through the occasioning of perceptions' (*CPR* A453/B481 n.). And the same goes for the representation of space. The generation of temporal and spatial representations requires sensory inputs and the attendant triggering of our capacity for sensibility; and since those representations are necessary conditions of empirical intuition, they have direct empirical application. What Kant means by the 'purity' of a pure intuition, then, is only that the intrinsic content and structure of the representations of space and time do not include sensory components—not that they lack empirical sources or meaningfulness. Just as pure concepts of the understanding are both pure and experience-independent even though they have objectively valid application to possible objects of experience and are fully cognitively realized only by means of sensory inputs, so too pure intuitions are such that their content neither contains sensory elements nor is determined by their associated empirical intuitions despite their also being 'given only through the occasioning of perceptions' in the dual sense that they are generated via the generation of perceptions and also apply solely *to* these perceptions and their objects. Otherwise put, the representations of space and time are pure and a priori, yet also empirically real or objectively valid (*CPR* A27–8/B44, A36/B52–3).

Given this general picture of the apriority of the representations of space and time, what arguments does Kant give for it? The argument for necessity has two versions. In the first, he points out that particular empirical intuitions in outer or inner sense are not possible unless the representations of space and time are presupposed as fundamental individuating or discriminating factors in cognition. Just to take what he says about the representation of space as representative of this line of argument:

> In order for certain sensations to be referred to something outside me (i.e. to something in another region of space from that in which I find myself), thus in order for me to represent them as outside and alongside one another, thus not merely as different but as in different places, the representation of space must already be their ground. . . . This outer experience is itself first possible only through this representation.   (*CPR* A23/B38)

Thus the representation of space must be presupposed in order to distinguish other things from myself, and also to distinguish those other things from one another. This argument can obviously be merged with a point made earlier. The media of demonstrative reference to apparent objects are empirical intuitions, together with egocentrically structured actual contexts of perceptual experience; and every empirical intuition necessarily invokes one or another (or both) of the forms of intuition, the representations of space and time. In this sense, the representations of space and time are a priori just in so far as they are necessary conditions of all perceptual demonstration.

In the second version of the necessity argument, Kant insists that 'one can never represent to oneself that there is no space' (*CPR* A24/B38) and 'as regards appearances in general one cannot remove time' (*CPR* A31/B46). This is not an empirical psychological generalization, as many commentators have thought,[75] but instead a claim in general cognitive semantics about the nature of spatial and temporal representational content. The representations of space and time are representationally inalienable from appearances. But *in what sense* are they inalienable? Charles Parsons makes the promising suggestion that for Kant the representations of space and time are 'fundamental phenomenological givens'.[76] That is, despite their being a priori, they are somehow also literally given or immanent in the manifest objects of perceptual experience. One way of fleshing this out is indicated by Kant's remarks in the Inaugural Dissertation to the effect that the representation of time is 'the subjective condition which is necessary in virtue of the nature of the human mind, for the coordinating of all sensible things in accordance with a fixed law' (ID Ak. ii. 400), and that the representation of space 'issues from the nature of the

---

[75] See e.g. Kemp Smith, *Commentary to Kant's 'Critique of Pure Reason'*, 104; Strawson, *The Bounds of Sense*, 58–9; and Walker, *Kant*, 29.
[76] Parsons, 'The Transcendental Aesthetic', 69.

mind in accordance with a stable law as a scheme, so to speak, for coordinating everything that is sensed externally' (ID Ak. ii. 403). In the light of this, we can say that the representations of space and time are a priori and yet immanent in the manifest objects of our perceptual experience in the way that the rules of baseball are relatively a priori for, and yet also immanent in, actual baseball games—that is, as constitutive rules.[77] The representations of space and time do not belong to the raw data or inputs of our perception; rather, as generatively innate, they present themselves as constituting the actual structure of the objects encountered in our perceptual activity.

The argument for experience independence also has two versions. The first version is terse: 'one can quite well think that there are no objects to be encountered in [space]' (*CPR* A24/B38–9), and 'one can quite well take the appearances away from time' (*CPR* A31/B46). These passages have also been red flags to many of Kant's critics. What Kant is driving at, I think, is a crucial point that returns us to the text in which he says that it is possible to pick out a form of intuition by reflectively abstracting away from the conceptual and sensory components of the representation of an empirical object (*CPR* A21–2/B34–5). In transcendental reflection it is possible to focus exclusively on a certain structural component *within* an otherwise empirically saturated representational content. So in reflection we can abstract away from the empirical matter of intuition and detach the forms of intuition, as pure forms alone. But this is not an ordinary empirical cognition of an object: 'the mere form of outer sensible intuition, space, is not yet cognition at all' (*CPR* B137). Again, in the chapter on the Amphiboly of the Concepts of Reflection, Kant stresses that neither space nor time is represented as an enormous, determinate, and yet ghostly empirical object of cognition: 'the mere form of intuition, without substance, is in itself not an object (*Gegenstand*)' (*CPR* A291/B347). Instead, pure space or pure time is represented in intuition by the aid of the dedicated pure productive imagination, as a unified intuitional framework governing the appearance of empirical objects. Thus it is an 'empty intuition without an object (*Gegenstand*)', or an '*ens imaginarium*' (*CPR* A291/B347).[78] And in the same place he says that pure space and pure time 'are indeed something, as intuitional forms (*Formen anzuschauen*), but are not themselves objects (*Gegenstände*) which are intuited'. It is in precisely this sense, in a famous footnote in the B Deduction, that Kant claims that the representations of space and time must be taken not merely as 'form of intuition' (*Form der Anschauung*) but also as 'formal intuition' (*die formale*

---

[77] See Searle, *Speech Acts*, 33–51. 'Regulative' rules describe actual patterns of human activity; constitutive rules, by contrast, determine the internal structure or normative content of human activity.

[78] Allison speaks aptly in this connection of pure space as a 'preconceptual framework'; see *Kant's Transcendental Idealism*, 94.

Anschauung) (*CPR* B160–1 n.).[79] They are non-empirical structural frameworks of pure sensibility, represented by means of the transcendental imagination and its figurative synthesis or *synthesis speciosa* (*CPR* B151), not fabulous empirical objects.

Of course this may still seem rather vague. So fortunately in another domain we have an illuminating analogy for just the sort of thing Kant is talking about—in the domain of pure logic. We have already seen in Section 2.1 that Kant and Wittgenstein share a transcendentalist conception of logical form. Here I want to exploit a series of Wittgensteinian insights in the *Tractatus* in order to work out an analogy between pure intuitional form and pure logical form:

The facts in logical space are the world.[80]

(Nothing in the province of logic can be merely possible. Logic deals with every possibility and all possibilities are its facts.) Just as we are quite unable to imagine spatial objects outside space or temporal objects outside time, so too there is *no* object that we can imagine excluded from the possibility of combining with others.[81]

My fundamental thought is that the 'logical constants' do not represent. That the *logic* of the facts cannot be represented.[82]

The proposition *shows* the logical form of reality. It displays (*weist . . . auf*) it.[83]

The logical propositions describe the scaffolding of the world, or rather they exhibit it (*stellen es dar*). They 'treat' of nothing.[84]

Logic is transcendental.[85]

Wittgenstein's 'fundamental thought' is that logical form is necessarily implicit or immanent in propositions in just the way that the pure intuitional representations of space and time are implicit or immanent in empirical intuition. That is, logical form is not discursively represented or 'said' by propositions; rather, it is simply intuitionally given or 'shown' by propositions. So in the *Tractatus* Wittgenstein in effect transfers Kant's analysis of the a priori intuitional representations of space and time in the Transcendental Aesthetic

[79] Paton correctly observes that 'the form of intuition is or contains the relations (or system of relations) in which appearances stand' while 'the content of pure intuition is these same relations, abstracted from sensible appearances, and taken together as forming one individual whole'. See *Kant's Metaphysic of Experience*, i. 104. Allison makes a similar distinction between what he calls the 'form of intuiting' and the 'form intuited'; see *Kant's Transcendental Idealism*, 97. The representations of space and time as formal intuitions presuppose both the pure productive synthesis of the imagination and the original synthetic unity of apperception (*CPR* B150–2, B160–2), and so are fully set up to realize and interpret the discursive functions of the understanding by schematizing them (*CPR* B291).

[80] Wittgenstein, *Tractatus Logico-Philosophicus*, prop. 1.13, p. 31.

[81] Ibid., prop. 2.0121, p. 31.   [82] Ibid., prop. 4.0312, p. 69.

[83] Ibid., prop. 4.121, p. 79, translation modified slightly.

[84] Ibid., prop. 6.124, p. 165, translation modified slightly.

[85] Ibid., prop. 6.13, p. 169.

over to his own analysis of the representations of logical form, in order to get around the various problems created by the sort of metaphysics and epistemology of logic characteristic of Frege's commitment to non-spatiotemporal, non-mental logical objects and Russell's platonism.

Assuming for the purposes of argument the general correctness of a broadly Kantian–Tractarian or transcendentalist conception of logic,[86] this sets up the analogy I am interested in. The way in which the pure intuiter represents space and time as autonomous yet also phenomenologically immanent forms, by reflecting on the transcendental component of her capacities for representing things spatially or temporally, is fundamentally akin to the way in which the logician creates a formalized language for the representation of logical forms that are actually immanent in natural language. On this analogy, open coordinates for places or times correspond to free variables in logical schemata; place names and dates correspond to individual constants; descriptions of situations correspond to propositional constants; basic spatial and temporal properties and relations play the role of predicate terms; and basic types of spatial and temporal transformation correspond to logical operators. So when Kant says that space and time can be represented as 'empty intuition without an object' or as *entia imaginaria* he does not mean that these representations are null and void, but rather that space and time can be represented as *formalized*.

This analogy between pure formal intuition and the representation of logical form can be pushed even a little further. It is arguable that both sorts of a priori representation essentially require the use of the pure productive imagination. Only by means of the pure productive imagination can space and time be schematically represented as formal intuition. So too it is arguable that logical form can be represented comprehensibly in a formalized language only if it is expressed by means of a perspicuous ideographic symbolism.[87] That is, an adequate formalized language must clearly, distinctly, and isomorphically depict what it represents. In this way an ideal logical language, or *Begriffsschrift*, is also an *ens imaginarium*.

Otherwise put, then, the representations of both spatiotemporal forms and logical forms alike are (1) grounded in transcendental capacities of the cognizing subject, (2) encoded innately in the mind as formal systems of a priori rules, (3) 'shown', in that they are grasped immediately by the mind via transcendental reflective abstraction aided by the pure productive imagination, and yet (4) 'not said', in that they are conditions for the possibility of ordinary cognition, not the empirical objects or *Gegenstände* represented by empirical discursive representations.

---

[86] See also Goldfarb, 'Logic in the Twenties: The Nature of the Quantifier', and Ricketts, 'Frege, the *Tractatus*, and the Logocentric Predicament'.

[87] Lewis, *A Survey of Symbolic Logic*, 3.

As if he were well aware that his readers would have difficulty just grasping—not to mention accepting—his doctrine of the representations of space and time as pure formal intuitions, Kant provides a second argument for that doctrine. This argument is aimed at producing the conclusion that 'space is not a discursive or as we say general concept of relations of things in general, but a pure intuition' (*CPR* A24–5/B39) and similarly that 'time is not a discursive or what is called a general concept, but a pure form of sensible intuition' (*CPR* A31–2/B47). There are three parts to the argument: (*a*) that the representations of space and time are themselves intuitions and not just forms of intuition; (*b*) that, being the sort of intuitions they are, they are thereby pure and not empirical; and (*c*) that the representations of space and time, being pure intuitions, cannot be pure concepts. For simplicity, let us focus on the representation of space.

Kant presents the first two components—corresponding to (*a*) and (*b*) just above—as follows:

In the first place, one can represent to oneself only one space, and if one speaks of many spaces, one understands by that only parts of one and the same unique space. [Secondly], these parts cannot as it were precede the one all-embracing space, as its constituents (from which its composition would be possible), but rather are thought only *in it*. [Space] is essentially singular; the manifold in it, and therefore also the general concept of spaces, depends merely on limitations. From this it follows that in regard to [space] an a priori intuition . . . grounds all concepts of it. (*CPR* A25/B39)

The first part of this line of reasoning—'one can represent to oneself only one space'—of course relies heavily upon Kant's thesis that intuitions are singular terms. The representation of space is not merely a form of empirical intuition or a form of sensibility, but also itself an intuition. Like empirical intuitions that contain as their matter real or concrete objects, so too the representation of space as a form of intuition 'gives the manifold of intuition a priori for a possible cognition' (*CPR* B137); but even over and above that, as a formal intuition, the representation of space contains a 'unity of the synthesis of the manifold' (*CPR* B161). Thus the representation of space is a singular representation of a non-empirical individual—namely space itself (although not, of course, space *in* itself), the complete framework of all actual and possible empirical objects represented in outer sense.

Now the representation of space differs from an empirical intuition not merely in that it picks out a purely structural, as opposed to a material or real, object. More than that, it delivers its object without the possibility of ever delivering something different. Here, again, a semantic way of treating this issue proves helpful. I argued above that empirical intuitions are best construed as functioning semantically like demonstratives; by contrast, it appears, the pure intuition of space (and, correspondingly, of time) is best construed as functioning like an extraordinary proper name. As I mentioned, ordinary proper names on the Kripkean construal are special rigid designators, in that they hold reference fixed across all speech contexts and possible worlds; more-over, they apply to concrete or material individuals or events. But the rigidly designating function of a proper name can be extended beyond concrete or material individuals, to entities of many different types. In just the way, for example, that the proper name "Equator" rigidly picks out an abstract spatial entity that would not exist if the actual earth did not exist, so too the repres-entation of space rigidly picks out an abstract intuitional framework that would not be empirically real if actual human sensory experience did not exist. The only remotely plausible alternative to this interpretation is to treat "space" as a predicate term of some sort, ranging over many different spatial and tem-poral frameworks. But Kant believes that there is only one space and one time (*CPR* A188–9/B231–2),[88] and that each possesses its basic properties neces-sarily; hence "space" and "time" are proper names of the extraordinary sort.

The second part of the second experience-independence argument—corresponding to (*c*) above—begins to spell out more explicitly just what space is represented *as* by the pure intuition of space. Here Kant relies heavily not merely on his theory of intuition, but also on a mereology or theory of wholes and parts. Kant's claim is that space is represented by the representation of space as not only an individual, but as an individual whole composed of parts: 'if one speaks of many spaces, one understands by that only parts of one and the same unique space'. This whole, moreover, contains its spatial parts in a very special way, for 'space is represented as an infinite *given* magnitude' (*CPR* A25/B39). Space, in other words, is represented as an infinite totality of spaces, such that every particular space is *already* contained within the one comprehensive space. But it is not as though space were a sort of massive chess-board with all individual spaces predetermined as occupants of tidy rows and columns; rather, the manifold of spaces is represented as resulting essentially from various limitations of the total space. This implies that even a collec-tion of the individual parts of space as large as the complete set of natural numbers could not exhaust space, since counting the parts of space would be only one possible way of limiting it. Space is represented as a singular abstract totality that is logically irreducible and logically prior to any aggreg-ate of particular subspaces or spatial items that it encompasses: 'these parts cannot as it were precede the one all-embracing space, as its constituents (from which its composition would be possible), but rather are thought only *in it*'. So space is not represented as a countable aggregate or sum of spaces; rather it is represented as both infinite and non-enumerable. Contrary, then, to the familiar picture of Kant as the great-grandfather of constructivist finitism in mathematics merely by virtue of his being an intuitionist,[89] he is in fact neither a finitist nor a Cantorian infinitist. The finitist holds that we can directly

---

[88] For objections to Kant's view, see Walker, *Kant*, 55–9; but, for a defence of the unique-ness of time, see Swinburne, *Space and Time*, ch. 10.

[89] See Parsons, 'The Foundations of Mathematics', 204–5.

represent only limited objects or limited collections of objects, whereas Kant thinks that a representation of the unlimited infinity of space is immediately given via pure intuition. On the other hand, the Cantorian infinitist holds (1) that we can enumerate the infinite by establishing a one-to-one correlation between a collection of things and the series of natural numbers, and (2) that there exist some quantities larger than any enumerable infinity (= the transfinite). By contrast, Kant thinks that, while infinity is representable in pure intuition, it is not represented as enumerable (*CPR* B111), because that would be to represent infinity as a completed totality or a noumenon, which is impossible for creatures minded like us (*CPR* A430/B548); and since infinity cannot be enumerated, there automatically cannot exist quantities larger than any enumerable infinite. For Kant, non-enumerability is a necessary condition of infinity; but the possibility of real enumeration requires the a priori representation of infinity.[90] He also clearly conveys this point in the Second Antinomy, where he remarks that, 'properly speaking space should be called not a *compositum* but a *totum*, because its parts are possible only in the whole, and not the whole through the parts. In any case, it could be called a *compositum ideale*, but not a *compositum reale*' (*CPR* A438/B466). This is closely connected with Kant's idea that, although space is represented as a non-relational or singular whole, it is nevertheless represented as containing nothing but relations (*CPR* B66–7). In order for any enumerable set of particular spatial items to exist, each and every such item must be already relevantly defined within the relational framework of total space; otherwise it is not a determinate item. So total space is represented in such a way that it does not supervene on the aggregative set of all its particular spatial parts; on the contrary, each one of its particular spatial parts, and hence the aggregative set of all of them, must presuppose the complete relational framework of total space as the fundamental ground of spatial determinateness.[91]

---

[90] Parsons argues in 'Infinity and Kant's Conception of the "Possibility of Experience"' that, because pure intuition cannot account adequately for the representation of enumerably infinite quantities, Kant's philosophy of mathematics fails. The mistake here is to assume, without further argument, that the representation of infinity and the representation of an enumerably infinite quantity are the same thing. Kant's view is that the representation of infinity entails its non-enumerability; and, further, that the pure intuitional representation of infinity, as the schema of the category of limitation (*CPR* A80/B106), is an a priori condition for the possibility of real enumeration or measurement, just as the representation of causal necessity is an a priori condition for the possibility of experience. Numbers for Kant are neither intrinsically finite nor intrinsically infinite because they are merely ways of counting objects (*CPR* A142–3/B182). Finite or limited magnitude, in turn, is defined in terms of a possible enumeration of all parts or elements. So, if all the parts of an object or all the elements of a collection of objects can be put into a one-to-one correspondence with the series of natural numbers, then (odd as it sounds) that object or that collection is finite in Kant's sense.

[91] Nerlich argues in a similar way that space is not merely set-mereological in nature; see *The Shape of Space*, 16–20, 28.

On the assumption that space is represented as an ideal totality in the sense just suggested, then Kant's argument does indeed seem to be sufficient to show that the representation of space is an experience-independent, pure intuition. As a non-aggregative, non-enumerable singular structural whole containing nothing but spatial relations, space is ontically underdetermined by whatever fills it up—whether by statically occupying locations, or by motion across locations. Hence space is represented as ontologically and logically prior to any and all empirical objects *in* space. Correspondingly, the content of the representation of space is not determined by any sort of sensory filling, and does not require any special sensory content in order to exist. That is, the representation of space is in itself strictly underdetermined by experience and free of all sensory aspects. Moreover, the representation of space is the essential factor for determining what will count as a particular spatial thing, or as a set of particular spatial things. Therefore the representation of space is an experience-independent and pure intuition.

Having argued his way to the claim that the representation of space (and, *mutatis mutandis*, the representation of time) is a pure intuition, Kant responds immediately to an obvious objection—namely, that he has not yet shown conclusively that the representations of space and time are not pure concepts. He points out:

Space is represented as an infinite *given* magnitude. Now one must, to be sure, think of every concept as a representation that is contained in an infinite collection of different possible representations (as their common characteristic), and which therefore contains these *under itself*; but no concept, as such, can be thought as if it contained an infinite number of representations *within itself*. Nevertheless space is thought [in this very way] (for all the parts of space, to infinity, are coexistent). Therefore the original representation of space is an a priori *intuition*, not a concept.   (*CPR* B39–40; see also B136 n.)

The relevant point is that a concept is essentially a representation that contains in itself a finite ordered complex of characteristics—that is, its intension or conceptual microstructure—and that uniquely determines an infinite comprehension of actual or possible objects contained under that concept. As we know from the immediately preceding argument, however, space is represented as a single item—an abstract space whole, or space framework, that is both infinite and non-enumerable. Two contrasts are salient here: the first concerns the differing referential components of concepts and intuitions, while the second concerns their differing semantic contents.

First, despite the fact that space is represented as infinite, it is not represented as having an infinite *comprehension*. A concept, as an essentially general representation, is applicable to the infinitely many possible objects in its comprehension; hence it is infinitely reapplicable or multiply realizable. An intuition, by contrast, is applicable only once, and to an individual and empirically real (even if in this case also non-empirical) being. The representation of space presents space as an 'infinite *given* magnitude'; as Kant's emphasis indicates, it is the givenness or actuality of the object that determines the singular reference of the representation. Secondly, the representation of space is a singular representation of an object that can be endlessly measured and partitioned. By contrast, the intension of a concept contains only a finite complex of characteristics, terminating in subconceptual simples (VL Ak. xxiv. 835). If the intensional microstructure of a concept were infinite, then it could not be the result of a step-by-step generative conceptual synthesis and could not therefore be grasped in an act of decompositional insight by a finite thinker.[92] For these two reasons, then, the representation of space is necessarily an intuition, not a concept; and the same goes for the representation of time.

4.4. Frege's Intuitionism

Now back to Frege. We have already seen that Kant and Frege share a doctrine of the syntheticity of propositions; but where does Frege stand in relation to Kant's theory of intuition?

In *Foundations of Arithmetic* Frege correctly notes that in 'The Jäsche Logic' Kant describes an intuition as a singular representation (*einzelne Vorstellung*), while by contrast in the Transcendental Aesthetic in the first *Critique* he describes it somewhat differently as a representation given (*gegeben*) to us through sensibility. According to Frege, this latter doctrine of intuition stresses the 'connection with sensibility . . . without which intuition cannot serve as the principle of our knowledge of synthetic a priori judgments'.[93] Setting aside the implied criticism to the effect that Kant's doctrines in the *Critique of Pure Reason* and 'The Jäsche Logic' are at odds with one another,[94] it is clear enough that Frege is willing to accept that singularity and sense relatedness are two necessary features of intuition.

Later in *Foundations* Frege points up another necessary feature of intuition when he remarks that 'what is purely intuitable is not communicable (*nicht mittheilbar*)'; and that the incommunicable is to be directly contrasted to 'what can be conceived and judged, what is expressible in words'.[95] In this way, an intuition is sharply distinct from an 'objective notion' (*objective Idee*): 'The idea in the objective sense (*Vorstellung in dim objectiven Sinne*) belongs to logic and is in principle non-sensible . . . Objective ideas are the same for all.

---

[92] See Allison, *Kant's Transcendental Idealism*, 93.

[93] Frege, *The Foundations of Arithmetic*, 19, translation modified slightly.

[94] As Dummett points out, Frege's criticism here is misguided: in fact, the doctrine given in 'The Jäsche Logic' is perfectly consistent with the doctrine given in the first *Critique*; see *Frege: Philosophy of Mathematics*, 64–5.

[95] Frege, *The Foundations of Arithmetic*, 35.

Objective ideas can be divided into objects and concepts.'[96] Frege recognizes that intuitions are neither objective (in his sense) nor conceptual in character. This is not, however, to say that intuitions are merely subjective or never related to objects, but rather only that intuitions are not related to objects that are non-sensible in character. Frege says that he 'must also protest against the generality of Kant's dictum: without sensibility no object would be given to us'.[97] Frege is not thereby denying that objects can be given to us via sensibility, hence via intuition—he is denying only that all objects must be so given.

This leads us to a crucial point. It is generally assumed by Frege-interpreters that when Frege says that intuitions are incommunicable, and contrasts them with objective ideas, he is also saying that an intuition is essentially subjective.[98] On this interpretation, then, Frege is saying that intuitions belong to the domain of what he calls 'an idea in the subjective sense': 'An idea in the subjective sense is what is governed by the psychological laws of association; it is of a sensible, pictorial character. . . . Subjective ideas are often demonstrably different in different men.'[99] In his later papers 'On Sense and Meaning' and 'Thoughts', he strengthens the doctrine of subjective ideas by asserting their essential privacy, or strict epistemological and ontological dependence on individual minds:

My idea . . . is an internal image, arising from memories of sense impressions which I have had and acts, both internal and external, which I have performed. . . . The idea is subjective: one man's idea is not that of another.[100]

Ideas cannot be seen, or touched, or smelled, or tasted, or heard. . . . Ideas are something we have. We have sensations, feelings, moods, inclinations, wishes. An idea that someone has belongs to the content of his consciousness. . . . It seems absurd to us that a pain, a mood, a wish should go around the world without an owner, independently. A sensation is impossible without a sentient being. The inner world presupposes somebody whose inner world it is. . . . Ideas need an owner. . . . It is so much the essence of any one of my ideas that to be a content of my consciousness, that any idea someone else has is, just as such, different from mine. . . . Nobody else has my idea, but many people see the same thing. Nobody else has my pain. . . . Every idea has only one owner; no two men have the same idea.[101]

Leaving aside Frege's questionable thesis that subjective ideas or sensations are necessarily private,[102] what I want to disagree with instead is the interpretive claim that Fregean intuitions are equivalent with Frege's necessarily private ideas—just because intuitions are non-objective and incommunicable.

---

[96] Frege, *The Foundations of Arithmetic*, 37 n. 1.   [97] Ibid. 101.
[98] See e.g. Carl, *Frege's Theory of Sense and Reference*, 33.
[99] Frege, *The Foundations of Arithmetic*, 37 n. 1.
[100] Frege, 'On Sense and Meaning', 160.   [101] Frege, 'Thoughts', 360–1.
[102] Against this thesis, see Wittgenstein, *Philosophical Investigations*, paras. 243–315, pp. 88–104.

The most obvious reason for resisting this claim is that, given Frege's theory of geometry, which like Kant's is based on pure spatial intuition, Frege could not possibly reduce spatial intuition to essentially subjective ideas without completely relativizing the truths of geometry. Hence Fregean intuition cannot be the same as Fregean consciousness or *Bewußtsein*.

And this is closely connected with an important feature of Frege's concept of incommunicability. It is easily assumed when reading Frege's remarks about intuition that the incommunicability of intuition yields the necessary privacy of its objects; but that is a non sequitur. Necessarily private items are indeed incommunicable, but sometimes our mode of access to items is incommunicable merely because that mode is essentially indexical, not because that mode or those items are necessarily private. For example, what allows me to distinguish this actual computer I am now working on, from any actual or possible type-identical counterpart of it? The answer is of course that I can pick out this actual computer from all of its actual or possible counterparts by intuiting it through sense perception; my computer is *this* one. Here the intuition is incommunicable (it cannot be 'said', but only 'shown' through subject-centred, context-dependent ostension), but it is also not in any way necessarily private, since any other perceiver can also perform a similar discriminatory act of locating this self-same actual computer from her own incommunicable point of view. Indeed, Frege explicitly holds that actual physical objects can be given to us directly via sensible intuition. As we will remember, in *Foundations* Frege states that cognitive access to what is spatially actual or *wirklich*—as opposed to access to the non-actual, non-psychological realm of the objective—is provided only either by means of sense perception or by means of pure spatial intuition.[103] This is reaffirmed in *The Basic Laws of Arithmetic* when he observes that whatever is actual 'has to be capable of acting directly or indirectly on the senses'.[104] And in at least one place Frege makes the connection between the sense perception of an object and outer sensory intuition perfectly explicit: 'one may . . . understand intuition as including any object so far as it is sensibly perceptible or spatial'.[105]

That Frege takes intuition to be incommunicable because of its essential indexicality—and not because of any necessary privacy that it or its objects supposedly has or have—is further shown by his view that geometry is based on the pure intuition of our actual space and not specifically on our ability to think or conceive geometric axioms, be they Euclidean axioms or non-Euclidean axioms. He argues explicitly that it is possible for two thinkers to agree conceptually and therefore objectively about all geometrical axioms, yet simply fail to intuit the same space:

---

[103] Frege, *The Foundations of Arithmetic*, 34–8.
[104] Frege, *The Basic Laws of Arithmetic*, 16.
[105] Frege, 'On Sense and Meaning', 160 n. 5, translation modified slightly.

Let us suppose two rational beings such that projective properties and relations are all that they can intuit—the lying of three points on a line, of four points in a plane, and so on; and let what the one intuits as a plane appear to the other as a point, and vice versa, so that what for the one is the line joining two points for the other is the line of intersection of two planes, and so on with the one intuition always dual to the other. In these circumstances they could understand one another quite well and would never realize the difference between their intuitions, since in projective geometry every pro-position has its dual counterpart; any disagreement over points of aesthetic appreciation (*ästhetischen Werthschätzung*) would not be conclusive evidence. Over all geometric theorems they would be in complete agreement, only interpreting the words differently in terms of their respective intuitions. With the word "point", for example, one would connect one intuition and the other another. We can therefore still say that for them this word means something objective (*etwas Objectives bedeute*), provided only that by this meaning we do not understand any of the peculiarities of their respective intuitions.[106]

One might be tempted to infer from this that for Frege our knowledge of Euclidean geometry is exhausted by our conceptual or objective knowledge of Euclidean axioms—that spatial intuition is otiose, because intuitive differences consist merely in differences of aesthetic appreciation.[107] But, as we saw in Section 4.1, according to Frege our a priori knowledge of Euclidean geometry depends necessarily *on our intuition*: conceptual thought is not sufficient. Let us look again at some parts of a text I have already quoted in full:

The truths of geometry govern *all that is spatially intuitable* . . . The wildest visions of delirium, the boldest inventions of legend and poetry . . . all these remain, *so long as they remain intuitable*, still subject to the axioms of geometry. Conceptual thought alone after a fashion can shake off this yoke, when it assumes, say, a space of four dimensions or positive curvature. To study such conceptions is not useless by any means; but it is to leave *the ground of intuition* entirely behind. If we do make use of intuition even here, as an aid, it is still *the same old intuition of Euclidean space, the only one whose structures we can intuit.*[108]

To be sure, some objective conceptual knowledge of the Euclidean axioms can be had independently of our intuition; but our actual knowledge of Euclidean geometry is not possible unless we have intuitive access to the struc-tures of actual Euclidean space. As Frege puts it elsewhere in *Foundations*: 'every-thing geometrical must be originally given in intuition.'[109] Therefore, since our geometric knowledge is not in any way purely subjective or necessarily pri-vate but in fact quite general and a priori, the incommunicability of intuition is perfectly consistent with its epistemic generality and apriority.

Otherwise put, then, that which is objective for Frege is not only non-subjective or non-private, it is also non-indexical. This is to say that the objective transcends that which is concrete, or somehow bound up with actual

[106] Frege, *The Foundations of Arithmetic*, 35–6, translation modified slightly.
[107] This is Dummett's reading; see 'Frege and Kant on Geometry', 248–50.
[108] Frege, *The Foundations of Arithmetic*, 20–1, emphases added.   [109] Ibid. 75.

space or time: 'I distinguish what I call objective from what is handleable (*Handgreiflichen*) or spatial or actual (*wirklich*). The axis of the earth is objective, so is the center of mass of the solar system, but I should not call them actual in the way the earth itself is so.'[110] Frege is of course saying here that not everything objective is actual. And it is fairly natural to assume that his reason for saying this is that some things are objective although not actual (for example, the axis of the earth, the centre of mass of the solar system, and so on), while other things are both objective and actual (for example, the earth itself). But another equally textually supported way of reading it is to hold that Frege is saying that the objective is ontologically distinct from the actual because *what is objective is non-actual, and what is actual is non-objective*. Both the objective and the actual share the property of being mind-independent, but no objective (= non-spatiotemporal) things are also actual things, and no actual (= spatiotemporal) things are also objective things. Thus the objective in Frege's special sense is essentially the *conceptual*.[111] The axis of the earth, and the solar system's centre of mass, are both conceptual or abstract objects, and therefore objective, but the actual earth is not objective in that special sense. So, following out this line of thinking, for Frege the actual earth is *non-objective*. Hence that which is 'objective' transcends intuition; yet that which is accessed through outer intuition, even if it is incommunicable—because indexical—remains strictly non-subjective and publicly accessible.

This point is closely connected with Frege's view that the objective is essentially bound up with reason:

I understand objective to mean what is independent of our sensation, intuition and imagination, and of all construction of mental pictures out of memories of earlier sensations, but not of what is independent of the reason—for what are things independent of the reason? To answer that would be as much as to judge without judging, or to wash the fur without wetting it.[112]

In arithmetic we are not concerned with objects which we come to know as something alien from without through the medium of the senses, but with objects given directly to our reason and, as its nearest kin, utterly transparent to it. . . . There is nothing more objective than the laws of arithmetic.[113]

---

[110] Ibid. 35. The same distinction is drawn in 'Thoughts', 369–70, with the addition of a further distinction between actuality (which is now said to involve causality), and the 'inner world' or the purely subjective or psychological realm. This makes explicit what is merely implicit in *Foundations*—namely, a sharp distinction between the intuitively accessible actual world in space and time, and the essentially subjective or purely psychological world accessible only through consciousness.

[111] This interpretive claim can be sustained both in early and in later Frege, because in *Foundations* the notion of a concept ambiguously covers both what Frege later thinks of as the sense (*Sinn*) and Meaning (*Bedeutung*) of a predicate expression. I agree with Sluga's view in 'Frege: The Early Years', 342–3 that Frege probably modelled his notion of the objective on Lotze's notion of 'validity'; see Lotze, *Logic*, ii. 208–11.

[112] Frege, *The Foundations of Arithmetic*, 36, translation modified slightly.

[113] Ibid. 115.

Much could and should be said about Frege's conception of reason and its similarities to and differences from Kant's conception.[114] The crucial point here, however, is that for Frege all objective knowledge gained through reason has three basic features. First, it is based on mind-independent objects; secondly, it is intersubjective or non-idiosyncratic; and, thirdly, its objects are wholly conceptual or abstract. It is the third feature alone that distinguishes it from cognition gained through intuition. Intuition too is based on mind-independent objects (for example, actual spatial objects like this computer or the earth) and intuition too is intersubjective and non-idiosyncratic (for example, in the synthetic a priori knowledge supplied through geometry). Intuitions for Frege are therefore singular, sensibility related, non-conceptual, incommunicable, and non-objective; but they are also non-private or non-subjective cognitions of actual objects. Otherwise put, Frege's theory of intuition is equivalent to Kant's. And intuitions are necessary for Frege's semantics because they are intrinsic to his account of synthetic truths, be they a posteriori or empirical truths of natural science and everyday discourse or a priori truths in geometry.

4.5. Conclusion

According to Kant, a true proposition is synthetic if and only if it is consistently deniable and its truth and meaning are intuition-dependent. In turn, an intuition is an immediate, sensibility-related, thought-prior, singular, object-dependent (existential, actual) means of semantic reference. As I have stressed, the fundamental feature of Kantian syntheticity and intuition alike is their essential indexicality. That is, all synthetic propositions are irreducibly subject centred and context-dependent in that their semantic contents, by virtue of the inclusion of empirical or pure intuitions, cannot be fully determined without taking into account the unique constitution of our sensibility, the natural circumstances of actual sensory experience (the dynamical context), and the unique structural properties of the empirically real but also pure a priori space and time that govern all possible experiences of objects (the mathematical context). I have argued that Kant's doctrine of syntheticity and intuition is also held by Frege, both in *Foundations of Arithmetic* and in later writings as well. To the extent that the analytic tradition after Frege overlooks, suppresses, or soft-pedals the factor of essential indexicality, it is not only anti-Kantian but also, ironically enough, anti-Fregean.

Put another way, the philosophical significance of syntheticity is that Kant's and Frege's doctrines of synthetic propositions fully commit them to

---

[114] See Burge, 'Frege on Knowing the Foundation', and De Pierris, 'Frege and Kant on A Priori Knowledge'.

a full-strength semantic intuitionism standing in stark contrast with the extreme conceptualism of the analytic tradition that runs through early Moore's theory of judgement, through Russell's Theory of Descriptions,[115] and through Carnap's intensional-descriptivist semantics, all the way up to Quine's elimination of all singular terms. In turn, however, to recognize the special anthropocentric restrictions built into this full-strength semantic intuitionism is to raise vividly the question of how it can be possible that at least some synthetic propositions are necessarily true and cognizable independently of all sense experience by creatures minded like us. And this is to raise the fundamental question of how synthetic a priori propositions are possible—the Modal Problem.

[115] As opposed to his theory of acquaintance, which is quasi-intuitionistic; see Russell, *The Problems of Philosophy*, chs. 5, 11.

5.

Necessity Restricted: The Synthetic A Priori

> After a rather thick book was written trying to answer the question how
> synthetic a priori judgements were possible, others came along later who
> claimed that the solution to the problem was that synthetic a priori judge-
> ments were, of course, impossible and that a book trying to show other-
> wise was written in vain.
>
> *Saul Kripke*[1]

5.0. Introduction

If what I have argued in Chapter 3 is sound, it follows that an analytic
truth for Kant is far from being the 'miserable tautology' (*CPR* A597/B625) it
is often taken to be.[2] As we have seen, analytic truths expose intrinsic necessary connections between our objectively valid concepts and thereby express
'real cognition a priori (*wirkliche Erkenntnis a priori*)' (*CPR* A6/B10). They
are topic-neutral in the sense that their truth is strictly determined by the form
and content of concepts alone, not by intuitions of objects; but from this it
does not in any way follow that analytic propositions are irrelevant to empirical reality. Indeed, they have necessary application in every possible world
in which their constituent concepts are (as it happens) instantiated. So, for
example, necessarily in every world in which there are (as it happens) some
bachelors, they are unmarried.

But even in view of Kant's anti-tautological conception of analyticity, it
remains true that he assigns philosophical pride of place to the synthetic a
priori: 'synthetic a priori judgements are contained as principles (*Prinzipien*)
in all theoretical sciences of reason' (*CPR* B14). He holds explicitly that synthetic a priori truths can be found in mathematics, in natural science or physics,

---

[1] Kripke, 'Identity and Necessity', 162.

[2] Miserable tautologies are propositions that are analytic by their form alone yet lack
objective validity, hence are truth valueless—e.g. (assuming the Ontological Argument is
valid) 'God exists'.

and in the transcendental metaphysics of human experience (*CPR* B14–18, A148–62/B187–202, A737/B765; *CJ* Ak. v. 181–6; *MFNS* Ak. iv. 467–79; and *P.* Ak. iv. 294–5).[3] And, as we have seen in Chapter 1, he identifies the task of explaining and grounding the notion of the synthetic a priori with the positive project of transcendental philosophy itself: 'Much is already gained if one can bring a multitude of investigations under the formula of a single problem. . . . Now the real problem of pure reason is contained in the question: how are synthetic a priori judgements possible?' (*CPR* B19). Synthetic a priori truths are at once necessary, essentially directed to the world of human sensory experience, and yet cognizable by creatures minded like us apart from all experience. Otherwise put, they are substantive necessary truths accessible to the human mind a priori. For this reason they are at the very centre of traditional philosophy. But they are also deeply puzzling. How can a truth be necessary and cognizable by us apart from sense experience, and yet also essentially directed to the world? This is the Modal Problem.

Now, quite apart from the fact that Kant wrote (to use Kripke's droll phrase) a rather thick book precisely in order to solve this problem, one might well wonder whether such a thing as the synthetic a priori really makes any sense at all. And, according to the Tractarian Wittgenstein, the logical empiricists, and their descendants,[4] it makes *no* sort of sense. From this point of view, the first *Critique* 'was written in vain' because 'synthetic a priori judgements were, of course, impossible'. Thus, for example, in his highly influential 1936 manifesto of logical empiricism, *Language, Truth, and Logic*, A. J. Ayer tells us that 'While it is true that we have a priori knowledge of necessary propositions, it is not true, as Kant supposed, that any of these necessary propositions are synthetic'.[5] For Ayer and the other logical positivists, there exist two and only two kinds of properly meaningful propositions: (*a*) necessary analytic a priori propositions (that is, either truths of elementary logic, or else propositions translatable into truths of elementary logic by replacing synonyms by synonyms), and (*b*) contingent synthetic a posteriori propositions (= factual truths). Looked at this way, the label "synthetic a priori" is an oxymoron.

---

[3] Kant calls synthetic a priori truths in mathematics 'mathemata'; synthetic a priori truths in physics 'laws of nature' or 'empirical laws'; and synthetic a priori truths in the transcendental metaphysics of experience 'principles (*Grundsätze*) of pure understanding' or 'transcendental principles'.

[4] In fact, a general rejection of the synthetic a priori did not arise until the middle or linguistic phase of analytic philosophy. Despite their logicism, both Frege and Russell (from 1900 to 1912) openly accepted the existence of synthetic a priori truths. Frege held that geometric truths are synthetic a priori, as we saw in Ch. 4. And Russell, in his 1900 *Critical Exposition of the Philosophy of Leibniz*, sect. 11, in his 1903 *Principles of Mathematics*, 4–5, 457, and in his 1912 *Problems of Philosophy*, 82–3, held that the basic truths of logic and mathematics alike are synthetic a priori propositions.

[5] Ayer, *Language, Truth, and Logic*, 84.

The demise of the synthetic a priori within the analytic tradition can be traced to the combined impact of two somewhat distinct sorts of objections: (1) objections to Kant's theory of the synthetic a priori, and (2) objections to the very idea of synthetic apriority. Apart from more general worries about Kant's (supposed) psychologism and his idealism, arguments against Kant's synthetic a priori typically take the form of rejections of his theories of arithmetic and geometry: Frege's moderate logicism seemingly entails the falsity of the former; and non-Euclidean geometry (proven factually, it is claimed, by the Theory of Relativity) apparently yields the falsity of the latter. We have already had a critical look at Frege's logicism in Section 3.3; and I will deal directly with the famous objection(s) from non-Euclidean geometry in Section 5.5. More pertinent now, however, are the in-principle objections to the very idea of the synthetic a priori. These in turn can be divided into two somewhat different but equally forceful lines of criticism.

Both lines share a starting point in the work of the early Wittgenstein. Wittgenstein argues in the *Tractatus* that any sentence putatively expressing a meaningful synthetic a priori proposition can be shown to be nonsensical (*unsinnig*) strictly by virtue of its logico-grammatical form: 'Most questions and propositions of the philosophers result from the fact that we do not understand the logic of our language.'[6] Carnap fully developed this idea in the 1930s. Synthetic a priori propositions fail to express anything meaningful because they are ill constructed according to universal rules of the logical syntax of language.[7] The other line derives from Moritz Schlick, who during the 1920s independently developed views that gradually merged with those held by

---

[6] Wittgenstein, *Tractatus Logico-Philosophicus*, prop. 4.003, p. 63.

[7] See Carnap, 'The Elimination of Metaphysics through the Logical Analysis of Language'; *The Logical Syntax of Language*, pt. V; and *Philosophy and Logical Syntax*. Carnap's earliest work in philosophy fell within the neo-Kantian tradition, however, and explicitly left open a place for synthetic a priori propositions in geometry: 'I studied Kant's philosophy with Bruno Bauch in Jena. In his seminar, the *Critique of Pure Reason* was discussed in detail for an entire year. I was strongly impressed by Kant's conception that the geometrical structure of space is determined by our forms of intuition. The after-effects of this influence were still noticeable in the chapter on the space of intuition in my dissertation, *Der Raum*. . . . Knowledge of intuitive space I regarded at that time [of the writing of *Der Raum*], under the influence of Kant and the neo-Kantians, especially Natorp and Cassirer, as based on "pure intuition", and independent of contingent experience' (Carnap, 'Intellectual Autobiography', 4, 12). The double assimilation of the Theory of Relativity and the doctrines of the *Tractatus* gradually pushed Carnap towards a more sharply defined anti-Kantian outlook. Even so, Carnap's 1928 *Logical Structure of the World* is at least empirically idealistic via its appeal to methodological solipsism—and, arguably, is committed to some stronger form of idealism as well. See Richardson, *Carnap's Construction of the World: The Aufbau and the Emergence of Logical Empiricism*. A complete rejection of the synthetic a priori did not emerge in Carnap's work until the 1930s, in the form of a radically logico-linguistic approach to all philosophical questions about necessity and apriority.

Wittgenstein in the late 1920s and early 1930s.[8] Schlick argues that sentences apparently expressing meaningful synthetic a priori propositions are all vacuous by virtue of their illegitimate semantic content. More precisely, any proposition expressed by such a sentence could be neither analytically true nor verifiable in sense experience—but analyticity and verifiability exhaust the legitimate sources of cognitive significance.[9] Collecting together the formalist and verificationist objections under a single heading, I will dub it the 'Wittgenstein–Carnap–Schlick–Ayer Thesis' ('the WCSA Thesis', for short): 'Synthetic *a priori* truths, by virtue of their corrupt form and corrupt content —that is, by virtue of their violation of syntactic and semantic first principles —are impossible simply because they are unintelligible.'[10]

The philosophical importance of the WCSA Thesis cannot be underestimated, since it is essential to the emergence and flourishing of the analytic tradition in its middle and later phases. Dissidents within the tradition were (and are still) rather few and far between.[11] There was a brief reopening of the whole issue of the synthetic a priori in the 1950s, in the form of a surprisingly vigorous debate about the modal status of the so-called colour-incompatibility proposition—for example, 'Nothing can be simultaneously both red all over and green all over.'[12] But this window was gradually closed—in

---

[8] See Waismann, *Wittgenstein and the Vienna Circle*, 47, 227. Like Carnap, Schlick began his philosophical career as a neo-Kantian; but he sloughed off the last vestiges of a commitment to the synthetic a priori almost a decade earlier than Carnap did. See Coffa, *The Semantic Tradition from Kant to Carnap*, chs. 9–10.

[9] Schlick, 'Is there a Factual *A Priori*?' (1930).

[10] It is possible to defend a weaker version of logical empiricism, according to which synthetic a priori propositions are at least intelligible, although strictly speaking neither logically nor factually true. See e.g. Hanson, 'The Very Idea of a Synthetic-Apriori'. On this view, synthetic a priori propositions function as historically contingent non-empirical background assumptions for the development of scientific theories. This strongly resembles Kant's view that there is a legitimate hypothetical or regulative use of otherwise objectively invalid synthetic a priori propositions containing ideas of pure reason, for the purpose of promoting natural scientific enquiry (*CPR* A642–68/B670–96). Friedman fruitfully emphasizes this somewhat Kantian line of development within logical empiricism in *Reconsidering Logical Positivism*.

[11] There are, of course, some exceptions. See e.g. Langford, 'A Proof that Synthetic *A Priori* Propositions Exist'; Pap, 'Logic and the Synthetic A Priori'; Sellars, 'Is there a Synthetic A Priori?'; and Toulmin, 'A Defense of "Synthetic Necessary Truth"'. Generally speaking, the strategy of these arguments is to show that some class of prima facie necessary a priori propositions cannot be assimilated to the standard logico-linguistic criterion of analyticity; but little or no attempt is made to give a positive theory of synthetic a priori necessity. To this extent, they cannot be regarded as serious defences of modal dualism. See Beck, 'On the Meta-Semantics of the Problem of the Synthetic *A Priori*', 97–8.

[12] See e.g. Putnam, 'Reds, Greens, and Logical Analysis'; Pap, 'Once More: Colors and the Synthetic *A Priori*'; and Putnam, 'Red and Green All Over Again: A Rejoinder to Arthur Pap'. See also Katz, 'The Problem in Twentieth-Century Philosophy'; Wittgenstein 'Some Remarks on Logical Form', 168; and Wittgenstein, *Tractatus Logico-Philosophicus*, props. 6.375–6.3751, pp. 181–3.

the sense that the whole issue of the synthetic a priori began to seem moot or even pointless—by the emerging consensus in support of Quine's radically sceptical rejection of the analytic/synthetic distinction. Still, as we have seen, there are good reasons for challenging the logico-linguistic conception of analyticity, even quite independently of Quine's devastating attack on it. And, without its doctrine of analyticity, obviously logical empiricism cannot stand. We have also seen that Kant's doctrines of syntheticity and intuition, seconded by Frege, expose a semantic dimension—essential indexicality— not adequately recognized by early Moore, early Russell, the logical empiri- cists, or indeed Quine. Hence there are good philosophical grounds for re- reopening the long-closed case of the synthetic a priori. If clear theoretical sense can be made of Kant's doctrine of synthetic a priori propositions, and if it can be shown that at least some synthetic a priori propositions in the Kantian sense exist, then it will follow both that the WCSA Thesis is false and that the very assumptions lying behind this third dogma of empiricism (a dogma never challenged by Quine) are in need of some serious rethinking. Or even more positively put, it will follow that we have uncovered a strong Kantian argument for modal dualism—the thesis that there are two irreducibly different types of necessary truth[13]—by showing how Kant solves the Modal Problem.

So, using the conception of syntheticity developed in Chapter 4 as a start- ing point, in this chapter I want to make a new case for Kant's doctrine of the synthetic a priori. I begin by presenting and explicating the semantic and modal properties of Kantian synthetic a priori propositions, followed by a general formulation of synthetic and analytic apriority (Sections 5.1–5.3). A particularly striking feature of Kant's doctrine is a distinction between what I call 'strongly necessary' and 'weakly necessary' synthetic a priori truths. Philo- sophical and mathematical truths are strongly necessary synthetic a priori, while weak synthetic a priori necessity attaches to propositions expressing causal laws of nature. Having broken a discursive lance or two in support of the intelligibility of the Kantian synthetic a priori, I then offer a further argument for its existence, in two steps. First, in Section 5.4 I reconstruct Kant's argument for the synthetic apriority of geometry. Secondly and finally, in Section 5.5 I respond directly on Kant's behalf to the famous and highly influential objection—made in different ways by Russell, Hermann von Helmholtz, and Hans Reichenbach—that the Kantian theory of geometry is undermined by the existence of non-Euclidean geometries.

[13] This is not to be confused with the thesis that there is only one type of necessary truth but two distinct ways of *knowing* such truths. Even defenders of the necessary a pos- teriori can hold this thesis.

5.1. Possible Worlds and Experienceable Worlds

For Kant, a proposition is analytic if and only if it is necessarily true[14] by virtue of its conceptual form or content alone. Now for Kant the 'nominal'—that is, analytic and strictly correct—definition of truth is that it consists in the 'agreement' (*Übereinstimmung*) between a judgement and its proper object (*CPR* A58/B82). Hence, despite Kant's being a transcendental idealist, he also holds that every true judgement has an objective truth-maker and thereby defends a version of the correspondence theory of truth.[15] An analytic proposition, as we have seen, is topic-neutral in the sense that its meaningfulness and truth depend on no special ontological configuration in any possible world; on the contrary, its truth is determined by intrinsic conceptual connections alone. By contrast, a proposition is synthetic if and only if it is consistently deniable and strictly dependent on an intuitional relation either to the actual individual inhabitants of the empirical world or to its overarching empirically real spatiotemporal structure. In this way a synthetic proposition is essentially indexical. Now, since a true analytic proposition is concept based and topic-neutral, one might be inclined to say that it has no worldly truth-makers whatsoever because its truth-makers are all concepts. Yet, because for Kant our entire repertoire of concepts is implicit in every possible world—as I mentioned in passing in Section 2.2 but will recapitulate in more detail directly, every possible world is merely a maximal consistent selection from that total human conceptual repertoire—it is more correct to say that every possible world is its truth-maker. And, since a synthetic proposition is intuition-dependent and essentially indexical, it is equally correct to say that it is true only in one or more of the intuition-accessible worlds, so that only one or more members of this specially restricted class of possible worlds constitute(s) its truth-maker. In this sense, while an analytic proposition is meaningful and true absolutely without modal limitation, a synthetic proposition is meaningful and true only by virtue of a restriction to one or more intuition-accessible worlds. In order to understand these crucial points, however, we must get a better handle on the Kantian notions of (*a*) what it is to be a possible world, and (*b*) what it is to be an intuition-accessible possible world.

Possible Worlds

At this point a critic might well challenge me by asking what warrant I have for talking about possible worlds at all in a Kantian context: 'Aren't possible

---

[14] As usual, in this chapter I make the simplifying assumption that, unless otherwise noted, all of the propositions discussed are true.

[15] See Hanna, 'Kant, Truth, and Human Nature'; see also Van Cleve, *Problems from Kant*, 214–17.

worlds a strictly Leibnizian—or more recently, a strictly C. I. Lewis-ian, Carnapian, and Kripkean—conception? So isn't your whole discussion hopelessly anachronistic?' No, it is not anachronistic. Of course, the notion of a possible world that is so central in recent and contemporary philosophy does have its origins in Leibniz's philosophy. But that is precisely why it is deeply relevant to discuss it in a Kantian context. Kant's famous awakening from his dogmatic slumbers may have been Humean in inspiration, but those slumbers were filled to the brim with *Leibnizian* dreams. The metaphysics of Leibniz, as transmitted through the writings of Wolff and Crusius, was both intimately familiar to and vividly salient for Kant throughout his pre-Critical period.[16] Indeed, as Lewis White Beck and Henry Allison have persuasively argued, Kant frames his entire Critical, transcendental theory of analyticity and syntheticity in direct reaction to the Leibnizian theory of concepts, propositions, and truth.[17] Hence it is neither accidental nor odd that Kant discusses possible worlds explicitly as early as his 1755 dissertation 'A New Elucidation of the First Principles of Metaphysical Cognition' (NE Ak. i. 414), in his 1759 essay 'An Attempt at Some Reflections on Optimism' (O. Ak. ii. 29–35), in the 1763 essay 'The Only Possible Argument in Support of a Demonstration of the Existence of God' (OPA Ak. ii. 72), and yet again in the *Critique of Pure Reason*.

Because of the intimate connection between the notion of a possible world and Leibniz's metaphysical theology, however, Kant decides to treat them both, not at the beginning of the first *Critique* but instead in book II, chapter III, of the Transcendental Dialectic, 'The Ideal of Pure Reason' (*CPR* A567–642/ B595–670). Here he spells out the content of the concept GOD and famously criticizes the ontological, cosmological, and design arguments. In his preliminary analysis of the concept GOD as the 'ideal of pure reason', he identifies it as the concept of a being that is the ontological ground—or necessary and sufficient condition—of the 'complete determination' (*durchgängigen Bestimmung*) of every other being. Hence the concept of God is the concept of an '*ens realissimum*' (*CPR* A576/B604; see also NE Ak. i. 395 and OPA Ak. ii. 77–87). Correspondingly, the idea of an absolute or complete determination of a finite thing by an *ens realissimum* is in fact Kant's version of a Leibnizian possible world:

---

[16] See Beiser, 'Kant's Intellectual Development: 1746–1781'. Kant's later vigorous rejection of his early doctrinal infatuation (to use Beiser's amusing image) is evident, for example, in the relational theory of space and the intellectualist theory of sensibility he uses as critical foils in the Transcendental Aesthetic (*CPR* A40/B56–7, A43–4/B60–2). Moreover, the Amphiboly of the Concepts of Reflection in the first *Critique* (*CPR* A260–92/B316–49) is entirely devoted to a critique of the Leibniz–Wolff metaphysics. And he even takes a parting shot at Leibniz and Wolff from beyond the grave in the posthumously published 1804 book, *What Real Progress has Metaphysics made in Germany since the Time of Leibniz and Wolff?* (*RP* Ak. xx. 253–351).

[17] See Allison, *The Kant–Eberhard Controversy*, chs. I–III; and Beck, 'Analytic and Synthetic Judgments before Kant'.

Every concept, in regard to what is not contained in it, is undetermined, and is subject to the principle of *determinability*: that, of *every two* contradictorily opposed predicates, only one can apply to it, which rests on the principle of contradiction and is therefore a purely logical principle, which abstracts from every intensional content (*Inhalte*) of cognition and is concerned solely with its logical form. Every *thing*, however, as regards its possibility, further stands under the principle of *complete* determination, according to which, if *all the possible* predicates of *things* be taken together with their contradictory opposites, then one of each pair of contradictory opposites must belong to it. This [principle] does not rest merely on the law of contradiction, for, besides considering each thing in its relation to the two contradictorily opposed predicates, it also considers it in relation to the *sum total of all possibilities*—that is, to the sum total of all predicates of things in general; and, by presupposing that [relation to the sum total] as being an a priori condition, it represents everything as deriving its own possibility from the share that it possesses in this sum of all possibilities. The principle of complete determination concerns therefore the intensional content and not merely the logical form. It is the principle of the synthesis of all predicates that are to constitute the complete concept of a thing, and not simply [a principle] of analytic representation, through one of two contradictory predicates; and it contains a transcendental presupposition—namely, that of the material (*Materie*) *for all possibility*, which is supposed to contain a priori the data for the *particular* possibility of each thing.   (*CPR* A571–3/B599–601)

According to Kant, then, a finite or limited being—roughly, any being with an enumerable list of parts, or that is subject to spatiotemporal constraints— is completely determined just in case it is strongly equivalent with a special sum of universally co-instantiated concepts or predicates, according to Leibniz's laws of identity, the identity of indiscernibles,[18] and the indiscernibility of identicals.[19] In turn, every such special sum of predicates represents a selection from the 'sum total of all possibilities . . . the sum total of all predicates of things'. This sum total is partially generated by the law of non-contradiction, but also presupposes the categorial and intuitability constraints introduced by the original synthetic unity of apperception (see Section 2.2). In short, then, the sum total of all possibilities consists in a complete list of every well-formed, self-consistent, internally coherent concept in our total human conceptual repertoire, taken along with its contradictory. Relative to that sum total, a thing is completely determined when, for every such predicate pair or concept pair, C and non-C, either the concept C or its contradictory non-C applies to the thing, but not both. In addition, the total special sum of predicates or concepts itself leads to no contradictions. A Kantian possible world is thus a maximal non-contradictory set of co-instantiable concepts—that is, it is a *thinkable world*, or a conceptually consistent complete set of specifiable

[18] i.e., necessarily, if any two things share all the same properties then they are identical.
[19] i.e., necessarily, if any two things are identical then they share all the same properties.

circumstances. This idea of a possible world as a thinkable world is also captured in Kant's idea of the 'object in general'.[20]

As I mentioned in Chapter 2, however, there are some fundamental differences between Kant's notion of a possible world and the Leibnizian one. For Leibniz, a possible world is a transcendent metaphysical being, a maximal non-contradictory sum of compossible substances or monads whose unity is grounded in the 'science of vision' of the supreme monad, God.[21] For Kant, by sharp contrast, a possible world is primitively defined in terms of the far less ontologically loaded notion of a concept.[22] Among other things, this means that, since there can be well-formed but strictly meaningless conceptual complexes (for example, the concept of a furiously sleeping green idea), there can be barely thinkable and hence barely possible yet objectively impossible—because wholly unintuitable—worlds. In any case, Kant's conceptualist doctrine of possible worlds marks a significant advance beyond the Leibnizian doctrine in that it as it were de-noumenalizes possible worlds and makes them instead a function of our a priori cognitive capacities. So, as I put it in Chapter 2, Kantian possible worlds are transcendentally ideal, not transcendentally real.

Experienceable Worlds

Just as not every concept is objectively valid (empirically meaningful) or objectively real (actually empirically applied), so too not every possible or thinkable world is a world accessible to human experience. Our experience—via judgements of experience—involves not only discursive thought, but also an ineliminable factor deriving from our finite sensible capacity for intuition: '*Our sensible and empirical intuition alone can provide* [our concepts] *with sense and meaning* (*Bedeutung*)' (*CPR* B148–9). So there is an essential connection between experienceability and syntheticity. It will be remembered that Kant defines syntheticity in the following way:

This principle [of syntheticity] is completely unambiguously presented in the whole *Critique*, from the chapter on the schematism on, though not in a specific formula. It is: *All synthetic judgements of theoretical cognition are possible only through the relating of a given concept to an intuition.* If the synthetic judgement is an experiential judgement, the intuition must be empirical; if the judgement is a priori synthetic, there must be a pure intuition to ground it. (*PC* Ak. xi. 38)

Thus, again, syntheticity is the intuition dependence of a proposition; but what is crucial for us here is that the intuition dependence implies an intrinsic restriction on the cognitive-semantic scope of the synthetic proposition. Kant

[20] See also Gram, *Kant, Ontology, and the A Priori*, 21.
[21] See Leibniz, 'On the Ultimate Origination of Things', 150–2, and Leibniz, 'The Principles of Philosophy, or, the Monadology', 218–20.
[22] See also Parsons, 'Was ist eine mögliche Welt?', and Rescher, 'The Ontology of the Possible'.

allows for two different kinds of synthetic proposition, and therefore for two different kinds of intuitional constraint on semantic scope. A proposition is synthetic a posteriori if and only if its meaning and truth strictly require a relation to an object given in empirical intuition; and it is synthetic a priori if and only if its meaning and truth strictly require a relation to an object given in pure intuition. The actual, humanly perceived world—the one to which we bear empirical intuitive relations involving affection—is the humanly intuit*ed* world. But there are many different possible worlds sharing the same spatial and temporal framework (including the actual world) to which we can gain cognitive access only by means of pure intuition. If we add these worlds to the actual world, then we have the class of humanly intuit*able* worlds.

What, then, is a humanly intuitable world? Simply put, it is any thinkable world that also incorporates the special formal transcendental conditions of human sensibility. This is not to say that it must be a world in which the biological species *Homo sapiens* actually exists (for that is not necessarily but instead only contingently required for the existence of our cognitive constitution), but only that it must be a spatiotemporally structured world in which a finite, receptive sensibility structurally (hence functionally) just like ours is really possible:

[Our mode of intuition] is dependent upon the existence of the object and is therefore possible only in so far as the subject's faculty of representation is affected through that [mode]. This mode of intuiting in space and time need not be limited to human sensibility; it may well be that all finite, thinking beings necessarily agree with human beings in this respect (although we cannot decide this), yet even given such universal validity this mode of intuition would not cease to be sensibility . . .　(*CPR* B72)

But human experience is not only sensible; it is also discursive. And the whole point of the A and B Deductions of the pure concepts of the understanding, together with the schematism of the pure concepts, is to demonstrate that the formal conditions of sensibility presupposed by empirical intuition in turn presuppose a set of further transcendental conditions on the possible human experience of objects, including the transcendental (or pure productive, or figurative) synthesis of the imagination, the pure concepts of the understanding, and the original synthetic unity of apperception:

We cannot *think* any object except through the categories; we cannot *cognize* an object that is thought except through intuitions corresponding to those concepts. Now all our intuitions are sensible, and this cognition, in so far as its object is given, is empirical. But empirical cognition is experience. Consequently, there can be *no* a priori cognition, except exclusively of objects of possible experience.　(*CPR* B166)

[The transcendental deduction] is the exhibition (*Darstellung*) of the pure concepts of the understanding (and with them of all theoretical a priori cognition), as principles of the possibility of experience, but of [these principles] as the *determination* of appearances in space and time *in general*—and [this determination], finally, from the

principle of the *original* synthetic unity of apperception, as the form of the understanding in its reference to space and time, as original forms of sensibility.   (*CPR*
B168–9)

Thus the schemata of the pure concepts of the understanding are the true and
sole conditions for providing them with a reference to objects, thus with *meaning*
(*Bedeutung*), and hence the categories are in the end of none but a possible empirical use, since they merely serve to subject appearances to general rules of synthesis
through grounds of an a priori necessary unity (on account of the necessary
unification of all consciousness in an original apperception), and thereby to make them
fit for a thoroughgoing connection in one experience.   (*CPR* A145–6/B185)

In this way, pure intuition determines a special class of possible worlds,
membership in which is defined precisely by the members' severally satisfying
all the transcendental conditions necessary and jointly sufficient for the possibility of the human experience of objects. These conditions prominently include
the schematized necessary rules or laws for experiential objectivity laid down
as principles of pure understanding in the Axioms of Intuition, Anticipations
of Perception, Analogies of Experience, and Postulates of Empirical Thought.
In the light of these, a sensory object of our intuition can be an object of
experience if and only if it possesses extensive magnitude, intensive magnitude, permanence or endurance in time, diachronic causal relations, and syn-
chronic dynamic interconnection, and is either materially possible, materially
necessary, or materially actual (*CPR* A148–235/B187–294). Therefore the
empirically intuitable worlds are also the objectively humanly experienceable
worlds.

  Now we are in a position to see, in at least a preliminary way, Kant's general
doctrine of the synthetic a priori. Just as the actual, experienced world of individual empirical objects and facts—directly accessible only through empirical
intuition—is the fundamental ground of the truth of synthetic a posteriori
propositions, so in turn the total class of objectively humanly experienceable
worlds—directly accessible only through pure intuition and indirectly accessible
through the objectively valid schematized pure concepts of the understanding
under the original synthetic unity of apperception—is the fundamental ground
of synthetic a priori propositions.[23] Kant expresses the doctrine this way:

Here we now have one of the elements required for the solution of the general problem of transcendental philosophy—*how are synthetic a priori propositions possible?*—
namely, pure a priori intuitions, space and time, in which, if we want to go beyond
the given concept in an a priori judgement, we encounter that which is to be discovered a priori and synthetically connected with it, not in the concept but in the
intuition that corresponds to it; but on this ground [of pure intuition] such a judgement never extends beyond the objects of the senses and can be valid only for objects
of possible experience.   (*CPR* B73)

---

[23] See also Parsons, 'Kant's Philosophy of Arithmetic', 116–18.

The highest principle of all synthetic judgements is, therefore: every object stands under the necessary conditions of the synthetic unity of the manifold of intuition in a possible experience. In this way synthetic a priori judgements are possible, if we refer the formal conditions of a priori intuition, the synthesis of the imagination, and its necessary unity in a transcendental apperception to a possible experiential cognition (*Erfahrungserkenntnis*) in general, and say: the conditions of the *possibility of experience* in general are at the same time conditions of the *possibility of objects of experience*, and thereby have objective validity in a synthetic a priori judgement.   (*CPR* A158/B197)

Our theoretical cognition never transcends the field of experience. . . . If there is synthetic cognition a priori, there is no alternative but that it must contain the a priori conditions of the possibility of experience in general.   (*RP* Ak. xx. 274)

Synthetic a priori propositions include, as a constitutive part of their semantic content, the pure intuitions that alone supply direct access to space and time; they thereby invoke the 'formal conditions of a priori intuition'. The formal conditions of pure intuition in turn presuppose the transcendental imagination (which generates the transcendental schemata), the formal discursive conditions of cognition (the categories), and the transcendental principles (which result from the schematization of the categories). All are unified by transcendental apperception. And conjointly these factors carve out the special set of humanly intuitable, objectively experienceable worlds. This entire class of experienceable worlds functions as the global truth-maker for every synthetic a priori proposition. Analytic propositions are true in every logically and conceptually possible world without qualification. By contrast, a proposition is synthetic a priori if and only if it is true in all and only the humanly experienceable worlds—or, otherwise put, for all and only objects of experiential cognition. Thus synthetic a priori necessity is a strong modality that is essentially restricted by the sensory constitution of creatures minded like us. It is necessity for humans and not for gods.

So much for the general idea of the synthetic a priori; let us now look more closely at the crucial notions of apriority and necessity that are intimately involved in it.

5.2. Apriority and Necessity

Perhaps no philosophical concept in Kant's scheme has been less well understood than his concept of the a priori. One of the sources of misunderstanding is surely the powerful retroactive influence of the many non-Kantian conceptions of the a priori to be found in the analytic tradition from Frege to Quine.[24]

---

[24] Broadly speaking, non-Kantian theories of the a priori tend to be either platonist, conventionalist, or holist.

But there is also another and even more troublesome source of the inter-pretive difficulty. And this is that his a priori versus a posteriori distinction operates in (at least) two different modes at once—an epistemic mode and a semantic mode.[25] What especially makes this fact about Kant's view a cause of confusion is the further fact that virtually all recent and contemporary work on necessity and apriority assumes more or less without argument (*a*) that necessity is a strictly semantic (or 'metaphysical' in the sense of 'truth in all possible worlds') concept, and (*b*) that apriority is a strictly epistemological concept.[26] Kant's idea, by sharp contrast, is that semantic, epistemic, and meta-physical considerations cannot be wholly disentangled from one another and are ultimately fused in the more basic and comprehensive notion of cogni-tion or objective mental representation. Many things could be said about this difference in approach. But, for our purposes at the moment, what is crucial is that for Kant apriority is not only an epistemological notion but also equally a semantic notion.

This is not to say that the epistemic a priori and semantic a priori should be indiscriminately run together. Elsewhere I have discussed Kant's epistemic conception of apriority.[27] The main idea is that epistemic apriority concerns the justification of beliefs directed towards propositions taken to be neces-sary, while semantic apriority concerns the content of those same proposi-tions. The crucial point in this context is that it is possible for the content of a proposition to be a priori even if a belief in it is justified a posteriori. For example, I may justifiably believe a posteriori that every even number is the sum of two primes solely because I have laboriously tested out that thesis on the first *n* even numbers until I was too old and tired to keep going; but the truth or falsity of this thesis surely is not determined by anything empirical, including my ability to verify it by experiential means. This suffices to isolate the semantic a priori.

Kant's doctrine of semantic apriority begins with an assertion that could usefully be printed as a running head on every page of the first *Critique*:

There is no doubt whatever that all our cognition begins with experience . . . But, although all our cognition begins *with* experience, yet it does not follow that it all arises *from* experience. For it could well be that even our experiential cognition is a composite (*ein Zusammengesetztes*) of what we receive through impressions and what our own cognitive faculty (merely triggered [*bloss veranlaßt*] by sensible impressions) supplies from itself. (*CPR* B1)

---

[25] Patricia Kitcher usefully distinguishes between three different types of apriority (logical apriority, apriority of psychological origins, and epistemic apriority); see *Kant's Transcendental Psychology*, 15–17. Semantic apriority in my sense is in fact distinct from all of these.

[26] These assumptions are largely due to Kripke; see *Naming and Necessity*, 34–9.

[27] See Hanna, 'How Do We Know Necessary Truths? Kant's Answer'.

Two claims are salient. First, Kant is saying that all objectively valid contents of cognition—in that sense of 'cognition' that includes intuitions, concepts, and judgements alike (*CPR* A68/B93, A320/B377)—have empirical relations: they have empirical reference; and they are (in the order of time) occasioned by empirical causes. Secondly, however, it is perfectly consistent with an objectively valid cognitive content's having empirical relations that it be logically separable from the empirical items to which it is so related. And this separability is based on the fact that for Kant cognitive content is not monolithic, but rather essentially a composite that includes components deriving from a source other than sensory experience—namely, a source of content that the faculty of cognition 'supplies from itself'.

Now, according to Kant, the self-supplied aspects of cognition are precisely the transcendental epigenetic rule structures of cognition (see Section 1.3). But how are we to pick out, or isolate, the specifically transcendental components of a given cognition? His answer is that a cognition is transcendental just in so far as it is a priori: 'I call all cognition *transcendental* that is occupied not so much with objects but rather with our mode of cognition of objects in so far as this [mode of cognition] is to be possible a priori' (*CPR* A11/B25). And he further tells us that every a priori component in a cognition is marked by a certain feature: 'It is a question requiring closer examination . . . whether there is any such cognition independent (*unabhängiges*) of all experience and even of all impressions of the senses. One calls such [cognitions] a priori *cognitions*, and distinguishes them from *empirical* ones, which have their sources a posteriori—that is, in experience' (*CPR* B2). Again, he says that 'we shall understand by a priori cognitions, not [cognitions] that occur independently of this or that experience, but rather those that occur *absolutely* independently of all experience. Opposed to them are empirical cognitions, or those that are possible only a posteriori—that is, through experience' (*CPR* B2–3). The first feature of semantic apriority is the absolute independence of a cognition and its content from experience and all impressions of the senses, owing to the presence in that content of factors contributed by the innate or generative/productive capacities of the human mind. But what is it for a cognition and its content to 'occur absolutely independently of all experience'? Is Kant saying here that the apriority of cognitive content is the same as a given cognitive content's necessary *exclusion* of everything sensory—that is, the removal of all sensory relations whatsoever from that content? No: and for two reasons.

First, it would obviously and directly contradict Kant's view that 'there is no doubt whatever that all our cognition begins with experience'. Secondly, it would violate Kant's doctrine of the objective validity or empirical meaningfulness of all objective representational content. As we have already seen in Section 2.2, the meaningfulness of any cognition, including all a priori cognition, necessarily involves a reference to objects of actual or possible sensory experience:

If a cognition is to have objective reality—that is, to refer to an object—and is to have meaning and sense (*Bedeutung und Sinn*) in [regard to that object], the object must be able to be given in some way. Without that the concepts are empty, and through them one has, to be sure, thought but not in fact cognized anything through this thinking, but rather merely played with representations. To give an object, if this again means not only [to give an object] mediately, but rather [the object] is to be immediately exhibited (*darstellen*) in intuition, is nothing other than to refer its representation to experience (whether this be actual or still possible). . . . The *possibility of experience* is therefore what gives all of our a priori cognitions objective reality.   (*CPR* A155–6/B194–5)

Kant's considered view is therefore that an a priori cognition and its content can be at once causally occasioned by and meaningfully referred to sensory experiences and yet *also* absolutely experience-independent.

So as to be able to accommodate the possibility of a cognitive content's being absolutely experience-independent even while it is causally linked to actual experiencess and referentially linked to possible experience, I propose that what Kant intends by saying that a cognition can 'occur absolutely independently of all experience' is given in the crucial phrase 'although all our cognition begins *with* experience, yet it does not follow that it all arises *from* experience'. That is, a cognitive semantic content is a priori in the sense of being absolutely independent of all experience just in so far as it is strictly underdetermined by every particular collection or specific sort of sense experiences, even if it is both causally associated with actual sense experiences and necessarily referred to objects of possible sense experience. More explicitly (and now focusing only on propositions) what I mean is this:

> SEMANTIC EXPERIENCE-INDEPENDENCE: a proposition is a priori in the sense of being semantically experience-independent if and only if no particular set or sort of sensory experiences is either necessary or sufficient for the determination of its semantic content (including especially its truth conditions[28]), even though its cognitive generation is actually causally associated with some experiences and even though it requires as a condition of its empirical meaningfulness that it be verifiable by means of some set or sort of possible experiences.

Again, a proposition is a priori in the sense of being semantically independent of experience if and only if its semantic content and in particular its truth conditions are not supervenient upon its sensory verification conditions—including all the sets and sorts of causal sensory conditions under which it was, is, or ever will be actually acquired and confirmed. And this property of strict underdetermination or non-supervenience obtains perfectly consistently with the crucial semantic property of objective validity.

---

[28] See also Bennett, *Kant's Analytic*, 9.

Some examples might help to make this idea more concrete. Let us look at the independence from actual, causally implicated sensory verifications first. Consider the arithmetical proposition that $7 + 5 = 12$. Not being divine thinkers, we do not spontaneously build the proposition that $7 + 5 = 12$ in an informational vacuum, but must have our generative act triggered by something else. We originally acquire such truths in concrete sensory learning situations of various kinds, which in turn partially determine the psychological means by which we actually come to understand those truths. Even after an arithmetical proposition has been learned and understood, especially if the numbers we are dealing with are fairly large, we may need to run through some calculation process or use some supplementary calculating device, in order to frame it again. But this is consistent with the proposition's content or truth being logically independent of all those experiences: we can easily imagine learning, understanding, or reframing the very same true proposition in very different ways under very different empirical conditions. That is, creatures minded like us have an innate capacity for generating that arithmetic propositional content over an indefinitely large class of variants on the initial empirical input conditions. So, for any particular set or sort of experiences that can trigger our cognitive generation of that proposition, that set or sort can also fail to obtain, while at the same time some other quite distinct set or sort is able to trigger the generation of that proposition.

Turning now to the consistency of semantic experience independence with objective validity, the sharp contrast between a priori and a posteriori propositions proves itself to be instructive. It is easy enough to see that for Kant an a posteriori proposition—say, 'Bodies have weight'—has its meaning at least partially determined by a rule specifying a fixed range of past, present, and future actual empirical verification conditions.[29] By contrast an a priori proposition like '$7 + 5 = 12$' never invokes such a rule or such a specific range. Nevertheless '$7 + 5 = 12$' is empirically meaningful. It can be at least partially confirmed through experience (for instance, by counting on one's fingers), and is also necessarily associated with possible empirical verification conditions. So empirical confirmation is necessarily relevant to it.[30] Yet '$7 + 5 = 12$' can be neither wholly confirmed through past, present, or future experiences, nor wholly disconfirmed. The empirical verification conditions that it has do not wholly constitute its meaning. Nor do its verification conditions wholly determine its truth value. So, just because either mental or physical computational processes of adding 7 to 5 always and everywhere produced the result 12, it does not follow that '$7 + 5 = 12$' is true. It is possible—just

[29] This in fact leads to problems; see Hanna, 'The Trouble with Truth in Kant's Theory of Meaning'.

[30] This contrasts sharply with the conventionalist or logico-linguistic theory of necessity and apriority, according to which all experience is wholly irrelevant; see Craig, 'The Problem of Necessary Truth', 27–31.

possible—that calculation errors have become endemic. And even if sometimes the process of adding 7 to 5, as it occurs in particular minds or machines, leads to a sum other than 12, that manifestly does not entail that '7 + 5 = 12' is false. So we do not subordinate the truth of '7 + 5 = 12' to uniformly confirming experiences, nor do we withhold the attribution of truth in the face of recalcitrant or disconfirming experiences.[31] The truth of experience-independent propositional contents must instead be explained by appeal to other empirically irreducible (that is, transcendental and hence modal) factors.

Now is the time to bring in a basic point about experience independence that is often missed not only in critical discussions of Kant's doctrine of the a priori, but also in strictly systematic discussions of the concept of apriority. The point is that semantic experience independence does not itself exhaust the nature of apriority; for experience independence is at best a necessary condition of a proposition's being fully a priori. What am I driving at? Pre-theoretically, it seems fairly plausible that every a priori proposition is not only semantically experience-independent, but also necessarily true. Yet, clearly, just because a proposition is experience-independent in the semantic sense, it does not automatically follow that it is necessarily true, or even meaningful for that matter. All necessary falsehoods[32] are a priori according to SEMANTIC EXPERIENCE INDEPENDENCE. So, too, sortally incoherent or nonsensical pseudo-propositions such as Russell's 'Quadruplicity drinks procrastination' are semantically experience-independent. Their semantic contents, being not just accidentally but rather necessarily incoherent (by virtue of sortal incorrectness), are thereby strictly underdetermined by empirical relations. And the same goes for 'miserable tautologies' or pseudo-analytic propositions such as 'God exists' (*CPR* A592–602/B620–30).

So, because semantic experience independence is at best necessary but not in itself sufficient for full-blooded apriority, Kant gives us another, richer characterization of apriority. He writes:

At issue here is a characteristic by which we can securely distinguish a pure cognition from an empirical one. Experience teaches us, indeed, that something is constituted thus and so, but not that it cannot be otherwise. *First*, then, if we have a proposition

[31] This tendency to be unmoved in our patterns of belief by experiential contingencies provides a reliable indicator or external criterion—what Kant would call a 'touchstone' (*Probierstein*) (*CPR* A820/B848)—of apriority. See Ayer, *Language, Truth, and Logic*, 75–6; and Mates, 'Analytic Sentences', 531. But the reliable indicator does not constitute apriority. Indeed, the identification of it with apriority yields a purely sceptical or deflationary conception of the a priori. See Quine, 'Two Dogmas of Empiricism', 42–6, and Quine, *Word and Object*, 66.

[32] This terminology is not quite Kantian. As we will soon see, Kant defines "necessary" in such a way as to imply truth: so, strictly speaking, for him "necessary falsehood" is an oxymoron. The appearance of inconsistency can be easily avoided, however, by introducing a new bit of jargon—I propose "contra-necessary"—to apply to propositions that are the contradictories of necessary truths.

that is thought along with its *necessity* (*Notwendigkeit*), it is an a priori judgement . . . *Secondly*, experience never gives its judgements true or strict, but only assumed and comparative *universality* (through induction), so it must be properly said: as far as we have hitherto perceived, there is no exception to this or that rule. If, then, a judgement is thought in strict universality (*in strenger Allgemeinheit*)—that is, in such a way that no exception is allowed as possible—it is not derived from experience, but rather is valid absolutely a priori. Empirical universality is only an arbitrary extension of a validity holding in most cases to that which holds in all, as in, for example, the proposition 'all bodies are heavy', whereas strict universality is essential to a judgement; this points to a special source of cognition for it, namely a faculty of a priori cognition. Necessity and strict universality are thus secure criteria (*Kennzeichen*) of a priori cognition, and also belong inseparably to one another (*gehören . . . unzertrennlich zu einander*).   (*CPR* B3–B4)

Here Kant makes, or at least indicates, three very important points. First, he tells us that all necessary propositions are a priori: 'if we have a proposition that is thought along with its *necessity* (*Notwendigkeit*), it is an a priori judgement.' Now, since he also claims, conversely, that 'every cognition that is taken to be established firmly as a priori proclaims that it wants to be held as quintessentially necessary (*schlechthinnotwendig*)' (*CPR* Axv; see also A76/B101), it follows that, according to him, a proposition is a priori if and only if it is necessary.

Secondly, however, there is another crucial feature of apriority to consider —strict universality. As Kant explains it, there are two sorts of universality: (1) merely assumed, comparative, or empirical universality, according to which a proposition actually holds for every member of some given set of cases and is inductively projected onto other cases (*CPR* A91/B124); and (2) strict universality, according to which a proposition has no admissible possible counter-examples ('no exception is allowed as possible' (*keine Ausnahme als möglich verstattet wird*)). Now not only is strict universality a sufficient condition of apriority; Kant also holds that if a proposition is a priori then it has 'true universality' (*wahre Allgemeinheit*) (*CPR* A2). Assuming that strict universality and true universality are the same notions, then a proposition is a priori if and only if it is strictly or truly universal. Since, as we have just seen in the previous paragraph, a proposition is a priori if and only if it is necessary, it also follows that a proposition is necessary if and only if it is strictly universal. In fact, necessity and strict universality 'belong inseparably to one another', which is to say that they are at least necessarily biconditionally equivalent, even if, as Kant points out, they are not wholly identical concepts.

Thirdly and finally, this text also relates necessity and strict universality to experience independence. Both the necessity and the strict universality of a proposition do not logically require that particular sets or sorts of possible sense experiences belong to that proposition's content; nor are such set or sorts of experiences sufficient for its content or truth value, because at best 'experience teaches us . . . that something is constituted thus and so, but not that it cannot be otherwise'. More directly, any 'judgement [that] is thought in strict universality, that is, in such a way that no exception is allowed as possible . . . is not derived from experience, but rather is valid absolutely a priori'. In other words, both the necessity and the strict universality of a proposition entail its semantic experience independence, although the converse is not the case.

According to Kant, then, an a priori proposition is semantically experience-independent, necessary, and strictly universal. Now, adopting as a guide the Leibnizian, or metaphysical, conception of necessity as the truth of a proposition in all possible worlds (let us call this '*M*-necessity' for short), one might well be strongly tempted to conclude that strict universality too is just Kant's way of expressing *M*-necessity. But we must be very careful here. Strict universality is not explicitly defined as truth in all possible worlds but rather as (assuming of course that strict universality also entails necessity) the absence of admissible counter-examples: 'no exception is allowed as possible.' Does the absence of admissible counter-examples for a given proposition automatically entail its truth in all possible worlds? It does not seem trivially self-evident that it does; so we had better not assume that strict universality is merely Kant's prolix way of expressing *M*-necessity.[33] But then we had better also answer the following question: what is the nature of strict universality?

The Nature of Strict Universality. As we have seen, according to Kant a proposition is strictly universal if and only if (assuming that strict universality also entails necessity) it has no admissible possible counter-examples. To be a counter-example to a proposition is to be a logically and conceptually possible set of objective circumstances—a fully thinkable world—that makes that proposition come out false. So to be strictly universal is to be non-false in every possible world. What, however, is meant by the 'admissibility' of a possible counter-example? More precisely put, will not a counter-example be admissible just by virtue of its being logically and conceptually possible? This is a crucial issue for the following reason. If we assume that being admissible just redundantly means being logically and conceptually possible, and if we assume the truth of what can be called 'the strong principle of bivalence'— namely, for every proposition *P*, *P* is either true or false and not both—then to say that a proposition is strictly universal or always non-false is just to say that it is true in every possible world. So, on those assumptions, strict universality collapses into *M*-necessity.

But let us suppose that by the principle of bivalence we mean instead the slightly different principle that for every proposition *P*, if *P* takes a classical

---

[33] See also Patricia Kitcher, *Kant's Transcendental Psychology*, 258, and Robinson, 'Necessary Propositions'.

truth value,[34] then *P* is either true or false and not both. Then we need not assume that every proposition has a classical truth value. Some propositions might never receive a classical truth value at all; and some propositions might receive a classical truth value in some possible worlds but no classical truth value in others. Let us call this 'the weak principle of bivalence'.

Now Kant's conception of a pure general logic, as a version of classical logic, is explicitly committed to strong bivalence (*CPR* A571/B599 and also JL Ak. ix. 53);[35] but things would appear to be very different in transcendental logic—or, more precisely, in 'transcendental analytic' (*CPR* A62–3/B87–8). Transcendental logic (we will remember from Section 2.2) considers not only the logical and syntactical structure of concepts and propositions, but also their sortal or categorial coherence, and especially their objective validity. In accordance with transcendental logic, then, Kant explicitly holds that some experience-independent propositions (for example, 'God exists'), despite the fact that they are syntactically well formed, non-contradictory, and categorially coherent, nevertheless never receive a truth value because they are not objectively valid or empirically meaningful. Such propositions lack a restriction to the sensory conditions of human experience, and refer exclusively to noumenal entities; hence he dubs them 'transcendent' propositions or principles (*CPR* A295–6/B352–3).[36] Kant also holds that traditional philosophy contains antinomies—propositions that are not merely contradictory, but hyper-contradictory in that they are demonstrably true if and only if they are false (*CPR* A420–60/B448–88). Both transcendent and antinomous propositions are strictly unassertible. By sharp contrast to them, however, there are other experience-independent propositions Kant calls 'immanent' (*CPR* A296/B352). These are objectively valid or empirically meaningful in all and only those circumstances involving the possibility of experience: 'such a judgement never extends beyond the objects of the senses and can be valid only for objects of possible experience' (*CPR* B73). And he further states explicitly that 'apart from this reference [to objects of possible experience] synthetic

---

[34] Non-classical truth values include 'middle', 'indeterminate', 'true and false', all degrees of probability between 0 and 1, and so on. Truth-value 'gaps', by contrast, are propositions taking no truth valuation at all, classical or non-classical. See Haack, *Deviant Logic, Fuzzy Logic: Beyond the Formalism*, pp. xiv–xv, 47–71, 243–58.

[35] Kant, like other logicians prior to the development of non-classical logic, tends to run together bivalence (for every proposition *P*, *P* is either true or false and not both) and excluded middle (for every proposition *P*, 'either *P* or not-*P*' is always true). But they are logically distinct; see Haack, *Deviant Logic, Fuzzy Logic*, ch. 3, and Kneale and Kneale, *The Development of Logic*, 47.

[36] Despite their lack of truth value, however, some transcendent propositions—e.g. 'God exists', 'Human actions are free', 'The human soul is immortal', and the categorical imperative (*GMM* Ak. iv. 420)—play crucial roles in Kant's overall theory of human reason, as principles (*Grundsätze*) or postulates (enabling presuppositions) for pure practical reason (*CPrR* Ak. v. 19–57, 124–34).

a priori propositions are completely impossible (*gänzlich unmöglich*)' (*CPR* A157/B196), by which he must mean that, when sundered from the possibility of experience, they cannot possibly be true because they are truth valueless or objectively invalid, not that they are deemed necessarily false.[37] So, from the standpoint of transcendental logic, Kant is clearly a defender of the weak principle of bivalence.

Assuming weak bivalence, then, my proposal is that Kant's notion of admissibility is not just a redundant way of saying 'logically and conceptually possible'. Let us instead suppose that Kantian admissibility means a possible world's admissibility according to some rule of selection including, but not necessarily restricted to, logical and conceptual consistency. Then we can see that for Kant there are two quite different ways for a proposition to have no counter-examples, or to be non-false. (1) Taking into account all logically and conceptually possible worlds, none of them is a counter-example to the proposition, because every world makes the proposition come out true. (2) Taking into account all logically and conceptually possible worlds, at least some of them would have been counter-examples but for the fact that they are inadmissible according to some rule of selection and so are not legitimate counter-examples—instead, the proposition receives no classical truth value in those rule-excluded or inadmissible worlds. Let us call these two types of strict universality, respectively, 'absolute' and 'restricted': the former is absolute because the proposition's failure to have a possible counter-example entails its unqualifiedly universal truth; and the latter is restricted because the proposition's failure to have a possible counter-example implies a special semantic injunction or intervention and does not entail its totally universal truth but instead only its universal non-falsity. This way of distinguishing between the absolute and the restricted is also Kant's: 'It is in this extended meaning that I will employ the word *absolute* (*absolut*), opposing it to what is merely comparative, or valid in some particular respect. For while the latter is restricted (*restringiert*) by conditions, the former is valid without restriction (*ohne Restriktion*)' (*CPR* A326–7/B382).

At this point it is necessary to bring out a crucial yet implicit feature of Kant's characterization of strict universality—truth. This is important because of a possible ambiguity in the conception of restricted strict universality. If a proposition's failure to have any admissible counter-examples depends upon a special semantic rule that excludes possible worlds from being counter-examples by assigning the proposition no classical truth value in those peccant worlds, then we can easily imagine a rule that excludes *all* possible worlds in the same way. Then a proposition could be, technically, restrictedly strictly

---

[37] This interpretation fits well with a passage at *CPR* A139/B178, which reads 'concepts are entirely impossible, and cannot have any meaning (*Bedeutung*), where an object is not given . . .'. In his copy of the A edition (the *Nachträge*), Kant changed "impossible" to "are for us without sense (*Sinn*)" (*R.* LVIII E 28–A139; Ak. xxiii. 46).

universal even though it was otherwise completely unintelligible ('Quadruplicity drinks procrastination'), false in every possible world ('Socrates is and is not a philosopher'), or even paradoxical ('This very proposition is false'). Yet Kant clearly believes that every strictly universal proposition is true.

How can we show this? The answer is by way of an analysis of the concept of necessity, which of course is entailed by strict universality. Kant believes that the concept of necessity analytically contains the concept of truth. He states explicitly that the apodeicticity of a proposition entails it is also assertoric, and '*assertoric* judgments are those in which [the assertion or denial (RH)] is regarded as *actual* (true)' (*CPR* A75/B100). Now, since an apodeictic proposition is neither merely assertoric nor merely possible, it must be non-contingent. So the concept NECESSARY has the same intension as the concept NON-CONTINGENTLY TRUE. Since strict universality entails necessity, strict universality also entails non-contingent truth. But a strictly universal proposition can be either absolutely or restrictedly strictly universal. Hence, because necessity and strict universality are necessarily biconditionally equivalent concepts, just as there are two types of strict universality, there will correspondingly be two types of necessity or non-contingent truth—absolute necessity and restricted necessity. And this allows us to give an explicit formulation of the second and third essential features of semantic apriority, to go along with semantic experience independence:

> NECESSITY AND STRICT UNIVERSALITY: a proposition is a priori in the sense of being necessary and strictly universal if and only if it is non-contingently true, where this can involve either its being true in all logically and conceptually possible worlds (= absolutely necessary, absolutely strictly universal), or its being true in every member of a specially delimited set of possible worlds while it takes no classical truth value in every other logically and conceptually possible world (= restrictedly necessary, restrictedly strictly universal).

5.3. Analytic and Synthetic A Priori: A General Formulation

With the concept of semantic experience independence clutched in one white-knuckled hand, and with the distinction between absolute necessity and restricted necessity clutched just as tightly in the other, I am now in a position to reintroduce Kant's distinction between the analytic and the synthetic, and to interweave that distinction with the a priori/a posteriori distinction.

We have already seen that an analytic proposition is true by virtue of conceptual form and content alone, and topic-neutral. Since the truth of an analytic proposition does not depend on any special configuration of objects in any possible world, but only on intrinsic conceptual connections, there are no possible worlds able to stand as counter-examples to it. Therefore analytic propositions are a priori in the sense of being absolutely necessary—that is, true in every logically and conceptually possible world. This is precisely the modal notion Kant describes as the 'merely formal and logical necessity in the connection of concepts' (*CPR* A226/B279). Moreover, because the truth of an analytic proposition is not dependent on any sensory things or empirical facts found in any possible world, but only on intrinsic connections between or within concepts, it is obviously also a priori in the sense of being semantically experience-independent. Or, as he puts it, 'it would be absurd to ground an analytic judgement on experience, since I do not need to go beyond my concept at all in framing the judgement, and therefore need no testimony from experience for that' (*CPR* A7/B12). Therefore every analytic proposition is both absolutely necessary and semantically experience-independent.

Correspondingly, the very idea of a synthetic a priori proposition appears to line up perfectly with the notion of a restrictedly necessary, semantically experience-independent truth. This point can be gained in two easy steps. The first step is to recognize that, for Kant, a synthetic a priori proposition is necessary in a way that involves concepts, but not merely because of those concepts. In a synthetic a priori proposition, 'we *should* . . . add a certain predicate to a given concept in thought, and this necessity already attaches to the concepts' (*CPR* B17). But the connection of concepts in a synthetic a priori proposition is non-analytic, precisely because it depends for its meaning and truth upon intuition:

What usually makes us believe . . . that the predicate of such [synthetic] apodeictic judgements is already contained in our concept, and that the judgement is therefore analytic, is merely the ambiguity of the expression used. We *should*, namely, add a certain predicate to a given concept in thought, and this necessity already attaches to the concepts. But the question is not what we *should think* in addition to a given concept, but what we *actually* (*wirklich*) *think* in it, even if only obscurely, and there it is manifest that the predicate is indeed attached necessarily to those concepts, although not as thought in the concept itself, but it is so in virtue of an intuition that must be added to the concept.   (*CPR* B17)

At issue here is not analytic propositions, which can be generated by mere decomposition of concepts . . . but synthetic [propositions], and indeed those ones that are to be cognized a priori. For I am not to see what I actually think in my concept . . . (this is nothing more than its mere definition); rather I am to go beyond it to properties that do not lie in this concept, but still belong to it. Now this is impossible in any way but by determining my object in accordance with the conditions of either empirical or pure intuition.   (*CPR* A718/B746)

In other words, the meaning and necessity in a synthetically necessary proposition are strictly determined by the intuitive content it has, over and above its conceptual content.

The second step ties the necessity and intuition dependence of a synthetic a priori proposition directly to its modal restrictedness and to the conditions of the possibility of experience. A Kantian restrictedly necessary proposition, I have said, is one whose meaningfulness and truth evaluation is determined by appeal to a special rule for selecting a certain domain of possible worlds (= the admissible worlds). While in principle there is nothing to prevent Kant from specifying this rule in any one of a number of ways, in fact of course he adopts a rule that incorporates his special transcendental strictures on the meaningfulness and truth of synthetic propositions. That is, he adopts roughly the following rule for the selection of admissible worlds:

> Select all and only those worlds accessible to pure or empirical human intuition—that is, the worlds incorporating the formal structures of our (representations of) space and time and containing all and only those objects governed by the schematized categorial conditions of the possibility of human experience under the original synthetic unity of apperception.

This restricting rule functions as the semantic ground of the synthetic a priori proposition, as is made evident in the case of synthetic a priori truths specifically concerning objects in space and time:

> We cannot judge at all whether the intuitions of other thinking beings are bound by the same conditions as those that limit our intuition and are universally valid for us. If we add the restriction (*Einschränkung*)[38] of a judgement to the concept of the subject, the judgement is then unconditionally valid (*gilt das Urteil alsdenn unbedingt*). The proposition 'All things are side by side in space' is valid only under the restriction that these things be viewed as objects of our sensible intuition. If, here, I add the condition to the concept, and say: 'All things, as outer appearances, are side by side in space', then this rule is valid universally and without restriction (*allgemein und ohne Einschränkung*).   (*CPR* A27/B43)

> We cannot say all things are in time, because with this concept of things in general abstraction is made from every mode of intuition of them, but this is the genuine condition under which time belongs to the representation of objects (*Gegenstände*). Now, if the condition is added to the concept, and [the principle] says that all things as appearances (objects of sensible intuition) are in time, then that principle (*Grundsatz*) has its sound objective correctness (*gute objektive Richtigkeit*) and universality a priori. (*CPR* A35/B51–2)

The main point should now be clear and distinct. Pure intuition functions as a restricting representational content that not only determines the meaning of a synthetic a priori proposition, but also makes it necessary and strictly universal (under the assumption, of course, of cognitive or representational idealism). Evaluated with regard to all logically or conceptually possible

---

[38] In the *Nachträge*, Kant changed "restriction" to "restricting condition" (*R.* XXIII E 18–A27; Ak. xxiii. 45).

worlds, synthetic propositions will come out false in at least some of them, because their denials are logically consistent. But if we constrain the set of possible worlds appropriately to the experienceable worlds by means of pure intuition, then the would-be falsity-making worlds are thereby excluded. In this way, while a synthetic proposition is consistently deniable in relation to all logically and conceptually possible worlds, if we evaluate a synthetic a priori truth under the restriction to all and only the experienceable worlds, then it comes out exceptionlessly universal and necessary in the sense that each and every experienceable world is its truth-maker and no logically and conceptually possible counter-examples are allowed in as semantic spoilers. Since the proposition's truth is secured in all and only the worlds of possible sensory experience, it is clearly also a priori in the sense of being semantically experience-independent with regard to those worlds.

Having spelled out Kant's analytic a priori versus synthetic a priori distinction—his Special Theory of Necessity, as it were—we are now also in a good position to ask whether anything can be proposed by way of a General Theory. Here logical form provides us with an important working clue, since, in his discussion of the Table of Judgements, Kant speaks of a *single* class of judgements under the rubric of the 'apodeictic proposition': 'The apodeictic proposition thinks of the assertoric [proposition] as determined through these laws of the understanding, and as thus asserting a priori, and in this way expresses logical necessity' (*CPR* A76/B101). This notion of logical necessity must not be too hastily identified with analytic necessity, which as we will remember is the 'merely formal and logical necessity *in the connection of concepts*' (*CPR* A226/B279, emphasis added). This is because the classification of judgements in pure general logic—under the rubrics of quantity, quality, relation, and modality—is logically prior to the analytic/synthetic distinction, which has primarily to do with the content of judgements and not with their form (*P.* Ak. iv. 266). So the concept of logical necessity at A76/B101 must be the same as the concept of 'merely formal and logical necessity' at A226/B279, and range over all necessary propositions whatsoever.

For convenience, I will dub this comprehensive Kantian concept of necessity '*K*-necessity', in contradistinction to metaphysical necessity or *M*-necessity. We already know from our previous discussion that *K*-necessity is necessarily equivalent to strict universality, and that it entails non-contingent truth and semantic experience independence. Kant's general philosophical story about *K*-necessity thus begins with some true and experience-independent proposition, and adds to it a modal operator or logical predicate 'necessarily', expressing necessitation or strict universality. But how does the addition of necessitation or strict universalization logically affect a proposition? Here we must make sense of Kant's otherwise highly puzzling remark that the modality of a proposition 'contributes nothing to the intension of the judgement (for besides quantity, quality, and relation there is nothing more that constitutes the intension of a judgement) but concerns only the value (*Wert*) of the copula in relation to thought in general (*das Denken überhaupt*)' (*CPR* A74/B100). Now there are good reasons for taking this to mean that modal predicates are strictly 'logical' and not 'determining', not to mean that modal predicates are merely attitudes of the mind towards propositions.[39] Let us then take the phrase "value of the copula" to refer to a proposition's classical truth value. And let us take the phrase "thought in general" to refer to what is comprehended by full thinkability in the technical Kantian sense: whatever is logically and conceptually self-consistent, well formed, and sortally coherent. Then the Kantian logical predicate 'necessarily'—understood also as entailing strict universality—is nothing other than a truth-or-falsity-determining operator on propositions, an operator whose function it is to quantify universally over the domain of possible worlds.

But what sort of universal possible worlds quantifier is it? What precisely are its truth conditions? As we have seen, Kant explicitly says that 'if we add the restriction of a judgement to the concept of the subject, the judgement is then unconditionally valid' (*CPR* A27/B43). This appears to be a feature of all necessary propositions whatsoever. In other words, a proposition is necessary or strictly universal only in relation to some qualification of the universal possible worlds quantifier. As we have seen, analytic propositions are true in every conceptually possible world; but synthetic a priori propositions are true in all and only experienceable worlds and lack a classical truth value otherwise. So in order to be able to express the basic distinction between absolute (analytic) and restricted (synthetic) necessity, Kant implicitly allows for two different possible qualifications of 'necessarily' when it is added to a propositional content—'absolutely necessarily' and 'restrictedly necessarily'. The former qualifier ranges over the class of all logically and conceptually possible worlds and introduces the null restriction, while the latter qualifier picks out a class of worlds smaller than that. Using these notions, then, we can see that a Kantian analytic proposition is most accurately represented by the form

(Absolutely Necessarily) *P*

and this means simply that *P* is true in all logically and conceptually possible worlds. By contrast, Kantian synthetic a priori propositions are represented by the form

(Restrictedly Necessarily*) *P*

---

[39] Many interpreters read this text as saying that, for Kant, modality is a function of propositional attitudes; see e.g. Pap, *Semantics and Necessary Truth*, 23 n. But my alternative way of looking at the modal concepts is strongly borne out by Kant's careful distinction between logico-semantic modality (as discussed in the 'The Logical Function of the Understanding in Judgments') and epistemic modality. The latter is expressed by propositional attitudes, or the modes of 'taking-to-be-true' (*Fürwahrhalten*) (*CPR* A821–2/B849–850).

where this means that P is restrictedly necessary according to the special constitution of our sensibility, or true in all and only humanly experienceable worlds and without a classical truth value otherwise. The asterisk indicates that the modal scope of synthetic necessity is fully determined by the anthropocentric restriction, even though, in principle, there could be other ways of restricting it.

But this immediately suggests another important question. Does Kant think that there must be only one kind of synthetic necessary truth? Perhaps surprisingly, no. In fact, he holds that there are two kinds. This point is made quite explicitly in the third Postulate of Empirical Thought, where he discusses the schematized category of necessity:

That which in its connection with the actual (*Wirklichen*) is determined in accordance with the universal conditions of experience, is (exists (*existiert*)) *necessarily*.   (*CPR* A218/B266)

As far as the third postulate is concerned, it pertains to material necessity in existence (*die materiale Notwendigkeit im Dasein*), not to the merely formal and logical necessity in the connection of concepts.   (*CPR* A226/B279)

Necessity therefore concerns only the relations of appearances in conformity with the dynamical law of causality, and the possibility grounded on it of inferring a priori from some given existence (a cause) to another existence (the effect).   (*CPR* A227–8/B280)

This material or dynamical necessity of causal laws is clearly a weaker kind of synthetic necessity than that possessed by mathematical truths and transcendental principles of possible experience. What I will call the 'strong' synthetic necessity of mathematical truths and transcendental principles is that they are true in all and only worlds in which human experience is possible. But the weak synthetic necessity of causal natural laws is that they are true in all and only members of a doubly restricted class of possible worlds—more precisely, all and only those experienceable worlds containing physical stuff or matter:

Metaphysics of nature . . . occupies itself with the special nature of this or that kind of things, of which an empirical concept is given in such a way that, besides what lies in this concept, no other empirical principle is needed for cognizing the things. For example, it lays the empirical concept of a matter . . . at its foundation and searches the range of cognition of which reason is a priori capable regarding these objects. Such a science must still be called metaphysics of nature—namely, of corporeal . . . nature. (*MFNS* Ak. iv. 470)

This double restriction implies that laws of nature are not only consistently deniable, like all synthetic propositions, but also contingent on the existence of the special sort of matter we find in the actual world: *inert* matter. Indeed, 'the possibility of a natural science proper rests entirely upon the law of inertia' (*MFNS* Ak. iv. 544), because, if matter were alive or vital, then the mechanical laws of action and interaction could not predict how a body would move under determinate initial causal conditions. Because for Kant all life is spontaneous to some degree or another, vital matter would, in effect, have a life of its own. In such a hylozoic world, empirical physical motions and influences could indeed be described, after the fact, by inductive causal generalizations conforming to the transcendental principles. Nevertheless, such generalizations would not support strict counterfactuals, and so could not be dynamically necessary truths. If all matter were alive, colliding billiard balls might do any old thing at all—just as they might in a Humean world lacking all necessary connections whatsoever. Therefore laws of nature in Kant's sense are what Gareth Evans aptly calls 'deeply contingent',[40] in the sense that they presuppose the existence of the totality of actual inert matter. Or, as Kant puts it explicitly in 'The Dohna–Wundlacken Logic': 'What is physically necessary can be logically only contingent. For example, it is physically necessary that all bodies fall, but this lies only in the thing and logically is only contingent' (DWL Ak. xxiv. 727).[41]

---

[40] See Evans, 'Reference and Contingency', 185. A proposition P is 'superficially' contingent if and only if there is some possible world such that P comes out not-true; but a proposition P is 'deeply' contingent if and only if any interpretation of its non-logical constants requires a commitment to some actual individuals or states of affairs—so P's very meaning requires an indexical commitment to actual existence. Thus, e.g., on Kant's theory of geometry, truths of Euclidean geometry are superficially contingent because they are not true in some logically and conceptually possible worlds (see Sect. 5.4); but they are nevertheless necessarily true in the sense of being true in all and only worlds containing space, as represented by our pure intuition—i.e. in all and only worlds of possible experience. Laws of nature are deeply contingent because they are existentially committed to the totality of actual inert matter.

[41] On the nature and status of causal laws of nature in Kant's philosophy of science, see e.g. Allison, 'Causality and Causal Laws in Kant: A Critique of Michael Friedman'; Buchdahl, 'The Conception of Lawlikeness in Kant's Philosophy of Science'; Buchdahl, *Metaphysics and the Philosophy of Science*, 651–65; Friedman, 'Causal Laws and the Foundations of Natural Science'; Friedman, *Kant and the Exact Sciences*, chs. 3–4; Guyer, 'Kant's Conception of Empirical Law'; Harper, 'Kant on the a Priori and Material Necessity'; Philip Kitcher, 'The Unity of Science and the Unity of Nature'; and Walker, 'Kant's Conception of Empirical Law'. There is, I think, a general scholarly agreement on the idea that causal laws for Kant must have a weaker synthetic modality than mathematical truths and transcendental principles. The remaining sticking points are (a) whether Kant can consistently hold this view, and (b) how such propositions can be a priori. If I am right, both problems are solved by the thesis that causal laws have doubly restricted necessity. This is because (a*), the notion of a double-restricted necessity is perfectly consistent with Kant's general analysis of synthetic or restricted necessity, and (b*) so long as a proposition is necessary, then by the Kantian principle that all necessary truths are a priori, causal laws must also be a priori. The second point is obviously the hardest to swallow. But— and this bears repeating—semantic apriority is perfectly consistent with the presence of a significant amount of empirical content in the meaning of a proposition, so long as that empirical content does not determine the meaning or truth conditions of that proposition. See Sect. 5.2 above, Kant's remarks about 'Gold is a yellow metal' at P. Ak. iv. 267, and Hanna, 'A Kantian Critique of Scientific Essentialism'.

Before moving on, I want to stop briefly to consider an illuminating misconception about Kant's theory of synthetic necessary truth, and also a possible objection to his theory.

The misconception is this. It is undeniably true that a two-types-of-necessity thesis is nowadays a fairly familiar one; logicians and semanticists frequently distinguish between absolute necessity and relative (hypothetical, conditional, and so on) necessity.[42] Their absolute necessity is the same as metaphysical necessity (M-necessity) or truth in all possible worlds. But the conception of relative necessity developed by these philosophers is explicitly parasitic on the notion of absolute or metaphysical necessity. On this view, a relatively necessary truth P is a proposition that is strictly implied (logically entailed) by a certain set S of logically independent propositions: hence it is absolutely necessary that if S, then P:

$$\text{(Absolutely Necessarily) } (S \rightarrow P).$$

In this way, P is absolutely necessary in a way that is logically materially conditioned upon S, because P is guaranteed to hold only in every possible world in which the members of S conjointly obtain. That is, relative necessity is a logically materially conditioned absolute or metaphysical necessity. In worlds in which some or all of the members of S fail to hold, their conjunction is false and then the logical material conditional relation between S and P is trivially satisfied. But it remains a stubborn logical fact that P can be false in some or all of the worlds in which some or all of the members of S do not obtain. P is not made true just because the material conditional '$S \rightarrow P$' is true.[43] By contrast, Kantian synthetic necessary truths, despite their not being true in every logically and conceptually possible world, are also non-false in every possible world; hence they are not merely relatively necessary.[44] This point is displayed in the formal representation of a synthetic a priori truth as '(Restrictedly Necessarily*) P', which obviously contains no material conditionals.

Exposing this misconception brings us to an illuminating point, however. Far from regarding synthetically necessary truths as definable in terms of absolute or metaphysical necessity plus the logical material conditional, in a

---

[42] Not too surprisingly, the distinction between absolutely and relatively necessary truths can be traced back at least as far back as Leibniz; see his 'On the Ultimate Origination of Things', 150. But the contemporary use of it stems from Lewis and Langford's formulation in 1932; see their *Symbolic Logic*, 161. More recent versions, influenced equally by conventionalism and by pragmatic (i.e. speaker-centred, context-oriented) considerations in formal semantics, can be found in Montague, 'Logical Necessity, Physical Necessity, Ethics, and Quantifiers'; Smiley, 'Relative Necessity'; and Stalnaker, 'Pragmatics'.

[43] See Sect. 3.4 for a similar point in connection with Carnap's theory of meaning postulates.

[44] Guyer, by contrast, has argued influentially in *Kant and the Claims of Knowledge*, 6–7, 53–61, 362–9, that Kant's synthetic a priori truths are relative necessities.

Kantian light we must instead regard *M*-necessity as less fundamental than, and indeed definable in terms of, the alternative Kantian doctrine of necessity. According to this doctrine, necessity is truth in at least all experienceable worlds and non-falsity in all logically and conceptually possible worlds. An *M*-necessary truth is one that is true in all the possible worlds in which synthetically necessary truths are true (= the experienceable worlds) but that is *also* true in all those possible worlds in which the synthetic necessities are merely non-false because lacking a classical truth value (= the non-experienceable or negatively noumenal worlds).

And here is the possible objection:

> As far as the machinery of Kant's modal theory is concerned, *any* sort of restriction placed on possible worlds might do, right? So, from a purely formal point of view, then, why not restrict the necessity-operator to all and only the logically and conceptually possible worlds in which, say, the proposition that Socrates is a philosopher is true? Then *that* proposition will come out synthetically necessary. In other words, given the right restrictions, any old non-analytic proposition will come out synthetically necessary. Thus Kant's theory of synthetic necessity is deeply open to radical arbitrariness in the choice of admissible worlds.

Not accidentally, this line of criticism contains an echo of the 'selection problem' I ascribed to Carnap's theory of meaning postulates (Section 3.4). But here is the crucial difference between Kant and Carnap: whereas Carnap can appeal only to a radically arbitrary decision or stipulation, or else to an external pragmatic motivation, as a ground for the selection of meaning postulates, Kant can solve the analogous selection problem for his restriction rule because he has independent reasons built right into cognitive semantics, for restricting the necessity-operator to all and only worlds of possible experience, in order to ground the synthetic a priori. These reasons derive directly and naturally from his substantive transcendental analyses of the conditions of the possibility of experiential cognition, as given in the Transcendental Aesthetic, the Metaphysical Deduction, the Transcendental Deduction(s) of the Categories, the Schematism, and the Analytic of Principles. These analyses tell us what we essentially are—we, the meaning-generating beings. The theories of empirical concepts and non-empirical categories, of empirical and pure intuition, of the original synthetic unity of apperception, of the transcendental imagination and the transcendental schematism, and of the Axioms, Anticipations, Analogies, and Postulates, and so on, are thus all in aid of justifying the limitation of synthetic necessity to all and only humanly objectively experienceable worlds. Drawing directly on these theories, then, Kant can argue that mathematical truths are legitimately synthetic a priori and that both the metaphysics of nature and natural science or physics contain synthetic a priori propositions as principles (see Sections 5.4 and 5.5).

So Kant's reading of the modal qualifier '(Restrictedly Necessary)' as '(Restrictedly Necessary*)' is in no sense arbitrary.

Unless, of course, being human is an arbitrary fact about us. Kant certainly assumes without special argument that actual human experiences exist, and that the 'we' of philosophy picks out actual human beings and also all and only creatures sharing our cognitive constitution. Yet this is not arbitrary. Kant holds that it is indeed a logically contingent fact, but not an accidental one, that we exist and have concept-soaked sensory experiences of just this specific sort. It is non-accidental, indeed *transcendental*, because the very possibility of framing relevant alternatives to the human standpoint presupposes just those conceptual and sensory capacities that are definitive of that standpoint. Therefore nothing will count as an alternative form of experience unless it somehow belongs to, or at least bears some near or distant analogy to, our special human sensory and discursive capacity for cognition:

Even if they were possible, we could still not conceive of and make comprehensible other forms of intuition (than space and time) or other forms of understanding (than the discursive form of thinking, or that of cognition through concepts), and even if we could, they would still not belong to experience, as the sole [type of] cognition in which objects are given to us.   (*CPR* A230–1/B283)

The argument so far has been aimed exclusively at showing the intelligibility of Kant's notion of the synthetic a priori. What is needed now is a defensible proof of the existence of some synthetic a priori propositions in Kant's sense. What I will argue in the next two sections is that such a proof can in fact be found in Kant's philosophy of mathematics.

5.4. Why Geometry is Synthetic A Priori

In the *Prolegomena* Kant tells us that the question 'how is pure mathematics possible?' constitutes 'the first part of the main transcendental question' regarding the possibility of synthetic a priori truth (*P*. Ak. iv. 279–80; see also *CPR* B14). The short and snappy version of Kant's answer to his own question is that pure mathematics depends on our pure intuitional representations of space and time, which in turn are the a priori forms of human sensibility. But it is precisely the struggle against Kant's attempt to ground mathematics in pure intuition that largely determines the philosophical programme created and relentlessly pursued by Frege, Moore, Russell, early Wittgenstein, Carnap, and the other logical empiricists, right up to Quine. This is illustrated vividly by one of Russell's pithy remarks in *The Principles of Mathematics*: 'The Kantian view . . . asserted that mathematical reasoning is not purely formal, but always uses intuitions, i.e., the *a priori* knowledge of space and time. Thanks to the progress of Symbolic Logic . . . this part of the Kantian philosophy is now capable of a final and irrevocable refutation'.[45] And Russell's remark is appropriately generalized by Coffa and applied to what he calls the 'semantic tradition'—that part of the analytic tradition that begins with Frege and ends with the Vienna Circle: 'The semantic tradition may be defined by its problem, its enemy, its goal, and its strategy. Its problem was the a priori; its enemy, Kant's pure intuition; its purpose, to develop a conception of the a priori in which pure intuition played no role; its strategy, to base that theory on a development of semantics'.[46] Therefore in an important sense all the issues and distinctions we have been exploring so far—semantics and cognition, the logical and the psychological, idealism versus realism, analytic versus sythetic, necessary truth versus contingent truth, the a priori versus the a posteriori, transcendental philosophy versus analytic philosophy, and so on—are wrapped up within the single question of whether pure mathematics is really synthetic a priori in Kant's sense or not.

In the light of the momentous importance of this question, however, it may seem passing strange that Kant rarely discusses it head on. Typically, he merely assumes the synthetic apriority of mathematical propositions, and then advances arguments intended to show how mathematics is possible:

Time and space are accordingly two sources of cognition, from which different synthetic cognitions can be derived a priori, of which especially pure mathematics in regard to the cognitions of space and its relations provides a brilliant example. Both [time and space] taken together are, namely, the pure forms of all sensible intuition, and thereby make synthetic a priori propositions possible. But these a priori sources of cognition determine their own limits by that very fact (that they are merely conditions of sensibility)—namely, that they apply to objects only insofar as they are considered as appearances, and do not exhibit (*darstellen*) things as they are in themselves. (*CPR* A38–9/B55–6)

Why did Kant apparently place so little emphasis on justifying the synthetic apriority of mathematics? One reason surely derives from historical context. The doctrine that mathematics is synthetic a priori was far less shocking to the eighteenth-century philosophical sensibility than it is to ours. This is because, although both the logical tradition stemming from the Leibniz–Wolff school and the laconic remarks of Hume somewhat favoured the analyticity of mathematics, other contemporary theoretical advances equally suggested its syntheticity. For example, Locke explicitly held in the *Essay* that mathematical propositions, which are characteristically known only through demonstration, should be carefully distinguished from mere trifling propositions (that

[45] Russell, *The Principles of Mathematics*, 4. See also his 1901 essay, 'Mathematics and the Metaphysicians', 74.
[46] Coffa, *The Semantic Tradition from Kant to Carnap*, 22.

is, definitional predications and simple logical truths).[47] And, as Michael
Friedman has shown, the Newtonian interpretation of the calculus implied
an essential connection between the concept of quantity and spatiotemporal
factors.[48] So Kant quite naturally did not regard his thesis as terribly controversial, even if he was justifiably proud of its originality. Indeed, his thesis
did not become a matter of philosophical controversy until his doctrine of
the analytic/synthetic distinction was vigorously challenged by the Leibnizian
Eberhard in that otherwise uneventful year 1789.[49]

Kant's relative lack of concern for defending what may seem to us to be a
terribly controversial thesis is especially evident in the particular case of the
apriority of mathematics. He writes:

It must first be noted that properly mathematical propositions are always a priori judgements and are never empirical because they carry necessity with them, which cannot
be derived from experience. But, if one does not want to concede this, then I am willing to restrict my proposition to *pure mathematics*, the concept of which already implies
that it does not contain empirical, but only pure a priori cognition.   (*CPR* B14–15)

Here [in pure mathematics] is a great and established branch of cognition . . . carrying with thoroughly apodeictical certainty . . . which therefore rests on no empirical
grounds.   (*P.* Ak. iv. 280)

These remarks seem at first to rest entirely on some pre-established analytic
connections Kant finds between the concepts of apriority, necessity, experience independence, and purity. But what independent justification could he
offer for the apriority of mathematics? Historical context is again directly
relevant. No major figure in the European tradition from Plato to Kant—not
even Hume—ever explicitly denied that truths of mathematics are a priori.
The thesis that mathematics is empirical did not even make an appearance
in the European tradition until Mill's 1843 *System of Logic*. But Frege's 1884
Foundations of Arithmetic supplied a knock-down reply to Mill. So in fact
it was not until Quine's 'Two Dogmas of Empiricism' had been published
in 1951 that the claim that mathematics is not a priori began to be taken
seriously by philosophers.[50] Put in this perspective, we can see that it was
perfectly appropriate for Kant, in his time and place, to assume that mathematics had been 'upon the secure path of a science' (*CPR* Bx) since the time of
the ancient Greeks, and to take the apriority of mathematics to be as firmly
established as anything ever is in philosophy. Moreover, given the broad

[47] Locke, *Essay concerning Human Understanding*, bk. IV, ch. ii, sects. 2–10, pp. 531–5;
and IV. viii. 8, p. 614.   [48] Friedman, *Kant and the Exact Sciences*, chs. 1–4.
[49] See Allison, *The Kant–Eberhard Controversy*.
[50] Even so, Quine's attack on the a priori was not widely recognized to extend all the way
to mathematics until somewhat later. Indeed, Putnam appears to have been the first to grasp
it fully; see *Mathematics, Matter, and Method: Philosophical Papers, Vol. 1*, esp. pp. viii–xiii
and essays 1–4 (all of which were published or written in the 1960s and early 1970s).

historical consensus among philosophers and mathematicians, even today, in favour of the apriority of mathematics, the heavy burden of proof should be fully on Mill and Quine to show that mathematics is not a priori, rather than on Kant to show that it is.

Obviously—since it relies on a merely historical argument—this defence of Kant's right to assume the apriority of mathematics is not decisive; but it does, I think, carry sufficient weight to allow Kant to get on with his business for the time being. (And I will come back again to Quine's radical apriority scepticism in the Concluding Un-Quinean Postscript.)

Now for Kant's crucial thesis that mathematics is synthetic. His argument for this must depend directly upon his cognitive-semantic theory of analyticity and syntheticity. Three points made earlier are especially pertinent. First, all analytic truths are such that their denial leads to contradiction. Therefore the negative criterion of a synthetic proposition is that its denial is conceptually and logically consistent. Secondly, the intuition dependence (whether pure or empirical) of a proposition is the positive mark of its syntheticity. And, thirdly, synthetic a priori truths are necessary, but they are not absolutely necessary. Rather they are restrictedly* necessary, or true in all and only humanly intuitable or objectively experienceable worlds while lacking a classical truth value otherwise. Granting these points, it follows immediately that any effective Kantian argument for the syntheticity of mathematics must show that mathematical truths are (1) consistently deniable or logically contingent, (2) intuition-dependent, and (3) nevertheless necessarily true under the restriction that they are assigned a classical truth value in all and only the experienceable worlds.

Kant offers at least one fairly explicit and arguably sound demonstration of the syntheticity of mathematical truth, in the special case of geometry. So I shall concentrate on this demonstration.[51] More precisely, I will give a reconstruction of the famous 'incongruent counterparts' argument in the *Prolegomena* (P. Ak. iv. 285–8).[52] For clarity's sake, I will spell out the argument

---

[51] The case for the syntheticity of arithmetic is not well presented by Kant (*CPR* B15–16); nor does he offer an account of the connection between arithmetic and the pure intuition of time that parallels his argument for the necessary connection between geometry and the pure intuition of space in the Transcendental Exposition of the Concept of Space (*CPR* B40–1); and the things he does explicitly say about the connection between arithmetic and pure intuition seem to point in very different directions (*CPR* A142–3/ B182; *P.* Ak. iv. 283; and *PC* Ak. x. 554–7).

[52] The upshot of Kant's argument from incongruent counterparts is a matter of some controversy—not least because he used it in several quite different ways over the course of his writings. See Buroker, *Space and Incongruence*, chs. 2–5. Its first use in 1768 in the 'Directions in Space' essay (DS Ak. ii. 377–83) is primarily aimed at showing the truth of Newton's absolute conception of space as against the Leibnizian relational theory. In the Inaugural Dissertation, by contrast, he uses it to argue that the representation of space is necessarily intuitional (ID Ak. ii. 403). And in the 1783 *Prolegomena* (P. Ak. iv. 285–6)

step by step; and, where it is relevant, I will also quote the texts upon which my glosses are based.

The Syntheticity of Geometry

(1) Assume the existence, in ideal three-dimensional Euclidean space, of two 'spherical triangles' (that is, cones), X and Y, which meet the following conditions: (i) X and Y are identical in their defining measurements; and (ii) X and Y are perfect mirror images (that is, enantiomorphs) of one another. (Premiss.)

> Two spherical triangles on opposite hemispheres that have an arc of the equator as their common base may be quite equal, both as regards sides and angles.   (*P*. Ak. iv. 285–6).

(2) Necessarily X and Y are incongruent. (From (A1).)

> Yet the one cannot be put in the place of the other (on the opposite hemisphere).   (*P*. Ak. iv. 286)

(3) But there is at least one logically and conceptually possible world in which X and Y are congruent; that is, it is at least thinkable that X and Y are congruent. (Premiss.)

> Nothing is to be found in either, if it be described for itself alone and completed, that would not be equally applicable to both.   (*P*. Ak. iv. 286)

(4) So it is not necessary that X and Y are incongruent. (From (3).)

(5) If and only if our pure intuition of space is invoked, can (2) and (4) be made consistent with one another. First, the enantiomorphs X and Y are incongruent in any possible world representable by our pure intuition of 3-D Euclidean space—that is, (2) is made true by all such worlds. But in some possible worlds that are conceivable, but not representable by our pure intuition, it is not the case that X and Y are incongruent—that is, (4) is made true by some of those thinkable yet non-intuitable worlds. Secondly, no other factor can establish this consistency, because only our pure intuition of space can restrict the scope of geometry in this way. (Premiss.)

> Here, then, is an internal difference between the two triangles; this difference our understanding cannot show to be external but only manifests itself by external relations in space. . . . Space is the form of the external intuition of this sensibility, and the internal determination of any space is possible only by the determination of its external relation to the whole of space, of which it is a

and again in the 1786 *Metaphysical Foundations of Natural Science* (*MFNS* Ak. iv. 484) he uses it to argue for the ideality of space. See also Van Cleve, *Problems from Kant*, ch. 4. I will employ it here solely to show that true geometric propositions are synthetic. I agree with Allison that the mere fact of incongruent counterparts, without extra premisses, does not itself entail ideality and is on the contrary perfectly consistent with Newton's spatial metaphysical realism; see *Kant's Transcendental Idealism*, 99–102.

part (in other words, by its relation to external sense). . . . Pure mathematics, and especially pure geometry, can have objective reality only on condition that it refers merely to objects of sense. But in regard to the latter the principle holds that our sense representation is a representation not of things in themselves, but of the way in which they appear to us. Hence it follows that the propositions of geometry . . . are necessarily valid of space, and consequently of all that may be found in space, because space is nothing but the form of all external appearances, and it is this form alone in which objects of sense can be given to us.   (*P. Ak.* iv. 286–7)

(6) Since (2) is both a necessary proposition and consistently deniable, but its necessity is grounded on our pure representation of space as the form of outer sensible intuition, it follows that it is synthetic a priori. (From (2), (4), (5), and the definitions of syntheticity and apriority.)

(7) The argument used in reference to (2) can be applied, *mutatis mutandis*, to any truth of geometry—for example, the proposition that the straight line between two points is the shortest. (Generalization of (6).)

Just as little is any principle (*Grundsatz*) of geometry analytic. That the straight line between two points is the shortest is a synthetic proposition. For my concept of *straight* contains nothing of quantity, but only a quality. The concept of the shortest is therefore entirely an addition to it, and cannot be derived by any decomposition from the concept of the straight line. Assistance must be gained here from intuition, by means of which alone the synthesis is possible.   (*CPR* B16)

(8) Therefore all geometric truths are synthetic a priori. (From (7).)

So the general strategy of Kant's argument for syntheticity is this: first, assume the existence of a necessary (hence a priori) truth of geometry; secondly, show its consistent deniability; thirdly, demonstrate that the necessity and consistent deniability of the proposition can both be maintained if and only if the truth of the proposition depends strictly upon the pure intuition of space; fourthly, assert the synthetic apriority of the proposition on the strength of the first three steps; and, fifthly, generalize the result to all other truths of geometry.

Obviously, the most important and controversial stage in Kant's argument strategy is the second, as instanced by step (3) above. It is in this step that consistent deniability is established, thereby showing automatically (if only negatively) that the geometrical truths are non-analytic necessities. But what sort of a possible world would permit the congruence of the enantiomorphic cones X and Y? Here we need think only of a possible spatial world in which some of the special geometric conditions laid down in (1) are removed or suspended. More precisely, what we need is a possible world in which X or Y can be taken through the looking glass, Alice-wise—that is, a world in which X and Y are homomorphic, not enantiomorphic. In the *Tractatus*, Wittgenstein correctly observes that X and Y are homomorphic in any possible world whose global spatial architecture permits a four-dimensional analogue of the three-dimensional Euclidean rotation of objects.[53] (In a precisely analogous way, a closed belt or cylinder in 3-D Euclidean space can be made to yield a Möbius strip by systematically deforming it in such a way as to produce a 'one-sided' or 'non-orientable' surface.[54]) So the mathematical possibility of any such spatial world, and furthermore the possibility of an alien spatial intuition of such a world,[55] are at least thinkable; but actually intuiting or imagining that higher-dimensional Euclidean space is impossible for creatures just like us. Curiouser and curiouser!

Through the process of conceiving a counter-example to the geometric proposition in question, we see reflectively that what must be notionally left out of that possible world is precisely what is necessarily included in every admissible world in which that proposition is true—namely, what is supplied only by the representation of space, the a priori form of our outer sense. Our pure intuition represents space as exclusively three-dimensional, orientable, and Euclidean. So it supplies all the conditions necessary and sufficient for representing the incongruence of X and Y, and for intuitionally ruling out any conceivable but not experienceable four-dimensional looking-glass world in which X and Y are congruent.

5.5. The Challenge from Non-Euclidean Geometry

It is, of course, philosophically notorious that—as I have just indicated—Kant holds the view that necessarily space is three dimensional (*CPR* B41) and also Euclidean (*CPR* B16). Let us call this 'the Strong Euclidean Thesis'. Kant's Strong Euclidean Thesis directly entails what might be called 'the Weak Euclidean Thesis', to the effect that as a matter of actual fact space is 3-D Euclidean; but it is, of course, possible to hold the Weak Thesis without holding the Strong Thesis. Now the Strong Euclidean Thesis has been almost universally (except by Frege) rejected by analytic philosophers, and held up as a perfect example of the failure of Kant's transcendental account of mathematical necessity. It is argued that the very fact of consistent non-Euclidean geometries (as discovered

---

[53] Wittgenstein, *Tractatus Logico-Philosophicus*, prop. 6.36111, p. 179. See also Nerlich, *The Shape of Space*, ch. 2.

[54] See Tietze, *Famous Problems of Mathematics*, ch. IV.

[55] For Kant, congruence is a relation possible only relative to some type of spatial intuition: 'Complete similarity and equality in so far as they can be cognized only in intuition is congruence. All geometrical construction of complete identity rests on congruence' (*MFNS* Ak. iv. 493). And he also explicitly allows for the thinkability of alien forms of spatial or temporal sensible intuition (*CPR* B72). Nevertheless we cannot even conceive of forms of sensible intuition other than spatial or temporal ones (*CPR* A230/B283).

not long after Kant's death by Gauss, and developed later by Riemann, Lobachevsky, and others) shows immediately that the Strong Thesis is false. Not only that, the argument continues, but, assuming that Einstein's General Theory of Relativity is true, it follows that space is actually non-Euclidean (with variable curvature). So even the Weak Thesis is apparently false.[56]

The failure of these theses, it is often held, casts doubt on the Kantian theory of necessity and apriority *überhaupt*. The underlying reasoning is roughly this:

> If Kant's theory of the synthetic *a priori* makes any sense at all, it surely would make sense in the special case of his doctrine of space and geometry; so if this doctrine fails, then that supplies a sufficient reason to reject the overall view. Now the Strong and Weak Euclidean Theses are both entailed by Kant's doctrines of space and geometry; and the Theses are both false, as Non-Euclidean Geometry and the General Theory of Relativity show: so not only must Kant's doctrines of space and geometry be specifically rejected but his whole theory of synthetic apriority must go down in flames as well.[57]

But why should Kant be obliged to accept this two-step inference from the assumed falsity of Kant's views on the 3-D Euclidean character of space, (1) to the failure of his overall doctrine of space and geometry, and then (2) to the universal collapse of his theory of synthetic apriority? He could, of course, be wrong about the two theses, yet right elsewhere. So it cannot be that Kant's whole theory of the synthetic a priori stands or falls on the tenability of the Strong and Weak Euclidean theses alone. The critics do, however, correctly draw attention to the fact that geometry is a crucial instance of a science that presents its results as both self-evidently necessarily true and a priori, yet also immediately empirical in its applications and implications.[58] In short, even if we reject the critics' two-step inference, we must also admit that the case of space and geometry provides a crucial philosophical test case for Kant's doctrine of the synthetic a priori.

In point of fact my reference to 'the' challenge from non-Euclidean geometry in the title of this section is not quite accurate, since the attack comes in several somewhat distinct forms and at least two different levels. The first distinction we must make is between (i) attacks on the Strong Euclidean Thesis, and (ii) attacks on the Weak Euclidean Thesis. The second distinction is between different strategies of attack within each of (i) and (ii). Since the attack on

---

[56] Very few contemporary philosophers—including Kant scholars who are otherwise very sympathetic to transcendental idealism—are willing to defend either the Strong and Weak Euclidean theses. See e.g. Longuenesse's reluctance in *Kant and the Capacity to Judge*, 290.

[57] This formulation is mine; but see also Coffa, *The Semantic Tradition from Kant to Carnap*, esp. chs. 3, 10, and Friedman, *Reconsidering Logical Positivism*, chs. 1–4.

[58] Carnap explicitly makes this point in the introduction to Reichenbach's *Philosophy of Space and Time*, pp. v–vii.

the Weak Euclidean Thesis depends on the assumption that General Relativity is true, and since this is obviously a highly complex issue—involving not only factual elements but also foundational topics in the philosophy of science—which is certainly not to be settled here, I will leave it aside, and focus instead on three important counter-arguments to the Strong Thesis. In each case, I will briefly unpack the counter-argument and then provide a Kantian reply. If these counter-arguments can be undermined, then we will have good reason to hold that the Strong Thesis is true. And, if the Strong Thesis is true, then obviously the Weak Thesis is also true—no matter how we might ultimately deal with the philosophical meaning of General Relativity.

Counter-Argument I. It is not absolutely necessary that space is Euclidean. In his 1897 *Essay on the Foundations of Geometry*, Russell clearly articulates a very common objection to Kant's theory of geometry: 'Now it must be admitted, I think, that Metageometry[59] has destroyed the legitimacy of [Kant's] argument from Geometry to space; we can no longer affirm, on purely geometrical grounds, the apodeictic certainty of Euclid.'[60] The rationale for Russell's assertion here is obvious. Kant is indeed committed to the view that it is necessarily and strictly universally true that space is Euclidean. And, certainly, it is no truth of logic that space is Euclidean. According to Russell, however, if it is absolutely necessary that space is Euclidean, then it must be true in all logically or conceptually possible worlds. But it is both logically and conceptually possible that space is non-Euclidean. Indeed, the patent fact of consistent non-Euclidean geometries based on differing denials of Euclid's Parallel Postulate entails that there are logically and conceptually possible worlds in which space is not Euclidean; so Kant's Strong Euclidean Thesis is false.

Reply to the First Counter-Argument. The error in this objection turns on a misconstrual of Kant's theory of necessary truth. It is directly entailed by Kant's modal dualism that only analytic propositions are absolutely necessary. A synthetic proposition, by definition, is one that is not absolutely necessary but instead only restrictedly necessary—it is consistently deniable yet true in all and only humanly experienceable worlds. Now necessary truths about space and in geometry are held by Kant to be synthetic a priori. So they are consistently deniable, which is to say that by hypothesis there exist logically and conceptually worlds in which they are not true. Therefore the bare fact of the consistency of non-Euclidean geometry is no defeater of Kant's view. Indeed, Kant states explicitly that non-Euclidean spaces are thinkable: 'In the concept of a figure that is enclosed within two straight lines there is no contradiction, since the concepts of two straight lines and their intersection contain no

---

[59] This is Russell's technical term for non-Euclidean geometry.
[60] Russell, *An Essay on the Foundations of Geometry*, 63.

negation of a figure . . .' (*CPR* A220/B268).⁶¹ Kant's doctrine about Euclidean space is that space is Euclidean in all and only humanly experienceable worlds, not that space is Euclidean in all logically and conceptually possible worlds. Thus the proposition that two straight lines determine a closed figure is both consistently thinkable and yet also impossible; but 'the impossibility rests not on the concept itself, but on its construction in space—i.e. on the conditions of space and its determination; but these in turn have their objective reality—i.e. they pertain to possible things, because they contain in themselves a priori the form of experience in general' (*CPR* A220/B268). Since Russell does not admit that Kant's Euclidean thesis could be modally weaker than absolute necessity, he does not actually consider the truth or falsity of *Kant's* doctrine.⁶²

Counter-Argument II. Non-Euclidean spaces are visualizable. According to Kant, a synthetic a priori proposition is true in all and only possible worlds in which creatures with cognitive constitutions like ours can have sensory experience of objects. The Strong Euclidean Thesis is a synthetic a priori proposition. Let us assume that, as things are, we do not intuitively experience non-Euclidean spaces. Nevertheless, a critic of Kant might say, there are arguments that show us that we can in fact imaginatively represent or 'visualize' non-Euclidean spaces. If this is so, then there are worlds in which the experience of creatures like us is possible, but which are non-Euclidean. But that entails that the Strong Euclidean Thesis is not even synthetically necessary, far less analytically necessary.

Unlike the first counter-argument, which was based on a simple misinterpretation of Kant's theory of necessity, this second one is a serious challenge to Kant's view. The rationale for it, which was originally proposed by Helmholtz

⁶¹ Friedman argues that 'there can be no question of non-Euclidean geometries for Kant', because the logical resources of Kant's theory make it impossible to construct a formalized non-Euclidean geometry; see *Kant and the Exact Sciences*, 82. Friedman's point is well taken. But, even granting it, Kant can still allow for the bare logical and conceptual possibility of non-Euclidean spaces: it is just that he cannot represent those spaces in an axiomatized polyadic predicate calculus. But, on the other hand, anyone who worked out a logic powerful enough to handle multiple quantification and relational predicates—say, Frege—could also work out a purely thinkable formal non-Euclidean geometry within an otherwise Kantian framework. See Frege, *The Foundations of Arithmetic*, 20–1, and Frege, 'On the Foundations of Geometry', 107–11.

⁶² Russell's doctrine in *An Essay on the Foundations of Geometry* is that there are three basic axioms about space ('homogeneity, dimensions, and the straight line' (p. 197)) and that 'these axioms, and these only, are necessarily true of any world in which experience is possible' (p. 177). This is strikingly similar to Kant's doctrine—as opposed to the one Russell ascribes to Kant—about the modality of synthetic a priori truths. So the young Russell's *Essay* is a neo-Kantian treatise, very like the young Reichenbach's *Theory of Relativity and A Priori Knowledge* (1920) and the young Carnap's *Der Raum: Ein Beitrag zur Wissenschaftslehre* (1922) two decades later.

in his seminal 1870 paper 'On the Origin and Significance of the Axioms of Geometry',[63] runs in essence as follows:

(1) Let us assume for the purposes of argument that it is true that actual space is Euclidean. What we want to challenge is the claim that this is anything other than a contingent, empirical fact.

(2) We, as inhabitants of three-dimensional Euclidean space, are in the same cognitive position as regards four-dimensional (or higher dimensional) Euclidean spaces as fictional creatures living on a two-dimensional Euclidean surface would be as regards three-dimensional Euclidean space. Just as those fictional creatures would find it psychologically impossible, owing to the limitations of their two-dimensional sense organs, to perceive or form imaginative representations of the third dimension, so we find it impossible for the same reasons to intuit or represent imaginatively any higher dimensional Euclidean space. It would be just as if blind people were to try to imagine colours.

(3) But things are different for us when we restrict ourselves to three-dimensional spaces. We can mathematically compare and contrast the properties of three-dimensional Euclidean spaces and three-dimensional non-Euclidean spaces of positive curvature (Riemannian space) or negative curvature (Lobachevskian space). Not only that, but we can also map the structures of those non-Euclidean spaces onto Euclidean models: Riemannian space, for example, isomorphically maps onto the outer surface of a Euclidean sphere; similarly, Lobachevskian space isomorphically maps onto the interior surface of a Euclidean sphere.

(4) Now suppose that there exists a Euclidean sphere that is a mirror on both its outer surface and its interior, and a Euclidean viewer is placed either in front of or inside this mirror sphere in such a way that it dominates his visual field. The images in the mirror sphere will in either case represent to the Euclidean viewer a perfect analogue of a non-Euclidean world.

(5) It is a plain fact about us Euclidean cognizers that, were we to make instantaneous and exactly proportionate changes in size or shape to all the bodies and spaces we experience, including the devices we use to measure those bodies and spaces, then we would not be able to notice the changes. Moreover, creatures living inside the non-Euclidean mirror images mentioned in (4) would experience their world in a perfectly parallel fashion to the way we experience ours. So suppose now an instantaneous but proportionate deformation and transformation of the Euclidean viewer and the bodies around him into the space of the non-Euclidean mirror image mentioned in (4). The resulting space with all

[63] See also Helmholtz, 'The Facts in Perception', and Helmholtz, 'On the Facts Underlying Geometry'.

its non-Euclidean bodies and properties would at first appear somewhat unfamiliar and strange to the deformed and transformed viewer,
but would soon begin to look exactly as ordinary Euclidean space did
before the deformation and transformation. Therefore, non-Euclidean
space is imaginatively representable for us, and the Strong Euclidean
Thesis is false.

Reply to the Second Counter-Argument. There are at least two things wrong
with Helmholtz's argument.

First, it is not at all clear that Helmholtz's thought experiments are
fully intelligible. In particular, the claim made in (2) seems to cut directly
against the claim made in (5). In (2) we are told that as three-dimensional
Euclideans we are severely limited in our actual intuitive scope and in our
psychological capacity for forming imaginative representations, to our own
special type of space; that is, lower dimensions are intuitable, but not higher
ones. Nevertheless, in (5) we are told that we can, in fact, visualize non-Euclidean
spaces. But there seems to be no good reason to believe that the phenomenological differences between the experience of 'flat' (= Euclidean)
three-dimensional space and the experience of 'curved' (= non-Euclidean)
three-dimensional space are any less sharp than the phenomenological differences between the experience of three-dimensional Euclidean space and the
experience of four-dimensional Euclidean space. While it is true that in our
(by assumption) familiar Euclidean space instantaneous and proportionate
changes to us and the environment would produce no phenomenological difference for us Euclideans, and while it is true that by hypothesis a non-Euclidean
creature living in the mirror image would have an exactly parallel experiential life to the Euclidean in front of the mirror, it certainly does not follow
that a trip to the non-Euclidean side of the mirror would be in any way
experientially possible for Euclideans. To take the analogy of the blind person,
suppose that an isomorphic mapping of sounds (and their properties) into
colours (and their properties) is possible, and suppose further that a given
sighted person is able to have a series of colour experiences that is, on this
mapping, perfectly parallel with the series of sound experiences that a blind
person has. It just does not follow that the blind person can imaginatively
visit the coloured world of the sighted person. Isomorphism is not *translation*. The two worlds are experientially incommensurable.

Secondly, even granting that Helmholtz's thought experiments are intelligible, they seem to show only that there can exist Euclidean visualizations
of Euclidean spaces that have isomorphic mappings into non-Euclidean
spaces. But what is needed in order to provide a counter-example to the Strong
Euclidean Thesis (properly construed as a synthetic a priori proposition) is
an imaginative representation that is itself non-Euclidean—that is, a non-
Euclidean visualization of a non-Euclidean space. But the possibility of this

has not been supplied by Helmholtz's argument. Indeed, recent empirical studies of the conscious manipulation of mental imagery show that, as a matter of fact, while the human visual system can smoothly adapt to global rigid transformations of mental images, it breaks down completely for non-rigid transformations and for non-Euclidean transformations more generally.[64]

At this point in the debate, then, we can usefully invoke on Kant's behalf an apt comment of Russell's in the *Essay*: 'Unless non-Euclideans can prove, what they have certainly failed to prove to this point, that we can frame an *intuition* of non-Euclidean spaces, Kant's position cannot be upset by Meta-geometry alone, but must also be attacked, if it is to be successfully attacked, *on its purely philosophical side*.'[65] In other words, assuming that the visualiz-ability of non-Euclidean space has not been established by Helmholtz's argument—and we have just seen some reasons why it would be very difficult if not impossible to establish it—then the only remaining line of attack against Kant's Strong Euclidean Thesis must be 'purely philosophical' and depend on non-ostensive or conceptual considerations alone. A powerful version of this conceptual non-Euclidean criticism of Kant was later worked out by the log-ical empiricist Hans Reichenbach; so let us turn to a sketch of that argument.

Counter-Argument III. The question of just which geometry applies to space is purely conventional, and fixed relatively to physical theory. According to Reichenbach in *The Philosophy of Space and Time* (1928), it is a mistake to think that our perceptual experiences are essentially either Euclidean or non-Euclidean in character. It is true that our ordinary experience tends to favour Euclid, but it is also true that our ordinary experience of objects does not necessitate Euclid, especially for those parts of space that are not directly access-ible to perception. So perceptual experience wholly underdetermines our choice of a geometry for physical space. Our application of a geometry to physical space is at bottom a theoretical construct—a conventional decision that is both based on broadly pragmatic grounds and determined relatively to the working scientist's choice of physical theory. More precisely, as Relativity Theory has shown, a given geometry for physical space depends entirely on the rigidity or deformation of the measuring instruments used by the physical theory. This is what Reichenbach calls the 'principle of the relativity of geometry':

It is meaningless to speak about one geometry as the *true* geometry. We obtain a statement about physical reality only if in addition to the geometry G of the space its universal field of force F is specified. Only the combination

$$G + F$$

is a testable statement.[66]

---

[64] See Shepard *et al.*, *Mental Images and their Transformations*, 4.

[65] Russell, *An Essay on the Foundations of Geometry*, 63, second emphasis added.

[66] Reichenbach, *The Philosophy of Space and Time*, 33.

Now, since General Relativity strongly favours a non-Euclidean interpretation of total physical space, says Reichenbach, we should adopt it.[67] But it is quite consistent with this that we adopt a Euclidean geometry for most everyday purposes and small physical distances. The precise determination of the geometric properties of the physical space under investigation is, therefore, an empirical matter, under a certain interpretation of the relevant physical axioms.[68] It is even possible to adopt a non-Euclidean interpretation of certain sequences of visual experiences that would otherwise lead to intolerable causal anomalies if interpreted in a Euclidean way,[69] and in this narrow sense a non-Euclidean visualization is possible. Reichenbach concludes that Kant is wrong that space is Euclidean in every experienceable world; and therefore that the Strong Euclidean Thesis is not even synthetic a priori, far less analytic.

Reply to the Third Counter-Argument. Everything turns here on the question of whether ordinary perceptual experience of space is really Euclidean or not. It is admitted by all parties to this controversy that experienced space normally presents itself as Euclidean. Moreover, it would not be denied by Kant that non-Euclidean geometries are conceptually possible relative to certain conceptual stipulations as to the a priori formal conditions under which non-Euclidean possible worlds are conceived. This would allow for non-Euclidean speculation. But, if human perceptual experience *must* at some basic level be 3-D Euclidean, then for any possible world of human experience space must also be 3-D Euclidean (= the Strong Euclidean Thesis). The Kantian thesis to the effect that perceptual experience must at some basic level be Euclidean should be distinguished from the Weak Euclidean Thesis, which concerns actual physical space and not necessarily the mode of our experience of it. To be sure, Kant also holds the view that our pure intuition correctly picks out the formal properties of actual physical space, because via the thesis of the ideality of space he identifies space with the total system of external extensive properties and relations applying to all and only the objects of experience; but that is not what is at issue here.

The historical fact that Euclid's starting points—the axioms and postulates—were so long accepted without question and as self-evident, provides at least prima facie support for Kant's claim that ordinary perceptual experience is 3-D Euclidean. What, however, can be said in favour of the opposing Reichenbachian claim that perceptual evidence underdetermines the geometric characteristics of what is experienced? The only argument here seems to be that it is always possible to interpret perceptual experiences in a non-Euclidean manner. That can be granted by Kant, since it is possible to adopt various non-Euclidean interpretations or conceptualizations of perception. There are logically and conceptually possible worlds in which perceivers quite unlike us—creatures

<hr/>

[67] Ibid. 36.   [68] Ibid. 37.   [69] Ibid. 66–7.

having different forms of spatial sensibility—have non-Euclidean modes of perception. But the crux of the matter really has to do with the geometric character of the nonconceptual or nondiscursive perceptions, if any, of creatures like us. If there are nonconceptual or nondiscursive perceptions, then they are automatically prior to any theorizing; and, if those nonconceptual perceptions must be 3-D Euclidean in character, then we have no good reason to believe that our ordinary perceptual experience underdetermines its geometry.

In Section 4.2 I have already unpacked Kant's doctrine of the concept independence of some empirical intuitions and perceptions, so the thesis that there exist concept-independent intuitions need not be redefended here. What must be defended is the stronger thesis that concept-independent sense perception is 3-D Euclidean.

Now one primary mode of concept-independent perception is our capacity to orient and move our own bodies in space. We know that kinaesthetic experience is concept-independent, because non-discursive non-human animals with sensory capacities like ours can do it just as easily as we can; because nondiscursive human infants are capable of moving and perceiving their own bodies; and because even adult human discursive thinkers can move themselves around when sleep-walking or hypnotized, despite their failing to have self-conscious thoughts. As early as his 1768 'Directions in Space' essay (DS Ak. ii. 378–80) and as late as his 1786 essay 'What is Orientation in Thinking?' (OT Ak. viii. 134–5), Kant argues explicitly that the possibility of immediately, intuitionally, and concept-independently experiencing incongruent counterparts like our own right and left hands supports the 3-D Euclidean interpretation of space. This argument seems to be cogent. If I have a direct or nonconceptual awareness of my right and left hands, then the phenomenal space centred on my body is not a non-3-D or non-orientable space: on the contrary, it must be a 3-D orientable space.[70] This does not logically entail that my phenomenal space is 3-D Euclidean, since there can be 3-D orientable spaces that are non-Euclidean; but it is certainly consistent with its being 3-D Euclidean.

More importantly for our purposes, however, if the phenomenal space centred on my body must be 3-D orientable, it follows that it is false that human sensory experience underdetermines the choice of geometry. More positively put, it follows that my conscious experience of my own body—indeed, even my conscious experience of myself as determined in inner sense[71]—partially determines the choice of geometry because it partially determines the properties of physical space: it must be locally 3-D and orientable. So Reichenbach is wrong that the choice of a geometry for physical space is underdetermined

[70] See Nerlich, *The Shape of Space*, ch. 2, and Van Cleve, *Problems from Kant*, 231–3.

[71] As I read it, the Refutation of Idealism shows that my conscious experience of myself as determined in inner self entails my conscious experience of my own body in outer sense; see Hanna, 'The Inner and the Outer: Kant's "Refutation" Reconstructed'.

by sense perception, purely conventional, and relative to physical theory. Human sense perception does not wholly determine the choice of geometry, but it does not *under*determine it either. It is to that extent non-conventional and not relative to physical theory. As a consequence, and, finally, because Reichenbach's thesis is wrong, Kant is thereby entitled to hold the thesis that space is necessarily 3-D Euclidean until further notice, given (1) the prima facie evidence in favour of the claim that our phenomenal space is 3-D Euclidean, and (2) the failures of Russell's and Helmholtz's criticisms.

5.6. Conclusion

As we have seen, according to Kant a proposition P is synthetic a priori if and only if P is (i) semantically experience-independent, (ii) intuition-dependent, (iii) consistently deniable, yet (iv) restrictedly necessary in the special sense that P is true in every humanly objectively experienceable world and lacks a classical truth value in any other possible world. In turn, a synthetic a priori truth can be either strongly necessary (= it is true in every experienceable world *überhaupt*) or weakly necessary (= it is true only in every experienceable world that contains the matter of the actual world and is governed by its causal laws). Truths of Euclidean geometry are strongly synthetic a priori; for they are demonstrably consistently deniable yet also necessary and experience-independent, in that they are true in all and only possible worlds in which our pure intuition of space obtains. Various important objections to Kant's doctrine from the fact of non-Euclidean geometry do not in fact hold up under critical scrutiny. Since Kant's view is certainly intelligible, and since there are good reasons for holding that synthetic a priori truths exist in geometry, it follows that the WCSA Thesis—the third and longest-lasting dogma of logical empiricism—is false. More positively, it follows that Kant's modal dualism is true and that the Modal Problem has been solved.

Well, that conclusion possibly sounded a little too confident. It must, of course, be admitted that Kant's philosophy of mathematics was, is, and will remain controversial. We have seen that there are some quite good arguments in favour of his theories of space and geometry. But suppose for a brief moment that Kant is wrong about mathematics, and that the existence of synthetic a priori truths has not yet been decisively established. Even then there is still good reason to prefer Kant's conception of necessity (K-necessity) over the standard modal monism according to which all necessary truth is metaphysically necessary (M-necessary). A K-necessary truth is a proposition that is true in all members of an experienceability-restricted set of possible worlds and is always non-false (either true or else lacking a classical truth value) otherwise. Supposing that the proposition is allowed to be always true otherwise, then it has precisely the same modal force as an *M*-necessary truth. It follows that *K*-necessity includes the very idea of *M*-necessity as a special case. In this way the Kantian or dualistic conception of necessity is inherently more comprehensive and flexible than the standard or monistic conception of necessity; hence Kant's modal dualism is to be rationally preferred over modal monism on those grounds alone.[72]

---

[72] In 'Semantical Considerations on Modal Logic', 66, Kripke remarks in passing that there are two fundamentally different ways of construing the necessity-operator in modal logic: 'Should we take □ *A* (in **H**) to mean that *A* is *true* in all possible worlds (relative to **H**), or just *not false* in any such world? The second alternative merely demands that *A* be either true or lack a truth-value in each world.' A similarly tantalizing remark is made in *Naming and Necessity*, 110. Since a proposition could be non-false in all logically possible worlds by never taking a classical truth value at all, Kant's theory of necessity in effect suggests a third way of construing the necessity-operator: that *A* is true in every member of the class of admissible worlds (relative to **H**), and non-false (i.e. either true or lacks a classical truth value) in all the rest.

Concluding Un-Quinean Postscript

> Our notion of rationality cannot be quite as flexible as Quine suggests.
>
> *Hilary Putnam*[1]

In this book I have unpacked Kant's positive philosophical project in the *Critique of Pure Reason* by working out his solutions to what I dubbed the Semantic Problem[2] and the Modal Problem;[3] I have argued that Kant's views on meaning and necessity played a crucial role in determining the historical foundations of analytic philosophy from Frege to Quine, if only (although not by any means always) by being repeatedly criticized and rejected; and I have also tried to offer some sort of a Kantian reply to each of those foundational criticisms and rejections.[4] But we are not quite finished yet. For there is one remaining fundamental worry that should be addressed. In Section 5.4, in the context of my discussion of Kant's unargued assumption that pure mathematics is a priori, I forestalled fully answering a certain radical sceptic by making an appeal to the history of philosophy and deploying a burden-of-proof-switching tactic. Although that provided a temporary fix, a more durable solution is required.

What we are dealing with here is a sceptic who rejects the very idea of the a priori in Kant's sense—who rejects, that is, the very idea of a necessary and experience-independent truth—but not because this sceptic, like Mill, unjustifiably assumes the truth of classical empiricism. What we are dealing with here, in short, is a sceptic who rejects platonism, classical empiricism and classical rationalism, Kantianism, and the conventionalism of the logical empiricists alike; a sceptic who does not merely think that apriorism is false, but instead that the very idea of the a priori is incoherent and untenable. Of the leading analytic philosophers, only Quine will qualify under this stringent criterion.[5]

---

[1] Putnam, 'Analyticity and Apriority: Beyond Wittgenstein and Quine', 138.

[2] How are objective mental representations possible? And, more specifically, how are necessary a priori objective mental representations possible?

[3] How are synthetic a priori judgements possible?

[4] For a cumulative list of the main worries, see Sects. 2.3, 3.0, and 4.0.

[5] What about the later Wittgenstein? The problem is that the precise scope and import of his views on necessary truth and apriority are matters of significant and unresolved controversy. See e.g. Dummett, 'Wittgenstein's Philosophy of Mathematics'; Stroud, 'Wittgenstein and Logical Necessity'; Putnam, 'Analyticity and Apriority: Beyond Wittgenstein and Quine'; and finally Dummett again, 'Wittgenstein on Necessity: Some Reflections'. My own rather tentative feeling is that, while later Wittgenstein is definitely an anti-rationalist, he is not altogether an enemy of the a priori.

Now it is clear to anyone who has read even only the first few pages of the first *Critique* that Kant simply assumes the fact of a priori cognition, and especially the fact of a priori cognition in logic and the exact sciences. His philosophical stategy is not to prove that the a priori exists, but rather to explain how it is possible. So what could Kant say to the Quinean sceptic, who attacks Kant's starting points themselves? If I am right and Kant can effectively escape Quine's critique of the analytic/synthetic distinction, then the remaining question is: can Kant also avoid Quine's broader critique of the very idea of apriority?

Here is one possible line of argument in defence of Kant's position. In the fifth section of 'Two Dogmas of Empiricism' Quine somewhat abruptly switches from his attack on the analytic/synthetic distinction, to an attack on what he calls '*reductionism*: the belief that each meaningful statement is equivalent to some logical construct upon terms which refer to immediate experience'.[6] The rejection of reductionism enables Quine to move from the semantic atomism of the verificationists to a semantic holism (of beliefs), which in turn sets up his new form of radical empiricism in the sixth and last section, aptly dubbed 'empiricism without the dogmas'.[7] In this section he argues that what traditional philosophers had regarded as necessary a priori truths and beliefs— especially logical truths and beliefs, and mathematical truths and beliefs —differ from contingent a posteriori truths and beliefs only by their high degree of centrality or indispensability in our overall scientific conceptual scheme (our web of beliefs), not by any fundamental semantic or epistemological difference in kind. So, according to Quine, in some loose and unsystematic sense, talk about the a priori will always be with us; but, at bottom, that way of talking is ultimately holistic, altogether continuous with the natural sciences, and above all revisable. It is this thesis of universal revisability, or fallibilism, that expresses the quasi-pragmatic dimension of Quine's view.

Now it has been occasionally noticed that there exists a peculiar gap in this view. Quine must presuppose and use the canonical notation of elementary logic in order to establish his holistic, behaviouristic, quasi-pragmatic, or fallibilistic naturalism,[8] yet it is not at all obvious just how his holism, behaviourism, fallibilism, and naturalism apply *to* elementary logic. Indeed, the very same argument he uses to such tremendous effect against the conventionalist theory of logical truth in his 1935 paper 'Truth by Convention' seems to apply directly to his own positive doctrine. Just as unreduced, preconventionalized logic is required in order to give the reductive conventionalist definition of a logical truth,[9] so it appears that an unreduced, prenaturalized logic is required to naturalize logic.

One way of seeing this point vividly is to raise three questions. What sense could be made of holism itself without logic? What sense could be made of

---

[6] Quine, 'Two Dogmas of Empiricism', 20.   [7] Ibid. 42.
[8] See Quine, *Word and Object*, 157–61.   [9] Quine, 'Truth by Convention', 104.

the revisability of beliefs or propositions without logic? And what sense could be made of the natural sciences without logic? The doctrine of holism, after all, claims that every belief or proposition is related to every other by consistency or entailment; but consistency and entailment are notions straight out of logic. So too the very idea of the revisability of a belief or proposition is that its denial is logically consistent, hence it is able to be rationally discarded by the believer under suitable conditions. And, finally, by Quine's own admission, the natural sciences themselves are partially defined by their shared possession of a logic: 'All sciences interlock to some extent; they share a common logic and generally some common part of mathematics, even when nothing else.'[10] So the very idea of a naturalized logic presupposes a common or universal logic—more precisely, what Quine calls 'orthodox logic' or 'sheer logic': 'If sheer logic is not conclusive, then what is? What higher tribunal could abrogate the logic of truth-functions or of quantification?'[11]

This leads to a more direct question: can logic really be at bottom empirical, as Quine insists? A closer look at the texts suggest that Quine is in fact a moving target on this crucial issue; for he has said at least two very different things about the revisability of logic.[12] In 'Two Dogmas', and in chapter 7 of his 1970 book *Philosophy of Logic*, Quine says explicitly that even the most basic logical truths are subject to possible revision;[13] but then in chapter 6 of *Philosophy of Logic* he says this of any 'deviant logician' who tries to reject the principle of non-contradiction (PNC): 'Here, evidently, is the deviant logician's predicament: when he tries to deny the doctrine he only changes the subject.'[14] That is, a deviant logician's attempted revision of the PNC is self-undermining; he cannot continue to be a logician in the strict sense and seriously deny it. The denial of the PNC would imply that the deviant logician has changed the very meanings of the logical constants he is using. Or, to put the same idea more positively: to be a logician is to presuppose the absolute unrevisability of some principles of orthodox or sheer logic, including the PNC.[15] In my opinion, Quine's 'deny the doctrine, change the meaning' argument about the absolute unrevisability of the most basic parts of logic is directly on target. But it has some Kantian implications he could not happily accept.

---

[10] Quine, as quoted in Fogelin, 'Quine's Limited Naturalism', 550–1.

[11] Quine, *Philosophy of Logic*, 81.

[12] See Dummett, 'Is Logic Empirical? (1976)', 269–70; Levin, 'Quine's View(s) on Logical Truth'; and Morton, 'Denying the Doctrine and Changing the Subject'.

[13] See Quine, 'Two Dogmas of Empiricism', 43, and Quine, *Philosophy of Logic*, 100.

[14] Quine, *Philosophy of Logic*, 81.

[15] This is especially the case if one assumes the strong law of bivalence (= every proposition P is either true or false and not both). But, even if one assumed only the weak law of bivalence (= if P has a classical truth value, then P is either true or false and not both), one could not coherently assert the possibility that every proposition and its denial are both true. See also Van Cleve, *Problems from Kant*, 30.

Putnam gives us a nudge in the direction of fully grasping this point in his important paper 'Analyticity and Apriority: Beyond Wittgenstein and Quine'. Here he aptly observes that sceptical attacks on the very possibility of a priori truths in classical logic or simple arithmetic are, at bottom, direct challenges to our self-defining conception of human rationality.[16] But I think that, from a Kantian point of view, the situation is even worse than that. The Quinean sceptic claims to be able to conceive the revisability of all truths, including all the laws of orthodox or sheer logic. But conceivability presupposes the PNC (*CPR* Bxxvii); hence it implies pure general logic in Kant's sense, and Quine's orthodox or sheer logic more specifically, assuming that this includes at least monadic logic. So the Quinean sceptic is challenging our self-defining conception of rationality by covertly using an element of that conception— classical logic—as a critical weapon. But, by Quine's own account, classical logic is absolutely unrevisable. So this is to fall into the most extreme form of pragmatic contradiction—self-stultification or cognitive suicide. You are using your own sceptical weapon on yourself. As Kant puts it in 'The Vienna Logic': 'Proceeding sceptically nullifies all our effort, and it is an antilogical principle . . . For if I bring cognition to the point where it nullifies itself, then it is as if we were to regard all human cognitions as nothing' (VL Ak. xxiv. 884). If I am right, then this was the unhappy, paradoxical, and ultimately self-defeating predicament of analytic philosophy by 1950—the year Quine first presented 'Two Dogmas of Empiricism' in public. In this sense, the analytic tradition has been living on borrowed time for fifty years.[17]

Now, what is to be done? The positive message of the first *Critique* to contemporary analytic philosophers, telegraphically reduced, has two parts.

The first part is that the central topics and obsessions of the analytic tradition from Frege to Quine—above all, meaning and the logico-linguistic theory of necessary truth—can be adequately treated only from the standpoint of a general cognitive semantics in Kant's sense. This means that meaning and necessity can be properly treated only from a mentalistic and aprioristic standpoint.

The second part is that a Kant-style general cognitive semantics can itself be properly understood only within a broader theory of human theoretical and practical reason (*CPR* Avii–xiii, A795–831/B823–59). And this implies that the central topics and obsessions of the analytic tradition up to Quine

---

[16] Putnam, 'Analyticity and Apriority: Beyond Wittgenstein and Quine', 110–11.

[17] In 1998 at the World Philosophy Congress in Boston, Quine was asked by a *New York Times* reporter, 'what have we learned from philosophy in the twentieth century?' Quine replied: 'I should have thought up an answer to that one. I'm going to have to pass.' Later he was given a second chance but admitted, 'I really have nothing to add.' See Boxer, 'At the End of a Century of Philosophizing, the Answer is Don't Ask'. I think that Quine gave exactly the right answer in the light of his own views.

are to be subsumed under the most synoptic and fundamental philosophical topic of all: what is the nature of our specifically human (that is, sensible or embodied) capacity for theoretical and moral rationality? For Kant, this is the same as the question, 'what is the human being?' (JL Ak. ix. 25), which both encapsulates and subsumes under itself the three leading questions of traditional philosophy: (1) what can I know?, (2) what ought I to do?, and (3) what may I hope? (*CPR* A805/B833). In other words, the second part of the positive message of the first *Critique* is that analytic philosophy is ultimately subsumable under rational anthropology.[18]

Now, if post-Quinean analytic philosophers were to adopt the Kantian view that the synoptic and fundamental topic of their enquiry is the nature of human rationality, this would in effect close the great historical circle by reconnecting them directly to their Fregean origins in *The Foundations of Arithmetic*, with all the benefits of critical historical hindsight: 'On this [logicist] view of numbers, the charm of work on arithmetic and analysis is, it seems to me, easily accounted for. We might say, indeed, almost in the well-known words: the reason's proper study is itself.'[19] What Frege's very Kantian remark implies is that only a self-conscious and self-regulating appeal to our specifically human capacity for reason can properly vindicate the very idea of a philosophical analysis.

But I am not saying 'Back to Kant!',[20] if by that it is meant that we should try to turn the philosophical clock back 200 years. That would be absurd. Far too much brilliant and basic philosophy has been written since the 1880s by the leaders of the analytic tradition—Frege, Moore, Russell, Wittgenstein, Carnap, Quine—and of course by many others too. What I am suggesting is only that contemporary analytic philosophers will not be able to resolve their foundational crisis, and move ahead, until they come more fully to terms with their own intellectual past and in particular with the book that made the analytic tradition possible.

---

[18] Rational cognition is cognition from principles (*CPR* A836/B864), or strict rules. So rational anthropology in the Kantian sense is the study of human beings—creatures minded like us—in so far as their thought, feeling, or action is open to governance or evaluation by strict rules. [19] Frege, *The Foundations of Arithmetic*, 115.

[20] This was, of course, the call to arms of the German neo-Kantians; see Beck, 'Neo-Kantianism', 468–9.

BIBLIOGRAPHY

ADAMS, R. M., 'Things in Themselves', *Philosophy and Phenomenological Research*, 57 (1997), 801–25.

ALLISON, H., 'Causality and Causal Laws in Kant: A Critique of Michael Friedman', in P. Parrini (ed.), *Kant and Contemporary Epistemology* (Dordrecht: Kluwer, 1994), 291–307.

—— *The Kant–Eberhard Controversy* (Baltimore: Johns Hopkins University Press, 1973).

—— *Kant's Transcendental Idealism* (New Haven: Yale University Press, 1983).

—— 'The Originality of Kant's Distinction between Analytic and Synthetic Judgements', in R. Chadwick and C. Cazeaux (eds.), *Immanuel Kant: Critical Assessments* (4 vols.; London: Routledge, 1992), ii. 324–46.

—— 'Transcendental Idealism: The "Two Aspect" View', in B. Den Ouden (ed.), *New Essays on Kant* (New York: Peter Lang, 1987), 156–76.

—— 'Transcendental Schematism and the Problem of the Synthetic *A Priori*', *Dialectica*, 35 (1981), 57–83.

ALPERS, S., *The Art of Describing: Dutch Art in the 17th Century* (Chicago: University of Chicago Press, 1983).

AMERIKS, K., *Kant's Theory of Mind* (Oxford: Oxford University Press, 1982).

AQUILA, R., *Intentionality: A Study of Mental Acts* (Philadelphia: University of Pennsylvania Press, 1977).

—— *Matter in Mind* (Bloomington, Ind.: Indiana University Press, 1989).

—— *Representational Mind* (Bloomington, Ind.: Indiana University Press, 1983).

AYER, A. J., *Language, Truth, and Logic* (2nd edn., New York: Dover, 1952).

—— (ed.), *Logical Positivism* (New York: Free Press, 1959).

BALDWIN, T., *G. E. Moore* (London: Routledge, 1990).

—— 'Moore's Rejection of Idealism', in R. Rorty *et al.* (eds.), *Philosophy in History* (Cambridge: Cambridge University Press, 1984), 357–74.

BAR-HILLEL, J., 'Bolzano's Definition of Analytic Propositions', *Theoria*, 16 (1950), 91–117.

BEALER, G., 'The Incoherence of Empiricism', *Proceedings of the Aristotelian Society*, supp. vol. 66 (1992), 99–138.

—— *Quality and Concept* (Oxford: Oxford University Press, 1982).

BECK, L. W., 'Analytic and Synthetic Judgments before Kant', in Beck, *Essays on Kant and Hume*, 80–100.

—— 'Can Kant's Synthetic Judgments be made Analytic?', in M. S. Gram (ed.), *Kant: Disputed Questions* (Chicago: Quadrangle, 1967), 228–46.

—— 'Did the Sage of Königsberg have no Dreams?', in Beck, *Essays on Kant and Hume*, 38–60.

—— *Essays on Kant and Hume* (New Haven: Yale University Press, 1978).

—— 'Kant's Strategy', in Beck, *Essays on Kant and Hume*, 3–19.

—— 'Neo-Kantianism', in P. Edwards (ed.), *The Encyclopedia of Philosophy* (7 vols.; New York: Macmillan, 1967), 468–73.

—— 'On the Meta-Semantics of the Problem of the Synthetic A Priori', in Beck, *Studies in the Philosophy of Kant*, 92–8.

—— 'Remarks on the Distinction between Analytic and Synthetic', in Beck, *Studies in the Philosophy of Kant*, 99–107.

—— *Studies in the Philosophy of Kant* (Indianapolis, Ind.: Bobbs-Merrill, 1965).

BEISER, F., *The Fate of Reason* (Cambridge, Mass.: Harvard University Press, 1987).

—— 'Kant's Intellectual Development: 1746–1781', in Guyer (ed.), *The Cambridge Companion to Kant*, 26–61.

BELL, D., and COOPER, N. (eds.), *The Analytic Tradition* (Oxford: Blackwell, 1990).

BENACERRAF, P., 'Frege: The Last Logicist', in French *et al.* (eds.), *The Foundations of Analytic Philosophy*, 17–35.

—— 'Mathematical Truth', *Journal of Philosophy*, 70 (1973), 661–79.

BENNETT, J., 'Analytic–Synthetic', *Proceedings of the Aristotelian Society*, 59 (1959), 163–88.

—— *Kant's Analytic* (Cambridge: Cambridge University Press, 1966).

BERMUDEZ, J. L., 'Scepticism and the Justification of Transcendental Idealism', *Ratio*, NS 8 (1995), 1–23.

BIRD, G., *Kant's Theory of Knowledge* (London: Routledge & Kegan Paul, 1962).

BLOCK, N. (ed.), *Readings in Philosophy of Psychology* (2 vols.; Cambridge, Mass.: Harvard University Press, 1981).

BOGHOSSIAN, P., 'Analyticity Reconsidered', *Nous*, 30 (1996), 360–91.

BOLZANO, B., *Theory of Science*, trans. B. Terrell (Dordrecht: D. Reidel, 1973).

BONJOUR, L., *In Defense of Pure Reason* (Cambridge: Cambridge University Press, 1998).

BOOLE, G., *The Laws of Thought* (Cambridge: Macmillan, 1854).

BOOLOS, G., and JEFFREY, R., *Computability and Logic* (3rd edn., Cambridge: Cambridge University Press, 1989).

BORING, E. G., *A History of Experimental Psychology* (2nd edn., New York: Appleton-Century-Crofts, 1950).

BOXER, S., 'At the End of a Century of Philosophizing, the Answer is Don't Ask', *New York Times*, Saturday, 15 Aug. 1998.

BRADLEY, F. H., *Principles of Logic* (London: G. E. Stechert, 1883).

BRANDT, R., *The Table of Judgments: Critique of Pure Reason A67–76; B92–101*, trans. E. Watkins (Atascadero, Calif.: Ridgeview, 1995).

BRENTANO, F., *Psychology from an Empirical Standpoint*, trans. A. C. Rancurello *et al.* (London: Routledge & Kegan Paul, 1973).

BRITTAN, G., *Kant's Theory of Science* (Princeton: Princeton University Press, 1978).

BROOK, A., *Kant and the Mind* (Cambridge: Cambridge University Press, 1994).

BUCHDAHL, G., 'The Conception of Lawlikeness in Kant's Philosophy of Science', in L. W. Beck (ed.), *Kant's Theory of Knowledge* (Dordrecht: D. Reidel, 1974), 128–50.

—— *Metaphysics and the Philosophy of Science* (Oxford: Blackwell, 1969).

BURGE, T., 'Belief *De Re*', *Journal of Philosophy*, 74 (June 1977), 338–62.

—— 'Frege on Knowing the Foundation', *Mind*, 107 (1998), 305–47.

—— 'Frege on Knowing the Third Realm', *Mind*, 101 (1992), 633–50.

Burge, T., 'Philosophy of Language and Mind: 1950–1990', *Philosophical Review*, 101 (1992), 3–51.

—— 'Sinning against Frege', *Philosophical Review*, 88 (1979), 398–432.

Buroker, J. V., *Space and Incongruence* (Dordrecht: D. Reidel, 1981).

Butts, R., 'Kant's Schemata as Semantical Rules', in L. W. Beck (ed.), *Kant Studies Today* (La Salle, Ill.: Open Court, 1969), 290–300.

Campbell, J., *Past, Space, and Self* (Cambridge, Mass.: MIT Press, 1994).

Candlish, S., 'The Unity of the Proposition and Russell's Theories of Judgment', in R. Monk and A. Palmer (eds.), *Bertrand Russell and the Origins of Analytical Philosophy* (Bristol, UK: Thoemmes, 1996), 103–33.

Carl, W., *Frege's Theory of Sense and Reference* (Cambridge: Cambridge University Press, 1994).

Carnap, R., *Der Raum. Ein Beitrag zur Wissenschaftslehre* (Kant-Studien Ergänzungsheft, 56; Berlin: Reuther and Reichard, 1922).

—— 'The Elimination of Metaphysics through Logical Analysis of Language', in Ayer (ed.), *Logical Positivism*, 60–81.

—— 'Intellectual Autobiography', in Schilpp (ed.), *The Philosophy of Rudolf Carnap*, 3–84.

—— *The Logical Structure of the World*, trans. R. George (Berkeley and Los Angeles: University of California Press, 1967).

—— *The Logical Syntax of Language* (London: Kegan, Paul, Trench, Teubner, 1937).

—— *Meaning and Necessity* (2nd edn., Chicago: University of Chicago Press, 1956).

—— *Philosophy and Logical Syntax* (London: Routledge & Kegan Paul, 1935).

—— 'Replies and Systematic Expositions', in Schilpp (ed.), *The Philosophy of Rudolf Carnap*, 859–1013.

Carroll, L., 'What the Tortoise Said to Achilles', *Mind*, 4 (1895), 278–80.

Cassirer, E., *Kant's Life and Thought*, trans. J. Haden (New Haven: Yale University Press, 1981).

Chomsky, N., *Aspects of the Theory of Syntax* (Cambridge, Mass.: MIT Press, 1965).

—— *Cartesian Linguistics* (New York: Harper & Row, 1966).

—— 'Quine's Empirical Assumptions', in D. Davidson and J. Hintikka (eds.), *Words and Objections: Essays on the Work of W. V. Quine* (Dordrecht: D. Reidel, 1971), 53–68.

—— *Reflections on Language* (New York: Pantheon, 1975).

—— *Syntactic Structures* (The Hague: Mouton, 1957).

Church, A., 'A Note on the Entscheidungsproblem', *Journal of Symbolic Logic*, 1 (1936), 40–1, 101.

Coffa, A., *The Semantic Tradition from Kant to Carnap*, ed. L. Wessels (Cambridge: Cambridge University Press, 1991).

Craig, E., 'The Problem of Necessary Truth', in S. Blackburn (ed.), *Meaning, Reference, and Necessity* (Cambridge: Cambridge University Press, 1975), 1–31.

Cummins, P., and Zoeller, G. (eds.), *Minds, Ideas, and Objects: Essays on the Theory of Representation in Modern Philosophy* (Atascadero, Calif.: Ridgeview, 1992).

De Pierris, G., 'Frege and Kant on A Priori Knowledge', *Synthese*, 77 (1988), 285–319.

Descartes, R., 'Meditations on First Philosophy', in Descartes, *Philosophical Writings of Descartes*, ii. 3–62.

—— *Philosophical Writings of Descartes*, trans. J. Cottingham *et al.* (3 vols.; Cambridge: Cambridge University Press, 1984).

—— 'Principles of Philosophy', in Descartes, *Philosophical Writings of Descartes*, i. 179–291.

—— 'Rules for the Direction of the Mind', in Descartes, *Philosophical Writings of Descartes*, i. 9–78.

DIAMOND, C., *The Realistic Spirit: Wittgenstein, Philosophy, and the Mind* (Cambridge, Mass.: MIT Press, 1991).

DUMMETT, M., 'Can Analytical Philosophy be Systematic and Ought it to Be?', in Dummett, *Truth and Other Enigmas*, 437–58.

—— 'Frege and Kant on Geometry', *Inquiry*, 25 (1982), 233–54.

—— *Frege: Philosophy of Language* (2nd edn., Cambridge, Mass.: Harvard University Press, 1981).

—— *Frege: Philosophy of Mathematics* (Cambridge, Mass.: Harvard University Press, 1991).

—— 'Frege's Distinction between Sense and Reference', in Dummett, *Truth and other Enigmas*, 116–44.

—— 'Is Logic Empirical? (1976)', in Dummett, *Truth and other Enigmas*, 269–89.

—— *Origins of Analytical Philosophy* (Cambridge, Mass.: Harvard University Press, 1993).

—— 'Oxford Philosophy', in Dummett, *Truth and other Enigmas*, 431–6.

—— *The Seas of Language* (Oxford: Oxford University Press, 1993).

—— 'The Significance of Quine's Indeterminacy Thesis (1973)', in Dummett, *Truth and other Enigmas*, 375–419.

—— *Truth and other Enigmas* (London: Duckworth, 1978).

—— 'What is a Theory of Meaning? (I)', in Dummett, *The Seas of Language*, 1–33.

—— 'What is a Theory of Meaning? (II)', in Dummett, *The Seas of Language*, 34–93.

—— 'Wittgenstein's Philosophy of Mathematics', *Philosophical Review*, 68 (1959), 324–48.

—— 'Wittgenstein on Necessity: Some Reflections', in Dummett, *The Seas of Language*, 446–61.

EASTON, P. (ed.), *Logic and the Workings of the Mind: The Logic of Ideas and Faculty Psychology in Early Modern Philosophy* (Atascadero, Calif.: Ridgeview, 1997).

EDWARDS, P. (ed.), *The Encylopedia of Philosophy* (7 vols.; New York: Macmillan, 1967).

EVANS, G., 'Reference and Contingency', *Monist*, 62 (1979), 161–89.

—— *The Varieties of Reference* (Oxford: Oxford University Press, 1982).

FALKENSTEIN, L., 'Kant's Account of Intuition', *Canadian Journal of Philosophy*, 21 (1991), 165–93.

—— *Kant's Intuitionism* (Toronto: University of Toronto Press, 1995).

—— 'Was Kant a Nativist?', *Journal of the History of Ideas*, 51 (1990), 573–97.

FODOR, J., *Concepts: Where Cognitive Science Went Wrong* (Oxford: Oxford University Press, 1998).

—— *The Language of Thought* (Cambridge, Mass.: Harvard University Press, 1975).

—— *Psychosemantics: The Problem of Meaning in the Philosophy of Mind* (Cambridge, Mass.: MIT Press, 1987).

FOGELIN, R., 'Quine's Limited Naturalism', *Journal of Philosophy*, 94 (1997), 543–63.

FRAENKEL, A., 'Set Theory', in P. Edwards (ed.), *Encyclopedia of Philosophy* (7 vols.; New York: Macmillan, 1967), vii. 420–7.

FREGE, G., *The Basic Laws of Arithmetic*, trans. M. Furth (Berkeley and Los Angeles: University of California Press, 1964).

—— *Collected Papers on Mathematics, Logic, and Philosophy*, trans. M. Black *et al.* (Oxford: Blackwell, 1984).

—— 'Comments on Sense and Meaning', in Frege, *Posthumous Writings*, 118–25.

—— 'Concept and Object', in Frege, *Translations from the Writings of Gottlob Frege*, trans. P. Geach and M. Black (Oxford: Blackwell, 1960), 42–55.

—— *Conceptual Notation and Related Articles*, trans. T. W. Bynum (Oxford: Oxford University Press, 1972).

—— *The Foundations of Arithmetic*, trans. J. L. Austin (2nd edn., Evanston, Ill.: Northwestern University Press, 1953).

—— 'Function and Concept', in Frege, *Collected Papers on Mathematics, Logic, and Philosophy*, 137–56.

—— 'Logic [1897]', in Frege, *Posthumous Writings*, 127–51.

—— 'Logic in Mathematics [Spring 1914]', in Frege, *Posthumous Writings*, 203–50.

—— 'A New Attempt at a Foundation for Arithmetic', in Frege, *Posthumous Writings*, 278–81.

—— 'On the Foundations of Geometry', in Frege, *On the Foundations of Geometry and Formal Theories of Arithmetic*, trans. E.-H. Kluge (New Haven: Yale University Press, 1971), 22–37, 49–112.

—— 'On Sense and Meaning', in Frege, *Collected Papers on Mathematics, Logic, and Philosophy*, 157–77.

—— *Philosophical and Mathematical Correspondence*, trans. H. Kaal (Chicago: University of Chicago Press, 1980).

—— *Posthumous Writings*, trans. P. Long *et al.* (Chicago: University of Chicago Press, 1979).

—— 'Review of E. G. Husserl, *Philosophie der Arithmetik I*', in Frege, *Collected Papers on Mathematics, Logic, and Philosophy*, 195–209.

—— 'Sources of Knowledge of Mathematics and the Mathematical Natural Sciences', in Frege, *Posthumous Writings*, 267–74.

—— 'Thoughts', in Frege, *Collected Papers on Mathematics, Logic, and Philosophy*, 351–72.

FRENCH, P., *et al.* (eds.), *The Foundations of Analytic Philosophy* (Midwest Studies in Philosophy, 6; Minneapolis: University of Minnesota Press, 1981).

FRIEDMAN, M., 'Causal Laws and the Foundations of Natural Science', in Guyer (ed.), *The Cambridge Companion to Kant*, 161–99.

—— *Kant and the Exact Sciences* (Cambridge, Mass.: Harvard University Press, 1992).

—— 'Kant and the 20th Century', in Parrini (ed.), *Kant and Contemporary Epistemology*, 27–46.

—— *Reconsidering Logical Positivism* (Cambridge: Cambridge University Press, 1999).

GAMUT, L. T. F. (a collective pseudonym for five authors), *Logic, Language, and Meaning* (2 vols.; Chicago: University of Chicago Press, 1991).

GAUKROGER, S., *Cartesian Logic* (Oxford: Oxford University Press, 1989).

GEORGE, A., 'On Washing the Fur without Wetting It: Quine, Carnap, and Analyticity', *Mind*, 109 (2000), 1–24.

GEWIRTH, A., 'The Distinction between Analytic and Synthetic Truths', *Journal of Philosophy*, 50 (1953), 397–425.

GIBBONS, S., *Kant's Theory of Imagination* (Oxford: Oxford University Press, 1994).

GLOCK, H.-J. (ed.), *The Rise of Analytic Philosophy* (Oxford: Blackwell, 1997).

GOLDFARB, W., 'Logic in the Twenties: The Nature of the Quantifier', *Journal of Symbolic Logic*, 44 (1979), 351–68.

GRAM, M. S., 'The Crisis of Syntheticity: The Kant–Eberhard Controversy', *Kant-Studien*, 71 (1980), 155–80.

—— *Kant, Ontology, and the A Priori* (Evanston, Ill.: Northwestern University Press, 1968).

GRICE, H. P., and STRAWSON, P. F., 'In Defense of a Dogma', *Philosophical Review*, 65 (1956), 141–58.

GUYER, P., 'Kant's Conception of Empirical Law', *Proceedings of the Aristotelian Society*, supp. vol. 64 (1990), 221–42.

—— *Kant and the Claims of Knowledge* (Cambridge: Cambridge University Press, 1987).

—— *Kant and the Experience of Freedom* (Cambridge: Cambridge University Press, 1993).

—— 'Psychology and the Transcendental Deduction', in E. Förster (ed.), *Kant's Transcendental Deductions* (Stanford, Calif.: Stanford University Press, 1989), 47–68.

—— 'The Transcendental Deduction of the Categories', in Guyer (ed.), *The Cambridge Companion to Kant*, 123–60.

—— (ed.), *The Cambridge Companion to Kant* (Cambridge: Cambridge University Press, 1992).

HAACK, S., *Deviant Logic, Fuzzy Logic: Beyond the Formalism* (Chicago: University of Chicago Press, 1996).

HACKER, P. M. S., *Insight and Illusion: Themes in the Philosophy of Wittgenstein* (2nd edn., Oxford: Oxford University Press, 1986).

—— 'The Rise of Twentieth Century Analytic Philosophy', in Glock (ed.), *The Rise of Analytic Philosophy*, 51–76.

—— *Wittgenstein's Place in Twentieth-Century Analytic Philosophy* (Oxford: Blackwell, 1996).

HACKING, I., *Why Does Language Matter to Philosophy?* (Cambridge: Cambridge University Press, 1975).

HANNA, R., 'Conceptual Analysis', in E. Craig (ed.), *Routledge Encyclopedia of Philosophy* (10 vols.; London: Routledge, 1998), ii. 518–22.

—— 'Direct Reference, Direct Perception, and the Cognitive Theory of Demonstratives', *Pacific Philosophical Quarterly*, 74 (1993), 96–117.

—— 'Extending Direct Reference', *ProtoSociology*, 10 (1997), 134–54.

—— 'How Do We Know Necessary Truths? Kant's Answer', *European Journal of Philosophy*, 6 (1998), 115–45.

—— 'How Ideas Became Meanings: Locke and the Foundations of Semantic Theory', *Review of Metaphysics*, 44 (1991), 775–805.

—— 'The Inner and the Outer: Kant's "Refutation" Reconstructed', *Ratio*, NS 13 (2000), 146–74.

—— 'Kant, Truth, and Human Nature', *British Journal for the History of Philosophy*, 8 (2000), 225–50.

—— 'A Kantian Critique of Scientific Essentialism', *Philosophy and Phenomenological Research*, 58 (1998), 497–528.

HANNA, R., 'Kant's Theory of Empirical Judgment and Modern Semantics', *History of Philosophy Quarterly*, 7 (1990), 335–51.
—— 'The Trouble with Truth in Kant's Theory of Meaning', *History of Philosophy Quarterly*, 10 (1993), 1–20.
HANSON, N., 'The Very Idea of a Synthetic–Apriori', in Sumner and Woods (eds.), *Necessary Truth*, 65–70.
HANSON, P., and HUNTER, B. (eds.), *The Return of the A Priori* (Calgary, Ala.: University of Calgary Press, 1992).
HARMAN, G., 'Analyticity Regained?', *Nous*, 30 (1996), 392–400.
HARPER, W., 'Kant on the A Priori and Material Necessity', in R. Butts (ed.), *Kant's Philosophy of Physical Science* (Dordrecht: D. Reidel, 1986), 239–72.
HARRIS, J. F., and SEVERENS, R. H. (eds.), *Analyticity: Selected Readings* (Chicago: Quadrangle, 1970).
HATFIELD, G., 'Empirical, Rational, and Transcendental Psychology: Psychology as Science and as Philosophy', in Guyer (ed.), *The Cambridge Companion to Kant*, 200–27.
—— *The Natural and the Normative: Theories of Spatial Perception from Kant to Helmholtz* (Cambridge, Mass.: MIT Press, 1990).
HEIDEGGER, M., 'What is Metaphysics?', in Heidegger, *Basic Writings* (New York: Harper & Row, 1977), 95–112.
HELMHOLTZ, H., *Epistemological Writings*, ed. R. S. Cohen and Y. Elkana (Dordrecht: D. Reidel, 1977).
—— 'The Facts in Perception', in Helmholtz, *Epistemological Writings*, 115–63.
—— 'On the Facts Underlying Geometry', in Helmholtz, *Epistemological Writings*, 39–58.
—— 'On the Origin and Significance of the Axioms of Geometry', in Helmholtz, *Epistemological Writings*, 1–26.
HINTIKKA, J., 'Are Logical Truths Analytic?', *Philosophical Review*, 74 (1965), 178–203.
—— *Logic, Language-Games, and Information: Kantian Themes in the Philosophy of Logic* (Oxford: Oxford University Press, 1973).
—— 'On Kant's Notion of Intuition (*Anschauung*)', in Penelhum and MacIntosh (eds.), *The First Critique*, 38–53.
HOWELL, R., 'Intuition, Synthesis, and Individuation in the *Critique of Pure Reason*', *Nous*, 7 (1973), 207–32.
—— 'Kant's First *Critique* Theory of the Transcendental Object', *Dialectica*, 35 (1981), 85–125.
HUMBOLDT, W., *On Language*, trans. P. Heath (Cambridge: Cambridge University Press, 1988).
HUME, D., *A Treatise of Human Nature* (Oxford: Oxford University Press, 1975).
—— *Enquiry concerning Human Understanding* (Indianapolis: Hackett, 1977).
HURLEY, S., 'Kant on Spontaneity and the Myth of the Giving', *Proceedings of the Aristotelian Society*, 94 (1994), 137–64.
HUSSERL, E., 'Prolegomena to Pure Logic', in Husserl, *Logical Investigations*, i. 53–247.
—— *Logical Investigations*, trans. J. N. Findlay (2 vols.; London: Routledge & Kegan Paul, 1970).

—— 'A Reply to a Critic of my Refutation of Logical Psychologism', in *Husserl: Shorter Works* (Notre Dame, Ind.: University of Notre Dame Press, 1981), 152–8.

HYLTON, P., 'Logic in Russell's Logicism', in Bell and Cooper (eds.), *The Analytic Tradition*, 137–72.

—— 'The Nature of the Proposition and the Revolt against Idealism', in Rorty *et al.* (eds.), *Philosophy in History*, 375–97.

—— *Russell, Idealism, and the Emergence of Analytic Philosophy* (Oxford: Oxford University Press, 1990).

JACKENDOFF, R., *Patterns in the Mind* (New York: Basic Books, 1994).

—— 'The Problem of Reality', in Jackendoff, *Languages of the Mind* (Cambridge, Mass.: MIT Press, 1995), 157–76.

—— *Semantics and Cognition* (Cambridge, Mass.: MIT Press, 1983).

JAMES, W., *Principles of Psychology* (2 vols.; New York: Dover, 1950).

KAPLAN, D., 'Demonstratives: An Essay on the Semantics, Logic, Metaphysics, and Epistemology of Demonstratives and Other Indexicals', in J. Almog *et al.* (eds.), *Themes from Kaplan* (New York: Oxford University Press, 1989), 481–614.

KATZ, J., 'Analyticity and Contradiction in Natural Language', in J. Katz and J. Fodor (eds.), *The Structure of Language* (Englewood Cliffs, NJ: Prentice-Hall, 1964), 519–43.

—— 'Analyticity, Necessity, and the Epistemology of Semantics', *Philosophy and Phenomenological Research*, 57 (1997), 1–28.

—— *Cogitations* (New York: Oxford University Press, 1986).

—— *The Metaphysics of Meaning* (Cambridge, Mass.: MIT Press, 1990).

—— 'The New Intensionalism', *Mind*, 101 (Oct. 1992), 689–719.

—— 'The Problem in Twentieth-Century Philosophy', *Journal of Philosophy*, 95 (1998), 547–75.

—— *Semantic Theory* (New York: Harper & Row, 1972).

—— 'Some Remarks on Quine on Analyticity', *Journal of Philosophy*, 64 (1967), 36–52.

KELLER, P., *Kant and the Demands of Self-Consciousness* (Cambridge: Cambridge University Press, 1998).

KEMP SMITH, N., *Commentary to Kant's 'Critique of Pure Reason'* (2nd edn., Atlantic Highlands, NJ: Humanities Press, 1992).

KEYNES, J. M., 'My Early Beliefs', in Keynes, *Two Memoirs* (London: R. Hart-Davis, 1949), 78–103.

KITCHER, PATRICIA, 'Kant's Dedicated Cognitivist System', in Smith (ed.), *Historical Foundations of Cognitive Science*, 189–209.

—— *Kant's Transcendental Psychology* (New York: Oxford University Press, 1990).

KITCHER, PHILIP, 'Frege's Epistemology', *Philosophical Review*, 88 (1979), 235–62.

—— 'How Kant almost Wrote "Two Dogmas of Empiricism" (and Why He Didn't)', *Philosophical Topics*, 12 (1981), 217–50.

—— 'The Naturalists Return', *Philosophical Review*, 101 (1992), 53–114.

—— 'The Unity of Science and the Unity of Nature', in Parrini (ed.), *Kant and Contemporary Epistemology*, 253–72.

KNEALE, W., and KNEALE, M., *The Development of Logic* (Oxford: Oxford University Press, 1986).

KÖHNKE, K., *The Rise of Neo-Kantianism*, trans. R. J. Hollingdale (Cambridge: Cambridge University Press, 1991).

KOSSLYN, S., *Image and Mind* (Cambridge, Mass.: Harvard University Press, 1980).

KRETZMANN, N., 'Semantics, History of', in Edwards (ed.), *Encyclopedia of Philosophy*, 358–406.

KRIPKE, S., 'Identity and Necessity', in Moore (ed.), *Meaning and Reference*, 162–91.

—— *Naming and Necessity* (2nd edn., Cambridge, Mass.: Harvard University Press, 1980).

—— 'Semantical Considerations on Modal Logic', in L. Linsky (ed.), *Reference and Modality* (Oxford: Oxford University Press, 1971), 63–72.

KUKLICK, B., *The Rise of American Philosophy* (New Haven: Yale University Press, 1977).

—— 'Seven Thinkers and How They Grew: Descartes, Spinoza, Leibniz; Locke, Berkeley, Hume; Kant', in Rorty *et al.* (eds.), *Philosophy in History*, 125–39.

KUSCH, M., *Psychologism* (London: Routledge, 1995).

LACKEY, D., 'Russell's 1913 Map of the Mind', in French *et al.* (eds.), *The Foundations of Analytic Philosophy*, 125–42.

LANGFORD, C. H., 'A Proof that Synthetic *A Priori* Propositions Exist', *Journal of Philosophy*, 46 (1949), 20–4.

LEIBNIZ, G. W., 'Discourse on Metaphysics', in Leibniz, *Philosophical Essays*, 35–68.

—— 'Meditations on Truth, Knowledge, and Ideas', in Leibniz, *Philosophical Essays*, 23–7.

—— 'On Freedom', in Leibniz, *Philosophical Essays*, 94–8.

—— 'On the Ultimate Origination of Things', in Leibniz, *Philosophical Essays*, 149–55.

—— *Philosophical Essays*, trans. R. Ariew and D. Garber (Indianapolis: Hackett, 1989).

—— 'The Principles of Philosophy, or, the Monadology', in Leibniz, *Philosophical Essays*, 213–34.

—— 'The Source of Contingent Truths', in Leibniz, *Philosophical Essays*, 98–101.

LEVIN, M., 'Quine's View(s) on Logical Truth', in R. W. Shahan and C. Swoyer (eds.), *Essays on the Philosophy of W. V. Quine* (Norman, Okla.: University of Oklahoma Press, 1979), 45–67.

LEWIS, C. I., *Mind and the World Order* (New York: Dover, 1956).

—— 'The Modes of Meaning', *Philosophy and Phenomenological Research*, 4 (1943–4), 236–49.

—— *A Survey of Symbolic Logic* (Berkeley and Los Angeles: University of California Press, 1918).

—— and LANGFORD, C. H., *Symbolic Logic* (2nd edn., New York: Dover, 1959).

LINSKY, L., 'The Problem of the Unity of the Proposition', *Journal of the History of Philosophy*, 30 (1992), 243–73.

LOCKE, J., *Essay concerning Human Understanding* (Oxford: Oxford University Press, 1975).

LONGUENESSE, B., *Kant and the Capacity to Judge*, trans. C. Wolfe (Princeton: Princeton University Press, 1998).

LORENZ, K., 'Kant's Doctrine of the A Priori in the Light of Contemporary Biology', in H. C. Plotkin (ed.), *Learning, Development, and Culture* (New York: John Wiley & Sons, 1982), 121–43.

LOTZE, H., *Logic*, trans. B. Bosanquet (2 vols.; Oxford: Oxford University Press, 1888).

McCulloch, G., *The Game of the Name* (Oxford: Oxford University Press, 1989).

McDowell, J., 'Having the World in View: Sellars, Kant, and Intentionality', *Journal of Philosophy*, 95 (1998), 431–91.

—— *Mind and World* (Cambridge, Mass.: Harvard University Press, 1994).

Marcus, R. B., 'Modalities and Intensional Languages', in I. Copi and J. A. Gould (eds.), *Contemporary Philosophical Logic* (New York: St Martin's Press, 1978), 257–72.

Marc-Wogau, K., 'Kants Lehre vom analytischen Urteil', *Theoria*, 17 (1951), 140–54.

Martin, M. G. F., 'Perception, Concepts, and Memory', *Philosophical Review*, 101 (1992), 745–63.

Mason, S., *A History of the Sciences* (2nd edn., New York: Collier, 1962).

Mates, B., 'Analytic Sentences', *Philosophical Review*, 60 (1951), 525–34.

Meinong, A., *On Assumptions*, 2nd end., trans. J. Heanue (Berkeley and Los Angeles: University of California Press, 1983).

Meerbote, R., 'Kant on Intuitivity', *Synthese*, 47 (1981), 203–28.

—— 'Kant's Functionalism', in Smith (ed.), *Historical Foundations of Cognitive Science*, 161–87.

Mill, J. S., *A System of Logic* (London: Longmans, Green, and Co., 1879).

Miller, G., 'The Magical Number Seven Plus or Minus Two: Some Limits on our Capacity for Processing Information', *Psychological Review*, 63 (1956), 81–97.

Monk, R., *Bertrand Russell: The Spirit of Solitude* (London: Jonathan Cape, 1996).

—— 'Was Russell an Analytic Philosopher?', in Glock (ed.), *The Rise of Analytic Philosophy*, 35–50.

—— 'What is Analytical Philosophy?', in Monk and Palmer (eds.), *Bertrand Russell and the Origins of Analytical Philosophy*, 1–22.

Monk, R., and Palmer, A. (eds.), *Bertrand Russell and the Origins of Analytical Philosophy* (Bristol, UK: Thoemmes, 1996).

Montague, R., *Formal Philosophy* (New Haven: Yale University Press, 1974).

—— 'Logical Necessity, Physical Necessity, Ethics, and Quantifiers', in Montague, *Formal Philosophy*, 71–83.

Moore, A. W. (ed.), *Meaning and Reference* (Oxford: Oxford University Press, 1993).

Moore, G. E., 'An Autobiography', in P. Schilpp (ed.), *The Philosophy of G. E. Moore* (New York: Tudor, 1952), 3–39.

—— 'Critical Notice of B. A. W. Russell, *Essay on the Foundations of Geometry*', *Mind*, 8 (1899), 397–405.

—— 'Kant's Idealism', *Proceedings of the Aristotelian Society*, 4 (1904), 127–40.

—— 'The Nature of Judgment', in Moore, *Selected Writings*, 1–19.

—— 'Proof of an External World', in Moore, *Selected Writings*, 147–70

—— 'The Refutation of Idealism', in Moore, *Selected Writings*, 23–44.

—— *Selected Writings*, ed. T. Baldwin (London: Routledge, 1993).

—— 'The Subject Matter of Psychology', *Proceedings of the Aristotelian Society*, 10 (1909–10), 36–62.

—— 'Truth and Falsity', in Moore, *Selected Writings*, 21–2.

Morton, A., 'Denying the Doctrine and Changing the Subject', *Journal of Philosophy*, 70 (1973), 503–10.

Moser, P. (ed.), *A Priori Knowledge* (Oxford: Oxford University Press, 1987).

NEISSER, U., *Cognitive Psychology* (New York: Appleton-Century-Crofts, 1967).

NERLICH, G., *The Shape of Space* (Cambridge: Cambridge University Press, 1976).

NORRIS, C., 'Doubting Castle or the Slough of Despond: Davidson and Schiffer on the Limits of Analysis', *Review of Metaphysics*, 50 (1996), 351–82.

O'NEILL, O., 'Vindicating Reason', in Guyer (ed.), *The Cambridge Companion to Kant*, 280–308.

PAP, A., *Elements of Analytic Philosophy* (2nd edn., New York: Hafner, 1972).

—— 'Logic and the Synthetic *A Priori*', *Philosophy and Phenomenological Research*, 10 (1950), 500–14.

—— 'Once More: Colors and the Synthetic *A Priori*', *Philosophical Review*, 66 (1957), 94–9.

—— *Semantics and Necessary Truth* (New Haven: Yale University Press, 1958).

PAPINEAU, D., *Philosophical Naturalism* (Oxford: Blackwell, 1993).

PARRINI, P. (ed.), *Kant and Contemporary Epistemology* (Dordrecht: Kluwer, 1994).

PARSONS, C., 'The Foundations of Mathematics', in Edwards (ed.), *The Encyclopedia of Philosophy*, iii. 188–213.

—— 'Infinity and Kant's Conception of the "Possibility of Experience"', in Parsons, *Mathematics in Philosophy*, 95–109.

—— 'Kant's Philosophy of Arithmetic', in Parsons, *Mathematics in Philosophy*, 110–49.

—— 'Mathematical Intuition', *Proceedings of the Aristotelian Society*, 80 (1980), 145–68.

—— *Mathematics in Philosophy* (Ithaca, NY: Cornell University Press, 1983).

—— 'The Transcendental Aesthetic', in Guyer (ed.), *The Cambridge Companion to Kant*, 62–100.

—— 'Was ist eine mögliche Welt?', *Kant-Studien*, 65 (1974), 378–96.

PASSMORE, J., *A Hundred Years of Philosophy* (London: Duckworth, 1966).

PATON, H. J., *Kant's Metaphysic of Experience* (2 vols.; London: George Allen & Unwin, 1970).

PEACOCKE, C., *A Study of Concepts* (Cambridge, Mass.: MIT Press, 1992).

PENELHUM, T., and MACINTOSH, J. J. (eds.), *The First Critique* (Belmont, Calif.: Wadsworth, 1969).

PERRY, J., 'The Problem of the Essential Indexical', *Nous*, 13 (1979), 3–21.

PIPPIN, R., 'Kant on the Spontaneity of Mind', *Canadian Journal of Philosophy*, 17 (1987), 449–76.

—— *Kant's Theory of Form* (New Haven: Yale University Press, 1982).

POTTER, M., *Sets: An Introduction* (Oxford: Oxford University Press, 1990).

POWELL, C. T., *Kant's Theory of Self-Consciousness* (Oxford: Oxford University Press, 1990).

PRAUSS, G., *Erscheinung bei Kant* (Berlin: de Gruyter, 1971).

—— *Kant und das Problem der Dinge an Sich* (Bonn: Bouvier, 1974).

PRICHARD, H. A., *Kant's Theory of Knowledge* (Oxford: Oxford University Press, 1909).

PRIOR, A. N., 'Determinables, Determinates, and Determinants', *Mind*, 58 (1949), 1–20, 178–94.

PROUST, J., *Questions of Form: Logic and the Analytic Proposition from Kant to Carnap*, trans. A. Brenner (Minneapolis: University of Minnesota Press, 1989).

PUTNAM, H., 'The Analytic and the Synthetic', in Putnam, *Mind, Language, and Reality: Philosophical Papers, Vol. 2,* 33–69.

—— 'Analyticity and Apriority: Beyond Wittgenstein and Quine', in Putnam, *Realism and Reason: Philosophical Papers, Vol. 3* (Cambridge: Cambridge University Press, 1983), 115–38.

—— 'The "Innateness Hypothesis" and Explanatory Models in Linguistics', in Putnam, *Mind, Language, and Reality: Philosophical Papers, Vol. 2,* 107–16.

—— *Mathematics, Matter, and Method: Philosophical Papers, Vol. 1* (Cambridge: Cambridge University Press, 1975).

—— 'The Meaning of "Meaning"', in Putnam, *Mind, Language, and Reality: Philosophical Papers, Vol. 2,* 215–71.

—— *Mind, Language, and Reality: Philosophical Papers, Vol. 2* (Cambridge: Cambridge University Press, 1975).

—— 'Red and Green All Over Again: A Rejoinder to Arthur Pap', *Philosophical Review,* 66 (1957), 100–3.

—— 'Reds, Greens, and Logical Analysis', *Philosophical Review,* 65 (1956), 206–17.

—— *Words and Life* (Cambridge, Mass.: Harvard University Press, 1994).

QUINE, W. V. O., 'Carnap and Logical Truth', in Schilpp (ed.), *The Philosophy of Rudolph Carnap,* 385–406.

—— 'Epistemology Naturalized', in Quine, *Ontological Relativity,* 69–90.

—— *From a Logical Point of View* (2nd edn., New York: Harper & Row, 1961).

—— *Methods of Logic* (4th edn., Cambridge, Mass.: Harvard University Press, 1982).

—— 'Mind and Verbal Dispositions', in Moore (ed.), *Meaning and Reference,* 80–91.

—— 'On Mental Entities', in Quine, *The Ways of Paradox,* 221–7.

—— 'Ontological Relativity', in Quine, *Ontological Relativity,* 26–68.

—— *Ontological Relativity* (New York: Columbia, 1969).

—— 'On What There Is', in Quine, *From a Logical Point of View,* 1–19.

—— *Philosophy of Logic* (2nd edn., Cambridge, Mass.: Harvard University Press, 1986).

—— 'The Problem of Meaning in Linguistics', in Quine, *From a Logical Point of View,* 47–64.

—— 'Reference and Modality', in Quine, *From a Logical Point of View,* 139–59.

—— 'Three Grades of Modal Involvement', in Quine, *The Ways of Paradox,* 159–76.

—— 'Truth by Convention', in Quine, *The Ways of Paradox,* 77–106.

—— 'Two Dogmas of Empiricism', in Quine, *From a Logical Point of View,* 20–46.

—— *The Ways of Paradox* (2nd edn., Cambridge, Mass.: Harvard University Press, 1976).

—— *Word and Object* (Cambridge, Mass.: MIT Press, 1960).

RAMSEY, F. P., *The Foundations of Mathematics and Other Essays* (London: Routledge & Kegan Paul, 1931).

REICH, K., *The Completeness of Kant's Table of Judgments,* trans. J. Kneller and M. Losonsky (Stanford, Calif.: Stanford University Press, 1992).

REICHENBACH, H., *The Philosophy of Space and Time,* trans. M. Reichenbach (New York: Dover, 1958).

—— *The Rise of Scientific Philosophy* (Berkeley and Los Angeles: University of California Press, 1951).

—— *The Theory of Relativity and A Priori Knowledge,* trans. M. Reichenbach (Berkeley and Los Angeles: University of California Press, 1965).

RESCHER, N., 'On the Status of "Things-in-Themselves" in Kant's Critical Philosophy', in Rescher, *Kant and the Reach of Reason* (Cambridge: Cambridge University Press, 2000), 5–20.

—— 'The Ontology of the Possible', in M. Loux (ed.), *The Possible and the Actual* (Ithaca, NY: Cornell University Press, 1979), 166–81.

RESNIK, M., 'Frege and Analytic Philosophy: Facts and Speculations', in French *et al.* (eds.), *The Foundations of Analytic Philosophy*, 83–103.

RICHARDSON, A., *Carnap's Construction of the World: The Aufbau and the Emergence of Logical Empiricism* (Cambridge: Cambridge University Press, 1998).

RICKETTS, T., 'Frege, the *Tractatus*, and the Logocentric Predicament', *Nous*, 19 (1985), 3–15.

ROBINSON, R., 'Necessary Propositions', *Mind*, 67 (1958), 289–304.

RORTY, R. (ed.), *The Linguistic Turn* (Chicago: University of Chicago Press, 1967).

—— 'Metaphilosophical Difficulties of Linguistic Philosophy', in Rorty (ed.), *The Linguistic Turn*, 1–39.

—— *Philosophy and the Mirror of Nature* (Princeton: Princeton University Press, 1979).

—— *et al.* (eds.), *Philosophy in History* (Cambridge: Cambridge University Press, 1984).

ROSSI-LANDI, F., 'Peano, Giuseppe', in Edwards (ed.), *Encyclopedia of Philosophy*, 67–8.

RUSSELL, B., *A Critical Exposition of the Philosophy of Leibniz* (2nd edn., London: George Allen & Unwin, 1967).

—— *An Essay on the Foundations of Geometry* (Cambridge: Cambridge University Press, 1897).

—— *Introduction to Mathematical Philosophy* (London: Routledge, 1993).

—— 'Knowledge by Acquaintance and Knowledge by Description', in Russell, *Mysticism and Logic* (Totowa, NJ: Barnes & Noble, 1981), 152–67.

—— *Logic and Knowledge* (New York: G. P. Putnam's Sons, 1971).

—— 'Mathematical Logic as Based on the Theory of Types', in Russell, *Logic and Knowledge*, 59–102.

—— 'Mathematics and the Metaphysicians', in Russell, *Mysticism and Logic*, 59–74.

—— 'Meinong's Theory of Complexes and Assumptions', in Russell, *Essays in Analysis* (New York: George Braziller, 1973), 21–76.

—— *My Philosophical Development* (London: Allen & Unwin, 1959).

—— *Mysticism and Logic* (Totowa, NJ: Barnes & Noble, 1981).

—— 'On Denoting', in Russell, *Logic and Knowledge*, 41–56.

—— 'On the Nature of Truth and Falsehood', in Russell, *Philosophical Essays* (London: Allen & Unwin, 1966), 147–59.

—— *Our Knowledge of the External World* (London: Allen & Unwin, 1914).

—— 'The Philosophy of Logical Atomism', in Russell, *Logic and Knowledge*, 177–281.

—— *The Principles of Mathematics* (2nd edn., New York: W. W. Norton, 1996).

—— *The Problems of Philosophy* (Indianapolis: Hackett, 1995).

—— *Theory of Knowledge: The 1913 Manuscript*, ed. E. R. Eames and K. Blackwell (London: Routledge, 1992).

RYLE, G., 'The Theory of Meaning', in Ryle, *Collected Papers* (2 vols.; New York: Barnes & Noble, 1971), ii. 350–72.

SACKS, O., *The Man who Mistook his Wife for a Hat* (New York: Harper Perennial, 1990).

SCHIFFER, S., *Remnants of Meaning* (Cambridge, Mass.: MIT Press, 1987).

SCHILPP, P. (ed.), *The Philosophy of Rudolf Carnap* (La Salle, Ill.: Open Court, 1963).

SCHLICK, M., 'Is there a Factual *A Priori*?', in H. Feigl and W. Sellars (eds.), *Readings in Philosophical Analysis* (New York: Appleton-Century-Crofts Inc., 1949), 277–85.

SCHWYZER, H., *The Unity of Understanding: A Study in Kantian Problems* (Oxford: Oxford University Press, 1990).

SEARLE, J., 'Determinables and Determinates', in Edwards (ed.), *Encyclopedia of Philosophy*, ii. 357–9.

—— *Intentionality* (Cambridge: Cambridge University Press, 1983).

—— *Rediscovery of the Mind* (Cambridge, Mass.: MIT Press, 1992).

—— *Speech Acts* (Cambridge: Cambridge University Press, 1969).

SELLARS, W., 'Is there a Synthetic A Priori?', in Sellars, *Science, Perception, and Reality* (London: Routledge & Kegan Paul, 1963), 298–320.

—— *Science and Metaphysics: Variations on Kantian Themes* (London: Routledge & Kegan Paul, 1968).

—— 'Some Remarks on Kant's Theory of Experience', *Journal of Philosophy*, 64 (1967), 633–47.

SHEFFER, H. M., 'Review of *Principia Mathematica*, Volume I, second edition', *Isis*, 8 (1926), 226–31.

SHEPARD, R., *et al.*, *Mental Images and their Transformations* (Cambridge, Mass.: MIT Press, 1982).

SLEIGH, R. (ed.), *Necessary Truth* (Englewood Cliffs, NJ: Prentice-Hall, 1972).

SLUGA, H., 'Frege: The Early Years', in Rorty *et al.* (eds.), *Philosophy in History*, 329–56.

—— *Gottlob Frege* (London: Routledge & Kegan Paul, 1980).

SMILEY, T., 'Relative Necessity', *Journal of Symbolic Logic*, 28 (1963), 113–34.

SMITH, E. E., 'Concepts and Thoughts', in R. Sternberg and E. E. Smith (eds.), *Psychology of Human Thought* (Cambridge: Cambridge University Press, 1988), 19–49.

SMITH, J.-C., *Historical Foundations of Cognitive Science* (Dordrecht: D. Reidel, 1990).

STALNAKER, R., 'Pragmatics', in G. Harman and D. Davidson (eds.), *Semantics of Natural Language* (Dordrecht: D. Reidel, 1972), 380–97.

STERNBERG, R., *Cognitive Psychology* (Fort Worth, Tex.: Harcourt Brace, 1996).

STICH, S. (ed.), *Innate Ideas* (Berkeley and Los Angeles: University of California Press, 1975).

STRAWSON, P. F., *The Bounds of Sense* (London: Methuen, 1966).

—— *Individuals* (London: Methuen, 1959).

—— *Introduction to Logical Theory* (London: Methuen, 1963).

—— 'Logical Form and Logical Constants', in Strawson, *Entity and Identity* (Oxford: Oxford University Press, 1997), 142–61.

—— 'Propositions, Concepts, and Logical Truths', *Philosophical Quarterly*, 7 (1957), 15–25.

—— *Subject and Predicate in Logic and Grammar* (London: Methuen, 1974).

STROUD, B., *The Significance of Philosophical Scepticism* (Oxford: Oxford University Press, 1984).

—— 'Transcendental Arguments', *Journal of Philosophy*, 65 (1968), 241–56.

—— 'Wittgenstein and Logical Necessity', *Philosophical Review*, 74 (1965), 504–18.

SUMNER, L. W., and WOODS, J. (eds.), *Necessary Truth* (New York: Random House, 1969).

SWINBURNE, R., *Space and Time* (London: Macmillan, 1968).

TARSKI, A., 'The Concept of Truth in Formalized Languages', in Tarski, *Logic, Semantics, and Metamathematics*, 152–278.

—— *Logic, Semantics, and Metamathematics* (Oxford: Oxford University Press, 1956).

—— 'On the Concept of Logical Consequence', in Tarski, *Logic, Semantics, and Metamathematics*, 409–20.

—— 'The Semantic Conception of Truth and the Foundations of Semantics', *Philosophy and Phenomenological Research*, 4 (1943), 342–60.

TAYLOR, C., 'Philosophy and its History', in R. Rorty *et al.* (eds.), *Philosophy in History* (Cambridge: Cambridge University Press, 1984), 17–30.

TETENS, J. N., *Philosophische Versuche über die menschliche Natur und ihre Entwicklung*, 2 vols. (Berlin: Kantgesellschaft Verlag, 1911).

THOMPSON, M., 'Singular Terms and Intuitions in Kant's Epistemology', *Review of Metaphysics*, 24 (1972–3), 314–43.

TIETZE, H., *Famous Problems of Mathematics* (Baltimore: Graylock Press, 1965).

TOULMIN, S., 'A Defense of "Synthetic Necessary Truth"', *Mind*, 58 (1949), 164–77.

TUGENDHAT, E., *Traditional and Analytical Philosophy*, trans. P. A. Gorner (Cambridge: Cambridge University Press, 1982).

VAN CLEVE, J., 'Analyticity, Undeniability, and Truth', in Hanson and Hunter (eds.), *The Return of the A Priori*, 89–111.

—— *Problems from Kant* (New York: Oxford University Press, 1999).

VAN HEIJENOORT, J. (ed.), *From Frege to Gödel: A Source Book in Mathematical Logic, 1879–1931* (Cambridge, Mass.: Harvard University Press, 1967).

WAISMANN, F., *The Principles of Linguistic Philosophy* (London: Macmillan, 1965).

—— *Wittgenstein and the Vienna Circle*, trans. J. Schulte and B. McGuinness (New York: Harper & Row, 1979).

WALKER, R. C. S., *Kant* (London: Routledge & Kegan Paul, 1978).

—— 'Kant's Conception of Empirical Law', *Proceedings of the Aristotelian Society*, supp. vol. 64 (1990), 243–8.

—— (ed.), *Kant on Pure Reason* (Oxford: Oxford University Press, 1982).

WALSH, W. H., *Kant's Criticism of Metaphysics* (Chicago: University of Chicago Press, 1975).

WARD, J., 'Psychology', in *Encyclopedia Britannica* (11th edn., 29 vols.; New York: Encyclopedia Britannica Co., 1911), xxii. 547–604.

WARMBROD, K., 'Logical Constants', *Mind*, 108 (1999), 503–38.

WAXMAN, W., *Kant's Model of the Mind* (New York: Oxford University Press, 1991).

WEISKRANTZ, L., *Blindsight* (Oxford: Oxford University Press, 1986).

WHITE, M., 'The Analytic and the Synthetic: An Untenable Dualism', in S. Hook (ed.), *John Dewey: Philosopher of Science and Freedom* (New York: Dial Press, 1950), 316–30.

WHITEHEAD, A. N., and RUSSELL, B., *Principia Mathematica to *56* (Cambridge: Cambridge University Press, 1962).

WILSON, K. D., 'Kant on Intuition', *Philosophical Quarterly*, 25 (1975), 247–65.

WITTGENSTEIN, L., *Philosophical Investigations*, trans. G. E. M. Anscombe (New York: Macmillan, 1953).

—— 'Some Remarks on Logical Form', *Proceedings of the Aristotelian Society*, supp. vol. 9 (1929), 162–71.

—— *Tractatus Logico-Philosophicus*, trans. C. K. Ogden (London: Routledge & Kegan Paul, 1981).

WOLFF, R. P., *Kant's Theory of Mental Activity* (Cambridge, Mass.: Harvard University Press, 1963).

WOOD, A., 'Kant's Compatibilism', in A. Wood (ed.), *Self and Nature in Kant's Philosophy* (Ithaca, NY: Cornell University Press, 1984), 73–101.

ZOELLER, G., 'Main Developments in Recent Scholarship on the *Critique of Pure Reason*', *Philosophy and Phenomenological Research*, 53 (1993), 445–66.

INDEX

acquaintance/description distinction,
   Russell's 233
Adams, R. 111 n.
affection:
   outer 47–8, 54, 113–19, 198
   self 155 n.
Allison, H. 13 n., 14 n., 37 n., 84 n.,
   104 n., 108–9, 113, 124 n., 132 n.,
   133, 145 n., 193 n., 202 n., 212 n.,
   219 n., 221 n., 240, 261 n., 266
Alpers, S. 37
Ameriks, K. 16 n.
Amphiboly of the Concepts of Reflection
   220, 240 n.
amplification:
   phenomenological 157
   semantic 133, 191
Analogies of Experience, the 12, 87, 94,
   263
analysis:
   analytic philosophy lacks a cogent
      conception of 11
   atomistic 5, 7–8, 120
   conceptual 172–3
   decompositional 134–5, 142–4
   expositional 134 n.
   see also reduction
analyticity:
   and absolute necessity 256, 259
   and the analytic tradition 120–1
   Carnap's theory of 165–71
   as conceptually necessary truth 154,
      180
   and containment 127–41
   and contradiction 145–54
   Frege's theory of 159–65
   history of the concept of 171
   and identity 141–5
   Kant's theory of 121, 125–54
   logico-linguistic theory of 122, 172–3
   philosophical legitimacy of the concept
      of 180

privileging of 181
Quine's critique of 122–3, 171–7
   see also analytic/synthetic distinction
Analytic of Concepts, the 29
Analytic of Principles, the 30, 94, 263
analytic philosophy:
   crisis in 11, 284–5
   has implicit foundation in general
      cognitive semantics 284
   origins and nature of 4–6
   as post-Fregean philosophy 182
   subsumable under rational
      anthropology 285
   see also analytic tradition
analytic/synthetic distinction 10–11,
   123–4, 156–7, 160–1, 165–6, 181–5,
   239
analytic tradition:
   as history of the concept of analyticity
      120–1
   schematic history of 6–11
   its underprivileging of the synthetic
      181–3
   see also Carnap, R.; Frege, G.; Moore,
      G. E.; Quine, W. V. O.; Russell, B.;
      Wittgenstein, L.
Anthropocentric Condition, the 104
anthropocentrism, Kant's 89, 91, 104,
   233, 243–5, 260, 263–4
Anticipations of Perception, the 12, 94,
   263
Antinomy of Pure Reason, the 21 n., 23,
   94, 114, 115 n.
appearance(s) 20–2, 47–54, 59–60,
   98–102, 216
   form of 212–13
   undetermined vs. determined 20 n.,
      49–51
apperception 32, 38, 42–3, 45, 64–5,
   202
apprehension, synthesis of 47–9,
   201–2